BUILDING MATERIALS
(MATERIALS OF CONSTRUCTION)

GURCHARAN SINGH
Formerly Joint Director
Directorate of Technical Eduction
(Rajasthan)
And
JAGDISH SINGH
M.E.
Water Pollution Board
Udaipur (Raj.)

STANDARD PUBLISHERS DISTRIBUTORS
1705–B, Nai Sarak, Delhi-110006
P.O. Box : 1066 Phones : 3262700, 3285798

Published by:
For A.K. Jain
Standard Publishers Distributors
1705-B, Nai Sarak, Delhi-110006

4581/15 G.F., Agarwal Road,
Daryaganj, New Delhi-110002

First Edition	:	1979
Second Edition	:	1992
Third Edition	:	1996
Fourth Edition	:	2000
Reprint	:	2004
Reprint	:	2007
Reprint	:	2009
Reprint	:	2010
Reprint	:	2012
Reprint	:	2013
Reprint	:	2014
Reprint	:	2017
Reprint	:	2019
Fifth Edition	:	2022

Price Rs : 175-00

ISBN: 978-81-8014-154-6

Printed by: Giriraj Offset Press, Delhi

PREFACE TO THE FIRST EDITION

The object of writing this book on "*Materials of Construction*" has been to present this subject to the students in most systematic manner and in simple understandable language. The sound knowledge of this subject is necessary for any engineer. Without this an engineer cannot predict the properties and behavior of the materials, which he is going to use. All the materials existing in the universe are useful in one field or the other. It is not possible to deal all the materials in one volume. The materials in most common use in engineering works have only been discussed in treatise. I.S.I. specifications have been quoted wherever found appropriate.

The book covers the syllabi prescribed by various Indian Universities, Technical Boards, and A.M.I.E. (India) examinations. The book is completely in M.K.S. system.

Being first edition, there may be some printing errors. The authors will be grateful if such errors are brought to their notice. The authors would sincerly welcome the constructive criticism of the book and also the suggestions, useful for bringing about improvement in the book.

In the last, the authors would like to express their deep sence of gratitude to Standard Publishers Distributors Delhi-6 for bringing out the book in such a nice form.

November, 1979 **Authors**

PREFACE TO THE FIFTH EDITION

In the third edition, the subject matter has been thoroughly revised and many new articles have been added. Latest Indian Standards Recommendations and codes have been incorporated in the text.

Two new chapters "*Properties of Building Materials*" and "*An Introduction to Material Science of Metals*" have been added. The authors are thankful to many readers for their useful suggestions. Further suggestions will be greatly appreciated

15th July, 1996 **Authors**

CONTENTS

1

STONE

1.1. Introduction

All the engineering structures are made from some materials. Each material which is used in the construction, in one form or the other, is known as *engineering material*. Engineering materials are also, sometimes, termed, as *building materials* or *materials of construction*. Every engineer has to come across various materials, in carrying out various engineering works and projects and as such he is supposed to be fully conversant with their properties and behaviour.

No material, existing in the universe, is useless. Every material has its own field of application. An engineer has to be conversant with the properties of most of them. Stone, bricks, timber, steel, lime, cement, metals etc. are some commonly used materials by a Civil Engineer. Even engineers in branches of Mechanical Electrical, Electronics etc. are required to know the properties of these materials. *Selection of building material, to be used in a particular construction, is done on the basis of strength, durability, appearance and permeability*. In order to carry out safe constructions, some standards for the materials to be used, are fixed. These standards are fixed by Indian Standards Institutions (ISI). These standards are continuously reviewed and modified from time to time to suit to the changed conditions. All the commonly used Engineering Materials have been discussed in this book, in regard to their properties, place of occurance, manufacture, and uses. In the first chapter stone has been discussed.

It is likely that our country may face shortage of common building materials like cement, lime, bricks, aggregates, plywood, plastics etc. It is therefore an urgent need to handle the situation by manufacturing cheap building materials and also by developing new building materials. Shortage of building materials and the high costs are likely to hamper many projects and developmental programmes. It is therefore imperative to lay greater emphasis on the growth of such industries which use local raw material resources for producing less costly building materials.

1.2. Rock and Stone

Rock is the term used to name a solid portion of the earth's crust.

It has no definite shape and chemical composition. It is generally very big in size..The *rocks have one or more than one minerals. Rocks having only one mineral is known as monomineralic rock and those having several minerals as Polymineralic rocks.* Quartz, sand, pure gypsum, magnesite are examples of *monomineralic rocks* and granite, basalt, etc. those of *polymineralic rocks.* The rocks are named after the predominant mineral present in it.

A rock having *calcium carbonate mineral as predominant mineral, is termed as calcarious rock. Similarly rock predominant in clay is called argillaceous rock.* Quartz, felspar, hornblend, mica, augite, dolomite are some of the common rock forming minerals.

Stone. The stone is always obtained from rock. *The rock quarried from quarries is called stone.* Quarried stone may be in form of stone blocks, stone aggregate, stone slabs, stone lintels, stone flags, etc. Stone has to be properly dressed and shaped before it is used at the place of its use.

1.3. Formation of Rocks

Solar system consists of sun as the centre and all other planets revolve around it. Our earth is one which originally was in form of mass of incandescent gases. The mass of gases after cooling, first converted into molten mass and then on further cooling, the surface of the molten mass converted into solid crust. The process of cooling of earth is still continuing and thus process of solidification of molten matter is also continuing. Existance of molten matter under earth's crust is reflected by eruption of volcanos from time to time. *The molten matter, of which the earth and other planets were originally made up and, existance of which is confirmed by the volcanic eruptions, is known as Lava or Magma.*

1.4. Classification of Rocks

The stone which is used in the construction works, in one form or the other, is always obtained from the rocks. The rocks may be classified in following four ways.

1. Geological classification
2. Physical classification
3. Chemical classification and
4. Classification based on hardness of the stone.

1. Geological classification. According to this classification, rocks may be divided into following three categories.

(i) Igneous rocks *(ii)* Sedimentary rocks and
(iii) Metamorphic rocks.

(i) Igneous rocks. As already explained in article 1.3 "formation of rocks," the in side portion of the earths surface is very hot and it can cause fusion even at ordinary pressures. The molten lava or magma, occasionally tries to come out of the earth's surface through cracks or other weak spots. *This magma when gets exposed to the outside cooling effect, solidifies in the form of a rock, known as igneous rock.* Hence igneous rocks are formed as a result of solidification of molten lava lying below or above the earth surface due to cooling effect. Depending *upon the cooling effect, following different types of igneous rocks are formed.*

(a) Volcanic igneous rocks. This type of igneous rock is formed when molten lava or magma gets exposed to atmosphere, at the surface of the earth. In this case, *cooling of magma is very rapid and, hence, structures of these rocks are extremely fine grained.* This rock may contain some quantity of glass which is non-crystalline. Example of *volcanic igneous rock is Basalt.*

(b) Hypa-byssal rocks. This rock is formed when magma is allowed *to cool at, comparatively, slower rate.* Such conditions of cooling, generally, prevail at relatively shallow depth under earth crust. Since rate of cooling is not as fast as in case of volcanic rocks, the structure of *resulting rocks, is fine grained and crystalline*, but not as fine as in case of volcanic rocks. The best example of *hypa-byssal rock is Dolerite.*

(c) Plutonic rocks. These rocks are formed when *cooling of magma takes places at a very slow rate.* Such conditions of cooling generally, exist *at a considerable depth from the surface of the earth. The structure of these rocks is coarse grained, and crystalline.* Stone, obtained from Plutonic rock is most commonly used in building industry. The best example of *plutonic igneous rock is granite.*

All the igneous rocks contain minerals like Augite, Felspar, Horn blende, mica, quartz etc. Before solidification, all these minerals are in molten state, along with some gases, forming magma.

(ii) Sedimentary rocks. The rocks are formed by the deposition of broken up materials like sand, clay, disintegrated rocks, dead sea organisms etc., with the aid of water, wind, frost etc. on the pre-existing rocks. *Earth's crust, when subjected to weathering cause disintegration, which results in the formation of clay, sand and pebbles. The disintegrated mass is carried by rain water, streams, wind etc. and settles as and when conditions become favourable to it. The process of deposition of new disintegrated matter continues in regular layers. With age this deposited mass becomes a rock, known as Sedimentary rock.* Since the sediments get consolidated in horizontal or nearly horizontal layers, these rocks show different layers distinctly. All the

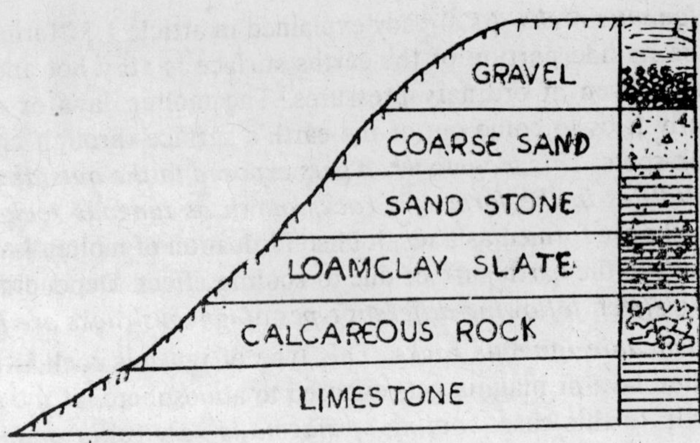

Fig. 1.1. Sedimentary Rock formation

layers of this rock may have same or different composition, colour and structure, as all the layers have deposited under varying conditions. *The formation of these rocks is shown in Fig 1.1.* These rocks can be easily split, along the bedding plane. Sand stone, limestone, slate and shale, are some common sedimentary rocks.

(iii) Metamorphic rocks. These rocks are formed, *when igneous as well as sedimentary rocks are subjected to a very large heat and pressure. The process of change due to heat and pressure is known as Metamorphism.* The rocks change their character, due to metamorphism, and the resulting mass of rock change into hard and durable foliated structure; Marble, quartzite and slate are common examples of metamorphic rocks.

Metamorphism. All the rocks of igneous and sedimentary origin, represent a mass of mineral composition. This mass remains in equilibrium under the general atmospheric conditions. When either temperature, or pressure, or even both are increased, the equilibrium of the mass gets disturbed and its minerals realign themselves to re-establish the equilibrium. *Re-alignment of minerals change the texture of the rock. This process is known as metamorphism.* It should be remembered that weathering action and sedimentation action, are not included in metamorphism.

Heat, pressure, and chemically active fluids, are the three agents which bring about the changes of metamorphism. Heat may be supplied by the general rise of temperature inside the earth or by hot magma and pressure may be caused due to heavy overlay rocks or due to movement of the earth during earth-quakes. Chemical liquids do not take any active part in the process of metamorphism. Following four types of metamorphisms occur.

(*a*) Plutonic metamorphism.

(*b*) Thermal metamorphisms.

(*c*) Cataclastic metamorphisms.

(*d*) Dynamo-Thermal metamorphisms.

(a) Plutonic metamorphism. The metamorphic *change takes place at large depths under the earth. Uniform pressure and high temperature* are responsible for this change. This is due to the fact that rocks become plastic mass at certain depths, and plastic mass can be in equilibrium only under uniform pressure.

(b) Thermal metamorphism. The changes brought about in this metamorphism are predominantly *due to high temperature.*

(c) Cataclastic metamorphism. This metamorphism or change is brought about by *directed pressure only and temperature,* uniform *pressure do not play any role in it.* This change takes place at the surface of the earth.

We have used two terms above–uniform pressure and directed pressure. Directed pressure can be applied to solids only. Directed pressure when applied to liquids is converted into uniform pressure. Uniform pressure can be applied to liquids and solids both.

(d) Dynamo-thermal metamorphism. Temperature increases with depth inside the earth. The changes brought about in the rock by *combination of heat and directed pressure are known as Dynamo-Thermal metamorphism*. This change takes place not at very large depths, *but at moderate depths.*

As a result of metamorphosis, limestone and marl become marble, Basalt and trap are converted to schist and laterite and granite becomes Gneiss.

2. Physical classification of rocks. According to general structure, the rocks may be classified into following three categories.

(i) Stratified rocks

(ii) Unstratified rocks and

(iii) Foliated or laminated rocks.

(i) Stratified rocks. These are such rocks which possess *planes of stratification or cleavage*. These rocks can be easily split along these planes. An experiences supervisor at the quarry site, can easily locate these planes. All the sedimentary rocks have distinct layers of stratification and thus are stratified rocks.

(ii) Unstratified rocks. *The structure of these rocks is compact granular.* They do not show any layers of stratification or cleavage. All the igneous rocks of volcanic origin, are the *examples of unstratified rocks*

(iii) Foliated or laminated rocks. These rocks comprise of thin laminations. *They can be split in definite direction and size*. Metamorphic rocks come under the category of foliated rocks.

3. Chemical classification. Based upon chemical composition, the rocks can be classified into following three categories:

(i) Silicious rocks

(ii) Argillaceous or clayey rocks

(iii) Calcareous rocks.

(i) Silicious rocks. These rocks *consist of silica*, as their predominant constituent. These rocks are very hard and durable and *are not easily affected by weathering agencies.*

Granite, quartzite, trap, basalt, sand sone, etc. are the examples of silicious rocks. Presence of weaker materials may cause their disintegration.

(ii) Argillaceous rocks. Predominant *constituent of these rocks is clay*. The principle constituent alumina, which is nothing but clay, remains mixed up in varying proportion with siliceous, calcareous and carboneous matter. These rocks are hard, durable, dense and brittle, in nature. Laterite, slate, porphyry, are the best example of argillaceous rocks.

(iii) Calcareous rocks. The *predominant constituent of these rocks is calcium carbonate*. The durability of these rocks is greatly dependent upon the constituents of surrounding atmosphere. Lime stone, marble, dolomite, Kankar etc. are the examples of this type of rocks.

4. Classification based upon hardness of the stone. According to this classification stone may be classified as soft, medium, hard and very hard.

Very hard rocks. Granite, trap, taconite, are the very hard varieties of rocks.

Hard rocks. Granite, basalt, trap, gravel, quartzite are the hard varieties of rocks.

Medium rocks. Dolomite and lime stone are the medium varieties.

Soft rocks. Talc, gypsum, sand stone, slate etc. are the soft varieties of stones.

Scale of hardness of various minerals, starting from hardest to softest, have been given as follow.

Diamond (Hardest)–Corundum–Topaz–quartz–Felspar–Apatite–Flouspar–Calcite–rocks salt–Talc (softest).

1.5. Composition of Stone (Rock-forming Minerals)

Chemically the rocks are composed of mineral earths, alkalies, oxides or iron and manganese etc. Silica (SiO_2), alumina (Al_2O_3), lime (CaO), and magnesia (MgO) are the mineral earths, which are usually found is rocks in one form or the other . Soda (Na_2O) and Potash (K_2O) are the usual alkalies present in the rocks. Presence of alkalies in the rocks is not preferred, as it causes stone to disintegrate when exposed to weather. Generally stones comprise of more than one mineral earth. Following are the materials of which igneous and sedimentary rocks are composed of.

Igneous rock forming minerals

(i) Quartz (SiO_2). Common sand is a variety of quartz. Pure quartz is crystalline and translucent. Its specific gravity is 2.65 and hardness 7. Pure quartz is usually colourless, but it may have some colour due to presence of metallic oxides. Flint, chalcedony and agate are the coloured varieties of quartz. It is good resistant to weathering agencies. It can withstand the action of acids except action of hydrofluoric acids. Stones having larger percentage of quartz are generally very hard and durable.

(ii) Felspar ($K_2O\ Al_2O_3\ 6SiO$). All the igneous rocks have felspar as an important constituent. It is essentially a silicate of aluminium combined with varying amounts of potash, soda or lime. The colour of felspar depends upon the oxide of the metal present in the rock. Red colour is imparted by small amount of iron oxide. Felspar has many varieties, the common being that of microline, orthoclase, and plagioclase.

(a) Orthoclase. It is whitish, greyish or pinkish in colour. It has well defined faces. It is a straight-spliting mineral. If orthoclase is present in the rock in large amounts, it can easily disintegrate.

(b) Microline Felspar. It is found alongwith orthoclase. It has deep green or flesh-red colour. Excessive amount of it is also a sign of weakness of the stone.

(c) Plagioclass Felspar. It is not one type of felspar, but it is the name given to a series of felspar. Albite which is sodium aluminium silicate and anorite which is calcium aluminium silicate are the examples of this type of felspar. This mineral splits obliquely and straightly.

(iii) Horn blende [5 (CaMg) 6 SiO_2]. It is very heavy, strong and durable mineral of igneous rocks. Its S.G. various from 2.9 to 3 and hardness from 5 to 6. It is black or dark green in colour. It is however brittle. It has glassy lustre. It changes to chlorite. when exposed to weather.

(iv) Mica. Mica occurs in form of thin transparent plates or laminae Its S.G. varies between 2.7 and 3.2 and hardness from 2 to 3. The mica flakes shine with metallic lusture. The presence of mica in a stone reflects, its weakness. The mica occuring in igneous rocks may be of two types-biotite and muscovite. Both the varieties may occur together or separately.

Muscovite mica. It is white in colour. It may have light colours also. Its S.G. varies from 2.76 to 3.10.

Biotite mica It is also known as black mica. It has metallic lusture and dark colours. It has some iron content and hence when exposed to weather it changes to chlorite and loses its elasticity. Its S.G. varies from 2.8 to 3.2.

(v) Olivine. It has yellow, olive-green or black colour. When found in thin sections, it is colourless. It frequently changes to *serpentine*.

(vi) Serpentine. This mineral has yellow or pale-green colour. It resembles chlorite and presents a massive appearance.

(vii) Chlorite. This mineral is the resultant of decomposition of horn blende, augite and biotite mica. It is green in colour.

(viii) Augite (Ca. Mg. SiO_2). This mineral is similar to horn blende. But it is heavier than it. Its. S.G. is as much as 3.6 and occurs abundantly in Deccan trap. Its crystals are octagonal which change to chlorite by hydration.

Sedimentary Rock Forming Minerals

Various minerals of which sedimentary rocks are composed of, are enumerated as follows :

(i) Calcite. Chemically calcite is calcium carbonate. It gives out carbon dioxide when attacked by mineral acids. It is generally colourless, but presence of certain impurities may impart yellow, brown, or red colours, to it. Waters containing dissolved Carbon dioxide (CO_2) are injurious to this mineral. This is because, carbon dioxide while acting on calcium carbonate, converts it into calcium bi-carbonate which is several times more soluble in water than calcite. Its S.G. is 2.7 and hardness 3.

(ii) Dolomite. This mineral is stronger and heavier than calcite. It is bicarbonate of magnesium and calcium (Mg CO_3 $CaCO_3$). It is insoluble in ordinary water, but acid charged waters are injurious to it. It is brittle and is available in various shades.

(iii) Magnesite. The chemical composition of magnesite is $MgCO_3$. It is sparingly found in rocks. It is harder than calcite and also less soluble in water.

(iv) Limonite. This mineral is insoluble in ordinary water, but dissolves in acidic waters. It has earthy appearance and its colour varies from yellow to reddish brown.

(v) Glauconite. This mineral is practically insoluble in acids. It has yellow to green colour. It has no definite crystal form.

(vi) Gypsum. Gypsum is the hydrated sulphate of calcium. *Its chemical composition is* $CaSO_4\ 2H_2O$. Basically it is white, but it may be available in any colour depending upon the nature of impurities present in it. It is a crystalline substance, having very poor solubility in water. Its density is 2.3 and hardness 2.

When H_2O *content from gypsum is removed by heating it is then called anhydrate of gypsum.* When anhydrate of gypsum is kept in contact with water for a long time, it converts back into gypsum. In this process volume is slightly increased. Density of anhydrate of gypsum varies from 2.8 to 3.0 and hardness from 3.0 to 3.5.

1.6. Texture of the Rocks

The way the particles of rock forming minerals, are arranged in the rocks is termed as texture or structure of the rock. Following may be different forms of textures. Texture of the stone can be visualized from the freshly fractured surface of the stone.

(i) Compact crystalline. In this texture, grains forming the mass of the stone are very fine and tightly held together. Quartzite, marble etc., are the examples of stone having such a texture.

(ii) Granular crystalline. This texture is formed when all the particles are of similar size and all are held together by some cementing materials is such a way, that all the grains are separately recognizable. Sandstone, Gneiss, has this type of texture.

(iii) Conglomerate. This texture consists of rounded grains of different sizes which remain held together by some cementing material.

(iv) Glass texture. This texture does not exhibit any grain or crystal at the fractured surface. Fractured surface is just like a glass.

(v) Foliated texture. This texture consists of all the grains arranged in form of parallel layers.

(vi) Porous granular. This texture is just like granular crystalline, with the only difference, that small perforations can be easily noticed at the fractured surface of the stone. The rocks having such a texture are not durable.

(vii) Vesicular texture. This texture exhibits small irregular depressions or cavities on the fractured surface of the rock.

(viii) Porphyritic texture. In this texture crystals of some minerals are larger than the crystals of other rock forming minerals. They can be easily recognized by nacked eye.

(ix) Pisolitic texture. This texture shows large size grains of peas size. uniformly distributed at the fractured surface.

1.7. Types of Fractures of Rock

When a rock is broken, the fractured surface of the stone or rock shows the type of fracture. Fractured surface of the stone helps in recognition of the texture of the rock. Fractured surfaces are generally irregular. Different types of fractures may be as follows.

(i) Uneven. This type of fracture shows minute *depression and elevations*. This type of fracture generally takes place in case of granular textured rocks.

(ii) Even. This type of surface of fracture is obtained in case of crystalline textured stones. The fractured surface is more or less plane.

(iii) Conchoidal. In this type of fracture a set of *concentric rings is formed. Quartz and flint generally present such a surface when freshly fractured.*

(iv) Fibrous. In this case, fractured surface presents fibrous, texture. *For example, when asbestos is fractured,* it presents a fibrous fracture.

Besides above said fractures, Hackly and earthy types of fractures are also there. Hackly fracture shows rough and broken surface having sharp edges. Earthy fracture resembles earth. Chalk when broken indicates earthy fracture.

1.8. Uses of Stone

Following are the various uses, of stones :

1. For masonry work.
2. For lintels and vertical columns.
3. For covering floors of building
4. For paving of roads and foot paths.
5. For the construction of roads in form of boulders and aggregate.
6. As an aggregate in cement as well as lime concretes.
7. Base material for water and sewage filters, in case of water works and sewage treatment plants.
8. As stone patties for roofing of buildings.
9. For the manufacture of cement and lime.
10. Stone may be used to give massive and pleasing appearance to the building.
11. Ballast used in railway tracks is also obtained from stone.
12. Lime stone is also used as a flux in the blast furnaces.
13. In the construction of a masonry dam, stones of good quality and durability are of vital importance.
14. Coarse sand obtained at stone quarry sites, is an excellent natural substitute for natural sand.

1.9. Natural bed of Stone

The stone used in buildings is obtained from rocks. The rocks, *particularly sedimentary type, have distinct planes of division along* which stones can be easily split. *The plane along which stones can be easily split is known as natural bed of stone.*

In stone masonry work, the stone should be used in such a *way that the direction of applied load is perpendicular to the natural bed of the stone.* In other words, the position of the stone blocks in the walls should be same in which they were originally deposited. This position gives maximum strength to the stone work in the walls. Stone in the walls should further be placed with layers at right angle to the face of wall. This will offer greatest resistance to disintegration of the stone by frost and other weather actions. See. Fig. 1.2 (*a*).

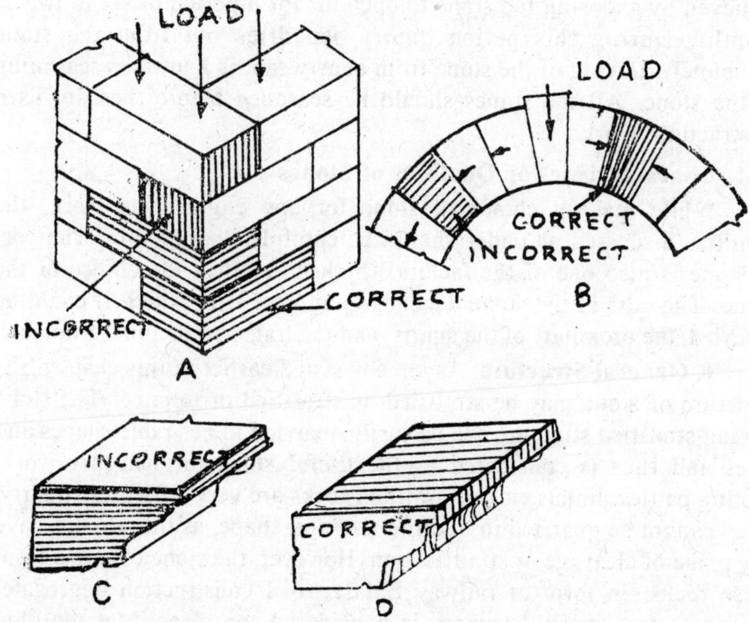

Fig 1.2. *(a)* **Stone in Walls** *(b)* **Stone in arch** *(c)* **&** *(d)* **Stone is cornice**

In the case of arches, the bedding plane should be radial and at right angles to the face of the arch. Such an arrangement causes the thrust of arch, act normal to the direction of the natural bed. See. Fig. 1.2 (*b*).

In the case of cornices and strong courses, stones remain unsupported. In their case, natural bed of the stone should be kept vertical. Correct and incorrect positions of stones in the case of wall, arch and cornice are shown in Fig. 1.2. In the case of corner stones neither of the principles given before will hold good, as it has two exposed faces. In such circumstances it is preferable to use stones, without any natural bed.

1.10. Seasoning of Stones

Freshly quarried stones have natural moisture. *This moisture is known as quarry sap. Quarry sap renders the stone blocks comparatively soft and makes them easily workable. So the stones should be dressed soon after quarring.* The quarry sap is a mineral solution which reacts chemically with the mineral constituents of stone during drying and makes the stone hard and compact. Thus it is important to achieve full hardening of freshly quarried stones, before they are allowed to be used in the masonry work. The full hardening of stone is achieved by exposing the stone to open air for a period of six to twelve months. During this period quarry sap dries out from the stone completely. Drying of the stone from quarry sap, is known as seasoning of the stone. All the stones should be seasoned before they are used in structural work.

1.11. Characteristics or Qualities of Stones

While making choice of stone for any engineering work, the qualities discussed as under should be carefully looked into. The cost of stone is also one of the factors which may affect the choice of the stone. The cost of the stone depends upon ease with which it could be quarried, the proximity of the quarry, and the transport facilities available.

1. General Structure. As already stated earlier in this chapter, the structure of stone may be stratified, unstratified or foliated. The stone having stratified structure can be easily quarried in desirable shapes and sizes and thus is considered as the useful stone for masonry work, roofing patties, lintels etc. Unstratified rocks are very difficult to quarry. They cannot be quarried in definite size and shape, as they do not have any plane of cleavage or stratification. However, the stone obtained from these rocks, in form of railway Balast, road construction aggregate, aggregate for cement concrete is considered top class. Metamorphic rocks have foliated structure. The layers in this case are not formed due to deposition but due to metamorphic action. The stone obtained from this rock is not very strong.

2. Fineness of grains. For carving and moulding works, fine-grained stones are considered most suitable. Stones having non crystalline or amorphous texture are liable to be easily disintegrated. A good building stone should have crystalline structure, because such stones are generally durable and strong.

3. Compactness. Compact stones are generally more durable. The stones found at larger depths under earth are considered the best stones, as they have been subjected to a larger pressure of earth above them.

4. Durability. A good building stone *should be durable*. The power of resistance *against wear and tear*, atmospheric and other agencies is called durability. The durability of stone *depends on its chemical composition, physical structure, homogenity and closeness of grains and type of cementing material*. Location of the stone in the structure also affects durability.

Alternate heating and cooling, alternate wetting and drying dissolved gases in rain water, high wind velocity, are some of the natural causes which affect durability adversely.

5. Strength. For ordinary building works, the strength need not be-considered. This is because maximum compressive stresses in such cases are very small as compared to the crushing strength of even the weakest variety of the stone. For example the crushing strength of soft lime stone which is considered a very week variety of stone has a crushing strength of *about 100 kg/cm^2, but the maximum compressive stress in a three storeyed building would be only about 4.5 kg/cm^2. Hence, it is clear that in ordinary works, strength is not a very important aspect*. However, in case of structures like dams, major bridge piers and abutments, retaining walls, etc. considerably higher stresses are likely to develop and as such strength becomes an important aspect to be considered. *As a thumb rule*, the maximum stress developed in the stone, *when subjected to severest possible conditions, should not exceed* $\frac{1}{10}$ *the crushing strength of the stone*. Average crushing strengths of some of the building stones are as follows.

Name of Stone	*Density in kg/m^3*	*Crushing strength in kg/cm^2*
Granite	2640-2750	1040-1400
Basalt	3000	1530-1890
Diorite	—	900-1500
Trap	2500	3000-3500
Laterites	2400	18-32
Lime stone	2000-2750	550
Marble	2650	720
Sand stone	2650-2950	650
Shale	—	2-6
Gneiss	2690	2100
Slate	2890	710-2110

6. Hardness. When stone is subjected to severe wear, and abrasion, as in the case of floors and pavements, the hardness of the stone is considered a very important property. Hardness of stone can be estimated roughly by the scratch with the finger nail or scratch by knife. Soft rocks having very small hardness can be scratched by finger nails, where as those of considerable hardness of knife. Coefficient of hardness as worked out in hardness test, should be greater than 17, when stone is to be used in road work. Stones having coefficient of hardness less than 14 are considered very poor and such stones should not be used in road work. Stones whose coefficient of hardness lies between 14 and 17 are considered of medium hardness.

7. Weight. Weight of the stone is related to the density of the minerals of which stone is composed of and also with the compactness and fineness of the grains. Heavy stones are generally more strong and durable. Heavy weight of the stone carries importance especially in marine engineering works. Heavy weight is preferred in case of dams, retaining walls, major bridge piers and abutments and marine engineering works. Vaults, arches etc. prefer light weight stone.

8. Percentage of wear. Resistance to wear is measured by Attrition test. Good stone should not show wear of more than 3%. This property is useful for the stone, to be used as road aggregate and railway ballast.

9. Ease in dressing or working. This property of stone is important from economy point of view. The stone which could be easily worked or dressed, proves economical. It is economical to dress the stone soon after its quarrying, as it is soft due to presence of quarry sap.

10. Appearance. This characteristic is important for the stones to be used for the face work of the building. Beautifully coloured stones provide architectural appearance at the face work. Such stone should be durable, uniform in colour and structure. Hard crystalline stone, having a very dense structure, can be easily carved, moulded or polished and thus preferred for face work. Marble, granite, slate etc. take very good polish.

11. Porosity and absorption. Porosity and absorption are two terms which are inter-related to each other. Porosity depends upon the void space between the mineral particles, whereas water absorbed by mineral constituents of the stone is known as absorption. Porosity is expressed in terms of absorption of water in relation with the dry weight of the stone.

All the stones have some porosity. The stones which are less porous are considered good stones. Porous stones can be destroyed by decomposition or by frost action. For a good stone, percentage absorption by weight after 24 hours, should not exceed 0.60.

12. Resistance to Fire. The stone should be composed of such minerals which could withstand the action of fires satisfactorily. Disintegration of stone due to fire may be by any of the following actions.

(i) Sudden rise in temperature.

(ii) Sudden cooling due to water poured for extinguishing fire.

(iii) Different coefficients of linear expansions of minerals.

Sand stone having silicate as binding material can withstand the fires satisfactorily. Stone having clay as the predominant mineral although have poor strength, but they can resist fires very well. At temperatures more than 600°C, free quartz expands suddenly, causing its disintegration. On the other hand limestone can resist fires very well upto about 800°C but then it disintegrates into calcium oxide and carbon dioxide. When water, being used for extinguishing fires, comes in contact with CaO, it expands a lot and causes collapse of the structure.

13. Weathering. The capability of the stone to withstand the adverse affects of various atmospheric and external agencies, such as rain, frost, wind etc., is termed as weathering. *Good weathering stones should be used for face work, so that existing appearance of the building may be maintained for a long time to come.*

14. Toughness The stones used for road work and other situations, which are subjected to very adverse conditions, should be tough. The power of the stone is to resist effect of impact is called toughness. *Toughness of the stone is determined by impact test and represented by toughness index. Stones having toughness index above 19, are very tough stones while those, having its value below 13 are not enough tough stones.* Stones having toughness index *between 13 and 19 are known as moderately tough stones.*

It should be remembered that one kind of stone cannot suit to the requirements of all types of constructions. Hence, it is very essential to make thorough study of the situations in which stones are to be used for making any definite recommendation.

Characteristics and qualities of good building stone have been enumerated in short, ones again.

1. The stone should be easily and economically obtainable in bulk.

2. The stone should be hard, strong and durable.

3. It should be able to withstand the deteriorating action of rough weather. In other words, it should weather well.

4. It should have fine grained compact texture. The shade of the stone should be of pleasing nature especially, where it is to be used in face work.

5. It should be capable to withstand the effects of smoke and acidic atmosphere. This point is specially important for the stones to be used in very industrialized cities, having polluted atmosphere.

6. The stone should be free from soft patches, flaws, cavities and cracks.

7. The stone should be in position to withstand the effects of ordinary fires, without suffering any serious damage.

8. It should be well seasoned and easily workable.

9. It must not absorb more than 5% of its weight when kept immersed in water for 24 hrs.

10. Its structure should be crystalline and homogeneous.

11. S.G. of stone should not be less than 25.

12. The fracture of the stone should be sharp, even and clear.

1.12. Characteristics of Principle Building Stones

1. Granite. This stone is obtained from igneous rock. It consists of minerals like quartz, Felspar, mica, hornblende, pyroxene etc. It has about 60% to 80% of silica, which acts as a binder. Silica is present more in form of felspar than in form of quartz. As granite is found at very large depths, it is also sometime called plutonic igneous rock.

Properties:

(i) It is hard, strong and durable unstratified type of stone.

(ii) It is a heavy stone having S.G. varying between 2.64 and 2.75.

(iii) Granite having fine grained structure can be very nicely polished.

(iv) It is very difficult to dress this stone and as such should not be used in ordinary works.

(v) Ordinarily its colour is grey, but actually it depends upon the presence of type of felspar in the stone. It is also available in green, red, pink, and brown colours also.

(vi) It splits badly, when it comes in contact with fire.

(vii) Its crushing strength varies from 1000 to 1400 kg/cm^2

(viii) Weathering properties and strength depend upon the amount of quartz and also on the type of felspar present in granite. A stone having larger amount of quartz and good type of felspar, is stronger and more resistant to atmospheric agencies.

(ix) Medium or coarse-grained granite, on account of tis hardness, strength, weathering qualities combined with good appearance, is considered to be the best stone for the construction of bridges, piers, marine works, and other exposed massive structures.

(x) Highly coarse grained granites are mostly used in form of crushed stones such as road metal, railway ballast and aggregate for concrete.

Granite is mainly found at Ajmer, Jhansi, Jabbalpur, Kagra in H.P., Bangalore, Sikanderabad, Dalhousie, Assam and Gujarat.

2. Gneiss or stratified granite. It is granite, which has been converted into stratified layers by the metamorphic action. This stone can be quarried in form of patties. This stone is even more stronger than the granite.

This stone may have white, light grey, pink, green or black colours. Its S.G. is 2.69 and crushing strength 2100 kg/cm^2. It can be used for rough masonry work and street pavings. This stone is not very good looking, and as such should not be used for face work of buildings. It can be very well adopted for pitching work and also as coarse aggregate in concrete.

This stone is quarried in Madras, Gujarat. Bihar, Andhra Pradesh, Maharashtra, Kerala, Bengal and Mysore.

3. Trap and Basalt. Both these stone are of igneous rock origin. Both are formed by sudden cooling of molten lava, when exposed to open atmosphere. They contain 40 to 60% of silica. Trap consists of Felspar and hornblende as the predominant mineral, whereas basalt has Felspar and pyroxene as the main minerals. When stone has some olivine present, it is known as *olivine basalt.*

These stones are hard, compact and strong. Their S.G. is 3 and crushing strength between 1530 and 1.90 kg/cm^2. These stones cannot be excavated in form of blocks as they have amorphous texture. The colour of these stones may be grey, dark grey, green, blue, black, red and yellow. Red and yellow coloured varieties are softer are therefore, recommended for ornamental work. Remaining coloured basalts are usually hard to work. These stones are not suitable for masonry and paving works, as they are not tough. However at places, where they are excavated in very large amounts, they can be used for masonry work also. These stones cannot be dressed.

These stones are obtained in Maharashtra, Madras, U.P. Bengal, Bihar, M.P. and Rajasthan. A Janta, Eulora, and Elephanta caves are made of this stone.

The uses of these stones is recommended for road metal, rubble masonry, foundation work, etc.

4. Sand stone. This stone is obtained from stratified sedimentary rocks. This stone contains quartz as the principle mineral which remains cemented together by a colloidal Matrix of silicate of alumina, lime, magnesium and some proportions of oxide and carbonate of iron. Durability, hardness, and the strength of this stone, depends upon the quality of cementing material. Stones having calcium carbonate as the cementing material have low weathering properties. Like stones of other rock sandstone also occurs in a veriety of formations such as fine grained, coarse grained, comapct or porous. Fine grained, silica bound sand stone, is considered strong and durable. Sand stone is available in white, green, blue, black, red and yellow colours. Sand stone can be very finely dressed. The best quality sand stone is used for ashlar work. Compact and fine grained sand stone is used for carvings. Sandstones, unless of very hard variety, cannot withstand abrasion and hence should not be used as road metal. S.G. of the sand stones varies from 2.65 to 2.95. The compressive strength is taken as 650 kg/cm^2.

Depending upon the type of cementing material, sand stones may be classified as *Calcareous sand stone, Argillaceous sand stone* and *ferruginous sand stone*. All these sand stones have lime, clay and oxide of iron, as the cementing materials, respectively. Argillaceous sand stone is generally very porous and thus very weak.

Sand stone is used for steps, facing work, columns, flooring, walls, ornamental carvings etc. This stone is available in A.P., M.P., Punjab, Rajasthan, Maharashtra, Gujarat, Bengal, Bihar, Himachal Pradesh, Kashmir, Madras and U.P.

5. Flag stone. It is also a type of sand stone available in form of thin slabs or patties. Its colour is grey or bluish grey. It is very hard and compact. It can be very nicely polished.

6. Tile stone. This stone is similar to flagstone. It is also available in form of thin slabs. This stone can be used in form of tiles, for covering roofs. There is one more variety of sand stone named *free stone*. This stone could be worked freely with the help of chisel and hammer.

7. Lime stone. This stone is also obtained from sedimentary rocks. It contains large proportions of calcium carbonate. Following four types of lime stones can occur. All these stones have different compositions, texture, and hardness.

(i) Compact lime stone

(ii) Granular lime stone.

(iii) Magnesium lime stone or Dolomite

(iv) Kankar.

(i) Compact lime stone. This stone is a veriety of an impure lime stone. Calcium carbonate, the principle ingredient of the stone, remains mixed up with impurities like sand and clay. It is generally found in seams of large thickness. Its texture is non-crystalline or amorphous. This stone may have grey, blue or black colour. This stone is easily workable, and as such can be easily adopted in construction works. However it should not be used in industrial cities because the atmosphere of such cities is heavily charged with acidic gases, which are injurious for this stone. This stone is quite tough and durable. This stone is extensively used as road metal for light traffic. It is also used in blast furnace and also for bleaching and tanning operations.

(ii) Granular lime stone. This stone consists of purely calcium carbonate or calcium carbonate cemented with silca or alumina. Its particles are quite large and some of its grains are of the size of peas. It has white light yellow or light grey colour. This stone is soft. light and absorbent. This stone should not be used in open situations. It can absorb 4% to 12% of water, when kept immersed in water for 24 hours.

(iii) Magnesium lime stone. The lime stone consists of calcium carbonate and magnesim cabontate predominetly. Iron silica and alumina are also present is small quantities. Magnesium limestone, consisting of about 45% of magnesium carbonate and about 45% calcium carbonate. It is also known as *Dolomite*. The colour of this stone containing larger proportion of megnesia is considered more durable. This stone is not considered suitable for acidic gases charged atmosphere.

(iv) Kankar. It is a form of impure lime stone containing about 30% of clay or sand. It is found at small depths either in form of solid layer, or irregular shaped nodules. It is very porous and has greyish colour. Hydraulic lime is manufactured by burning the nodules of Kankar. Hard and tough kankar can be used in the construction of roads also.

All the types of lime stone have S.G. varying from 2.0 to 2.75 and crushing strength of about 550 kg/cm^2.

Slabs of lime stone are used for flooring and roofing purposes. It can also be used for general construction works. This stone is predominently used in the manufacture of lime and cement.

It is available in Maharashtra, Rajasthan, Punjab, Gujarat, Bihar, A.P., H.P., M.P. and U.P.

8. Marble. It is a metamorphic rock. It has highly crystalline formation of lime stone or dolomite. Marble is usually white, but it acquires other colours also due to presence of certain minerals during its formation. If lime stone is heated red hot and no gas is allowed to escape from it, the stone gets converted into marble. No change takes place during heating, but only structure changes.

Marble is available in white, grey, black, red, brown, yellow blue and green colours. White marble is available in Rajasthan at Makrana and also at Jabbalpur. Green marble is excavated in Gujarat near Baroda, while black and yellow coloured marble is found near Jaipur and Jaisalmer in Rajasthan. Marble is also found in U.P., M.P., A.P. and Mysore.

S.G. of marble in 2.65 and crushing strength 720 kg/cm^2.

It is very costly stone and as such it cannot be used for ordinary works. It is used in costruction of very high class building temples, and mosques, and structures erected in the remembrance of elders. It can be used at the face work of building and also in form of flooring tiles, stair steps, wall lining. Table slabs, Electrical swtich boards, columns, pilasters etc. Wastes obtained during quarrying and dressing of marbles, may be used in the manufacture of lime. Mosaic chips can also be obtained from marble.

9. Laterites. It is a metamorphic rock of sedimentary origin. Chemically it is Argillaceous type of rock. It may be called sandy clay stone having high percentage of iron oxide. It has visicular texture. It is soft porous stone. Its colour may be dark grey or red. When freshly quarried it has lot of sap and thus very soft. It can be easily quarried in form of rectangular blocks. It should be allowed to season for at least six months in open before it can be used. Its S.G. is 2.4 and compression strength varies from 18 to 32 kg/cm^2. This stone can be used for building walls, as road metal and as aggregate in concretes.

It is found in Bihar, Orissa, Mysore, M.P., A.P., Madras. Kerala and Maharashtra.

10. Slate. It is originally a sedimentary rock which has been converted into metamorphic rock having laminations. This is mostly composed of silica and alumina. During metamorphic action, its original planes of stratification, completely vanish and new planes of cleavage are formed. This stone can be split easily along the cleavage lines in form of thin laminations. $\frac{1}{2}$ cm. thick laminations can be easily obtained from this stone. It is non-absorbent, compact fine grained stone, which produces metallic ringing sound, when lightly struck. It can be available in colours like grey, black, dark-blue and reddish brown. It can be used as tiles in roofs and paving slabs in floors, slates are also used for D.P.C. dados, and in bathrooms. Its S.G. is 2.89 and compressive strength varying from 710 to 2110 kg/cm^2. This stone is found in U.P., Bihar, Rajasthan (Alwar), Madras, Mysore (Bijapur), Baroda, A.P. (Cuddapah) and Kangra in H.P.

11. Quartzite. When silicious type of sand stone (sedimentary) is subjected to metamorphic action, quartzite, which is metamorphic stone, is obtained. This stone consists of quartz as predominent constituent, but fels-par may also be present in small amounts. This stone is found in various colours like, red, yellow, white and brown. It is dense, strong, hard stone, having stratified nature and crystalline texture. Being very hard, it breaks up irregularly and thus it cannot be worked upon.

This stone can be used in rubble masonry and also as road metal. It also provides a very good coarse aggregate for concretes. It is mainly found in Mysore, Gujarat, Punjab, Madras, Rajasthan, Bengal, A.P., H.P., U.P.

12. Sale. This stone is not used for engineering works. It is also a sedimentary stone which consists of calcium carbonate, and organic matter, cemented together with the help of clay.

13. Moorum. It is a gritty silicious material which is obtained as a resultant of disintegration of laterite stone. Moorum is abundently found near the quarry sites of laterite stone. Its colour is red and thus, sometimes it is also called by name 'red earth'. It is mainly used as blindage in the construction of water bound macadam (WBM) roads. It is also spread on foot-paths in gardens and in front of posh buildings so as to beautify these places. Moorum is a material obtained from metamorphic rock.

14. Chalk. It is pure white lime stone of sedimentary origin. It is very soft and can be converted into powder easily. This stone is unsuitable for engineering costruction works. It is vey much used in the manufacture of cement and glazier's putty. It is available at places, where lime stone is found.

15. Shingles. These are water-borne pebbles found in river beds. The size of pebbles is greater than those of gravel. It is also found near sea shores. Brosin shingles are used as road metals and in concretes, where no other aggregate is available.

16. Gravel. It is a mixture of water-borne pebbles with sand. It is found in river beds and also in alluvial tracts. It is used for surfacing roads, blindage, and also in concretes.

17. Schists. It is a name given to a group of stones which can be easily split. All the stones of this group are of metamorphic type, having their original origination from igneous as well as sedimentary rocks. It is not a name of any individual stone.

18. Conglomerate. When small pieces of gravel and shingle are cemented together by means of clay or lime, *conglomerate* is formed. The texture of conglomerate is pebbly non-uniform and porous. Conglomerate is not suitable for construction works. It is mainly used for revetment or pitching.

19. Kaolin or China clay. This material is obtained by the disintegration of felspar mineral, presence it in igneous rocks. It is also called hydrated silicate of aluminium (Al_2O_3 $2SiO_2$ $2H_2O$). Pure Kaolin's colour is light white and one has the feeling of smoothness like soap when touched with finger. It is a principle constituent of porcelain, used for making cups and soucer plates, and also for electrical and sanitary goods.

20. Syenite. This stone is of igneous origin. It consists of quartz, felspar and horn blende. It is tough and durable stone which can be finely polished. It is used for pavings and ornamental works.

21. Serpentine. It is also an igneous rock stone. It is soft, but compact. It has stripped appearance resembling the skin of a serpent. This stone is used for decoration purposes.

22. Porphyry. It is igneous rock stone. It is very hard and tough equivalent to granite. It is used as road metal and also as ornamental building stone.

1.13. Tests for Stones

Building stones are required to be tested for their different properties before they may be recommended for any specific use. Following are the tests which can be carried out on stones.

1. Smith's test.
2. Freezing and thawing test.
3. Frost action test.
4. Acid test.
5. Water absorption test.
6. Microscopic examination
7. Impact test.
8. Attrition test.
9. Crushing test.
10. Crystallization test.
11. Hardness test.

All these tests have been explained one by one.

1. Smith's test. This test is carried out to find out the presence of soluble matter in the stone. Few small chips of a freshly quarried stone are put in a glass tube containing water. After a lapse of about one hour the tube is briskly stirred for about half an hour. If water continues to remain clear, it reflects the stone free from soluble matter. If water becomes dirty, it shows presence of earthy matter in the stone. Presence of earthy matter reflects weakness of stone.

2. Freezing and thawing test. In this test, the effect of freezing and thawing on the stone are observed. Take specimen of stone to be tested and keep it immersed in water for 24 hours. The specimen is then transferred in a freezing mixture having–12°C temperature for 24 hours.

The specimen is maintained in freezing mixture for 24 hours. After this the specimen is warmed. This completes one cycle of freezing and thawing. This process is repeated several times and behaviour of stone is carefully observed.

3. Frost action. This test is also known as Brard's test. Take few damp stones and put them in boiling, concentrated solution of sulphate of soda. After this, the stone is kept suspended for several days and reweighed. The loss in weight of stone represents effects of frost action.

4. Acid test. This test is carried out on sandstone, to assess their weathering qualities. In this test, a sample of stone weighing about 100 gm. is taken and put in a solution having 1% strength of hydrochloric acid. It is maintained in the solution for seven days and during this, solution is periodically agitated. After this the specimen is taken out and its surface examined. If the sharpness of edges and corners is maintained it is considered that stone can withstand the weathering effects satisfactorily.

5. Water absorption test. This test is carried out to determine percentage absorption, by weight as well as by volume. It is also used to determine percentage porosity by volume, Density, S.G. and saturation coefficient. The test procedure is as follows.

(i) Take about 50 gm to 100 gm of cube of stone specimen and weigh (W_1 gms) it in air after drying in oven at 105°C for 72 hrs. and then cooling it to room temperature in a descicator.

(ii) Immerse the cube in distilled water tube kept between 20°C and 30°C for 24 hours. Take out the sample, wipe off its surface and weigh again. Let this time weight be W_2 gms.

(iii) Place the specimen again in water tube and raise the temperature of the tube to boiling of water. The boiling of specimen in water is continued for five hours. Allow the specimen to cool in the tube to a temperature lying between 20°C and 30°C. Weight the specimen suspended in water. Let this weight be W_3 gms.

(iv) The cube is taken out of tub, wipe off with damp cloth and reweighted. Let this time weight of the specimen be W_4 gms.

Now values of various components can be found out as follows.

Weight of moisture absorbed $= W_2 - W_1$

(*a*) Percentage absorption by wt. $= \left(\frac{W_2 - W_1}{W_1}\right) 100$ ... (1)

Original volume of stone in C.C. = loss of wt. in gms.

$= (W_4 - W_3)$

Increase in weight due to absorption $= (W_2 - W_1)$ gms.

Volume of water absorbed $= (W_2 - W_1)$ C.C.

(*b*) Percentage absorption by volume in 24 hours.

$$= \frac{(W_2 - W_1)}{(W_4 - W_3)} 100.$$

After 5 hours immersion in boiling water,

wt. of soaked specimen $= W_4$

original weight of specimen $= W_1$

absorption by wt. $= \left(\frac{W_4 - W_1}{W_1}\right) 100.$

Volume of test specimen = wt. of water displaced in gm. of C.C.

Volume of test specimen $= W_4 - W_3$

wt. of water absorbed $= (W_4 - W_1)$ gms.

Volume of water absorbed $= (W_4 - W_1)$ cc.

Absorption by volume after 5 hrs. immersion in boiling water

$$= \left(\frac{W_4 - W_1}{W_1 - W_3}\right) 100.$$

Percentage porosity by volume $= \left(\frac{W_4 - W_1}{W_2 - W_3}\right)$

Saturation coefficient $= \frac{\text{Water absorption}}{\text{Total porosity}}$

$$= \frac{W_2 - W_1}{W_4 - W_1}$$

Specific gravity (S.G.) $= \frac{W_1}{W_2 - W_3}$

= density also.

6. Microscopic examination. In this, surfaces of freshly borken stone specimen, are examined by keeping them under powerful microscope. In this examination information is sought in regard to texture, nature of cementing material, mineral constituents, average grain size, existence of shakes, fissures and pores etc.

7. Impact test. This test is carried out to find out the toughness of the stone. Test requires a machine having C.I. anvil and system by which fall of a hammer weighing 2 kg. can be regulated. Test procedure is as follows.

(i) Prepare a test specimen cylinderical in shape. Specimen has diameter and height both 25 mm. Put this specimen on anvil of machine with its axis vertical.

Adjust the fall of the 2 kg. heavy hammer vertically in such a way that after every blow the next blow of the hammer will take place from 1 cm. increased hight of the fall. Fall of first blow is always kept 1 cm. Fall of hammer in case of subsequent blows will thus be 2 cm, 3 cm, 4 cm and so on. The blow at which specimen breaks is noted. If it is say *n* th blow, then *n* represents the toughness index of the stone.

8. Attrition test. This test is used for the stones to be used, particularly as road metal or railway ballast. This test, helps in the assessment of the resisting power of the stone against grinding or rubbing action. Following is the test procedure.

Take sample of broken stone about 6 cm size and weighing about 5 kg. The test specimen of stones is put in both the cylinders of Devels attriction testing machine. Cylinders of the machine are 20 cm in diameter and 34 cm long. The cylinders are so fixed on a rotating table that the axis of each cylinder makes an angle of 30° with the horizontal. See Fig. 1.3.

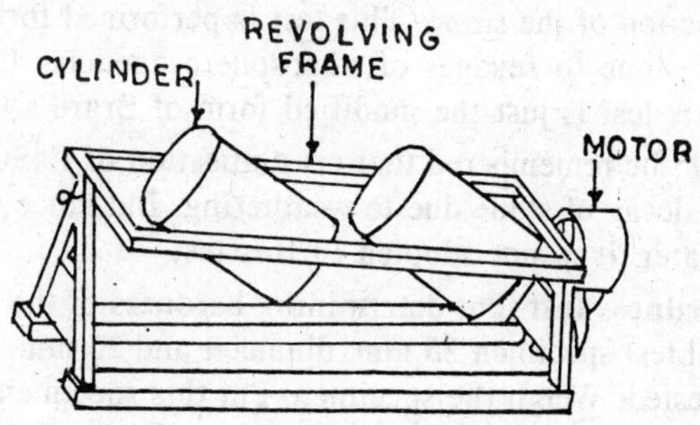

Fig. 1.3. Attrition test machine

Now the cylinders containing specimen of stone aggregate are rotated about horizontal axis for 5 hours at the rate of 30 R.P.M.

After this the test specimen is first sieved through 1.5 mm. sieve and then contents left over the sieve unpassed are weighed. Percentage of wear is found out as follows:

$$\text{Percentage wear} = \left(\frac{\text{Loss of weight in sample}}{\text{Original wt. of the sample}}\right)100.$$

9. Crushing strength test. This test is conducted to find out the compressive strength of the stone. For this test, specimen which may be inform of cube, cylinder or prism of diameter or lateral dimension equal to 50 mm, and of height less than 50 mm. are used. Mostly cubes of 40 mm. size are used as specimen. Three such specimen are prepared from the stone to be tested. All the test specimen are kept immersed in water of 20°C to 30°C for at least 72 hrs, before they are put to test.

All the test specimen are now tested in crushing test machine turn by turn. The rate of loading is maintained as 140 kg/cm^2 per minute. Crushing strength of the stone is taken as the average of crushing strength of all the three test specimen.

10. Crystallization test or Brard's test. For this test four specimen cubes, each having 40 mm. side are prepared. The cubes are dried for three days and then weighed. Prepare a solution of 14% strength of sodium sulphate. The specimen cubes are kept immersed for two hours in this solution and then taken out and dried at 100°C and reweighed. The difference in original weight and the weight after one cycle of immersion and drying, is noted. The process of immersion, drying and reweighing is repeated for at least five times and each time change in weight is noted and expressed as percentage of original weight. Visible changes that take place in the specimen also give some idea of disintegration. Sodium sulphate reacts chemically with the stone, and on drying, it crystallizes and expands in the pores of the stone and thus causes distruction of the stone. This test is performed for assessing the resistance of stone to revages of atmosphere agencies like sun, rain, wind etc. This test is just the modified form of Brard's test.

It should be remembered that crystallisation of $CaSO_4$ in pores of stone causes decay of stone due to weathering. But since $CaSO_4$ is less soluble in water, it is not adopted in this test.

11. Hardness test. For determining hardness of the stone prepare a cylinderical test specimen 25 mm. diameter and 25 mm. height, out of stone to be tested; Weigh the specimen. Put this specimen vertically on horizontal disc of Dorry's testing machine and kept pressed with a pressure of 1250 gm. Disc of the machine is then rotated at the rate of 28 R.P.M. During rotation of the disc. coarse sand is sprinked on the disc regularly. The specimen is taken out after completing 1000 revolutions and weighed. Determinine the loss in weight in gms. of the test specimen. Coefficient of hardness is found out as follows:

$$\text{Coefficient of hardness} = 20 \frac{\text{Loss in weight in gms.}}{3}$$

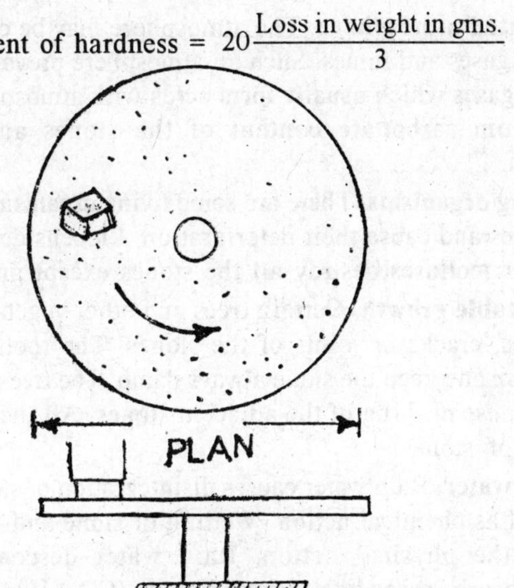

Fig. 1.4. Dorry's hardness testing machine

12. Shear strength test. For this test 5 cm × 5 cm and 18 cm long square bar is taken out from the stone to be tested for shear strength. The test specimen bar in fitted in the Johnson's shear tool of the machine and centred properly. Now the movable head is moved at a speed less than 1 mm. per minute. The shear strength is the total load divided by twice the area of the section sheared. Average of at least three tests should be taken as the shear strength.

1.14. Decay or Deterioration of stones

Exposed stones have to withstand the harmful efffects of atmospheric and external agencies. The stones may decay due to following causes:

1. Temperature variation. Stones are composed of several minerals which have different coefficients of thermal expansion. Rise or fall of temprature causes differential expansion or contraction of the minerals which cause deterioration or decay of stone. Alternate rise and fall of temperature without any differential expansion or contraction also causes deterioration of stone.

2. Wetting and drying of stone. Rain, dew and frost cause wetting of stones where are sunshine causes their drying. Alternate wetting and drying causes disintegration of stone.

3. Frost action. In hilly regions or other cold regions, water present in the pores of stone may freeze due to cold. Water expands after freezing , and thus causes the splitting of the stone.

4. Polluted atmosphere. The atmosphere may be charged heavily with harmful gases and fumes. Such an atmosphere prevails in industrial cities. These gases which usually form acids with atmospheric moisture, act on calcium carbonate content of the stones and cause their disintegration.

5. Living organisms. There are some living organisms which slowly act upon stones and cause their deterioration. Lichens destroy limeston, and worms or molluses destroy all the stones except granite.

6. Vegetable growth. Certain trees and other vegetation may grow at the fissures, cracks or joints of the stones. The roots of vegetation attract moisture and keep the stone always damp. The trees while growing expand and cause pushing of the adjacent stones. All these actions may cause decay of stones.

7. Rain water. Rain water causes disintegration of stone by physical action as well as chemical action. Wetting of stone and then drying by sunshine is the physical action. Rain water descending through atmosphere absorbs gases like carbon dioxide (CO_2) Hydrogen sulphide (H_2S) and others. CO_2 and H_2S both form acides with rain water and render water chemically, aggressive. This aggressive water reacts chemically with minerals of stone and causes their disintegration.

8. Wind. Winds also help in deterioration of the stone. Strong winds, cause fine particles strike against the stone and cause its decay. Winds also help rain water penetrate deep into the stone. Rain water at larger depth may not be evaporated and may freeze during winter. The frozen water expands and splits stone.

9. Stone coming in contact with some chemical. If stone happens to come in contact with some chemical, the stone may disintegrate. Dissimilar stones when used together may also affect each other and become the cause of disintegration.

10. Water. Sea water, river water, or ground water may also cause deterioration of stone. The water coming in contact of stone may dissolve some of the mineral constituents of stone and cause their decay.

1.15. Preservation of Stone

It is always good if policy of using good stone is adopted rather than preserving the inferior stone. However inferior stones may have to be used if good stone is not locally available. Secondly, even good stone requires preservation, when atmosphere where it is to be used is heavily polluted with sulphurous or carbonic acids. Hence, preservation of stones is required when either stone itself is poor or when atmosphere where it is to be used is very aggressive, as in industrial cities. A good preservative should possess following properties.

(i) It should be economical, non-corrossive and harmless for health.

(ii) It should maintain its effectiveness for long time.

(iii) It should easily penetrate into the surface of stone

(iv) It should be easy in applying on the surface of stone.

(v) It should not develop objectionable colour and it should not allow deep penetration of moisute into the stone.

(vi) Preservative should be hard enough to withstand the effects of atmospheric agencies.

Following are the preservatives which may be used.

(i) Paints. Painting of stone surfaces change the original colour of the stone. Painted surfaces, if painted with deep penetration paints may act as preservative.

(ii) Linseed oil. Like paints, the surface of the stone may be preserved by applying raw or boiled linseed oil. Raw linseed oil maintains the original shade of the stone, where as boiled one makes the surface dark. But boiled linseed oil is better preservative than raw linseed oil. It also lasts longer than raw linseed oil. Effectiveness of boiled linseed oil is further increased, when it is further coated by diluted ammonia in warm water.

(iii) Coaltar. If applied on the stone surface, it acts as perservative but because of its objectionable colour, it is not used. It also absorbs heat of sun.

(iv) Paraffin. Paraffin alone may act as preservative. It can also be used by dissolving in neptha.

(v) Alum and soap. Alum and soap are taken in proportion of $1\frac{1}{2}$: 1 and a solution with water is prepared. This solution when applied to the stone surface, acts as a good preservative.

(vi) Use of Baryta or barium hydroxide. This preservative proves most effective when stones are to be preserved in the atmosphere, charged with carbonic or sulphurous acids. Barium hydroxide solution, when applied on the surface of the stones fills the pores and causes the hardening of the surface. This hardened surface resists atmospheric absorptions. The coating of Barium hydroxide has to be renewed from time to time.

(vii) Pointing and plastering. Stone works can be preserved by pointing or plastering the exposed surfaces. Plasters prevent atmospheric agencies from coming in contact with stone surfaces. Pointing prevents ingress of moisture or rain water, and thus prevents decay of stone.

1.16. Artifical Stone

Cement has made it possible to cast artifical stones. Cast stone is nothing, but hardened plain cement concrete, moulded in suitable shape and size. Some times some colouring agent or some other ingredient may be added to the dry mixture of concrete to obtain the desired shade of the structure.

Artifical stone consists of 1.5 parts of coarse aggregate of size 3 mm to 6.mm and 1.5 parts of fine aggregagte of size less than 3 mm. Both, coarse aggregate and fine aggregate, are obtained from natural stones. Mix both the aggregates. This mass will form three parts. Now add one part of cement to three parts of mix of coarse aggregate and fine aggregate and mix them dry. If any specific colour effect is to be developed in the cast stone, add suitable pigment to the dry mix. Lastly add water to the dry mix to obtain a mixture of workable consistency. The plastic mix is then pressed into moulds, cured and dried. Artificial stone blocks are ready for use. The blocks may be polished, if required. In order to develop light shades, white cement may be used in place or ordinary cement.

The moulds used for manufacture of cast stone may be made of wood or steel. Sometimes 2.5 cm to 4 cm thick skin of facing is made of superior aggregates and cement, and the heart may be made of cheaper material. Cement concrete, Mosaic tiles and terrazo, are the good exampels of artificial stones. Precast concrete tiles, having top of marble chips, are known as mosaic tiles. R.C.C. may also be considered as a type of artificial stone.

Advantage of artificial stones. Following are the advantages which artificial stones have, over the natural stones.

(i) They can be cast in any shape and size.

(ii) They can be made stronger than natural stone.

(iii) They do not have any specific natural bed and as such they can be used in any position.

(iv) They can be easily moulded and seasoned at the site of work.

(v) They do not require any dressing

(vi) Holes may be kept at the time of casting. These holes may be required for pipe or electric wire fittings.

(vii) Their mass is more homogeneous and thus their properties, are more reliable.

(viii) They can be designed for any srength.

(ix) They can be cast in economical sizes which could be easily handled.

(x) They normally do not have any defect.

(xi) They are more durable than natural stone.

(xii) They do not require any transportation as they can be cast at site.

(xiii) The progress of work will be faster with precast stones.

1.17. Stone Quarrying

The site from where stones are excavated is known as simply *quarry* or *quarry site*. The process of taking out stones from quarry is known as *quarrying of stone*. There is difference between the terms quarry and the mine. In the case of mines, all the excavation processes are carried out under ground at large depths where as all the processes or operations are carried out at ground level under exposed conditions in case of quarry.

Selection of quarry site. Selection of site for quarrying the stones should be done very carefully. Following points should be considered while making selection of site.

(i) Distance of quarry from road, railways, etc. should not be very large.

(ii) Sufficient stone should be assured from the site.

(iii) Availability of equipment, labour, etc. also affect the selection of site.

(iv) Quality of stone available from quarry should be good.

(v) Drainage from quarry should be easy.

(vi) Adequate facilities for transportation of stone, should be available.

(vii) Geological formation of the site should be properly studied.

(viii) The site should be away from built up areas, in case blasting has to be resorted to.

1.18. Important point to be Considered before Starting Quarrying

(i) Equipment and labour. Before starting any quarry, the need of labour and equipment should be carefully studied. For this, experience of people engaged in other quarries in that area should be pooled. There should be proper co-ordination between equipment and labour.

(ii) Removal of overlay. The soft soil and soft rocks lying at the top, are first of all removed and surface of the stone to be excavated, exposed. The stone obtained from top surface is generally very soft and unsuitable for construction work and thus usually rejected. Good dense stone can be availed only at depths.

(iii) Lay Out. All the needs of the equipment are estimated before hand and a layout plan showing positions of each equipment or machines and processes envolved, is prepared. The lay out plan should be such that all the operations involved in stone quarrying are arranged in most logical manner.

(iv) Examination of rock surface. The exposed surface of the stone, after removing the over lay material, should be carefully examined. Position of natural bed, cracks, fissures etc. along which stones can be easily split, should be identified, so as to make the operation of quarrying economical.

(v) Stability of slopes. The slopes at the quarry site should be maintained such that their stability is not disturbed easily. If this precaution is not taken, landslides may take place, causing either serious accidents or some times, even blocking of the quarries.

1.19. Methods of Quarrying Stone

The methods of quarrying the stone may be five :

1. Digging or excavating
2. Heating
3. Wedging
4. Use of channelling machine and
5. Blasting.

1. Digging or excavating. This method is suitable when detached blocks of stone lay burried in earth or soft rock dust. Tools like crow bars, pick-axes, kassi, etc. are mainly required.

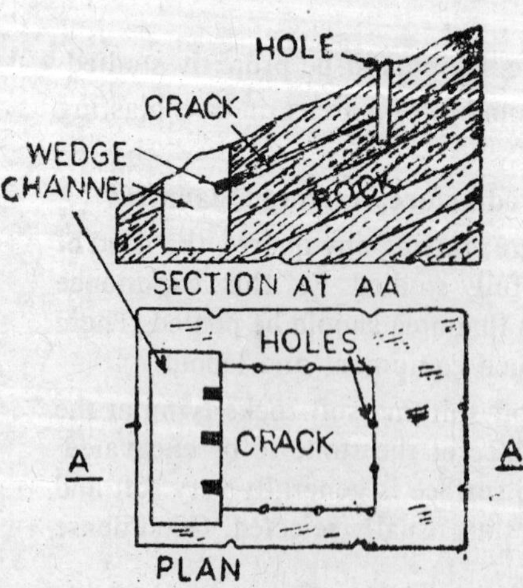

Fig. 1.5. Wedging method of excavation

2. Heating. In this method of quarrying, fire wood is piled on the surface of the stone to be excavated. The fire is burnt steadily for sometime. Heating of the stone causes upper layers of stone expand, in relation to the lower layers. Due to unequal expansion, upper layers of rock separate from the lower layers. Splitting of the rock is indicated by dull bursting sound. The detached stones are then taken out of quarry with the help of wedges and crow bars etc. This stone is suitably, shaped with the help of hammers and marketed. This method is found suitable where rock formation consists of thin horizontal layers. This method provides small blocks of stone of nearly regular shape.

3. Wedging. This method is mainly used for the rock of sedimentary type, which are comparatively soft, such as sand stone, limestone, marble, slate, laterite.

In this method, first of all naturally occuring cracks or fissures are located in the rocks, to be excavated. The steel wedges or points are then driven with the help of hammer, in such fissures or cracks and stones are detached. The split out blocks of stone can be converted into marketable forms and supplied to users.

If natural cracks or fissures do not happen to be there artifical cracks will have to be formed. For this, a line of holes is drilled along the rock surface. The holes are normally 12 mm in diameter and 20 to 25 cm deep depending upon the type of rock and also desired size or thickness of the excavated stone. Holes are generally spaced at 10 to 15 cm apart again depending upon the type of the rock. The holes are generally drilled with the help of pneumatic drill. After drilling, each hole in provided with two pieces of feathers and a conical steel wedge or plug inserted in each hole as shown in Fig. 1.6. Plug is nothing, but a conical steel wedge where as feather is half-rounded piece of steel flat, with its upper end slightly curved.

Now all the plugs or wedges are simultaneously driven by the hammer. The force exerted by all the wedges cause rock to crack along the line of the holes.

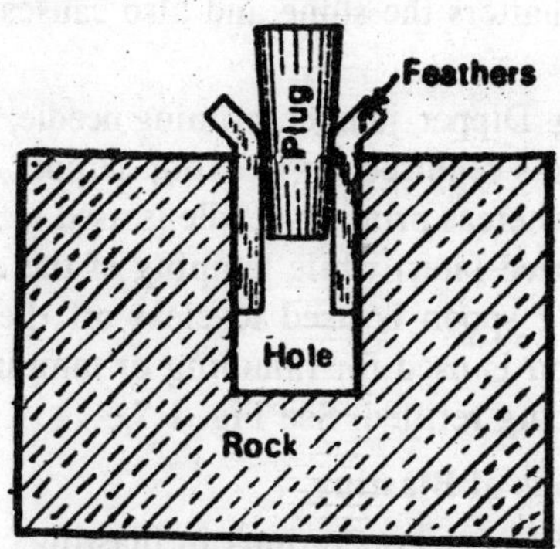

Fig. 1.6. Feather and Plug system

Sometimes, if rock to be excavated is soft, dry wooden plugs are inserted between the feathers put in the holes. After tightly fitting all the wooden plugs, water is sprikled on them. Wet wooden plugs swell and exert a large force to split the stone along the line of the holes.

After splitting, the stone is taken out and converted into desired forms.

4. Channelling machine method. This method of excavation of rocks is adopted when stone in definite large sizes is required, and stone involved is of softer variety. Marble, lime stone, and soft sand stones can be quarried by this method. In this method a special machine known as channelling machine is used. It is such a machine which can make vertical as well as oblique grooves in the stone. This machine can cut out 5 to 8 cm wide and 2 to 4 m deep grooves.

A groove is cut around the stone block to be excavated with the help of this machine. The stone block is then detached from the bottom by drilling horizontal holes and then wedging as explained earlier. In the case of stratified rocks drilling of horizontal holes is not required and blocks can be detached with the help of the wedges and hammer directly.

5. Blasting. This method is used when stone to be excavated is of very hard variety and it has no cracks or fissures. Moreover, if stone is to be excavated on very large scale, blasting method will have to be adopted. No definite size blocks can be excavated by this method. After blasting, the excavated stone is sorted out in different sizes and categories.

Blasting is a method in which quarrying of stone is done with the help of explosives. First of all, holes are drilled with the help of pneumatic drills. The holes are charged with explosive and fired. When explosives are fired, they cause shaking of the stone and solid rock is shattered in the form of various sized blocks. This method should be avoided for building stones, as it shatters the stone and also causes a good deal of wastage.

Tools for Blasting. Dipper, jumper, priming needle, scraping spoon, tamping bar, are the tools required for blasting. Dipper and jumper are used for making holes whereas priming needle is used to maintain a hole (for the fuse to be inserted later) while tamping of the clay in the hole is being done. Scraping spoon is used to clear off the dust from the blast holes. Tamping rod is used for ramming or tamping the material while blast holes are being refilled. See Fig. 1.7.

1.20. Various Operations of Blasting

Following are the various operations in blasting :

1. Boring or drilling of holes
2. Charging of the holes with explosive
3. Tamping of the holes with clay.
4. Firing.

1. Boring or drilling of holes. The holes in the rock are made either with the help of jumpers or with a pneumatic or percussion drilling machine. Jumper is, however, generally used. Its length and diameter, depend upon the depth and diameter of the hole required. It is usually 2 to 4 cm in diameter and 1 to 2.5 m long. While excavating hole, the jumper is slightly rotated every time after striking the rock. Water is also added in the holes to soften the rock. When the hole is drilled to the required depth, it is cleared of the loose matter by a scraping spoon. Holes of small depth can be made by jumper, but deeper holes in very hard rocks are drilled with the help of drilling machine.

2. Charging of the holes with explosive. First of all the hole is dried by rotating a small iron rod with a rag tied at its end. The charge of gun powder or dynamite (Gun-cotton) is placed at the bottom of the hole.

3. Tamping of holes with clay. The Priming needle which is a thin copper rod is greased and placed in the explosive. The remaining portion of the hole is filled with damp clay and rammed hard with the help of copper tamping bar. While tamping is being done, the priming needle should be frequently slightly turned. This facilitates easy withdrawal of priming needle when the hole is completely filled up. The priming needle is slowly with drawn, leaving a long narrow hole. Gun powder is then poured inside this hole. A fuse is inserted in whole and kept sufficiently projecting out of the hole. Thus a link is setup between the fuse at top and charge of explosive at the bottom. Detonators are used in placed of fuse when explosive used in dynamite.

4. Firing. The firing of the charge in the blast hole, is done either with a match box or with electric spark. Dynamite is always detonated with the help of detonators which act on electric spark, where as gun powder is fired with the help of fuse. Charge can be detonated from considerable distance with the help of long leads of electric wires. But in case of firing the charge, sufficient time is required for the man firing to retreat to safer place, before blast takes place. This time can be regulated with the length of the fuse projecting out of the hole. Even gun powder can be ignited, with the help of electric spark. But Dynamite cannot be ignited, but can only be detonated.

In case blasting holes are subjected to seepage of water, the holes must be made dry before charging them. The blasting powder may also be used by enclosing in water proof bags. Fuse is directly inserted into the explosive and kept projecting out of the hole. The explosive can be fired by igniting the projecting end of the fuse.

Firing by electric spark is advantageous because of following reasons :

(i) It is safe and time saving

(ii) It can even fire under water

(iii) Firing being simultaneous, the efficiency of explosive is very high.

(iv) Rock is shattered into small blocks.

1.21. Precautions in Blasting

While blasting, in order to avoid the possibilities of serious accidents, following precautions should be taken.

1. **Notice to Public**. The area affected by blasting should either be cordoned with the help of barbed wire or arrangements made to keep the cattle and general public away. Notices, visiable signs in form of red flags etc. should be displayed at suitable places along the boundary of such area. Blasting hours may be fixed and notified to general public so that they may keep off at assigned hours of blasting.

2. The people should be informed by syrons, or ringing of bells, well in advance of the actual blast. On hearing the syrons the labour working at the site should be instructed to move out of the danger zone.

3. One should not enter the blast zone immediately after blast has taken place. First of all, it must be ensured that all blast holes charged with explosives have been fired or not. If some charge has not fired, steps should be taken either to fire it or remove it, before entering the zone. Firing of misfires is preferred rather than taking it out of hole, unfired.

4. The main who is handling the explosives should put on polythine gloves on his hands.

5. The hole which is to be made in the explosive to house the detonator should be made with the help of wooden rod rather than metallic rod.

6. **Length of fuse.** The length of the fuse projecting out of the blast hole should be such that a worker may retreat to a safe distance after firing it.

7. **See page of water.** If seepage water is likely to enter the blast hole, the explosive charge should be placed in the hole either by enclosing in a water proof paper or in a thin iron plate.

8. **Expert supervision.** The responsibility of blasting should be entrusted to experienced persons only.

9. **Storing of explosives.** The explosives should be carefully stored in specially constructed magazines, located away from residential and other important buildings. Different explosives should be stored separately and detonators should be kept entirely away from the explosives.

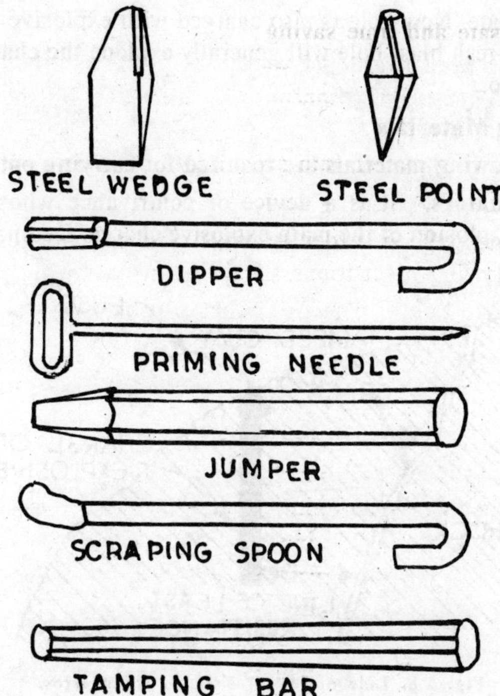

Fig. 1.7. Various rods and spoons used for filling explosing the hole

10. Tamping rod and priming needles. These should be made of bronze, brass or copper, and not of steel. The steel rod striking a rock may develop spark. This may result in premature explosion and serious accident.

11. Line of least resistance. It is the distance from the centre of the blast hole to the face of the rock exposed to air, along which the gases generated by the explosion of the charge will find least resistance to escape into the air,. Length of line of least resistance (L.L.R.) is important in determining the quantity of explosive required in the process of blasting. Hence location of the holes and their depths should be very skillfully decided. Depth of the hole should be equal to the line of least resistance. The quantity of powder or dynamite, required for each blast depends mainly on the nature of rock, the mass of rock to be removed and the position of the hole. Generally charge of powder in $\text{kg} = \dfrac{(\text{L.L.R.})^2}{8}$ where L.L.R. is in meters.

12. Failure of explosion. If a blast hold charge fails to explode due to any reason, a fresh new hole should be made near the hole that has failed to explode. New hole is also charged with explosive and blasted. Explosion in fresh blast hole will generally explode the charge of failed blast hole also.

1.22. Blasting Materials

The following materials are required for carrying out the blast.

1. Detonators. It is a device or contrivance whose explosion initiates the explosion of the main explosive charge. Detonators may be of two types.

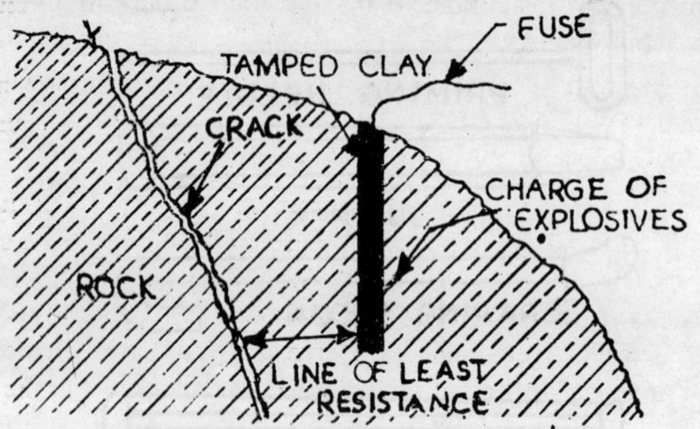

Fig. 1.8. Line of least resistance along arrow joining fuse hole with fissure

(i) Plain detonators also known as blasting caps.

(ii) Electric detonators also known as electric blasting caps.

(i) Plain Detonators. It consists of a copper or aluminium cylinderical tube, about 6 mm diameter and 25 mm long. It is closed at one end. It is partly filled with fulminate of mercury or any other sensitive explosive. The tube is only partly filled, since this detonator is always used in conjuction with safety fuse. Safety fuse is inserted in the tube, so that it comes in contact with the sensitive charge in the tube of the detonator. After putting the safety fuse, the detonator tube is slightly pressed at the mouth, so that fuse is held in position. The assembly of plain detorator with safety fuse in, is termed as a capped fuse. See Fig. 1.9.

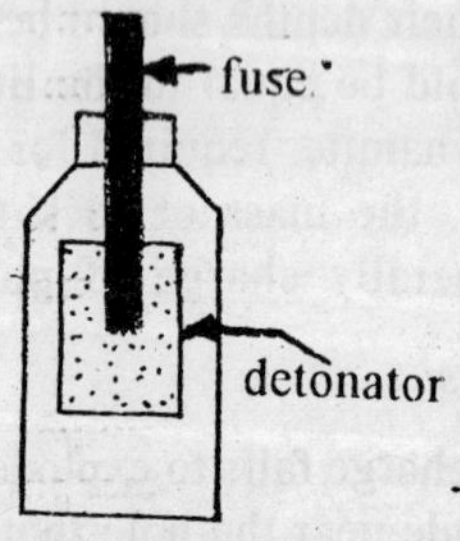

Fig. 1·9. Detonator

(ii) Electric Detonator. It is also just like plain detonator except that the length of the tube is slightly more and safety fuse is replaced by an assembly of fuse head and leading wires. This detonator thus has (*a*) detonator tube containing the explosive charge (*b*) the fuse head (*c*) the water proof seal at the open end and (*d*) the leading electric wires.

Detonators are used when dynamite explosive is to be fired. Detonators may be fired either by fuse as in case of plain detonators, or electric spark as in case of electric detonators.

2. Fuse. It is also called safety fuse. It is used for firing a charge or a detonator. It is in form of thin rope of cotton with a core of continuons thread of fine gun powder. The safety fuse may either be slow burning, or instantaneous buring. Rate of burning of slow burning fuse is about 1 cm per second.

3. Explosives. There are so many types of explosives, but in stone quarry work,. gun powder and dynamite are in most common use. Composition of each explosives is given in brief.

(i) Gun powder. It is also called blasting powder. It is a weak explosive and is mostly used in the blasting of soft rocks. Its composition consists 70% saltpetre (KNO_3), 15% charchoal, and 15% sulpher. The proportions of charcoal, saltpetre and sulpher by weight may be 15, 75 and 10%, respectively. This explosive does not cause shattering effect. It only causes separation of fairly large stone blocks from the rock mass. Its action is slow and not very shattering. Gun powder is fired either by a safety fuse or electric spark. This explosive is mostly used in the manufacture of safety fuses.

(ii) Dynamite. It consists of 25% of sandy earth saturated with 75% of nitro-glycerine. It is in the form of thick plastic mass and is sold in definite sized cartridges. It is always exploded by means of detonators. Explosion in detonator causes a shock wave which further leads to the explosion of main charge. It is a very powerful explosive powder. It is used under the circunstance, when very heavy work is to be under taken under wet conditions. It is instantaneous in explosion and thus causes lot of shattering effect. It is mostly used for excavation of tunnels etc., and not for quarrying stone, as stone excavated by this explosive will be available in small sizes.

(iii) Gun cotton. It is developed by impregnating clean cotton in a cool mixture of nitric acid and sulphuric acid. It is avilable in the form of blocks or stocks.

It is as strong as dynamite, but its shattering effect is less. It decomposes with rise of temperature. It is generally stored and transported in moist conditions.

(iv) Cordite. It is a product of nitro-glycerine. It is prepared from the mixture of nitro-glycerine and nitro-cellulose. It is cheaper than other explosives. It is also detonated with the help of gun powder, primer, and detonator. It is a powerful explosive and does not give smoke. It can be used under water.

(v) Blasting Gelatine. It consists of 93% nitro-glycerine and 7% gun cotton. It has explosive power about 50% more than that of dynamite.

(vi) Gelignite. Its composition consists of 65% blasting gelatine and 35% of absorbing powder. It is also a powerful explosive and can be used under water.

(vii) Rock-a-rock. It consists of 79% of pottassium chlorate and 21% of nitro-benzol. It is more effective under water. It is used in U.S.A.

In blasting of rocks mostly gun powder and dynamite are used and hence comparisons of their properties is given here.

Particular	*Blasting Powder*	*Dynamite*
1. Cost	It is very cheap	It is about 5 times costlier than gun powder.
2. Action in quarring	Its lifting power is high and as such large blocks of stone are obtained	Its shattering power is high and as such small stone blocks are obtained.
3. Tamping	Its required very hard tamping	It does not require hard tamping.
4. Use	It is used in quarrying of stone.	It is mostly used for mining and tunnelling operations. It can be used for quarrying under water.
5. Destructive Power	Weak.	As strong as 6 times that of gun powder.
6. Efficiency	Comparatively low (4 m^3 rock/1 kg. explosive)	Comparatively large 6m^3/1 kg of dynamite)

1.23. Making of Primer Cartridge

In order to explode the dynamite charge, generally a primer cartridge is first of all prepared. The primer cartridge is then embedded in the main charge of the dynamite.

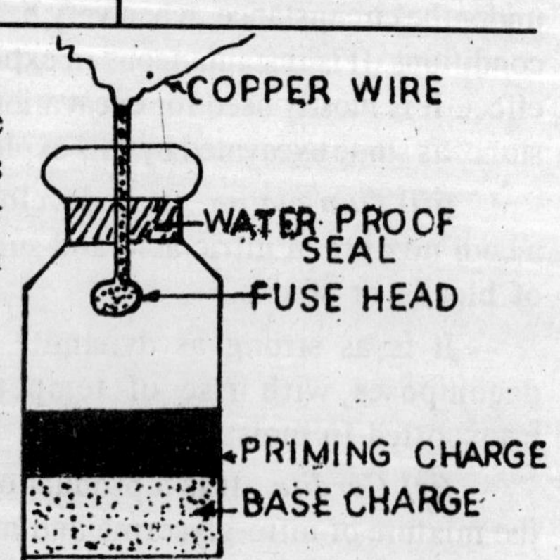

Fig. 1.10. Electric Fuse

To prepare a primer cartridge, first of all take a safety fuse in required length and insert its one end in the detonator. The open end of the detonator is slightly compressed with the help of nippers so that fuse remains in position in the detonator. The safety fuse should remain in touch with the explosive in the detonator tube. Now take dynamite cartridge, open its one end, insert the assembly of fuse and detonator gently and close up the dynamite cartridge. Now the primer cartridge is ready. This cartridge is embedded in the main charge which is to be detonated.

1.24. Storing of explosives

Explosives used for blasting the rocks should be stored very carefully. The store used for storing explosives is also called magazine. Following precautions should be taken while storing the explosives.

1. Detonators and explosives should be kept totally separately.

2. Different explosives should be placed in separate boxes.

3. In case of power failure only torches should be used for lighting. Flame lantern should not be used in any case.

4. No outsiders should be allowed to enter the magazine campus. The authorized persons must wear magazine shoes having no nails.

5. All the electric fitting and wiring should be properly concealed and frequently checked.

6. Explosives should be handled gently and gerks or drops of explosives should not be allowed.

7. Firing or smoking should be strictly prohibited with a radius of 50 m. from the magazine.

8. The magazine should be located away from residential buildings, important structures, public places and places of fuel storage.

9. The boundary area should be protected by a high barbed wire fencing and proper caution boards should be located. Watchman should guard the magazine round the clock.

10. Lightning conductors should be provide to safe guard the magazine.

11. The magazine should always be kept locked and the keys should be kept in the safe custody.

12. Under no circumstances the magazine should be constructed with a distance of 1/2 km from any working kiln or furnace.

13. Magazine should not be opened during or on the approaching thunderstorm and no person should remains in the vicinity of the magazine during such storm.

1.25. Handling of Misfires

In case explosion has not taken place in an explosive, charged blast hole when fired, it is known as *misfire* . Misfired explosive should not be removed from the balst hole. First of all one should wait for sufficient length of time, before approaching the misfired hole. Another hole should be drilled near the misfired hole and it should be fired by charging it with fresh explosive. The explosion in the new hole would cause explosion in the misfired hole also. This would avoid the chance of any accident.

1.26. Dressing of Stone

Stone blocks obtained from quarry, are in irregular sizes and shapes and cannot be used as such in masonry work, without dressing. Dressing of stones is a process, carried out with the help of hand tools, to give proper shape and surface to the stone, before its use in masonry or in any other work. The dressing of the stones is done for the following purposes.

(i) To get the good appearance of stone masonry.

(ii) To suit to the requirements of stone masonry.

(iii) To make transportation of stone easy and economical from the quarry.

(iv) To extract the advantage of trained local men in the trade of dressing.

(v) To take the advantage of softness in dressing due to presence of quarry sap in freshly quarried stones.

The degree of dressing of the stone, depends upon the type of masonry and the type of stone available. Following are the varieties of finishes that can be obtained by dressing of stones.

1. Quarry faced finish. Some of the stone blocks, as obtained from the quarry, can be used in masonry work directly without any dressing at the site of work. The large projections are knocked off from the stone blocks with the help of quarry hammer, as soon as the stone is quarried. The faces of such stone blocks are rough. The surface of such a stone is termed as self-faced, rock faced or hammer faced or quarry faced.

2. Scabbling finish. In this type of finish, the projections from the quarried stone blocks are removed using scabbling hammer. It is also a sort of rough dressing of stones.

3. Hammer-dressed finish. This finish is slightly more finer than qarrty and scabbling finishes. The stones in this dressing are made roughly square or rectangular and 2 cm to 5 cm wide margin is made about the edges of the exposed face.

4. Axed finish. This finish is mostly given to the surfaces of hard stones such as granite. This finish is given with the help of an axe.

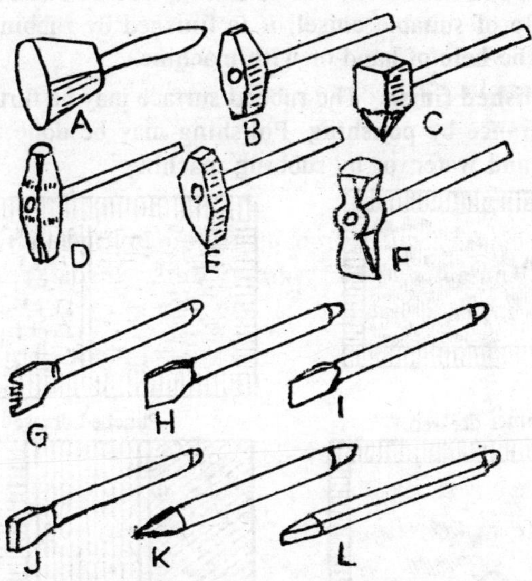

Fig. 1.11. Different types of hammers and chisels used for dressing the stones

5. Tooled finish. In this type of dressing, the surface of the stone is finished by means of a chisel. This finishing has continuous parallel chisel marks throughout the width and length of stone blocks. These marks may be made inclined also. By using different chisels, different patterns of finished surfaces can be obtained.

6. Punched finish. In this type of finishing, the surface of the exposed face of the stone is prepared by using punches. The full surface consists of uniformly distributed punch marks on its surface.

7. Cut stone finishing. In this type of dressing, the surface is finished using very sharpe chisel in such a way that chisel marks can hardly be recognized. It is a sort of very high class of finishing.

8. Furrowed finish. The surface of the exposed face is finished by making a number of vertical or horizontal grooves about 10 mm wide. 2 cm wide margin is also made around the edges of the exposed face.

9. Reticulative finish. In this finishing, 2 cm wide margin chamfered at 45° is marked around the edges and irregular depressions are developed on the enclosed space of the exposed face.

10. Vermiculated finish. This finished surface appears just like worm eaten surface. It is more or less similar to reticulated finish except that depressions in this surfacing are more curved and good looking in appearance.

11. Rubbed finish. In this finishing, instead of finishing surface with the help of suitable chisel, it is finished by rubbing the surface either with the help of hand or with machine.

12. Polished finish. The rubbed surface may be further improved in its appearance by polishing. Polishing may be done using pumice stone, sand and water, or by rubbing machine.

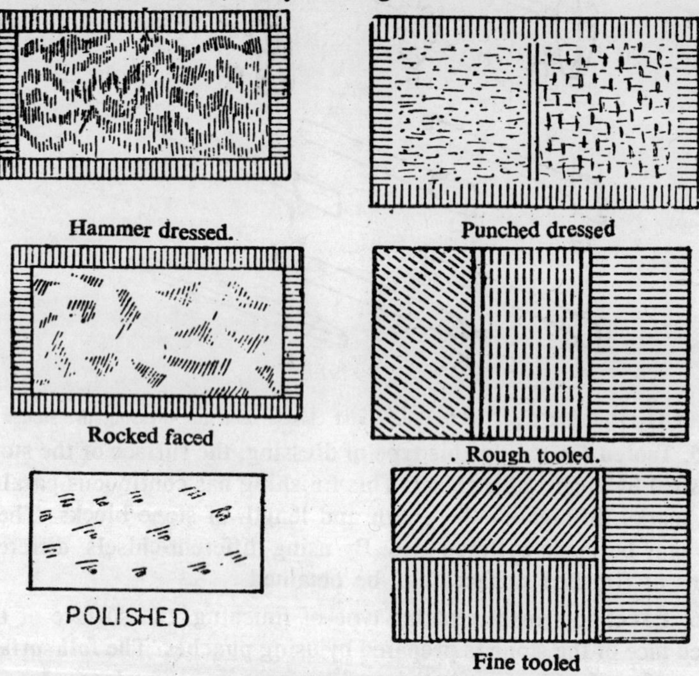

Fig. 1.12. Different types of Stone dressings

13. Chisel-draughted margin. In this case, a uniform margin about 2 cm wide is draughted around the stone with the help of chisel. Rest of the face may have any finishing.

Boasted finish, Dragged or combed finish, are some of the finishes which can be developed by using specific type of shisel in specific way.

1.27. Machines Required for Quarrying Stone

Following are some of the machines or equipment required at various stages in the quarrying of stone.

1. Channeller. It is a special machine used to cut deep grooves, vertical or oblique, around the stone to be quarried. It is used specially when massive blocks of stone are required to be excavated

2. Drilling machine. A pneumatic drill working on electric, mechanical or compressed air is requried to drill holes. The holes are required for blasting of stones or for wedging the stones, during quarrying.

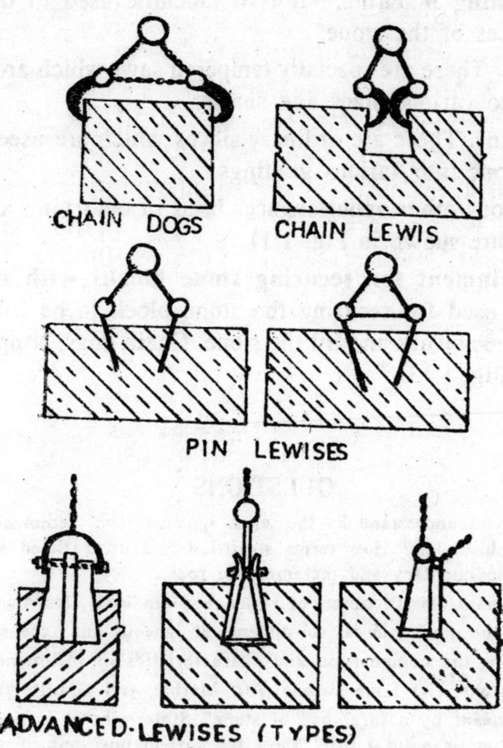

Fig. 1.13. Stone block lifting devices

3. Cranes and pulley blocks. They are used to lift and hoist the heavy stone blocks. The crane should be of adequate capacity so as to be in position to handle large size stones.

4. Tipping or dumper trucks. These are ordinary trucks having body of very small height. Even the sides and back of the body, remain hinged at the bottom and they can be opened as and when required for loading or unloading the trucks. They are used to transport the quarried stone to the place of use.

5. Crushers. If stone aggregate is required for road, railways, or concrete works, crushers may be installed near the quarry. When stone blocks are made to pass through the crusher, it gets converted into aggregate of specific size. There is provision in the machine to change the size of the aggregate as per requirements.

6. Moulding machine. It is a special machine which is used to engrave carved mouldings on the stone.

7. Polishing machine. It is a machine used to develop very smooth surfaces of the stone.

8. Saws. These are specially tempered saws which are used to cut the stones into various sizes and shapes.

9. Screens. These are ordinary sieves which are used to sort out the broken stone into various gradings.

10. Various other appurtenances used in quarrying and dressing of the stones are shown in Fig. 1.11.

11. Equipment for securing stone blocks with hoists. This equipment is used for securing the stone block to be lifted, so that lifting device may work and lift the stone. Chain dogs, Nippers, Lewish are shown in Fig. 1.13.

QUESTIONS

1. What do you understand by the terms igneous rock, sedimentary rock and metaphorphic rock? How terms stratified and unstratified are related to igneous, sedimentary and metamorphic rocks?
2. Give the main classifications of rocks. Explain each classification in brief.
3. What are the main mineral constituents of igneous and sedimentary rocks?
4. Write down the composition and characteristics of following stone:–
   (i) Sand stone, *(ii)* Lime swtone, *(iii)* Marble, *(iv)* Granite *(v)* Basalt.
5. What is meant by natural bed of stone? State, why it is necessary to set the stone on its natural bed? Show the correct positions of natural bed in case of cornice, arch, and corner stone.
6. What are the desirable qualities of building stone? Discuss all of them in brief?
7. Discuss the following tests used in stone :–
   (i) Smith's test, *(ii)* Water absorption test, *(iii)* Attrition test, *(iv)* Crushing test and *(v)* Hardness test.
8. Write short notes on following :–
   (i) Natural bed of the stone
   (ii) Line of least resistances
   (iii) Freezing test on stone.
   (iv) Artificial stone.
   (v) Texture or structure of the stone.
9. What are the different methods of quarrying stone? Explain each of the methods briefly.
10. *(a)* What are the different tests applied to test the suitability of stones for structural use and what are the factors affecting the durability of stones?
    (b) What are the materials required in blasting? Describe the process of blasting rocks. *(A.M.I.E. May 1952)*
11. Explain briefly what do you understand by *(i)* igneous rock, *(ii)* Sedimentary rock, *(iii)* Metamorphic rock.

Give example of each type and state their uses in building construction. (*A.M.I.E. Nov. 1966*)

12. What are the types of explosives generally used? Explain how they are normally obtained and stored before use?

How is blasting carried out and what precautions have to be taken for the safety of workmen? (*A.M.I.E. Nov. 1963*)

13. (*a*) What are the main principles to be observed in quarrying a rock? Illustrate your answer with sketch.

(*b*) State the sequence of a good building stone and mention any type of good building stone available in your state. Give the characteristics and Geological structure (*A.M.I.E. Nov. 1962*)

14. You have been asked by your boss to collect materials for the construction of a building having beautiful architectural features. State what points will you consider in selecting the quarry for supplying the stones?

15. Define a quarry what considerations you would suggest before making its site selections?

16. What are different explosives that can be used in blasting the rocks. Besides explosive what extra items are required for carrying out a successful blast of the rock? What precautions should be taken in the process of blasting?

17. Write short notes on :-

(*i*) Agencies that cause deterioration of stones.
(*ii*) Stone preservatives.
(*iii*) Impact test.
(*iv*) Fracture of the rock.

18. Distinguish between the following :-

(*i*) Stone and rock
(*ii*) Quarry and mine.
(*iii*) Lime stone and marble
(*iv*) Stratified and unstratified rocks
(*v*) Laterite and murum.

2

BRICKS

2.1 Brick

It is a regular sized rectangular unit, used for most of the building works. It is used as substitute for stone, where stone is not available. Bricks are obtained by moulding plastic mass of suitably proportioned earth in timber or steel moulds, Moulded bricks are first allowed to dry and then burnt in kilns designed for the purpose. *Bricks are always rectangular in shape and of such proportion that the length is generally twice the width plus the thickness of mortar joint.* Thickness of the brick is less than or at the most equal to the width of the brick. The size of the brick is such that it can be easily lifted and handled with one hand. They do not require any lifting appliances.

2.2. Comparison of Stone Work and Brick Work

Following are the points of comparison between stone work and brick work.

1. Stone is much more strong, durable and weather resisting than brick.

2. Because of more strength, durability and weather resisting characteristics, stone is used in the constructions, subjected to more severe and rigorous conditions. Under such conditions brick construction may not last long.

3. Stone work is generally not plastered to preserve the natural colour which is quite pleasing. But brick masonry is generally plastered to conceal the defects of the bricks.

4. Bricks, when subjected to dampness or other unfavourable conditions, may disintegrate and thus may affect the life and appearances of the brick work. Stone is not easily affected by such conditions.

5. Brick is a very good fire resistant material in comparision with stone. Hence in fire resistant structures bricks are preferred to stone.

6. Bricks absorb more water than stones and this moisture can easily reach inside the brick work. More over, brick will be easily affected by harmful salts in water.

7. Brick masonry is easy to raise where as stone masonry can be done by skilled masons only.

8. Stone masonry generally remains restricted at and around the area, where good type of stone is easily and locally available. Brick work can be done any where, because bricks can be manufactured any where by establishing brick kilns.

9. Bricks being is regular shape and size, can be used in definite pattern known as `bond'. Stone masonry does require any bond.

10. Progress of brick masonry is always more than that of stone masonry.

11. Bricks do not require any dressing etc., but stone masonry envolves lot of dressing.

12. Bricks can be moulded in any shape or size as per requirements, but dressing or shaping of stone to specific size or shape is not as easy.

13. Bricks being small, do not rquire any lifting device which may sometimes, be required in case of stones.

14. Brick work requires very little mortar, as joints in this case are very thin. Moreover structure also becomes more durable, because of thin joints.

15. Brick work does not create the feeling of massiveness, in comparison to stone work.

16. In case of monumental structures, stone work is found to be more useful than brick work.

17. Brick walls as thin as 10 cm can be constructed, but thickness of stone masonry is generally not less the 38 cm.

18. Good railway ballast can be obtained from stone only.

19. Good aggregate for concrete and road construction also can be had from stone only.

Seeing the points of comparison between stone and bricks, it can be easily appreciated that brick is in no way less useful building material than the stone. Both the materials have their own short comings and good points.

2.3. Ingredients of Good Brick Earth

A good brick earth mainly consists of silica (sand) and alumina (clay), mixed in such a proportion that the resulting mass with water is a plastic mass which could be easily moulded and dried without under going shrinkage, cracking or warping. It should contain a little finely divided lime which enables silica to melt at furnace heat and bind the particles of brick together. Bricks having more of lime become virtified.

It should also contain a small quantity of oxide of iron. It acts as a flux like lime, and more over gives red colour to the bricks on burning.

1. Alumina (clay). Alumina is the chief constituent of every kind of clay. A good brick earth should contain betwen 20 to 30% of alumina. Alumina provides plasticity to the earth, so that it can be moulded. If bricks contain excess amount of alumina, and insufficient sand they shrink, crack and warp on drying and burning.

2. Silica. It is present in the earth either in free or combined form. As free sand, it remains mechanically mixed with clay. In comined form, it exixts in chemical composition with alumina forming silicate of alumina. The percentage of silica in a good brick earth should lie between 50 to 60%. Presence of silica prevents cracking, shrinking and warping of raw bricks. Its excess amount distroys the cohesion between particles and makes the bricks brittle and weak. Hence, durability of the bricks depends largely on the proper proprotion of silica in brick earth.

3. Lime. Small quantity of lime in brick earth is desirable. It should be present in a finely powdered form and not in lump form. Excess amount of lime causes the brick to melt and thus its shape is lost. If lumps of lime are present, they are convered in to quick lime after burning. The quick lime thus formed slakes and expands due to moisture and causes splitting of bricks into pieces.

Silica or sand alone is infusible. But slight amount of lime acts as a flux and causes silica to fuse slightly at kiln temperature. Such slightly fused sand acts as a very hard cementing material, and the resulting bricks of very large strength and durability are obtained. hence, slight amount of lime in a very finely powdered from is good in brick earth, where as its larger porpotion in lump form is harmful. Lime present in small prorportion also prevents shrinkage of raw bricks.

4. Oxide of iron. Small quantity of oxide of iron to the extent of about 5 to 6% is considered desirable in good brick earth. It also helps silica to fuse at comparatively low temperature like lime. The colour of the brick depends largely on the proportion of oxide of iron present in the earth. The bricks having very small amount of iron oxide are yellow in colour. The colour of the bricks goes on darking with increase in the quantity of iron oxide. Too much iron oxide makes the bricks dark, blue or blackish. Iron also increases the durability and impermeability of the bricks.

5. Magnesia. A small proportion of it, decreases the shrinkage and gives yellow tint to the bricks. But larger amounts of magnesia cause bricks to decay.

2.4. Harmful Ingredients of Brick Earth

Some of the ingredients if present in the brick earth, render the resulting bricks unsitable for any safe construction. Following are such ingradients, presence of which in the brick earth is considered undesirable.

1. Lime. As already explained earlier, that its presence in small quantity and in powdered form is desirable. But its presence in large amount and that too in lump form is harmful. Calcium carbonate present in lumps is convered into quick lime (CaO) after burning of bricks. When these bricks come in contact of moistuse, quick lime present in the bricks slakes and causes disruption of bricks because of its expansion. Excess lime also causes the bricks to melt and hence disfigures them.

2. Pebbles of stone and gravel. Presence of pebbles and gavel in brick earth, is also harmful. They do not allow thorough mixing of the earth and the bricks containing pebbles and gravel are considered very week. Such bricks can not be broken at the desired section and they break very irregularly. Hence, while preparing brick earth all the stones, gravel, etc. should be either picked up or powdered, if possible.

3. Iron pyrites. Presence of iron pyrites in the brick earth cause crystallization and disintegration during burning of the bricks. It is a common impurity found in most of the clays. It causes discoloration of bricks in form of black slag.

4. Alkalies. The earth containing alkaline salts, is not considered good for brick earth. The alkalies are mainly salts of sodium and potassium. Alkalies act as flux in the kiln and cause fusion, warping and twisting of the bricks. Bricks may also lose their shape, because of fusion. Alkalies present in bricks also absorb moisture from the atmosphere. Such bricks when used for masonry work cause deposition of white powder on the surface, because of drying, the salts which have come to the surface with moisture get deposited. This action is known as efflorescence. This action seriously spoils the appearance of the building. Effloresecence can also be caused, if clay used for making bricks contains pyrites, or water used in the preparation of the brick earth contains dissolved gypsum.

5. Organic matter. Presence of organic matter and vegetation, in the brick earth render the bricks porous. The porocity in bricks is the result of burning carbonaceous matter present in the earth. In order to avoid the adverse affect of the organic matter, the bricks should be well burnt.

6. Presence of Reh or Kallar. These consists of sodium cholride, sodium carbonate and sodium sulphate. The bricks can not be properly burnt in the presence of sodium sulphate.These elements re–crystallize after buring of the bricks and deposit on the surface of masonry in form of whitishspots. This causes pealing off the plaster and bricks and ultimately leads to the failure of the structure. presence of reh or kallar in the earth can be detected inspecting freshly dug pits or by noticing the signs of effloresence.

2.5. Classification of Brick Earths

The brick earth may be classified into following categories depending upon the predominance of the constituent present in the earth.

1. Loamy mild or sandy clay. This earth consists of considerable free silica (sand) together with clay or alumina. Larger amount of silica helps in preventing cracking, shrinking and warping of the bricks. This earth requires addition of small amount of powdered lime. The powdered lime acts as a flux and helps in fusion of sand. Fused sand acts as a very hard cementing material to bind the particles of brick together. Bricks made from such earth are generally quite hard, if lime has been added. Otherwise they are week and sandy. This earth may have following composition.

Silica	66%
Alumina	27%
Lime and magnesia together	1.0%
Oxide of iron	1.0%
Organic matter	5%
	Total 100%

2. Marls, chalks, or calcareous clays. This earth consists of considerable amount of calcimum carbonate (chalk) along with alumina and silicia. This earth makes good bricks. But in order to avoid the undersirable affects of excess lime, additional sand may have to be added. Malm or washed earth which is an artificial imitation of natural marl, is a compound of clay and chalk and gives the best result when added to earths. Bricks of very superior quality can be made of this earth. A typical composition of this earth may be as follows.

Lime and magnesia	48%
Silica	35%
Alumina	10%
Iron oxide	3%
Alkalies	4%
	Total 100%

This composition is just a tentative one and percentage of different ingradients may change slightly this way or that way.

3. Plastic, strong or pure clay. This earth chiefly consists of silica and alumina with small percentages of lime, magnesia, and other salts. Raw bricks prepared from pure clays will crack, shrink and warp during drying. Hence, such clays require addition of sand and ash to modify their properties. Addition of extra sand prevents shrinkage, where as ash provides lime to act as flux. A typical composition of pure clay may be as follows.

Alumina	34%
Silica	50%
Lime and magnesia	6%
Iron oxide	8%
Organic matter	2%
Total	100%

Test of clay. If prepared brick earth in too clayey it will adhere to the finger when pressed between two finger tips. If instead of sticking to the finger tips the earth particles become segregated and each particle is individually recognizable, then earth in sandy. The best method of testing brick earth is to prepair some sample bricks, from it. If bricks crack on drying, it shows that earth has more of clay present in it and requires to be corrcted by addition of sand. If dried bricks are very soft and brittle it reflects more of sand present in the earth. If bricks are neither brittle nor crack on drying but still found unsatisfactory after burning in kilns, the chemical analysis of the brick only will reveal the real cause, which may be remedied. A good brick making earth should have following physical properties.

(i) Liquid limit	25 to 38%
(ii) Plasticity index	7 to 13%
(iii) Shrinkage	15 to 25%

However the following two field tests may be perfomed to ascertain the suitability of soil for the purpose of brick manufacture.

1. First field test. The soil to be tested is finely ground and mass is converted to a plastic mass by adding sufficient quantity of water. The plastic mass is kneaded and balls of about 80 mm diameter are moulded with hands. These balls are allowed to dry in sun. If dry balls deform in shape and crumble easily on pressing, it indicates the excessive sand content in the soil. If it is deficient in sand content, the balls will develop surface cracks on drying.

2. Second field test. The plastic mass as prepared in case of first test has platic consistency of such nature that it can be rolled in thread of 3 mm in diameter. the bricks of standard size are then moulded from this earth and allowed to dry in the sun for four days. The surface of the bricks is examined for cracks developed due to shrinkage.

2.6. Broad Classification of Bricks

Bricks may be classified into following five categories :–

1. Fist class bricks
2. Second class bricks
3. Third class bricks.
4. Over burnt or Jhama bricks.
5. Under burnt or pilla bricks.

1. First class bricks. Bricks of this category should possess the following properties.

(i) Size of the burnt brick *should be exactly 19×9×9 cm.*

(ii) The earth from which bricks have been made should be suitably proportioned. It should be free from small pebbles, lime lumps, organic matter, and sodium salts.

(iii) It should be well burnt.

(iv) Its colour should be uniform yellow or red.

(v) Its surface should be regular and sides parallel. Edges should be sharp and at right angles to each other.

(vi) It should have a firm, compact, and uniform texture.

(vii) Its fractured surface should not show fisures and bubbles or lumps of lime.

(viii) Its surface should be so hard that finger nails should not be able to make any impression on its surface.

(ix) It *should not absorb water more than 20% of its* own dry weight after 24 *hours of immersion in cold water.*

(x) Mettalic ringing sound should emit when two bricks are struck against each other.

(xi) Its crushing strength should not be less than 105 kg/cm^2.

(xii) No signs of efflorescence should be visible when bricks are dried after soaking in water.

(xiii) The brick should not break when it is dropped on a hard ground from a height of 1 metre.

First class bricks are used in all works of permanent nature. They are also used at exposed face work.

2. Second class bricks. Bricks of this category should possess the following properties.

(i) Like first class bricks, these bricks should also be well burnt. They can even slightly be over burnt.

(ii) Ringing sound should emit when two bricks are struck against each other.

(iii) They should not absorb water more than 22% of its own dry weight after 24 hours of immersion in cold water.

(iv) Minimum crushing strength should be 70 kg/cm^2.

(v) The shape, size and colour of the brick should be generally regular and uniform. Slight distortion and surface cracks may however be allowed.

(vi) Texture should be uniform. Presence of small pebbles may however, be allowd. Presence of lime stone and kanker should not be allowed to occur.

(vii) These bricks should not show appreciable signs of efflorescence when soaked bricks are dried.

3. Third class bricks

(i) These bricks are generally under burnt.

(ii) They are soft and light coloured.

(iii) They emit a dull sound when struck against each other.

(iv) Size and shape of these bricks is not regular. But the irregularities should not be so much that it may become difficult to have the course of uniform thickness, in masonry work.

(v) It should not absorb water more than 25% of its own dry weight when kept immersed in water for 24 hours.

(vi) They may suffer from intensive efflorescence.

(vii) Texture of the brick is not uniform and it may show lot of pebbles on freshly fractured surface of the brick.

These bricks are not used for important and permanent works. They are mostly used for temporary works.

4. Over burnt or jhama bricks. These are over burnt vitrified bricks. They are so distorted that they can not be used in construction works. They are used for making aggregate for lime concrete for foundations and as a road metal in the construction of roads.

5. Under burnt or pilla bricks. Under burnt bricks are known as pilla bricks. They are just half burnt and have yellow colour. These bricks do not have any strength. These bricks may be burnt by using them again in the kilns, or they can be ground to powder from and used as surkhi.

2.7. I.S.I. Classification of Bricks

This classification of bricks varies from man to man, who is classifying the bricks. The quality declared as Ist class by one person may be declared as IInd class or even III class by another person. To overcome this anamoly ISI has classified the bricks into *HI, HII. FI, FII, I, II, LI* and *LII* categories, primarly, according to the compressive strength. *HI* class bricks are most strong having accompressive strength of 440 kg/cm^2. The lowest category of bricks is *LII* which have a compressive strength of 35 kg/cm^2. The following Table 2.1 gives the I.S.I classification of bricks.

Table 2.1. I.S.I. classification of bricks.

Class of Bricks	*Minimum compressive strength in kg/cm^2*	*Minimum absorption in 24 hours in percent of dry weight*	*Efflorescence*	*Tolerance in dimension in percent*	*Shape and other properties*
HI	440	5	no	±3	Metallic sound, smooth, rectangular
HII	440	5	no	±8	Slight deformation in shape permited.
FI	175	12	very little	±3	Smooth, rectangular, metallic sound when two bricks strike.
FII	175	12	very little	±8	Slight deformation in shape permitted
I	70	20	very little	±3	Smooth, rectangular, metallic sound when two bricks strike.
II	70	20	very little	±8	Slight deformation in shape permitted.
LI	35	25	very little	±3	Rectangular, sharp edge, metallic sound on striking, need not be present.
LII	35	25	little	±8	Slight deformation in shape allowed..

I.S. 1077–1957 specified the strength of the bricks as below.

(i) Bricks having a compressive strength of minimum 35 kg/cm^2 must be used for any work of permanent nature.

(ii) Bricks having compressive strength 140 kg/cm^2 are classified as class AA bricks.

(iii) Bricks having a compressive strength between 70 and 140 kg/cm^2 are classified as class A bricks.

According to IS 1077–1976 common burnt clay bricks are classified on the basis of their average compressive strength as shown in Table 2.2.

Each class of brick is further sub-divided into two sub-classes A and B based on tolerances and shapes *e.g.* brick of classification 150 is further Sub-classified as 150 A and 150 B and so on. Bricks of Sub-class A shall have smooth faces, sharp edges and corners and uniformity in colour whereas bricks Sub-class B may be slightly distorted or may have slightly rounded edges subject to the condition that these distortions do not cause any difficult in laying of uniform courses.

Table 2.2. Classes of common Burnt clay bricks

Class Designation	*Average compressive strength kg/cm^2*	
	Not less than	*Less than*
350	350	400
300	300	350
250	250	300
200	200	250
175	175	200
150	150	175
125	125	150
100	100	125
75	75	100
50	50	75
35	35	50

2.8. Brick Sizes

According to I.S.I. the size of the brick without the thickness of mortar joint is 19 cm × 9 cm × 9 cm. The size with mortar joint be comes 20 cm × 10 cm × 10 cm. Hence, the effective size of brick is taken as 20 cm × 10 cm × 10 cm. If thinner bricks are required their standard size is 19 cm × 9 cm × 4 cm. and effective size as 20 cm×10 cm×5cm. The *minimum compressive strength of the standard bricks should be 35 kg cm^2.*

Bricks may be made in various sizes. But in all the cases, the length should be twice the width plus the thickness of one vertical joint, so that one stretcher (length of brick) along the wall will just cover two headers (width × height face of the brick) placed across it, with a joint between them.

The size of the brick is also fixed on the consideration that man of average physique can easily lift the brick with one hand. More over the brick dimensions should be such that they can be burnt to the core easily.

In the past various department of various states connected with construction works, have been using the bricks of varying sizes. In U.P. 24 cm × 11.4 cm × 7 cm was the usual size of bricks and each cubic meter of masonry required 475 bricks. Punjab P.W.D. used to adopt 23 cm × 10.8 cm × 7 cm size bricks and each cubic meter of masonry required 536 bricks. Punjab irrigation department used to adopt 23 cm × 11 cm × 7 cm bricks and it required 560 bricks for one cubic meter of masonry.

2.9. Manufacture of Bricks

The complete process of manufacturing the bricks can be broadly divided into following heads.

1. Preparation of clay
2. Pugging or tempering of the clay.
3. Moulding of bricks.
4. Drying of bricks.
5. Burning of bricks.

Each operation will now be discussed at length.

2.10. Preparation of Earth or Clay

Preparation of clay involves operations like unsoiling the top loose earth, then digging. cleaning, weathering and blending of the earth. The top layer soil about 20 cm thick contains lot of impurites and as such unsuitable for brick making. After removing the top unsuitable soil, the clay is dug out either with manual labour of with the help of power excavators. Dug out clay is spread on the levelled ground. Height of the heap of clay *may vary from 60 cm to 120 cm*. It will be preferred, if the operation of digging out clay is completed before the rains set in. All the pebbles, gravel, kankar, vegetable matter etc. are removed from the excavated clay. Lumps of clay if opresent, should be converted into powder form. Now, the clay is left exposed to atmosphere for softening or mallowing. This operation is known as weathering of the clay. The period of weathering may vary from few weaks to full season. Digging the earth before rains is advantageous in the sense, that full monsoon rains will be pouring on the dug out earth and earth will be subjected to weathering for full monsoon.

After weathering, the earth is chemically analysed and if there is any deficiency of any ingredient it is spread on the heap of the weathered earth and mixed with it with the help of phorah. Mixing is done by turning the mixture of earth and deficient ingredient for three times up side down. Now process of preparation of clay is compelete.

2.11. Pugging or Tempering of Clay

Tempering or pugging the clay means, breaking up of prepared clay, watering, and kneading till the earth becomes a homogeneous mass. Water is added to clay in required quantity and the whole mass is kneaded under the feet of men or cattle. But this method of tempering is out dated and not used much these days.

Where, good bricks are required to be manufactured on a large scale tempering of clay is usually done by pugg-mill which is described as follows.

Pug mill. It consists of steel tub *1.20 m to 2m. height* Its diameter at top end *is 90 to 120 cm* and that at the bottom end is slightly lesser which may be about 80 cm. *In elevation the steel tub looks like an inverted frustum of a cone.* The tub is covered at the top. It is fixed on a timber base which is made by fixing two wooden planks at right angles to each other. Bottom of the tub is covered except for the hole to take out pugged earth. Provision is made at the top to admit clay inside the pug mill. The steel tub is provided with a vertical shaft passing along the axis of the tub. The shaft consists of a number of horizontally radiating arms and each horizontal arm has a number of wedge-shaped knives of steel. When vertical shaft is rotated either by a pair of bullocks or by mechanical power and clay and water are admitted into the mill, the horizontal arms attached to shaft cause churning of clay while the knives cause kneading. After some time the clay in the mill gets fully tempered and collected near the bottom of the tub through the opening provided for the purpose. (See Fig. 2.1)

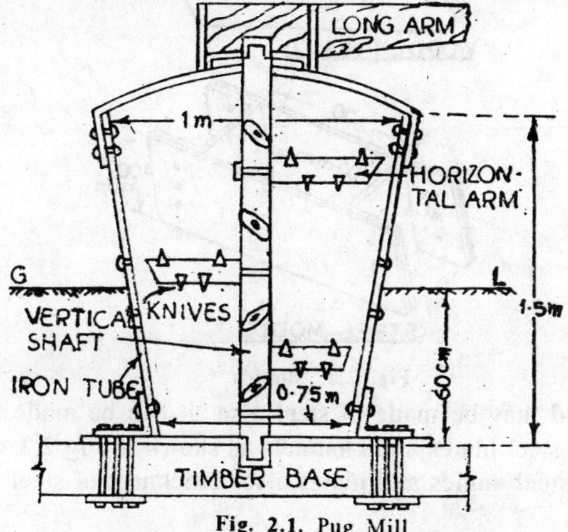

Fig. 2.1. Pug Mill

In fact at the time of starting the mill the bottom hole for pugged clay is closed and mill is run for some time by putting clay and water in it. When clay has been fully pugged, hole at the bottom of the tub is opened. Now mill is continued to run and feeding of clay and water from the top and operation of taking out pugged clay from the bottom hole are, simultaneously, carried out. Now pugged clay, ready for next process. *i.e.* moulding of bricks is available.

2.12. Moulding of Bricks

After tempering of the clay, bricks should be moulded as soon as possible, *as otherwise pugged clay may become stiff and moulding of bricks may become difficult*. The bricks can be moulded by following two methods.

(*i*) Hand moulding and (*ii*) Machine moulding.

Before we take up moulding of the bricks, let us discuss the mould used for moulding the bricks.

Moulds. Moulds are rectangular boxes without any top and bottom. They may be made of steel or timber. If of timber, it should be made from well seasoned timber. The longer sides of the mould are kept a few centimeter projecting on both the ends to act as handles for lifting the mould. *The edges of the timber mould are sometime protected by fixing steel or brass strips*. Sometimes complete internal faces of the mould are lined with steel or brass sheet, to increase the durability and also to ensure true shape of the bricks.

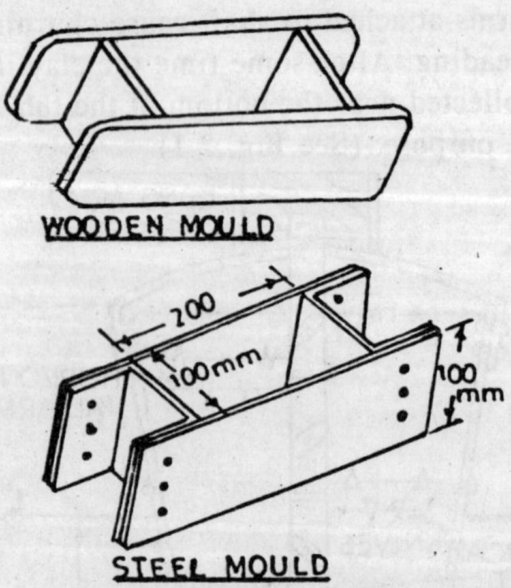

Fig. 2.2. Moulds

The mould may be made of steel also. It can be made from the combination of steel plates and channels as shown in Fig 2.2. It can be prepared from steel angles and plates also. Thickness of steel mould is generally 6 mm. Steel moulds are preferred, when bricks are to be manufactured on a very large scale. The bricks moulded by steel moulds are more uniform in size and shape.

Moulds are made in size slightly greater than the standard size of the brick. This is done because on drying and burning the bricks shrink. Increase in dimension of the mould should be about 10%. Exact percentage of increase in dimensions of moulds is determined by conducting actual experiment on the clay most likely to be used for moulding the bricks.

Hand moulding of bricks. The bricks moulded by hand may be of two types.

(*a*) Ground-moulded bricks (*b*) Table-moulded brick

(*a*) *Ground-moulded bricks.* The ground where bricks are to be moulded is first of all prepared by sweeping off all the loose matter. Sometimes, even pucca plateforms are prepared for moulding the bricks. But, generally, ground moulding of bricks is done on kucha-ground which has been prepared by sweeping the loose matter and sprinkling water over it. *Fine sand is always kept sprinkled on the ground.*

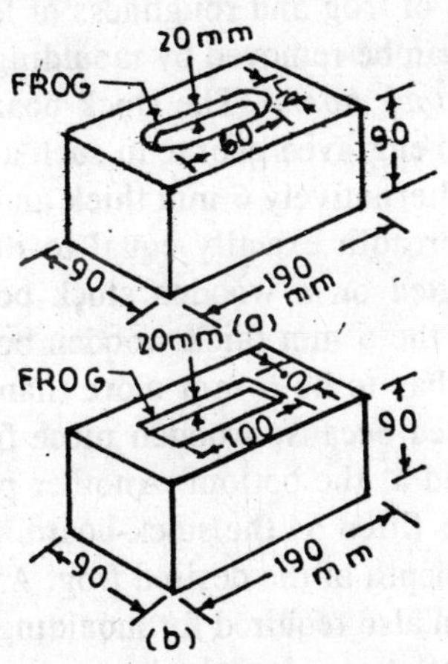

Fig. 2.3. Dimensions of standard bricks

Mould is directly placed on the prepared ground and lump of tempered clay is lifted by both the hands by the moulder and dashed in to the mould. Moulder then presses the clay in the mould with his fists and fingers, so as to fill all the corners of the mould throughly. Extra or superfluous clay is removed from the top of the mould either with *wooden strike or metal strike or wired frame. Strike is nothing, but a wooden or metal piece with a sharp edge..* After removing the superfluous clay, the mould is swiftly lifted up leaving the moulded brick on the ground. Now again moulder places the mould just by the side of the previously moulded brick and all the operations like dashing and pressing the clay in the mould are repeated and mould is lifted swiftly after striking the excess clay from the mould, leaving second brick moulded on the ground. Process is repeated till ground is covered with raw bricks or required number of bricks is moulded.

In order to avoid the sticking of pugged clay with the mould and also to facilitate *easy extrusion of moulded bricks from the moulds,* the inside surface of the *mould is always either swept with water or with fine sand before lump of pugged clay* is dashed in to it. If bricks are moulded *by washing the inside surface of the mould with water, the resulting bricks are called slop-moulded bricks.* If fine sand or ash is used on the inside surface of the mould instead of water, the moulded bricks are known as *sand-moulded bricks.*

Bricks, moulded directly on the ground have two draw backs. Firstly the lower face is very rough and secondly they can not have a frog. Frog is a depression of about 1 to 2 in depth made on the face of bricks during moulding. *Frog serves following two functions.*

(i) Frogged surface of the brick is generally kept on the upper side of the course of brick work. *The mortar accumulated in the frog forms a very good key for the* subsequent course of brick above it.

(ii) Manufacturers generally *engrave their trade name in the Frog which causes a very good* advertisement of the firm, manufacturing the bricks.

Both short comings *i.e.* formation of frog and roughness of lower surface of the ground moulded bricks, can be removed by moulding the bricks on a wooden block, called the *stock board.* The stock board is bigger than the mould. It has 6 mm deep engraved goorve in such a way that mould fits exactly in the groove. Alternatively 6 mm thick another wooden board having the length and breadth exactlly equal to inside length and breadth of the mould is fitted on a wooden stock board. Mould can exactly be placed enclosing the 6 mm thick wooden board. In both the cases height of the mould has to be 6 mm more than the normal height of the brick to be moulded because wooden piece fitted on stock board remains inside the mould at the bottom. Another piece of wood having trade name of the firm is fitted on the stock-board. Size of this piece depends upon the size and depth of the desired frog. Along with stock-board a pair of pallet boards in also required for moulding the bricks. Pallet board is nothing but thin flat wooden plank.

Now the stock-board having frog piece fitted over it, is placed on the ground and mould swept by water of fine sand, is fitted in the groove formed for the purpose.

Clay is dashed inside the mould and pressed into the corners of the mould. The top surface of the brick is covered by a wooden pallet board after having striken off superfluous clay with the help of wooden or steel strike. Now the whole assembly, consisting of stock board, mould filled with clay, and pallet board placed at the top, is lifted by the moulder and turned upside down and placed on table or moulding floor. The mould is lifted off leaving the moulded brick, lying on the pallet board. The helper of the mouldes then places second pallet board on the upper side of wet plastic brick and conveys, it to the drying shed. The bricks are placed on edge along longer face, in the drying sheds and both the pallet boards are removed and brought back to the moulder for using them again. As bricks are laid on edge they occupy less space, and more over, they dry quicker and better. The same process of moulding of the bricks is continued till required number of bricks are moulded.

(*b*) *Table moulding of bricks*. This method of moulding the bricks is more or less similar as ground moulding with the help of stock boards and pallets. The only difference is that the whole of the process of moulding has to be carried out on a specially designed table. *Moulder has to work in standing position and stock board which was loose in case of ground moulding is nailed to the* top of the table in table moulding.

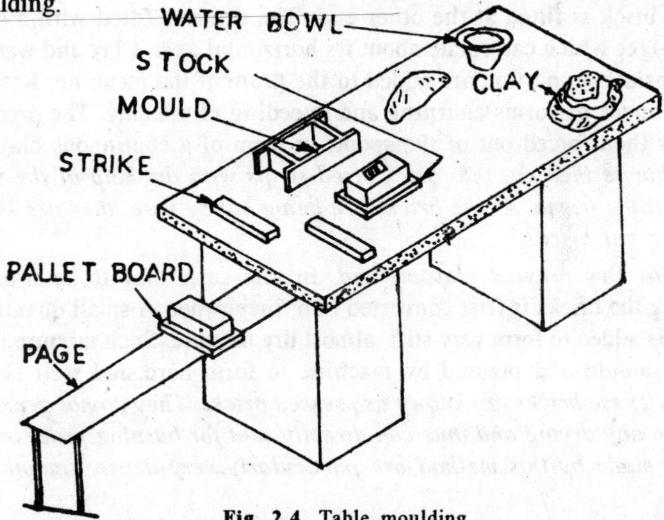

Fig. 2.4. Table moulding

In this case also mould is placed over the fixed stock board. *The stock board is already fitted with another wooden block for the development of frog.* After placing the mould on stock board, clay is dashed in the mould, pressed and excess clay cut off by strike. A pallet board is placed over the top, and mould filled with clay and pallet at the top are swiftly lifted up and turned up side down. Now pallet is at the bottom of the mould. Mould is taken out leaving moulded brick lying on the pallet board. The helper will place another pallet at the top of moulded brick and carry, it to the drying shed between the two pallets. The brick is placed on edge in drying shed and both the pallets become free which are again handed over to the moulder. The process of moulding is continued till space in the drying shed is filled with moulded bricks. A team of a moulder and a helper can mould about *1000 bricks in a day*.

(2) Machine moulding of bricks. Machine moulding of the bricks may be adopted when very large number of bricks are required to be manufactured at one place. This method proves economical only when bricks in huge quantity are to be moulded. The machine moulded bricks are hard and strong than table or ground moulded bricks. They are heavier in weight and have external surfaces smooth. Machine moulding of the bricks can be done by following two methods.

(*a*) Plastic clay method. (*b*) Dry pressed clay method.

(*a*) *Plastic clay method.* For this method, all the operations of mixing clay with water, pugging and moulding of bricks, are done by one machine. The machine consists of a large horizontal steel drum, one end of which is closed, while a rectangular spout equal to length and breadth of the brick is fitted at the other end. The drum is fitted with a screw type auger which can rotate about its horizontal axis. Clay and water in appropriate proportion are added to the drum of the mcahine. Rotating screw auger performs churning and kneeding of the clay. The prepared clay is then forced out of the spout, in form of a continuous clay bar. *Clay bar is then cut into brick sized strips with the help of the wires fixed in the frame. As the bricks are being cut by wire, they are known as wire cut bricks.*

(*b*) *Dry pressed clay method.* In this case, clay to be used for making the bricks is first converted into finepowder. A small quantity of water is added to form very stiff, almost dry mixture. Such mixture is put in the mould and pressed by machine to form hard and well shaped bricks. *These bricks are known as pressed bricks. They do not generally require any drying and thus can directly sent for burning process. The bricks made by this method are particularly very dense, smooth and strong.*

2.13. Drying of Bricks

Wet bricks have to be dried before they are fed for burning in the kilns. Following are the objects of drying the bricks.

(i) To remove as much of moisture from the bricks as possible, so as to save time and fuel during the burning.

(ii) To avoid the chances of cracking and distortion of bricks during the burning.

(iii) To increase the mechanical strength of the bricks, so that they can be handled and stocked without any damage to the bricks.

In the case of ground mounding, with out stock boards and pallets, the freshly moulded bricks are left in moulded position for one, or two days. After this, bricks acquire sufficient strength and then they are turned on edge. Brick on edge is subjected to more direct contact with air and hence drying takes place at much faster rate. After another two or three days, dried bricks are stacked.

In the case of table moulding or ground moulding with the help of stock board and pallets, the bricks are directly put on edge in drying yards or sheds. After three or four days, bricks acquire suffcient strength and they can be stacked. Similar is the case for plastic clay method of machine moulding of the bricks. Dry pressed clay bricks normally do not require any drying and hence, they can be directly sent for burning.

Bricks might have been moulded by any method, (except dry pressed method), they have to be stacked after two or three days of drying. Stacking makes space available for further moulding of the bricks. Although after two or three days of drying, bricks do not become dry and fit for burning, but they become sufficiently strong to get stacked. The bricks are stacked in such a way, that even in stacked position free circulation of air is maintained around them. Bricks are stacked in two brick (length wise) wide and 8 to 10 courses high stacks with sufficient space between individual brick. A specimen stack is shown in Fig. 2.5. Following important facts should be taken care of, while drying and stacking of the bricks.

Fig. 2.5. Stacking of bricks

(i) Drying yard. For drying of the bricks, special drying yards or sheds should be erected. Its level should be higher than the adjoining ground and it should be covered with tin shed to save the bricks from rains and direct sun.

(ii) Drying period. This period depends upon the prevailing weather conditions. It may, *however take one week to two, in normal conditions.*

(iii) Bricks should be stacked leaving sufficient space for free air circulation. This aspect will maintain drying of the bricks even in stacked position.

(iv) Artificial drying If bricks are to be supplied for burning immediately after moulding, artificial method of drying the bricks are adopted. In this case bricks are moulded with rather stiff clay. The moulded bricks are made to pass through special dryers where hot conditions (less than 120°C) are maintained and bricks dry in a matter of 1 to 3 days. Or alternatively the moulded bricks are put on edge in the drying shed. After the shed is full of freshly moulded *bricks, its doors are closed and steam or hot gases are forced inside the shed. The bricks get dried in a matter of few hours time.*

Drying bricks should not be subjected to direct sun or wind. If exposed, they may crack and warp. Hence drying sheds should be protected against direct sun and wind.

2.14. Burning of Bricks

Burning of the bricks is a very important operations in the manufacture of the bricks. It imparts strength and hardness to the bricks and makes them dense and durable. Most of the free moisture is driven out of the bricks during the process of drying but temperature of drying being small, *water in combined form or water of crystallization is not removed. Burning process also removes water of crystallization from the bricks.* When temperature of the bricks, being burnt, reaches about 650°, all the carbonaceous matter present in the bricks gets oxidized. Water of crystallization is also removed at this temperature. But *burning of bricks should not be stopped at this temperature otherwise on cooling the bricks get rehydrated by absorbing moisture from the atmosphere.* Hence burning or heating of the bricks is continued to higher temperature. At higher temperature different constituents of the brick react chemically and properties of bricks are completely changed. The bricks become hard, strong, and absorb very small amount of moisture.

At about *1100°C the two main constituents of brick, silica and alumina, combine with each other and bricks become dense and strong. At this temperature fusible glass which is a flowing* matter at high temperature is formed in very small amount which keeps clay particles binded together. Temperature of the bricks *should not be allowed to exceed 1100° C as* otherwise fusible glass will be formed in large amount. This will cause bricks to flow and make them destored and vitrified. Bricks should neither be *over burnt nor under burnt, as in both the cases quality of bricks suffers.*

Bricks are burnt either in clamps or in kilns. Clamps are temporary structures and are adopted when bricks are to be burnt on very small scale. Kilns are permanent structures and they are adopted when manufacture of bricks is to be carried out on a large scale.

1. Clamps. Clamps are also called pazawah. These are temporary kilns used for burning the bricks on very small scale. Generally people in villages burn the bricks for their own use by this method. There are so many types of clamps, which are being adopted in different parts of the country. A typical clamp is shown is Fig. 2.6.

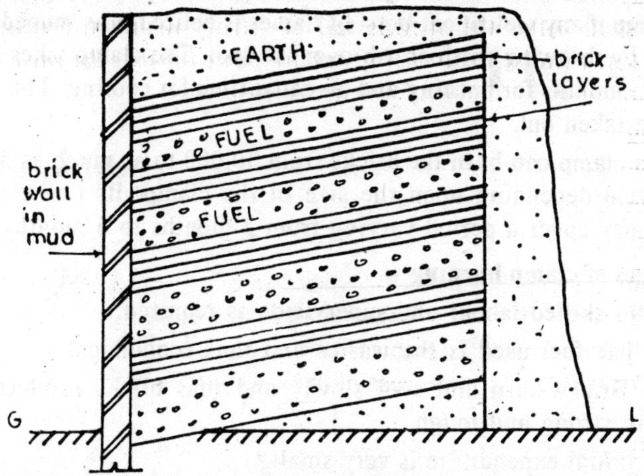

Fig. 2.6. Clamp.

The basic structure of the clamp consists of alternate layers of fuel and dried bricks. Size and shape of the clamp varies from place to place. The clamp's usual shape in plan is trapezoidal. The floor of the clamp is prepared in such a way, that short end is slightly in excavation and wider end is raised. The prepared floor should have a slope of about 15°. A brick wall in mud is constructed at the lower shorter end of the clamp.

The first layer immediately above prepared floor consists of fuel. Fuel is generally composed of grass, cow drug, litter, rice husk etc. Thickness of fuel layer is about 75 cms. Wood or coal dust may also be used as fuel.

Four to five courses of raw bricks are then laid on edge on the fuel layer. Bricks should be laid by leaving suitable space for circulation of hot gases.

A second layer of fuel is then placed and over it another stage of four or five layers of raw bricks is put up. Thus clamp is filled with alternate layers of fuel and raw bricks. Thickness of fuel layers gradually decreases as the height of the clamp increases. Total height of clamp may vary from 3 m to 5 m.

When clamp is loaded for about $\frac{1}{3}$rd height, it is fired from the bottom. The object of this is to burnt the bricks in the lower part when loading of upper part is in progress. After firing, the remaining loading of the clamp is carried out hurriedly so that clamp may be fully loaded- before fire reaches the top of the clamp.

After completely loading, the clamp in plastered with mud on sides and top is filled with earth to prevent escape of heat. During burning of the clamp if any violent out-burst of flames is noticed, it is immediately put down by throwing earth or ash-over the spot. The clamp takes about one to two months for burning and an equal time for cooling. The burnt bricks are taken out.

This clamp can burn the bricks from 30,000 to as much as 3 lakh in one cycle depending upon the size of the clamp. Its one cycle of working may cover a period varying from 2 months to 6 months.

Advantages of clamp burning

(i) No skilled labour and supervision is required.

(ii) The fuel used is the wastes and thus economical

(iii) Bricks burn and cool slowly and thus bricks produced by clamps are strong and tough.

(iv) Initial expenditure is very small.

Disadvantages of clamp burning

(i) It is very slow process.

(ii) There is no control on fire in the clamp.

(iii) Qualtity of bricks is not uniform as bricks near the bottom are over burnt and those near sides and top are under burnt.

(*iv*) Bricks are not of regular shape. It may be due to settlement of the bricks when fuel near bottom is burnt.

(*v*) Clamps yield about 60% first class bricks. The remaining *40% are either over burnt or under burnt.*

Kilns. The kiln is a system, designed more scientifically, to burn the bricks in very large numbers. The kilns used for burning the bricks may be classifieid into following types:

1. Intermittent kiln. 2. Continuous kiln.

1. Intermittent kiln. It is such a kiln, where operation of burning the bricks is not continuous. the kiln is loaded then fired, then allowed to cool and lastly unloaded. This completes one cycle of operations. Intermittent kilns may be rectangular or circular in plan, but mostly they are rectangular. They may be completely or partially under ground or completely over ground. Allahabad kiln shown in Fig. 2.7 is a typical example of intermittent kiln. It consists of a rectangular room 5m to 6m wide and 2 m to 3 m height. The length of the room is taken according to the number of bricks desired to be burnt in each cycle. However the length of the kiln is about 18 m.

The floor of the kiln consists of 30 cm deep and 40 cm wide trenches dug across the length at centre to centre spacing of about 140 cm. The unexcavated width left between two successive trenches is 100 cm. The unexcavated width in called the *rouse*. Raw dry bricks are stacked on edge on these rouses. Small spaces are left between the bricks, so as to cause circulation of hot gases around them. Excavated trenches act as fire houses. Seven courses of bricks are laid on edge at the rouses and then 8th, 9th and 10th courses of bricks are corbelled from both the sides to close the fire houses from the top. Fire houses are also called flues or chullahs. Small arched doors are provided in the longitudinal walls of the kiln corresponding to the flues. These doors are provided with suspended plate called damper. Fuel is supplied in the flues through these doors and dampers control the air supply in the flues. At the centre of each flue a partition wall of loose raw bricks is formed. The function of this partition is to deflected the draught from each side upwards into the body of the kiln.

The height above the arched flues is filled by laving bricks on edge with small spaces between them. The top most course of bricks is laid flat and covered with a 5 cm thick layer of earth to prevent the escape of heat.

After completing the loading, the kiln is fired from both the ends of each flue. The intensity of fire is kept slow for the first three days by properly manipulating the dampers of the flues. Slow fire-drives off the moisture from the bricks. After this, firing is made vigorous and maintained so, far about 2 days to 3 days. Draught of hot gases rises in the upward direction from bottom of the kiln and brings about burning of the bricks. The fire is regulated with the help of dampers fixed in the door openings. When bricks get throughly burnt, all the openings are closed and plastered with clay. The kiln is allowed to cool down for 8 days to 10 days and after this it is unloaded starting from the top. As soon as the unloading of burnt bricks is over, the kiln is charged again with raw bricks and procedure of burning is repeated for the next burning of the bricks.

Bricks burnt by intermittent kilns are better than those produced by clamps. This kiln suffers from following disadvantages.

(*i*) Supply of bricks is intermittent.

(*ii*) Quality of burnt bricks is not uniform. Bricks near bottom are over burnt and those near top are under burnt.

(*iii*) There is wastage of fuel as kiln is to be cooled down every time after burning.

Intermittent kilns may be *up-draught kilns* or *down draught kilns*. In case of up-draught kilns, fuel is burnt near the bottom of the kiln and hot gases rise upwards and escape through the chimney. Working of the down draught kilns is more or less similar to the up-draught kiln except that hot gases are released in the kiln near the top and they are forced to move downwards from where they escape out into the atmosphere. Movement of gases from top to bottom is made possible due to chimney draught. It is claimed that bricks burnt by down-draught kiln are evenly burnt and performance of the kiln is better than up-draught kiln. There is perfact control on heat in this method and as such down-draught kilns are mostly used for burning of clay tiles, terraycotta, etc.

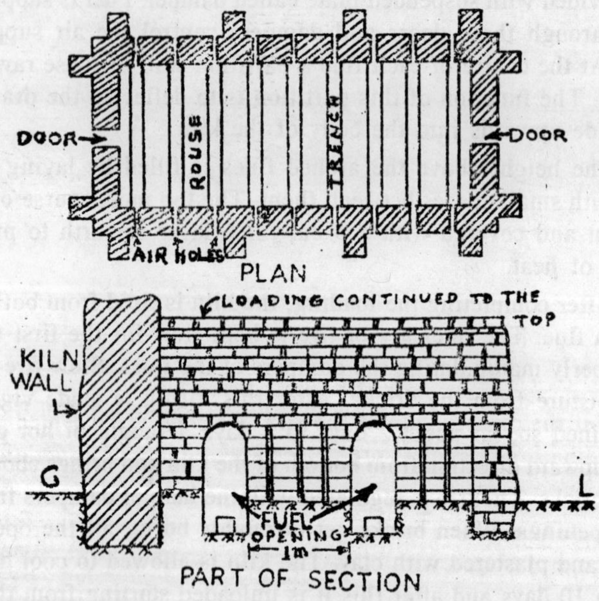

Fig. 2.7. Allahabad intermittent kilns

A typical sketch of an intermittent kiln is shown in Fig. 2.7.

Up-draught intermittent kiln generaly does not have roof, but down-draught kiln has permanent roof. The floor of down-draught kiln has openings which remain connected to common chimney stack through flues.

2. Continuous brick burning kilns. These kilns are continuous in operation and thus ensure continuous supply of burnt bricks. All operations like loading, firing, cooling and unloading are carried out simultaneously in these kilns. There may be various types of continuous kilns, but following three varieties are mostly used and hence discussed.

(*i*) Bull's trench kiln. (*ii*) Hoffman's kiln and

(*iii*) Tunnel kiln.

(*i*) **Bull's trench kiln**. This kiln is generally oval shaped in plan, although circular plan may prove more economical. The kiln may be built partly or wholly under ground. If kiln is partly under ground, as is the usual case, the ramps of earth should be provided on out side wall.

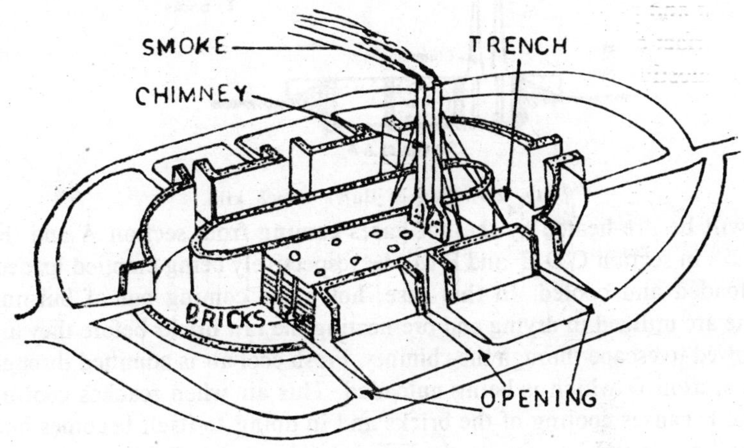

Fig. 2.8. Bull's trench kiln.

For the construction of the kiln, a trench is excavated. The depth and width of the trench is pre-decided taking into consideration the size of the kiln and also whether, it is to be wholly underground or partly undergound depending upon the local conditions. Outer and inner walls are constructed, in over burnt or rejected bricks, taken from near by kiln. Height of the walls constructed along the outer and inner faces of the trench should be about 2.5 m. Opening are generally provided in the outer walls to act as flue holes.

The kiln is divided into various sections, with the help of dampers which are nothing but simply iron plates. Each section of the kiln is in turn subjected to loading, drying, burning, cooling and unloading, operations. All these operations, are carried out simultaneously in the different sections of the kiln.

When bricks in section (A) are being burnt, the bricks in section

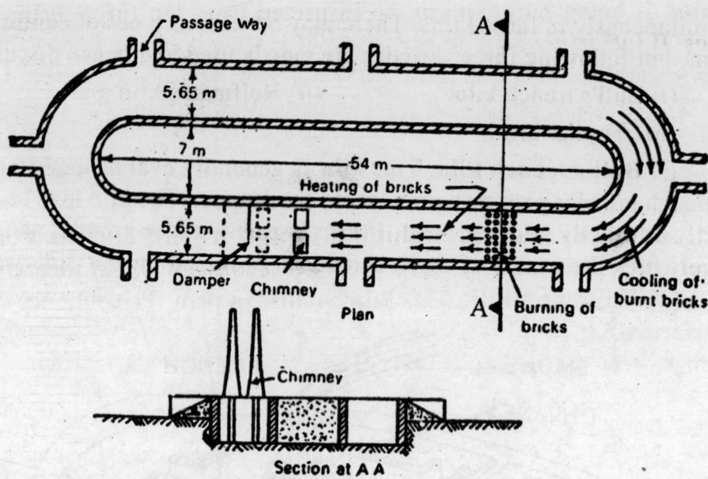

Fig. 2.9. Plan of Bull's trench kiln.

B will be pre-heated by the hot gases coming from section A and the bricks in section C.D.E. and F will be respectively being emptied loaded, unloaded and cooled. In this case, hot gases coming out of burning zone are utilized in drying and pre-heating the raw bricks before they are allowed to escape through the chimney. Fresh cool air is admitted through the section D which is being unloaded. This air when reaches cooling zone E causes cooling of the bricks and in doing so itself becomes hot. This hot air thus passes on the burning-zone and before escaping out through the chimney, it comes in contact of freshly loaded bricks, where they get pre-heated by hot air. Thus it is clear that thermal value of the fuel is utilized to its utmost value and thus consumption of fuel in this case is much less than the clamps and the intermittent kilns.

Depending upon the size of the kiln, there may be one or two movable chimneys which can be adjusted on the holes kept at regular distance apart on the kiln wall top. A clear space of about 15 cm is kept between the two successive sections over which the chimney is placed. The chimney is placed in advance of the section being fired. The quantity of coal dust required per lakh of bricks is about 25 tonnes.

Method of filling the raw bricks

Raw bricks are stacked on edge leaving suitable space between them. Stacking is done in such a way that flues are formed at the bottom. Flue holes are also maintained vertically above the flues. When this section is to be fired, the fuel is dropped down through the flue holes. Centre to centre spacing of the flue holes is usually kept as 90 cm. The flue holes are always kept covered by iron pans or lids. When any section is being burnt, it can be inspected from top through the flue holes. If intensity of fire at certain point is slow it can be intensified by dropping more of fuel from the top. Bricks have burned properly or not, is also controlled by visual judgement from top through the flue holes. When burning of one section is completed, the fire is advanced to the next chamber and the section containing the burnt bricks is allowed to cool, by closing its flue holes.

Although initial cost of this kiln is high, it yields first class bricks in very high percentage. This kiln requires a constant skilful supervision.

(*ii*) **Hoffman's kiln**. This kiln circular in plan. The chimney stack is placed at the central point and twelve compartments or chambers are arranged around the chimeny inform of a circular ring. Each compartment has a door in the external wall which is used for loading and unloading of the bricks. All the compartments have communicating doors in the walls separating each other and all the chambers have a connection with chimney with the help of radial flues. All the communicating doors and radial flues are provided with dampers with the help of which desired pattern of air draught can be established. This kiln has permanent roof, but fuel holes are provided to drop the fuel in the kiln from top. The fuel used in this kiln is powdered coal.

In this kiln also, all the chambers are subjected to loading, drying and pre-heating, burning, cooling and unloading operations successively, and all these operations remain going on all the time simultaneously, in the kiln. All the twelve chambers of the kiln may be functioning as follows.

Chambers 1	Loading
Chambers 2, 3, 4, 5,	Drying and preheating
Chambers 6 and 7	Burning
Chambers 8, 9, 10, 11,	Cooling
Chamber 12	Unloading.

With this arrangement, the circulation of flue gas will be as follows

Cool air enteres the kiln through open doors of chambers 1 and 12. This cool air passes through chambers 11, 10, 9, 8 and in course of time gets heated, while performing cooling of the hot burnt bricks in these chambers. Now this heated air or gases enter the burnig chambers 7 and 6 where it performs the burning of the bricks. Fuel is dropped in these chambers from the top. After performing burning of bricks hot gases are led to chambers 5, 4, 3, and 2 where they perform drying and pre-heating of freshly loaded bricks. The communicating door of chamber 2 is closed and cooled gases are lead to chimney through the radial flue of this chamber. Care should be taken that for the particular arrangement explained above all the radial flues except of chamber 2 remain closed and all the communicating doors except in the wall between chambers 1 and 2 remain, open. Outer loading and unloading doors remian closed

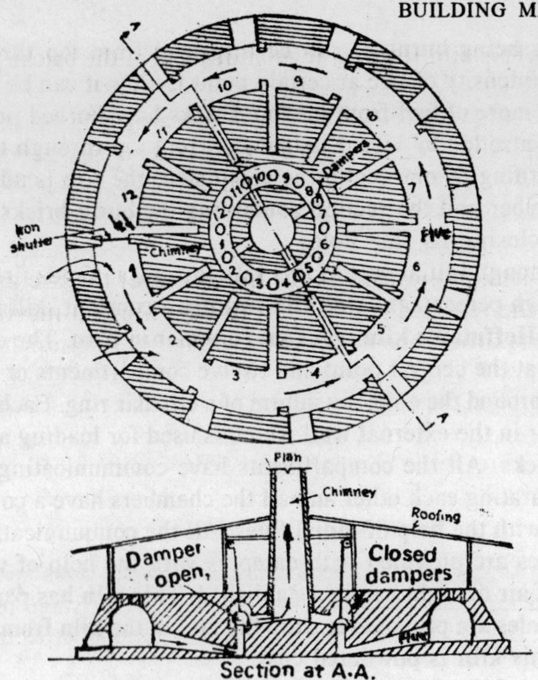

Fig. 2.10. Haff man's kiln

by rejected bricks and clay plaster except for the two chambers, which are being loaded and unloaded.

After some time when bricks of chambers 7 and 6 have been burnt the pattern of circulation will change and it will be as follows :

Chamber 12	**Loading**
Chamber 1, 2, 3, 4	**Pre-heating**
Chambers 5 and 6	**Burning**
Chambers 7, 8, 9, 10	**Cooling**
Chamber 11	**Unloading.**

In this case, all radial flues remain closed except that of chamber 1 and all the communicating doors remain open except that separating chambers 1 and 12. This kiln having each chamber of about 11 m long 4.5 m average width, 2.5 m height will yield about 25000 bricks daily. This kiln has following advantages and disadvantages.

Advantages :–

(*a*) There is perfect control on the heat.

(*b*) Supply of bricks is continuous and regular.

(*c*) Pre-heating of the bricks by hot gases before they escape into the atmosphere considerably reduce the consumption of the fuel.

(*d*) Bricks are burnt evenly and thus bricks of good quality are produced.

(*e*) Percentage of first class bricks is the highest.

Disadvantages :–

(*a*) Intitial cost of construction is high.

(*b*) This kiln requires regular demand of the bricks which may not be possible.

(*iii*) **Tunnel kiln**. As its name indicates, this type of kiln consists of a tunnel which may be straight, circular or oval shaped in plan. There is one fixed zone of fire. Unburnt raw bricks are loaded on a train of trolleys and this train is slowly moved on the track laid in the tunnel. As the trolleys approach zone of fire, the bricks loaded in trolleys get dried up and pre-heated. As the trolleys enter the fire zone, bricks are burnt to the required degree. The trolleys keep on moving and as they come out of firing zone bricks start cooling. When bricks have sufficiently cooled, they are un-loaded from trolleys and re-loaded by fresh load of raw bricks. This kiln also involves lot of expenditure and hence, proves economical only when bricks are required on a very large scale. Bricks of uniform quality are produced, as all the bricks are subjected to same degree of temperature.

2.15. Characteristics of Good Bricks

Bricks have already been classified into Ist class 2nd class and 3rd class and their characteristic explained at early stage of this chapter. However the general characteristics that a good brick should possess are given here again.

1. **Colour**. The colour of good brick should be uniform. It may be deep red, cherry or copper coloured. Uniformity of colour indicates uniformity of chemical composition.

2. **Shape**. Bricks should be uniform in shape with all its edges sharpe, straight and at right angles to each other. All the faces should be true in shape.

3. **Size**. Size of the bricks should be standard as prescribed by Indian standards.

4. **Txture and Compactness**. The bricks should have fine, dense, compact and uniform texture. Fractured surface of the brick should not show, lumps of lime, loose grit, fissures and cavities.

5. **Water absorption**. Ist class brick should not absorb water more than 15% of its dry weight when kept soaked in water for 24 hrs.

6. **Crushing Strength**. It should not be less than 105 kg/cm^2.

7. **Hardness**. The bricks should be so hard that finger nail should not be able to make any impression on its surface when scratched.

8. **Soundness**. Two bricks when struck against each other should emit ringing sound.

9. The earth used for moulding the bricks should be free from gravel, pebbles, kankar, salt-petre and other harmful ingredients.

10. Bricks should be sound proof and also of low thermal conductivity.

11. Bricks should not break when dropped flat an hard ground from a height of about 1m.

2.16. Comparison between clamp burning and kiln burning of the bricks

Comparison in respect of	*Clamp-burning*	*Kiln burning both bull's as well as hoffman's*
1. Initial expenditure	Minimum	It requires elaborate construction of masonry walls, dampers, chimneys, hence costly,
2. Cost of fuel	Fuel of cow dung, litter, grass, etc if used is economical. But if fire wood or coal is used it proves uneconomical	Generally coal dust is used. It proves economical than clamp where coal or fire wood is being used.
3. Capacity	About 30000 to 3 lakh bricks in one loading taking time varying from 3 months to 6 months.	About 25000 bricks are burnt daily
4. Mode of supply	Supply of bricks is intermittent	Supply of bricks is continuous.
5. Quality of bricks	Percentage of good bricks is about 60%.	Percentage of good bricks may be as high as 90 to 95%.
6. Suitability	It is suitable where dry fuel inform of grass, litter etc. is easily available and demand is small and periodic.	It is suitable when large number of bricks are required continuously.
7. Time in burning	It required 2 to 6 months time for burning one cycle.	Every chamber requires about one day for the burning and 8 to 10 days for cooling
8. Wastage of heat	There is considerable wastage of heat.	Heat is used very economically.
9. Structures	It require temporary arrangement.	It required permanent structure.
10. Supervision	Skilled supervision neither possible nor called for.	Continuous skilled supervision in necessary.
11. Control on fire	It is not possible to contol fire in clamps.	Fire is fully under control and can be regulated at will.
12. Effect of atmosphere agencies	Atmospheric agencies affect the working of clamps to a large extent.	They have no marked effect on the working of the kilns
13. Method employed	They employ crude methods of loading and unloading	They are more mechanized

2.17. Tests for Bricks

Certain tests are necessary to be conducted before any brick lot is accepted or rejected. Following are some of the tests which reveal the suitability of the bricks. These tests are :

1. Absorption test.
2. Crushing strength test.
3. Hardness test.
4. Shape and size test
5. Soundness test.
6. Test for presence of soluble salts.

1. Absorption of water test. In this test any brick is choosen from the heap and weighed dry. For dry weight the dry brick is kept in an oven at 105 to 115° C for some time. The brick is then kept immersed in water maintained at temperature of 27 ± 2° C for 24 hrs (according to I.S.I.) and reweighed after brick is whiped with damp cloth. The increase in weight of the brick after immersion in water, indicates the amount of water absorbed by the brick. This absorption can be expressed in terms of percentage of dry weight of the brick. The percentage of absorption should not exceed 20% of dry weight for bricks up to class 125 and 15% by weight for higher classes.

For absorption of water test five hour boiling water test may also be conducted. In it the specimen is oven dried and dry weight obtained. Then brick is immersed is boiling water for 5 hours. The water is allowed to cool to 27 ± 2° C with brick immersed. The brick is taken out, whiped class with damp cloth and reweighed. The absorption is then expressed in terms of percentage of dry weight of the brick.

2. Crushing strength test. In this test, well burnt bricks are selected. The bricks are slightly rubbed on both the flat faces, to render them smooth and even. The frog of the bricks is filled with 1:1 cement mortar. When mortar acquires sufficient strength, the bricks are tested for crushing by compression testing machine after taking them out of room temperature water. The minimum crushing strength of the bricks should not be below 35 kg/cm^2. The bricks of superior quality should exhibit a crushing strength varying from 70 kg/cm^2 to 140 kg/cm^2. While testing apply compression axial load at a uniform rate of 140 kg/cm^2 per minute till failure.

3. Hardness test. Hardness of the bricks can be estimated with the help of the scratch of the finger nail. If no nail scratch is left on the brick, it is considered to be having sufficient hardness.

4. Shape and size test. All the faces of the brick should be truely rectangular and size truely standard as specified by Indian standards. All the edges should be sharpe and right angled.

5. Soundness test. Soundness of the bricks is estimated by striking two bricks against each other or by a light hammer. They should emit ringing sound. Soundness of the brick is also tested by the fall of the brick. A good sound brick should not break, when made to fall flat on hard ground, from a height of about 1 m.

6. Test for presence of soluble salts. Soluble salts, if present in the brick cause efflorescence. Presence of such salts can be found out as follows.

A brick is taken and kept immersed in water for 24 hours. It is then taken out and allowed to dry. Soluble salts, if present in the brick, will get dissolved in water and when wet brick is allowed to dry, greyish or whitish powder of soluble salts will get deposited at its surface. If no white or grey powder is deposited, the brick is free from soluble salts. Amount of soluble salts is estimated from the salts that have deposited on the surface. If powdered salts cover only about 10% of the surface of the brick, amount of soluble salts are considered low. If they cover 50% surface, amount of salts are considered moderate. If the powder covers more than 50% of the surface, amount of salts present is considerable and thus considered very harmful.

2.18. Colouring of Bricks

The colour of the brick depends upon the following factors :—

1. Burning temperature of bricks.
2. Type of fuel used during burning.
3. Chemical composition of the earth.
4. Nature of sand used during moulding.
5. Degree of dryness achieved before burning
6. Amount of air admitted to the kiln during burning.

The colour attained by any of the above causes is known as the natural colour of the brick. Bricks can be coloured artificially also. This can be done either by dipping the bricks in colouring liquid or by addition of specific colouring material in the brick manufacturing earth.

For dipping method of colouring, a colouring liquid is formed by dissolving specific colouring pigment in mixture of lineseed oil, litharge and turpentine. This colouring mixture is put in an earthen ware pot and kept stirred. The bricks to be coloured are lightly heated by placing them on iron plate with fire underneath. Lightly heated bricks are taken one by one and dipped in colouring solution and kept aside to dry.

The bricks can be given desired colour by mixing appropriate colouring material in the earth itself at the time of preparation of brick earth.

2.19. Special Shapes of the Bricks

Ordinary bricks are always rectangular, but sometimes bricks of special shapes suiting to the specific requirements are required to be made. Some of the special shaped bricks are shown is Fig. 2.11.

1. Cow nose brick. It is a specially moulded brick having two vertical short corners rounded. These bricks are used in the construction of brick pillars, when sharpe corners are not required.

2. Bull nosed brick. This brick consists of one of the four vertical short edges rounded. It is used as a rounded quoin, where sharpe corner of the wall is not required.

3. Copping bricks. This brick is made according to the thickness of the parapet wall, it has to cover. This brick may have various shapes such as chamfered, half round, or saddle back etc. These bricks prevent the entry of rain water into the wall from the top.

4. Radial bricks. These bricks are inform of curved sector. The curvature of the bricks is fixed according to the conditions of their use. These bricks are used for the masonry work of circular pillars, circular chimneys and also for the construction of circular arches.

5. Queen closer. It is half of the full brick cut length wise. It is generally casted, but may be prepared from full sized bricks, also.

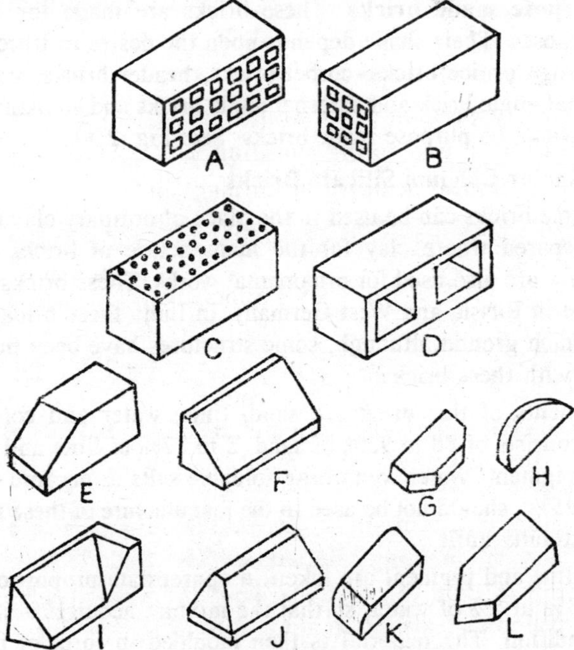

Fig. 2.11. Special bricks.

6. King closer brick. It is a full sized ordinary brick which has been cut along the line jointing the centre points of adjacent sides of the brick in plan when lying flat.

7. Splayed bricks. These bricks are used to form the splayed jambs of doors and windows.

8. Paving bricks. Paving bricks may be plain or chequered. These bricks are used for approaches to entrance of the building. They are manufactured from clay containing a higher percentage of iron. More iron oxide content vitrifies the bricks at a low temperature, which resist abrasive action of traffic more satisfactorily.

9. Hollow bricks. They are also known as cavity or cellular bricks. These bricks are not solid, but hollow. Their wall thickness may be 20 mm to 25 mm. They are light in weight and reduce transmission of heat, sound and dampness. They may be used for construction of brick partitions. These bricks can be burnt easily.

10. Perforated bricks. These bricks are also not solid, but they are also not very hollow. The hollowness in these bricks is comparatively small. The perforations in bricks may be holes of circular, square or rectangular shaped. These bricks are very easy to burn.

11. Purpose made bricks. These bricks are made for certain specified purposes. Their shape depends upon the desire in which they are to be used. Cornice bricks, corbel bricks, header bricks, stretcher bricks, internal angle brick and external angle bricks and so many other shaped bricks can be purpose made bricks. Sec. Fig. 2.11.

2.20. Sand-line or Calcium Silicate Bricks

Sand-lime bricks can be used in the place of ordinary clay bricks. They are prepared where clay for the manufacture of bricks is not available. They are also used for ornamental works. These bricks are in very wide use in Russia and West Germany. In India these bricks have not gained much ground although, some structures have been made in Kerala state with these bricks.

Constituents of this brick are sand, lime, water and colouring pigment. It consists of 88 to 92% of sand, 8 to 12% of lime and 0.2 to 0.3% as the pigment. Water containing soluable salts or organic matter more than 0.25%, should not be used in the manufacture of these bricks. Sea water is totally unfit.

Sand, lime and pigment are taken in appropriate proportion and mixed with 3% to 5% of water, so that the mixture acquires a state of semi-dry condition. The material is then moulded in form of bricks. Moulding of bricks is done by specially designed rotary table press machine. The machine is such in which, bricks are moulded with the aid of mechanical pressure. The bricks are moulded under a pressure varying from about 300 kg/cm^2 to 600 kg/cm^2. The bricks thus prepared do not require any drying. The prepared bricks are directly fed into an autoclave and subjected to a saturated steam pressure of about 8 to 16 kg/cm^2. This pressure is maintained for 6 to 12 hours. During, autoclaving operation, intraction between lime and sand takes place and both combine chemically. The bricks are now removed from the autoclave and sent for use. These bricks do not require burning as well as drying.

An autoclave is sealed steel cylinder having its diameter as 2 m and length 20 m. The process of subjecting, these bricks to a saturated steam pressure is known as *autoclaving* or *hydro-thermal treatment*.

Advantages of sand-lime bricks

1. They are quite hard and strong.
2. They are uniform in colour and texture.
3. The earth from which these bricks are prepared do not contain any soluble salts and these bricks are free from efflоresence.
4. Being very uniform in size, their masonry work requires a very thin layer of plaster.
5. They can be manufactured at places, where availability of clay is very difficult.
6. Thse bricks present such a pleasing appearance, that their plastering may be avoided.

Disadvantages

1. They are unsuitable for furnaces since they disintegrate, when subjected to prolonged hot conditions.
2. They are very weak, against abrassive action and hence can not be used for pavings.
3. Being less resistant against water, they are found unsuitable for use in foundations.
4. These bricks do not carry any significance at places, where clay is readily available for the manufacture of the clay bricks.

2.21. Making Bricks from Black Cotton Soil

Black cotton soil is abundently available in central western parts of India. It is very difficult to prepare bricks from black cotton soil as, it is very plastic. On drying, this soil shrinks a lot. If lime stone or kankar are further present in the raw bricks, they generally get oxidized during burning and when such bricks come in contact with water, they swell and get shattered into pieces. The measures to get good bricks from black cotton soil are the following.

1. Prepare the bricks by mixing 40 to 50% of coal ash into the black cotton soil. This measure gives very good bricks, but care should be taken that no piece of unburnt coal should be present in the coal ash.

2. Black cotton soil is pulverized and moulded in the spherical lumps by mixing necessary amount of water in it. These lumps are allowed to dry and then burnt at a temperature varying from 500° C to 600° C. The lumps are burnt till their colour turns red. These lumps are cooled and finely ground and to this 70 to 75% unburnt black cotton soil is added. Appropriate amount of water is added to the mixture of ground lumps and raw black cotton soil and bricks are moulded in usual moulds. But during moulding, the mould should be swept by burnt clay rather than usual sand. The bricks are allowed to dry and then they are burnt. The burnt bricks are allowed to coal down. Cooled bricks are put in to water, so that presence of lime if any is detected.

2.22. Fire Bricks or Refractory Bricks

These bricks are manufactured from specially designed earth, so that after burning, they may withstand very high temperatures without affecting its shape, size and strength. These bricks are used for lining of chimneys, furnaces etc., where usual temperatures are expected to be very high. These brick have been explained in detail in chapter 3.

2.23. Surkhi

It is nothing, but fine powdered under burnt bricks. it is also known as artificial puzzolana. Natural puzzolana is burnt silica and alumina. It will be economical, if surkhi is manufactured near brick kilns. It must be free from admixtures of foreign matter. Good surkhi should pass through 152 mesh. Lime–surkhi can be made from bricks prepared from clay to which 10 to 15% quick lime has been mixed prior to burning. Surkhi is very much used for making mortars.

Pozzolanas— These are silicious materials which, while having no cementitious values within themselves, will chemically react with calcium hydroxide at ordinary temperature and in the presence of moisture to form compounds possessing cementitious properties.

The term includes natural volcanic material having pozzolanic properties as also other natural and artificial materials, such as calcined clay (Surkhi) and fly ash.

Clay pozzolanas have the following advantages.

1. They replace cement to the extent of 20% in cement concrete and mortars without affecting the strength and also constitutes 20 to 30% of pozzolana cement. A cement sand mortar of 1 : 6 mix can be better replaced by a mortar made by mixing one part of hydrated lime, two parts of clay pozzolana and 8 parts of sand.

2. In conjuction with the standard quality dry hydrated lime. These can be used for preparation of mortar and plasters having the same strength as that of cement-sand mortars.

3. Lime pozzolana mortars are cheaper as compared to cement sand mortars.

4. They give improved workability.

5. They give increased water tightness.

QUESTIONS

1. Compare stone work with the brick work. In what respect each is superior to the other?
2. What are the chief ingredient of a good brick earth? State the harmful ingredients in brick earth.
3. How brick earth is classified. Give the composition of each type of earth.
4. Write down the properties of first class, 2nd class, and 3rd class bricks.
5. Describe briefly the various operations involved in the manufractured of bricks, pointing out the importance and necessity of each. Draw a neat sketch of a brick kiln. Explain the technique of glazing white ware products. *(A.M.I.E. Nov. 1856)*
6. Describe briefly the method of manufacture of bricks, using continuous kiln with suitable sketches. *(A.M.I.E. May 1963)*
7. Describe with sketches the manufacture of bricks by Bull's trench kiln. *(A.M.I.E. Nov. 1966)*
8. On what considerations the size of the brick is fixed? What relation should the breadth of a brick bear with length and why?
9. A very huge construction work requires large and continuous supply of bricks. Explain the type of kiln you would adopt for obtaining such supply. What are its advantages?
10. What is a pug mill? How is it set up? What are its uses and advantages? Describe its working with dimensioned sketch. What other appliances do you find arranged close to a pug mill?
11. Compare the burning of bricks in Bull's kiln and country clamp and discuss the reasons that would lead you to adopt one or the other of the systems in specific cases.
12. What are the tests of Ist class bricks? In what parts of buildings you would use Ist class, 2nd class and 3rd class bricks?
13. Explain the working of Hoffman's kiln in the burning of bricks.
14. What are the various operations involved in the manufacture of bricks? What is importance of chemical analysis of the brick earth?
15. Explain various methods of moulding the bricks. Explain the circumstances in which each method is found suitable?
16. Explain the various methods of drying the bricks. Why and how stacking of the bricks is done?
17. What are the characteristics of good bricks?
18. What are the usual tests which may be conducted to confirm the suitability of the bricks?

3

CLAY PRODUCTS AND REFRACTORIES

3.1. Clay products

It has already been explained in Chapter 1, that clay is obtained from the chemical weathering of igneous rocks. Felspar is a chief mineral of igneous rocks and there is one variety of Felspar known as orthoclase, which is whitish, greyish or pinkish in colour. The rocks containing considerable amount of orthocalse felspar disintegrate quite easily. Thus, it can be said, that orthoclase felspar, is mainly responsible, for the production of clay in nature. This mineral on further decomposition gives a product known as *kaolinite*. Kaolinite is free from alkalies and iron oxide. The product having a composition of pure kaolinite is termed as kaolin. In kaolin, silica and alumina compounds, are held in a colloidal state and these compounds form the basic constituents of all clays. In addition to these compounds, seveal other materials, such as iron oxide, free sand, silicates of magnesium and calcium etc., may also occur. but in very small prorpotion.

Clay when wet has a very high degree of plasticity and tenacity and as such, it can be moulded in any desired shape. Clay when wet contains water in two forms, namely, free water and combined water. Free water is removed by drying, but to remove combined water the clay has to be heated to a very high temperature. At high temperature, different consitituents combine with each other chemically and new products are formed. The new formed products are generally very compact and hard. If clay is further heated beyond certain limit of temperatue, it becomes soft and products lose their shape. The limit of this temprature, depends, on the quality of the clay.

Bricks, tiles, terra-cotta, stoneware, earthen ware, porcelains etc, are the main products which are commonly used in engineering works, one way or the other. Bricks, have already been discussed in chaper 2. The rest of the predominant clay products will be discussed one by one, under the heading clay products.

3.2. Tiles

Tiles are also a clay product, used mainly for roof covering and pavings. They are thinner than bricks. They are manufactures from superior type of clay.

Tiles being thinner than bricks, they should be carefully handled to avoid any damage to tiles. The tiles can be classified in following two groups :-

1. Common tiles. These tiles are of different shapes and sizes and are mainly used for flooring, paving and roofing.

2. Encaustic tile. These tiles are used for decorative purposes in floors, walls, roofs ceilings.

3.3. Manufacture of Tiles

Manufacture of tiles can be carried out in following four operations:

1. Preparation of clay.
2. Moulding of tiles.
3. Drying of tiles and
4. Burning of tiles.

1. Preparation of clay. The clay to be used, in the manufacture of tiles is taken and all the pebbles, grit, and other impurities, picked out from it. The clay is then pulverized in grinding machine. Water is added to the ground clay, and put in the pug mill to temper. For manufacturing tiles of superior quality, the ground clay is mixed with plenty of water in a large pucca tank. The mixture is allowd to stand quietly, during which coarse heavy particles settle at the bottom of the tank. Fine particles are held in suspension and mixture of fine particles and water is transferred to another tank. This mixture in allowed to dry in open during which water is evaporated and fine clay, is left at the bottom of the tank, which is used for the manufacture of the tiles. In order to make tiles imperivious and hard, a finely ground mixture of glass and pottery ware may be added to the clay.

2. Moulding of tiles. Tiles can be moulded by following three methods.

(i) Moulding by wooden moulds. *(ii)* Machine moulding

(iii) Potter's wheel moulding.

(i) Moulding by wooden moulds. In this method of moulding wooden moulds are prepared in shape and size of which tiles are required to be moulded. Moulding of the tiles is done in the similalr manner as has been explained in the moulding of bricks. Mould is placed in position and prepared clay is pressed in the mould. Care should be taken to preserve the shape of the tiles during the removal from mould. This method of moulding tiles is very common. Only plain tiles are generally moulded by this method. In this method tiles are first moulded plain and when they become a bit hard and dry, they can be given any shape with the help of. wooden patterns.

(ii) Machine moulding. In machine moulding of tiles, the clay is forced to come out of machine, under pressure and tiles are cut in specific size from the clay spout with the help of wire frame.

(iii) Potters wheel moulding. In this method, round tiles are first shaped on the potters wheel, and after taking out of wheel, when moulded cylinder in quite hard, it is cut longitudinally to develop two half round tiles. These tiles are not exactly cylindrical, but have varying diameter as tiles moulded on potter's wheel are not of same diameter through out.

3. Drying of tiles. The tiles, as they come out of mould are stacked one above the other and heaps of tiles, about 15 tiles high are formed. After about 2 days time when tiles slighly get hard, the irregularities developed due to warping are corrected with the help of flat wooden mallets. The tiles by now become hand-hard and they can be lifted. Each tile is lifted up and its edges and under surfaces cleaned. They are stacked on edge under a shade, to dry for about two-three days. It is very important to dry the tiles under shade as this will prevent cracking and warping of tiles, due to rain and direct sun.

4. Burning of tiles. After drying, the tiles are subjected to burning in kilns. A typical kiln capable of burning 30,000 to 40,000 tiles is shown in Fig. 3.1.

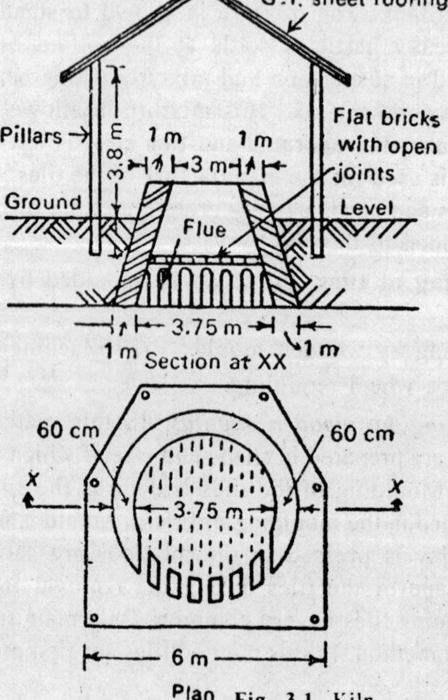

Fig. 3.1. Kiln

The kiln is circular in plan and is protected by a shed. Long narrow flues are formed at the bottom of the kiln and they are covered by a layer of bricks. The bricks are arranged in such a way, that open spaces are left between them. Dried tiles are now placed on edge, layer after layer on the layer of bricks. After loading the kiln to its full capacity, all the doors in the kiln are closed by brickwork in mud. Top of the kiln is covered with a layer of old tiles, placed in loose conditions. Heating or burning of the tiles is affected by firing wood in the flues.

Regulation of heat is very important in the furnace to acquire good results. In the beginning, fire in the kiln should be gentle, so that moisture is completely driven out of the tiles. The temperature is then raised to about 800°C. This temperature is known as red hot. The fire is kept slakened for about 5 hours and than it is raisied to about 1300°C. This temperature is maintained for 3 hours. The process of slakening the fire for 6 hours and then raising to about 1300° C, is repeated twice. 1300° C temperature is also called, white heat temperature. Finally the temperature of 1300° C is maintained for 3 hours and firing is stopped. The kiln is now allowed to cool gradually. In order to achieve gradual cooling of tiles in the kiln, the flues are filled with fire and their mouths closed with bricks in mud and fire is allowed to burn gradually. The complete process of burning the tiles may take about 3 days times.

Now kiln is started unloading. Good well burnt tiles are stacked separately and dispatched for use. Under burnt tiles are stacked separately, and they are used on the top of the kiln in next load of burning of tiles.

3.4. Properties of Good tiles

Good tiles should exhibit following properties :

1. Tiles should be true to shape and size.

2. They should possess uniform colour.

3. Clear ringing sould shound be emitted, when one tile is struck against another or with light hammer.

4. Fractured surfaces should show the compact and even structure.

5. It should be free from warps, cracks etc.

6. It should be strong, hard, sound and durable.

7. It should be well burnt.

8. Thickness (minimum) of machine made tiles should be 10 mm and hand mould tiles 12 to 15 mm.

3.5. Types of Tiles

The tiles may be classified in following three categories depending upon their use.

1. Drain tiles.
2. Floor tiles.
3. Roofing tiles.

1. Drain tiles. These tiles may be circular semi-circular or segmental. They are used for covering irrigation water, or for discharging surface rain water out of cities.

2. Floor tiles. These tiles may be square or polygonal in plan. They are flat tiles. Thickness of these tiles varies from 12 mm to about 50 mm. Size of the tiles may be 15 cm × 15 cm to as much as 30 cm × 30 cm. Floor tiles are used for covering surface of the floor of buildings. They may be of any type of finishing. The top surface of the tiles used in water closets, bath rooms, kitchens etc. should be glazed, where as under side in left unglazed, so as to adhere properly to the surface. They may be vitrified to prevent water absorption. They are manufactured in a variety of sizes, shapes and colours. Some of the floor tiles are explained as follows.

(i) Sanitary tiles. These are mostly of size 15 cm × 15 cm. They may be used on floor and also on walls. These are made with dry mixture of fire clay and crushed stone. Their top surface is generally glazed.

(ii) Mosaic tiles. These are ordinary tiles made from cement concrete, the top surface of which is finished by adding marble chips in cement mortar and grinding the surface smooth. They are very much used these days for flooring, in all types of buildings. The size of these tiles is 15 cm × 15 cm and 20 cm × 20 cm which may even be 25 cm × 25 cm.

(iii) Cement tiles. These are 20 cm × 20 cm rectangular tiles whose top surface is finished by cement. These tiles may be used in chowks and varandah of ordinary houses.

(iv) Porcelain or glazed tiles. They are manufactured either by dry or wet process. In dry process prepared clay is ground and pressed into shape. Very small quantity of water is added in clay in this case. The tiles made by dry process withstand firing better, but do not weather well. Size of these tiles is generally 10 cm × 10 cm.

3. Roofing tiles. These tiles are made for pitched roofs to act as a covering material. These are so many types of tiles available in the market. Some important varieties have been given here.

(i) Plain tiles. These are ordinary rectangular tiles. Their thickness varies from 10 mm to 17 mm and in plan their size is mostly 25 cm × 15 cm. One short edge of these tiles either remains turned downward or has two lugs projecting downwards. Turned edge or projecting lugs are used to help hang the tiles on the battens of the roof. Two nut holes are also provided in the tile near the nibs for fixing the tiles permanently to the battens. These tiles are not perfectly flat. but have slight curve to

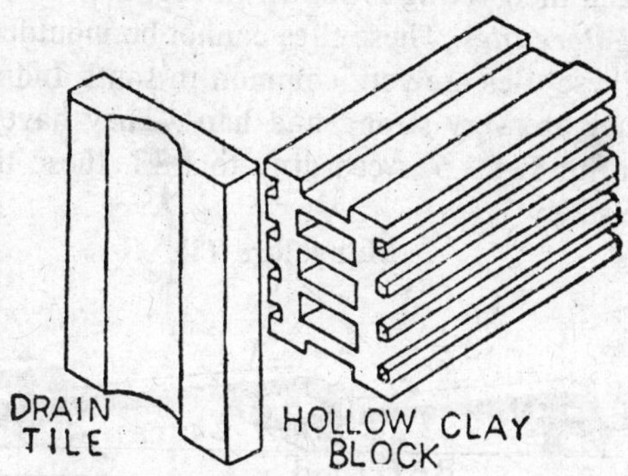

Fig. 3.2. Tile drain and hollow clay blocks

prevent water from being drawn up below the tiles by the capillary action. Size of the projecting lug should not be less than 2 cm × 2 cm and its projection not less than 1 cm.

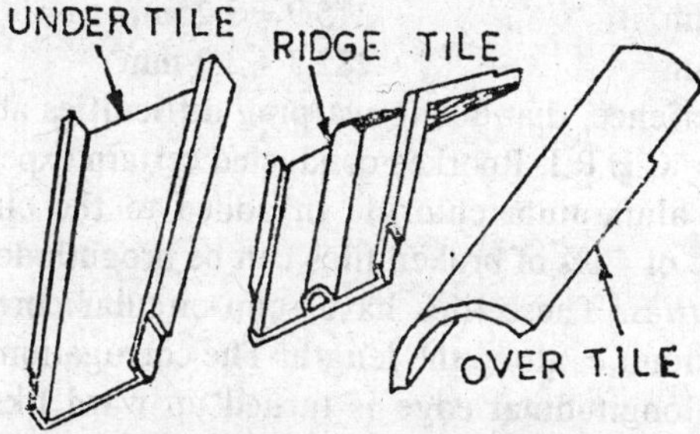

Fig. 3.3. Allahabad Tile

(ii) Allahabad Tiles. This tiles has two parts. One part is made channel shaped, where as the other part is semi-circular. Channel shaped, part is 38 cm. long 23 cm. wide at one end and 27 cm wide at the other

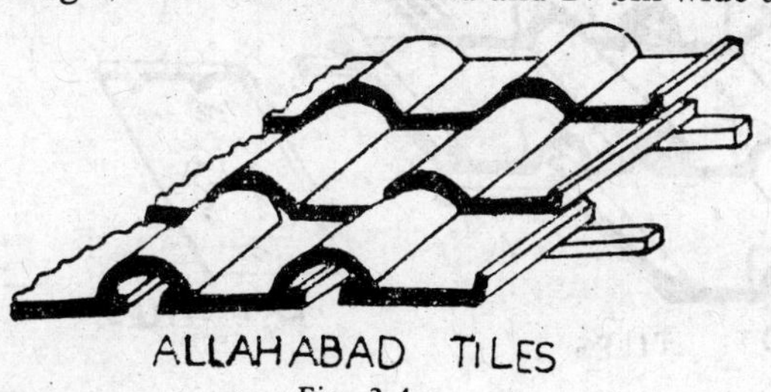

Fig. 3.4

end. Similarly, semi-circular part is also 38 cm long and it has diameter of 12 cm at one end and 16.5 cm at the other end. Channel part is also known *as under tile* and semi-circular part as *over tile.* The tiles are fixed on a ground work prepared by wooden battens on the roof slopes. Pattern of tile and their fixing is shown in Fig. 3.4.

(iii) Mangalore tiles. These tiles cannot be moulded by hand, but by machines. These tiles are very common in south India. Being made by machines they are very strong and hard. They have typical shape which is shown inf Fig 3.5. According to I.S.I. these tiles may be of following three sizes.

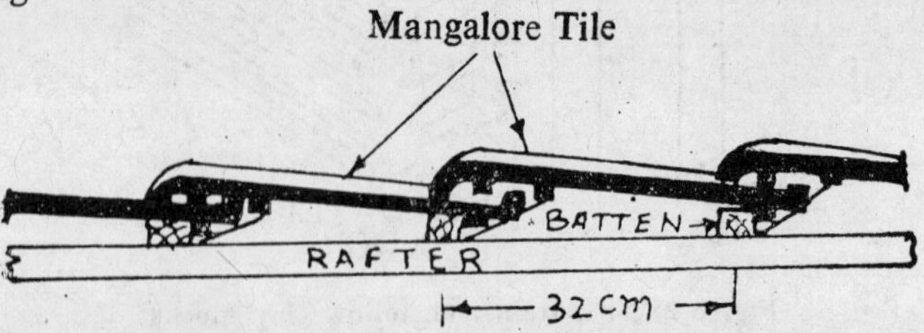

Fig. 3.5. Mangalore Tile

Effective length	Effective Width
317.5 + 6.4 mm	209.6 + 3.2 mm
342.9 + 6.4 mm	215.9 + 3.2 mm
349.3 + 6.4 mm	222.3 + 3.2 mm

It is the experience, that due to warping difficulties about 40% of the tiles get broken. C.B.R.I. Roorkee conducted certain experiments and suggested that, if aluminium chloride in added to the clay in small quantity, the figure of 40% of broken tiles can be broguth down to 15%.

(iv) Sialkot tiles. These tiles have semi-circular corrugations in longitudinal direction *i.e.* along the length. The corrugation faces down wards. The other longitudinal edge is turned up ward like a channel edge. Shape of the tile and its position on the roof is shown in Fig. 3.6.

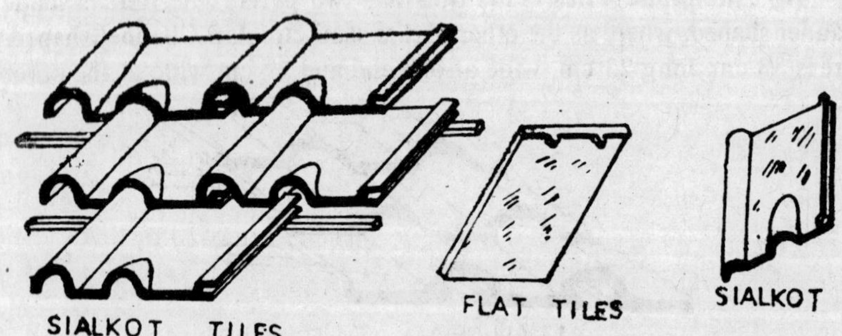

Fig. 3.6

(v) Pot tiles. These tiles are hollow half round and tapering in longitudinal direction. They are prepared on potter's wheel and tapered shape to the tiles is given by the potter with his wet hands. Polishing of inner and outer surfaces is done by wet cloth. The length of this tile varies from 15 cm to 20 cm. Its diameter varies between 11.4 cm to 14 cm at one end and between 8.9 cm to 11.4 cm at other end. They are used, on the roof with their concave and convex faces up ward alternately. These tiles are not of uniform size, as potter can mould them of smaller or larger diameter. These tiles are liable to break frequently and hence their replacement on the roofs, is a sort of permanent feature.

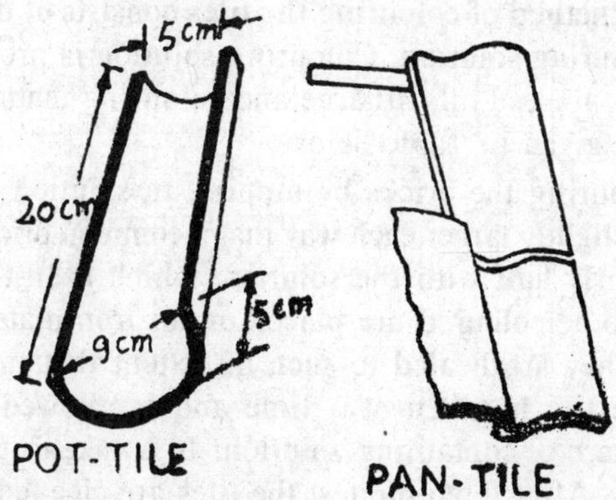

Fig. 3.7.

(vi) Pan tiles. These are rectangular tiles in plan. When it is cut across the length, it gives S shaped section. The length of this tile, varies from 33 cm to 38 cm and width from 23 cm to 28 cm. Moulding

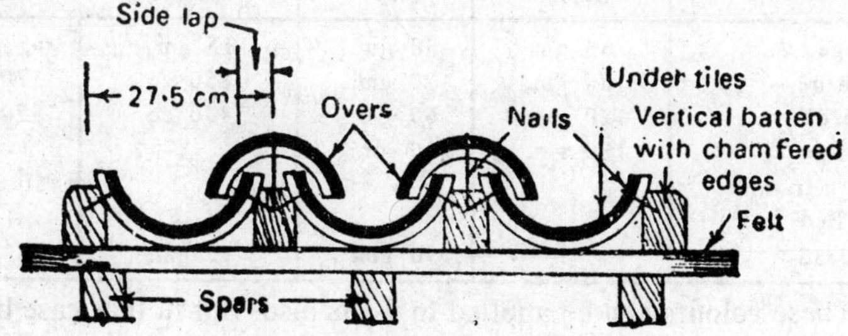

Fig. 3.8. Pot tiles of roof

of this tile requires a house, a bow, a strike, and mould. Prepared clay is first of all filled in mould and super-fluous clay removed by bow. The cut top surface is pressed by a strike. The strike should be swung two three times on the tile, so that its top surface becomes smooth. Now tile is slowly extracted from the mould and placed on the burnt tile When tile becomes slightly dry it is placed on horse wooden piece and slightly pressed to develop S curve in it. These tiles are comparatively heavier, stronger and durable. Position of pan tiles on roof slopes are shown in Fig. 3.7. Of course a ground work of wooden battens and rafters will have to be formed over which tiles can be fixed.

3.6. Colouring of Tiles

Tiles are coloured in same way as has been explain in colouring of bricks. In one of the methods, colouring matter is mixed with the clay during pugging. This method is suitable only when the colouring matter is cheap and easily available.

Second method of colouring the tiles consists of dipping the burnt tiles in a colouring solution. Colouring solution is prepared by mixing turpentine oil, linseed oil, litharge and colouring matter in appropriate proportion as given in Table below.

For colouring the bricks by dipping in solution an earthen ware box which is slightly larger each way that a common brick or tile, is taken and filled nearly half with the solution, which is in the form of thick paste. Tiles to be coloured are placed on an iron plate and with a fire underneath, they are heated to such an extent that they can be easily handled. One tile is taken at a time and is allowed to stay for few seconds in the box containing solution. It is taken out and placed on a Table to dry. After few minutes, the tiles are cleaned with cold water and placed aside to dry. The proportions of various ingredients of the coluring solution should be as follows:

Ingredient	*Name of the colour of colouring solution*			
	Black	*Grey*	*Dark red*	*Blue*
Litharage	60 gm.	30 gm.	115 gm.	15 gm.
Turpentine	180 gm.	120 gm.	850 cc	570 cc
Linseed oil	120 gm.	60 gm.	850 cc	570 cc
Manganese	180 gm.	30 gm.	—	—
French ultramine				450 gm.
Indian Red				
White lead		90 gm.	15 gm.	

These colours can be applied to walls also. But in that case brick work has to be carefully cleaned and the colouring solution applied hot with the help of brushes.

3.7. Terra-Cotta

The term terra means earth and cotta means baked. Hence terra-cotta means baked earth. It is thus an earthen ware or porous pottery made from clays and glazed with glazing containing galena. It can be scratched with this help of a knife.

Terra-cotta is prepared from the clay having sufficient percentage of iron and alkaline matter. Percentage of iron oxide may be about 5 to 8% and that of lime about 1%. Sand, ground glass, old terra-cotta or pottery, are also added to the clay to provide increasesd strength and rigidity to resulting terra-cotta products. These materials also prevent shrinkage during drying. The clay so prepared is made free from impurities like organic matter, pebbles, etc. The mixture is finely ground and ingredients thoroughly mixed with spades, after adding necessary amount of water. This wet clay is kept damp for several days, during which it thoroughly gets weathered and tempered. It is further kneaded in a pug mill. Now the clay is ready for moulding Terra-cotta. If any specific colour is desired, it should be added at the time of grinding the mixture.

After preparing clay, terra-cotta products are moulded in moulds. For moulding Terra cotta products, special moulds of plaster of paris or templates of zinc are used. While moulding fine sand is used for cleaning the surface of the moulds. The plaster of paris moulds are made to full scale size giving uitable allowance for shrinkage of clay during drying. The moulds filled with clay are not emptied immediately, but kept for some days in the mould itself for drying. After this terra-cotta is taken out of mould and allowed to dry further in a shaded area. Drying should be slow and under controlled temperature.

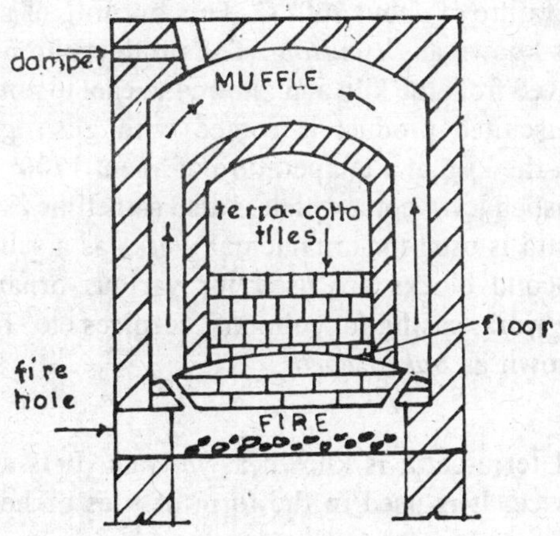

Fig. 3.9. Muffle furnace.

Dried products of terra-cotta are burnt in special muffle furnaces. A muffle is a box of the furnace constructed with the help of refractory bricks. Muffle chamber is sourrounded by an open space which is also lined with refractory bricks. The open space remains connected with the furnace. A typical muffle furnace is shown in Fig. 3.9. It is such a furnace in which any product can be heated without any contact of the product with the fuel. Dampers are provided near the top to regulate the draught of the hot gases.

Raw Terra-cotta to be burnt is stacked in the muffle chamber and its temperature raised slowly to a temperature of about 1200°C. This temperature is maintained for 4 days and then burnt Terra-cotta is allowed to cool down for next five days. If Terra-cotta products are required in form of glazed products, they are covered by glazing material before feeding into the furnace for burning.

Terra-cotta may be classified into two following categories.

1. Porous Terra-cotta and 2. Polished Terra-cotta.

3.8. Porous Terra-cotta

To obtain porous terra-cotta saw dust or ground cork, is mixed with the clay during preparation of clay. When terra-cotta prepared from such clay is burnt in a kiln, the saw dust or cork dust gets, burnt, leaving pores in the terra-cotta. Porous terra-cotta is sound proof and fire proof material. It can be nailed, screwed and sawn like timber. It is structurally weak and light in weight.

3.9. Polished Terra-cotta

In order to obtain polished terra-cotta, the product is first burnt at a lower temperature of about 700° C. This burning of products at lower temperature is known as *Biscuiting.* The products brought to biscuiting stage are removed from the kiln and allowed to cool to normal temperature. The cooled biscuited product is coated with glazing compound and burnt again in the kiln at a temperature of about 1200° C. The resulting product is polished terra-cotta which is also sometimes known as *faience.*

Terra-cotta is used for ornamental works as a substitute for stone. Hollow terra-cotta blocks are used for various ornamental purposes such as facing work, casing for columns, cornices etc. Terra-cotta is also some time known as *baked earth.*

3.10. Faience

Polished terra-cotta is known as *faience.* It is also called terra-cotta burnt-twice. It is used in the form of tiles or hollow cast units.

3.11. Earthen Ware

This term is used to indicate the articles or wares, prepared from brick earth or clays, which have been burnt at comparatively low temperature and cooled down slowly. The moulded product is burnt to such a temperature that the product has acquired a semi–vitrified stucture. Earthern wares are usually unglazed; but they can be glazed or enamelled.

Sometimes, clay, forming earthen wares, is also mixed with some sand and crushed pottery to increase the strength and also to prevent shrinkage during drying and burning. Glazed earthen wares are impervious to water and not affected by acids and atmospheric agencies. Terra-cotta is also a kind, of earthen ware. Ordinary drain pipes, cheap lavatary fittings, etc. are generally made from earthen wares.

3.12. Stone Ware

It is the name given to the articles used for sanitary purposes such as wash basins, sewer pipes, glazed tiles, water closets, gully traps, acid jars etc. These articles do not suffer from any corrosion. Stone ware articles are manufactured from refractory clays, to which powdered old stone ware (grog), ground flint, crushed pottery and other such material, have been added. A small percentage of iron oxide is also added in tne clay to impart colour and also to cause easy fusion. The moulded stone ware products, are burnt at high temperature to get a fused and vitrified body of the product. On cooling, the surface is covered with glaze solution and then fired again for fusing the glaze in the body of the product. Sound stone wares give clear ringing sound, when struck with each other. They are strong, durable, corrosion resistant, and easily capable, to withstand the affect of, atmospheric agencies. They are also used to hold the chemicals.

3.13. Porcelain

It is the term, used to indicate a fine earthen ware which is white this and semi-transparent. Since the colour of porcelain is mostly white, it is also sometimes called *white ware*. Porcelain may be classified into soft and hard categories. *Soft porcelain* is made from pure white clay, to which some percentage of crushed flint (melted glass) is added. In this case, firing is done in two stages. In first stage product is subjected to biscuiting at a temperature varying from 1000°C to 1200°C. The product is allowed to cool, coated with glaze solution and reburnt at a temperature of about 1500°C. Crockery like plates, dishes etc. come in this category of porcelain. *Hard porcelain* is made from china clay or kaolin, to which some percentage of felspar and quartz have been added. Hard porcelain is burnt only onces. If it is to be glazed, its coat is applied to the product before firing. This product is used mostly for electrical insulations and bathroom fixtures, sanitary wares, sotrage vessels, crucibles etc.

Procelain can also be divided into *low voltage category* and *high voltage category*. Low voltage procelain is mainly used for switch blocks, insulating tubes, lamp sockets etc. It is prepared by dry process and if sone quantity of alumina or silicate of magnesia is added it can resist quite high temperatures also. High voltage porcelain is prepared by wet process. Carbon brick, zircon porcelain, steatic porcelain, are the examples of high voltage porcelain.

3.14. Glazing

It is a process of covering the earthen ware, stone ware and procelain products with an impervious film of glaze. It is a glassy coat of about 0.1 to 0.2 mm thickness, applied on the surface and then fused into the product by burning at high tempertature. The glazed film improves the appearance, makes the articles impervious and durable, produce decorative effect, protect the articles from atmosphere and chemical actions, and provides smooth surface. Glazing may be *opaque like enamels* or *transparent like glass*. For obtaining desired coloured glaze, oxides of various metals are added. For instance copper oxides impart green colour where as iron oxide red or brown colours.

Opaque glazing. For this, superior clay is finely powdered and dried and sufficient water is added to make this clay plastic cream like mass. This mass is known as *slip*. Articles to be glazed are dipped in the slip, before burning. After burning an opaque glazed surface is obtained.

Transparent glazing. It may be *salt glazing* and *lead glazing*.

(*a*) **Salt glazing.** In this glazing, common salt (sodium chloride) is thrown in to the product in the kiln itself, when temperature is very high. At high temperature, salt vaporises and glass like film, called glazing is formed on the surface of the product. Extreme care should be exercised in regard to quantity of salt and the temperature at which it should be thrown in.

(*b*) **Lead glazing**. In this case, the product is pre-heated and dipped in bath containing oxide of lead and tin solution. The product is taken out of bath and reheated to a very high temperature. Because of high temperature oxide of lead and tin melt and form a glass like hard film on the exposed surface. This method is adopted for glazing Terra-cotta.

3.15. Clay Blocks

Clay blocks are also sometimes, prepared and used in the construction of partitions. Clay blocks may be solid or hollow. They are mostly hollow. Clay blocks may be made in various sizes and shapes suiting to the requirements. The usual section of the block may be 20 cm × 30 cm and thickness may vary from 5 cm to 15 cm. Blocks of larger dimensions can be cast and used. Thickness of wall of hollow blocks should not be less than 2 cm. The blocks may have various patterns of grooves on the surface. They help in the interlocking of the blocks with each other and also in making joints rigid. Hollow clay blocks, are very efficient in preventing fire and sound. They are generally light and non-shrinkable.

3.16. Fire Clay

Fire clays are clays which can resist very high temperature without getting soft or melting. They are composoed of nearly pure hydrated silicate of alumina (25 to 35%) and usually contain large proportion of silica (65 to 75%) with small percentage of alkalies. The higher percentage of lime, mangenese, iron oxide, or other alkalies, reduce the fire resisting capacity of the fire clay. They act as flux and cause fusion of the clay at high temperature. Fire clays are used in the manufacture of the fire brick chimney lining, etc. The fire-clays can be classified into three categories depending upon the fire resisting capacity. The categories are low duty, medium duty and high duty fire clays. Low duty, fire clays can resist temperatures up to 850°C, medium fire clays, up to 1500° C and high duty fire clays, up to 1650°C.

3.17. Fire Bricks

The bricks made from *fire-clays* are known as *fire bricks*. The processes involved in their construction are same as have been explained in the manufacture of ordinary bricks, but in case of fire bricks, processes of burning and cooling are kept rather slow. The colour of fire bricks is usually white, or yellowish white, and they weigh about 3 kg each. Fire bricks can resist high temperatures without undergoing any appreciable change in their structural properties. They are used for the lining of furnaces, and construction of chimneys, chambers etc. Fire bricks can be divided into following three categories.

1. Acidic fire bricks
2. Basic fire bricks and
3. Neutral fire bricks.

1. Acidic fire bricks. These bricks are used mainly, where acidic actions are mostly involved. Fire bricks and silica bricks are examples of these types of bricks.

(i) Fire bricks. These bricks are made from refractory earth contianing 50 to 75% silica and 20 to 40% of alumina. The percentage of fluxing matters should not exceed 10%. Smaller the percentage of fluxing matter, higher will be the percentage of alumina and more resistant will be the bricks. Percentage of alumina should not be allowed to exceed unnecessarily, otherwise bricks may become alkaline in nature. These bricks do not become soft even at a temperature of 1700°C.

(ii) Silica bricks. These bricks contain 95% pure silica and about 2% lime. Mixing of 2% lime is necessary to develop plasticity in the earth, while moulding the bricks. These bricks are burnt at 1483°C and they can with stand temperature upto 2000°C. These bricks should possess crushing strength of over 150 kg/cm^2. These bricks are used for lining the furnaces, used for melting the iron. These bricks have appreciable coefficient of expansion and as such wide mortar joints are used in the masonry work of these bricks.

2. Basic Bricks. These bricks are used for lining the furnances, where mostly alkaline actions are involved. Dolomite, magnesite, Bauxite bricks, are the examples of basic bricks.

(i) Magnesite bricks. The main constitutent of this brick is magnesium oxide. Other oxides, about 10%, may be mixed with it. Magnesite is calcined upto a temperature of about 800°C to drive out the carbon dioxide gas. Calcined magnesia is further heated to a temperature of about 1800°C and then allowed to cool down. Now the magnesite which has been cooled down after reaching 1800°C, is mixed with about 5% of magnesite clacined at 800°C and both are mixed to form an intimate mixture. This mixture is added with small amount of water, and since this prepared mixture has very small plasticity, it may be mixed with Tar or magnesium chloride to improve the plasticity. The bricks are moulded and allowed to get dry a little. They are then pressed and allowed to dry further. The bricks are then burnt. These bricks are widely used for the lining of Bessemer convertor, open hearth furnaces, blast furnaces, etc.

(ii) Dolomite bricks. These bricks are not as fire resistant, as megnesite bricks. These bricks have calcined dolomite, magnesium carbonate, and lime, as their main components.

(iii) Bauxite bricks. These bricks are manufactured from the mixture of powdered Bauxite, in which 15 to 30% fire clay has been mixed. The bricks are moulded as usual by adding suitable amount of water. Though, these bricks can withstand quite high temperatures, but at very high temperature, they suffer lot of shrinkage and hence, they are not used much as fire bricks.

3. Neutral bricks. Under the circumstances, where both acidic as well as basic actions may take place, neutral bricks are used for lining. Some of the types of neutral bricks may be as follows.

(i) Chrome bricks. These bricks are weaker, than the magnesite bricks and also less fire resistant than those. They are made from the earth containing 30 to 40% of chrome oxide and rest silica, alumina, and magnesium oxide. These bricks are very good resistant to corrosive action of slag and gases.

(ii) Chrome Magnesite bricks. They are made from mixture of chrome and magnesite.

(iii) Spinal bricks. These bricks are manufactured from a mixture of alumina and magnesia taken in equal proportion.

(iv) Forsterite bricks. These bricks are manufactured from magnesium silicon oxide mineral ($2\ MgO\ SiO_2$).

Neutral bricks are not very important as they are not much used for fire-resisting purposes.

The mortar to be used in the masonry work of fire bricks, should also be of refractory earth or clay. The crushing strength of these bricks should be of over 150 kg/cm^2. Their density is about 2400 kg/m^3 and their absorption coefficient varies from 4% to 10%.

3.18. Refractories

This term is used to indicate the materials which are able to withstand the effects of high temperatures, without affecting the structural strength of the material, by appreciable amount. Refractory materials can be classified according to their chemical properties and also according to temperature, they can withstand. Fire clay is also a form of refractory material. Fire bricks are also known as *refractory bricks*.

3.19. Efflorescence

Some of the soluble salts, may be present in bricks, or soils, coming in contact of the bricks or even water coming in the contact with bricks. When bricks containing soluble salts come in contact of water, the soluble salts get dissolved and when wet bricks dry the soluble salts are left at the surface in forms of white powder. This process of depositon of whitish powder on the surface of bricks, is known as *efflorescence*. Salts of sodium, potassium, and calcium, cause the efflorescence in the bricks. If efflorescence is not prevented in time, it will go on making bricks more and more porous and weak, and ultimately may lead to collapse of the structure. As a remedy of efflorescence all the materials used for the manufacture of bricks should be free from soluble salts. The surface more prone to this action may be plastered with cement.

QUESTIONS

1. (*a*) What are the different types of tiles? Mention their various uses in building industry.

   (*b*) What are the characteristics of good tiles?
2. Describe the complete process of manufacturing the good tiles.
3. State the components of earthen ware and stone ware products. What are their chief uses? (*A.M.I.E., May 1966*)

4. What is Terra-cotta? How is it manufactured? Discuss the varieties of Terra-cotta.
5. What is glazing? Mention the purposes of glazing and discuss its varieties.
6. What dò you understand by terms refractory clay, and fire bricks? What are various types of fire bricks?
7. Write short note on.

   (*i*) Pot tile (*ii*) Porcelain (*iii*) Muffle furnace and (*iv*) Salt glazing.
8. Explain the terms—white ware, stone ware, fire bricks; Biscuiting.

4

LIME

4.1. General

Lime is a very important building material. It has been in use since ancient times. Egyptions used to use lime for plastering works and Romans for plastering, mortar, and concrete works. In India, there are numerous historical constructions, where lime had been used in the form of cementing material. Even to-day, lime is a very important material not only for building purposes, but also in so many other manufacturing processess.

4.2. Propertieis of Lime

Following are the properties of lime which have made it, a very important Engineering material.

(i) It has good plastic properties.

(ii) It gives strength to the masonry, when used as mortar,.

(iii) It stiffens quite easily and in short time.

(iv) It is easily workable.

(v) It has good adhering properties with stone and bricks both.

(vi) Its shrinkage is comparatively low and hence masonry in lime mortar is more durable.

(vii) It can with stand moisture easily.

4.3. Uses of Lime

The lime can be used for following purposes.

1. As a binding material in mortar
2. As a binding material in concretes.
3. As an aggregate in form of crushed lime stone.
4. For plastering.
5. For white washing and also as a base coat for distempers.
6. It is used for preparing lime-sand bricks.
7. It is used as a fluxing material in so many manufacturing processes.

8. It may be used for masonry work in form of lime stone.
9. It is also a component of refractory clay.
10. It is used for soil stabilization.
11. It is used for improving soils for agriculture purposes.

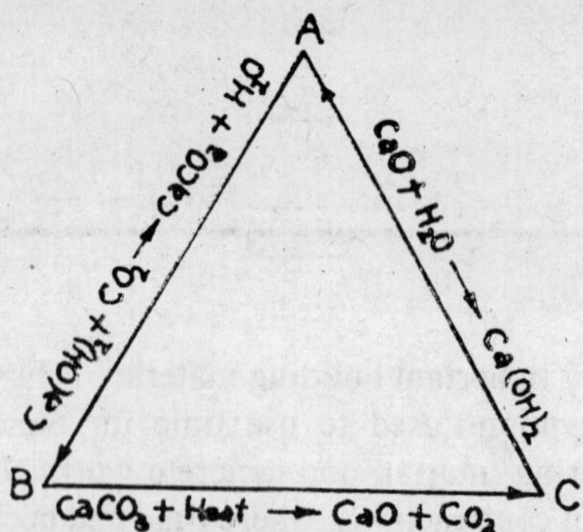

Fig. 4.1. Cycle of decomposition and reformation of calcium carbonate.

12. It is used for water purification and sewage treatment works.
13. When used in combination with cement, its properties are modified and lot of cement can be saved.
14. It is used even in paints.
15. It is used for the manufacture of glass.

So we see, that, there is no field in which lime is not used these days in one form or the other.

4.4. Source of Lime

Lime does not occur in nature in free state. It is obtained from substance having lot of calcarious content in it. Lime stone, chalk, Kankar are the usual raw materials from which lime is obtained. All the materials containing calcarious substance have calcium carbonate ($CaCO_3$) as the chief constituent. When calcarious materials are heated, carbon dioxide and moisture are driven out, leaving behind calcium oxide (CaO), which is called lime. Raw material from which lime is obtained by heating vary in chemical composition as well as physical properties from place to place and as such lime of uniform quality can not be obtained at all the places. Besides this, methods of burning, slaking, storing and using also affect the properties of the lime.

4.5. Some Important Terms and their Definitions

Following are some of the terms frequently used in regard to the lime:

1. Calcination. This is the process of heating the limestone to redness in the presence of atmospheric air. During calcination carbon dioxide in driven out and calcium oxide is left as the final product.

2. Lime. As already stated, from of limestone, when carbon dioxide is driven out the resulting product is calcium oxide (CaO), which is known as lime.

$$\underset{\text{(Limestone)}}{CaCO_3} \rightarrow \underset{\text{(Lime)}}{CaO} + \underset{\text{(Carbon-dioxide)}}{CO_2}$$

3. Quick Lime. The lime obtained from the calcination of pure lime stone is known as *quick lime*. Quick lime has great affinity for moisture. It is essentially calcium oxide, but some times small amount of magnesium oxide (MgO) may be present along with calcium oxide (CaO). Quick lime is also known as *Caustic lime*. The quick lime as it comes out from kilns is known as lump lime.

4. Setting of lime. When lime converted into paste form is exposed to atmosphere, it gradually hardens. This phenomenon of slow hardening of lime in exposed conditions is known as *setting of lime*. Drying should not be taken as hardening. In the case of drying evaporation of water takes place, where as in case of hardening chemical action takes place.

5. Slaking. Quick lime has very large affinity for moisture. Adding water in sufficient quantity to quick lime is known as *slaking*. When water is added to quick lime, it swells and cracks. Lot of heat is also generated during slaking and quick lime gets, converted into hydrated lime or calcium hydrate [Ca $(OH)_2$].

$$\underset{\text{(quick lime)}}{CaO} + \underset{\text{(water)}}{H_2O} \rightarrow \underset{\text{(Hydrated lime)}}{Ca(OH)_2}$$

6. Slaked lime. The product obtained by slaking of quick lime is known as *slaked lime* or hydrated lime. During slaking, lot of heat is generated with hissing sound. Water required for slaking quick lime, works out about 32% of the weight of quick lime, but due to various factors like method of slaking, degree of burning, and composition of lime, water required for slaking is taken 2 to 3 times, the volume of the quick lime. Rate of slaking is affected by the size of burnt lime lumps and temperature of atmosphere. Slaking can be done withg steam very speedily, under increased pressure in closed drums. Hydrated lime is thus obtained in form of dry powder, which is sold in market in packed bags. When sand and water is mixed with this lime, we get lime mortar. The slaked lime should be used fresh because it has the tendency to absorb carbonic acid from the atmosphere in presence of moisture. This leads to the formation of carbonates of lime particles as follows :

$$H_2CO_3 \rightarrow H_2O + CO_2$$
$$Ca(OH)_2 + CO_2 \rightarrow CaCO_3 + H_2O$$

The slaked lime thus gets converted into carbonate of lime and such slaked lime becomes useless because it losses setting property. Hence slaked lime should therefore be not kept in a damp place.

7. Hydraulicity. It is the property due to which lime sets in damp places or under water or in thick masonry walls, here there is no free access of air. Hydraulicity is due to the crystallizing power of the aluminate and the silicate of lime.

Following are some constituents that are chiefly responsible for producing hydraulicity in the lime.

(i) Clay. It is the most important constitutent that produces hydraulicity in lime. But the property of hydraulicity decreases if clay is present in more than the specified limit. A proportion 8 to 30% of clay is considered good for developing a good lime.

(ii) Soluble silica. Hydraulicity occurs, when both silica and alumina are present in chemical combination with limestone. Silicates of calcium, magnesium, and aluminium are responsible for hydraulicity. Such silicates are inert or inactive at low temperature, but they become active and combine with lime at high temperatures.

(iii) Carbonate of Magnesia. This constituent reduces slaking, but increases the setting process. It imparts more strength. The amount of expansion, and evolution of heat is also small.

(iv) Alkalies and metallic oxides. They tend to become soluble silicates at low temperature only and thus cause hydraulicity. They may be present up to 5% or so.

(v) Sulphate. It also tends to reduce slaking, but increases setting action, but only when it is not in excess amount.

4.6. Varieties of lime

Depending upon the sources, the limes may be of following three varieties.

1. **Stone lime**. It is almost pure lime.
2. **Kankar lime**. It is impure or adulterated lime.
3. **Shell lime**. It is purest form of lime.

4.7. Classification of Lime

The limes may be divided into three categories as follows:

1. Fat lime.
2. Hydraulic lime.
3. Poor lime.

1. Fat lime. This lime is known as fat lime, because it increases 2 to 2.5 times in volume, when slaked.This lime is obtained by burning comparatively pure lime stone. This lime is also sometimes known as *pure lime, rich lime, white lime* or *high calcium lime*. The lime stone from which this lime is obtained should contain about 95% calcium oxide and about 5% other materials inform of impurities after burning. When lime stone containing mostly calcium carbonate is burnt in atmosphere, carbonate dioxide is driven out, leaving back calcium oxide (CaO), known as *quick lime. Fat lime* is obtained by *slaking quick lime*.

Setting of this lime is entirely dependent upon the atmospheric oxygen. For setting, this lime absorbs carbon dioxide (CO_2) from atmosphere and after chemical reaction gets converted into $CaCO_3$ which is quite hard substance, insoluble in water. This reaction is known as setting of the fat lime. Setting and hardening actions of this lime, are very slow. The properties of fat lime may be enumerated as follows.

(i) Its hardening action is slow

(ii) Its setting action, being dependent upon atmospheric air is also slow.

(iii) It slakes vigorously with hissing sound and lot of heat is generated during slaking.

(iv) It swells 2 to 2.5 times of quick lime after slaking.

(v) It has a very high degree of plasticity.

(vi) It is soluble in water.

(vii). It is milky white in its purest form.

Uses of fat lime

Setting of this lime being dependent upon atmospheric air, it should not be used at interiors or internal situations, where approach of air is difficult. It may be used for following purposes.

(i) For white washing

(ii) For plastering

(iii) Its mortar with sand may be used for thin masonry works.

(iv) Its mortar with surkhi develops good setting and hydraulic properties. Such mortar, can be used for thick masonry works, foundations etc.

2. Hydraulic lime. This lime has the property of setting under water. It is obtained by burning lime stone, containing lot of clay and other substances which develop hydraulicity. Hydraulicity of this lime, depends upon the amount of clay and type of clay present in it. Silica, alumina and or iron oxide are present in chemical combination with calcium oxide (CaO). Depending upon the amount, of clay (silica and alumina) present, hydraulic limes may be further divided into following three categories.

(i) Feebly hydraulic lime

(ii) Moderately hydraulic lime.

(iii) Eminently hydraulic lime.

Feebly Hydraulic lime. It contains silica, alumina and/or iron oxide less than 15%. The usual percentage of these constituents varies between 5% to 10%. On slacking, it increases in volume by very small amount. It slakes slowly. This lime may be used in form of mortar with sand in not very important works.

Moderately Hydraulic lime. This lime contains 15 to 25% silica and alumina. It slakes very slowly and increases by very small amount on slaking. This lime provides a very good mortar with sand. It is mostly used as mortar in good type of masonry works.

Eminently hydraulic lime. This lime is of even better quality than moderatly hydraulic lime. It contains 25 to 30% clayey (silica and alumina) ingredients. It resembles very much to portland cement in chemical composition. Slaking of this lime is hardly noticable. Its initial setting starts after 2 hours and the final setting withing 48 hours. This lime is mostly used for structural purposes and for the works carried out under water or in damp situations.

Properties of hydraulic lime can be summarized as follows:

1. Increased percentage of clay renders lime more hydraulic and makes slaking more difficult.

2. With 30% clay content, its chemical composition resembles more or less that of cement.

3. It can set under water.

4. It can set under situations where free air can not reach. This is because, setting action of this lime does not depened upon atmospheric air.

5. This lime is not perfactly white and appears less sanitary than fat lime.

6. It does not dissolve in water but forms a thin plastic paste with water.

7. This lime, if used for plaster work should be finely ground, before mixing with sand. If lime is not ground, some of the thick particles of lime may slake even after a month (slaking action being very slow) and may spoil the plastered surface after wards. This action is known as *blistering*. It is good, if mortars prepared from this lime are kept heaped up for a weak or so before use.

3. Poor Lime. This lime contains more than 30% of clay. It slakes very slowly. It does not dissolve in water. It forms a thin plastic paste with water. This lime is also known as *lean lime* or *impure lime*. This lime hardens and sets very week slowly. This lime forms very week mortar and hence used for inferior works only.

4.8. Comparision Between Fat Lime and Hydraulic Lime

Table 4.1

	Item	*Fat lime*	*Hydraulic lime*
1.	Composition	It is obtained from pure lime stone in which other impurities do not exceed 5%.	It is obtained from kankar and other lime stones containing 5 to 30% clay contents and some amount of ferrous oxide.
2.	Colour	It is milky white when burnt or calcined without allowing it to come in contact of fuels like coal.	Its colour is not white because of presence of silica, alumina and iron oxide in certain proportion.
3.	Slaking	It slakes vigorously with hissing sound and lot of heat is generated. It increases 2 to 2.5 times in volume.	Slaking action is slow depending upon the amount of clay contents. No sound and heat is generated and increase in volume is also slight.
4.	Setting	It sets only in the presence of air. It absorbs CO_2 from air and forms $CaCO_3$.	It sets under water. It combines with water and forms crystals of hydrated tri-calcium aluminate and di-calcium silicate.
5.	Hydraulicity	It does not possess any hydraulic property (It does not set under water)	It possesses hydraulic property. (It sets under water)
6.	Strength	It does not have much strength and hence not used where strength is required.	It is strong and hence can be used where strength is required.
7.	Uses	It is mainly used for white washing, plastering, and for preparing mortar with surkhi and sand.	It is mainly used as mortar for thick walls. It can be used for plaster work also, but one has to be careful against blistering-effect.
8.	Shrinkage	It shrinks a lot on drying and hence to reduce the effect of shrinkage sand equal to two or three times of its volume is added to it.	It shrinks very small and as it can be added with comparatively small sand.

4.9. Classification of Lime According to I.S. 712-1984

According to I.S. 712-1984, lime has been classified into following six categories.

Class A– It is hydraulic lime which is mostly used for construction works. It is nothing, but eminently hydraulic lime.

Class B– It is semi-hydraulic lime which can be used as mortar in masonry works.

Class C– It is fat lime which is used for plastering and white washing. It can be converted into artificial hydraulic lime by mixing surkhi, or other Pozzolanic materials in it in suitable amount.

Class D–It is magnesium lime used for finishing coat in plastering white washing etc.

Class E–It is kankar lime and is used for masonry mortars.

Class F– It is siliceous dolomite lime which is used for under coat and finishing coat of plaster. It is to be supplied in hydrated or quick form.

Class A and Class E limes are always available in form of bydrated lime : Class B, C and D limes may be available in form of quick lime or hydrated lime. Chemical compositions of different limes as suggested by I.S. 712-1984 are given in Table 4.2. Variations in the quality of lime caused by the variations in the qualities of locally available lime stones are bound to be there. Regional standards for lime so as to cover regional differentiations are being compiled by the Indian Standards Institutions. I.S.I. has given following definitions of some terms used in context with lime.

1. Quick lime– The calcined material major part of which is calcium oxide in natural association with a relatively smaller amount of magnesium oxide and capable of slaking with water.

2. Hydraulic lime–Lime containing small quantities of silica and alumina and/or iron oxide which are in chemical combination with some of the calcium oxide content giving a putty or mortar which has the property of setting and hardening under water.

Hydrated lime– A dry powder obtained on treating quick lime with sufficient water to satisfy its chemical affinity for water under the condition of its hydration.

Milk of lime– A thin pourable suspension of slaked lime in water.

Lump lime– Quick lime as it comes from kilns.

$$\textit{Cementation value} = \frac{2.8A + 1.1B + 0.7C}{1.0D + 1.4E}$$

Table 4.2

Chemical composition of different types of limes

Types of test	Class A	Class B		Class C		Class D		Class E
	Hyd-rated	Quick	Hyd-rated	Quick	Hyd-rated	Quick	Hyd-rated	Hyd-rated
1. Calcium and Magnesium oxides percent Minimum	60	70	70	85	85	85	85	25
2. Magnesium oxides percent								
Max	5	5	5	5	5	—	—	5
Min	—	—	—	—	—	5	5	—
3. Silica, alumina and ferric oxide percent min	25	15	15	—	—	—	—	—
4. Unhydrated oxides percent max	—	—	—	—	—	8	8	—
5. Insoluble residue in hydrochloric acid less the silica, percent Max	2	3	2	—	—	—	—	—
6. Insoluble matter in sodium carbonate solution percent max	5	5	5	5	5	5	5	5
7. Loss on ignition percent (max)		5 for large lumps 7 for lime other than large lumps		same as for class B quick lime		same as for class B quick lime		
8. Carbon dioxide percent max	5	5	5	5	5	5	5	—
9. Comentation value Min	0.6	0.3	3.0	—	—	—	—	—
Max	—	0.6	0.6	—	—	—	—	—

where A = percentage of silica according to weight

B = percentage weight of alumina oxide.

C = percentage weight of iron oxide.

D = percentage weight of calcium oxide.

E = percentage weight of magnesium oxide.

Compressive strength of class A lime after 14 days, should be 17.5 kg/cm^2 and that after 28 days 28 kg/cm^2.

Compressive strength of class B after 14 days setting should be 12.5 kg/cm^2 and that after 28 days 17.5 kg/cm^2 and for class E it is 10.5 kg/cm^2 after 14 days and 17.5 kg/cm^2 after 28 days.

Modulus of rupture of class A and class B categories of lime is 10.5 kg/cm^2 and 7.0 kg/cm^2 respectively after 28 days of setting. It is 7 kg/cm^2 at 28 days for class E lime.

4.10. Indian Standard Specification for Lime.

Class A Lime. It consists of calcium and magnisium oxide minimum 60% and maximum 70%. Percentage of silica, Aluminia and iron oxide should be minimum 25%. Insoluble salts in hydrochloric acid except silica should not exceed 2% and on calcination amount of CO_2 should not exceed 5%.

When sieved through 240 Nos. I.S. sieve no residue should be left over it. When sieved through 95 Nos. and 30 Nos IS sieve the residue left over them should not respectively exceed 5% and 10%. Its initial setting time should not be less than 2 hrs and final setting should not exceed 48 hrs. When tested in Le-chatliers apparatus for soundness, its indicators should not show expansion of more than 10 mm. Its minimum compressive strength after 14 days and 28 days with lime sand mortar 1:3 by weight should be 17.5 kg/cm^2 and 28 kg/cm^2 respectively. Its modulus of rupture after 28 days should not be less than 10.5 kg/cm^2.

Class B lime. It should not contain calcium and magnesium oxides less than 70%. Percentage of silica, alumina and iron oxide should not be less than 15%. It should not contain insoluble content in hydrochloric acid, more than 3% in quick lime condition and 2% in hydrated condition. On calcination, amount of CO_2 should not be more than 5% and loss of weight on ignition should not exceed 5 to 7%. Soundness and fineness of this lime should conform to same specifications as class A lime. Its compressive strength at 14 days and 28 days setting be 12.5 kg/cm^2 and 17.5 kg/cm^2, respectively, and modulus of rupture for tensile strength should not be less than 7 kg/cm^2 after 28 days of setting.

Class C lime. It should not contain calcium and magnesium oxide, less than 85%. Evolution of CO_2 and loss on ignition should be same as for class B. In slaked form when sieved through 240 and 85 Nos I.S. sieves, no residue should be left. When sieved througth 30 and 20 Nos I.S. sieves the residue left over should not exceed 5% and 10%, respectively.

Class D lime. Calcium and magnsium oxide content should not be less than 85%. Loss on ignition and evolution of CO_2 is same as for class B and class C limes. In hydrated form it will leave no residue on 850 micron IS sieve, to percent on 300 micron IS sieve and the fraction passing through 300 micron I.S. sieve shall leave not more than 10% (of this fraction) on 212 micron sieve. This lime is not tested for compressive strength, transverse strength and soundness. Percentage of unhydrated oxides must not exceed 8% both in quick form and hydrated form.

Class E lime. Calcium and magnesium oxide content is very little about 25%. Evolution of CO_2 is nil. It is not tested for cementation value. The Le-chateliar moulds shall not exhibit more than 10 mm expansion. Modulus of rupture should not be less than 7 kg/cm^2 at 28 days. Compressive strength should be 10.5 kg/cm^2 after 14 days and 17.5 kg/cm^2 after 28 days. When sieved through 2.35 mm sieve, it must not leave any residue and when sieved through 850 micron sieved the residue must not be more than 5%. The fraction passing through 850 micron shall leave not more than 10% of this fraction on 300 micron I.S. sieve.

Soundness test is conducted only for class A class B (hydrated) and class E limes. In all these three cases the Le-chateliar moulds must not exhibit more than 10 mm expansion.

Workability test in done for class C and D limes. In quick lime form they shall require not less than 12 bumps to attain an average spread of 19 cm from an initial spread of 11 cm on the flow Table. In hydrated form they shall require not less than 10 bumps to attain the same average spread of 19 cm from an initial spread of 11 cm on the flow table.

4.11. Manufacture of Fat Lime

The manufacture of fat lime involves following three distinct stages:

1. Collection of lime stone.
2. Burning or calcination of limestone.
3. Slaking of calcined lime or quick lime.

1. Collection of lime stone. Bulk of limestone of pure variety is collected at the site of manufacture. The lime stone should contains 95% calcium carbonate. The lime stone collected at the site is broken into lumps of small sizes.

2. Burning or calcination. In this process, broken limestone is burnt to red hot temperature. Fuel used for burning may be charcoal,

coal, fire wood, or coal ash. Mostly charcoal is used, where lime is to be manufactured on large scale. The limestone should be heated slowly in the initial stage of burning as sudden heating results in the blowing of stones to pieces due to quick release of moisture and carbon dioxide. Cow-dung cakes or chips of dry wood, are used for initiating the firing of the limestone. Calcination of limestone may be carried out in clamps, or in kilns. Clamps are used when manufacture of lime is to be carried out on a small scale and also where fire wood is cheaply and abundently available. Kiln burning of limestone is adopted, where lime is to be manufactured on comparatively large scale. Kilns may further be divided into *intermittent kilns,continuous kilns*. Clamps, intermittent kilns and continuous kilns have been described one by one.

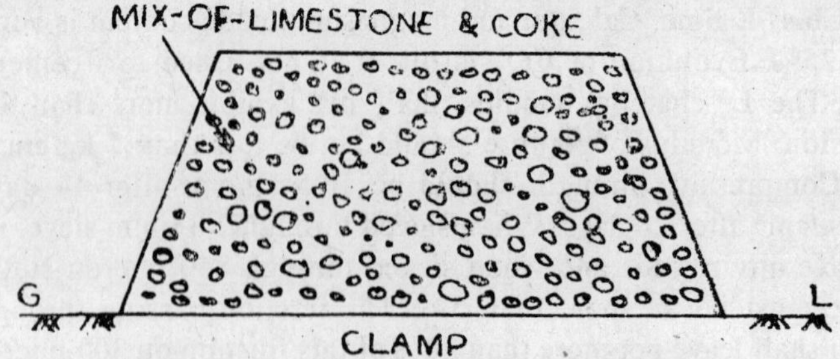

Fig. 4.2. Lime burning crude clamps

Clamp. Clamp is a very crude method of burning the lime stone. It consists of a stack of limestone and fuel, arranged either in alternate layers or in form of a mixture of limestone and fuel. The height of the stack is usually 3.5 to 4.0 m and its faces are sloped . The sloping faces are covered with mud plaster to prevent the escape of heat during the process of burning. Fire places are kept at the bottom of the stack or clamp, for firing. This method of burning suffers from following draw backs.

(i) More fuel is requried for burning as, it is wastefull method.

(ii) There is no control on temperature during burning.

(iii) Fire cannot be regulated properly.

(iv) Quality of lime is not uniform. Limestone pebbles near surface generally remain unburnt or under burnt, while those very near to the fire are over burnt.

(v) Supply of burnt lime is intermittent and small.

2. Intermittent kilns. There are many types of intermittent kilns in use. But the most commonly used kilns are following :

(i) Intermittent Flame kiln and *(ii)* Intermittent flare kiln.

(i) Intermittent Flame kiln. It consists of a round encloser, open at the top. The encloser is lined by fire clay bricks from sides. It has fire places and draw holes suitably located in the walls. The kiln is loaded by crushed lime stone and fuel, arranged in alternate layers. Horizonal as well as vertical flues are formed at the time of loading. The loaded kiln is lastly covered with some unburnt material, which may be clay. The kiln is fired and allowed to burn for about 3 days. The kiln is then allowed to cool and lastly unloaded. The processes of loading, burning, cooling and unloading have to be repeated for each charge of the kiln. In this case, thickness of each fuel layer is kept about 20 cm. and that of each crushed limestone about 40 cm. A kiln having 2 m diameter and 4 m depth can burn about 15 *t* of limestone in one charge.

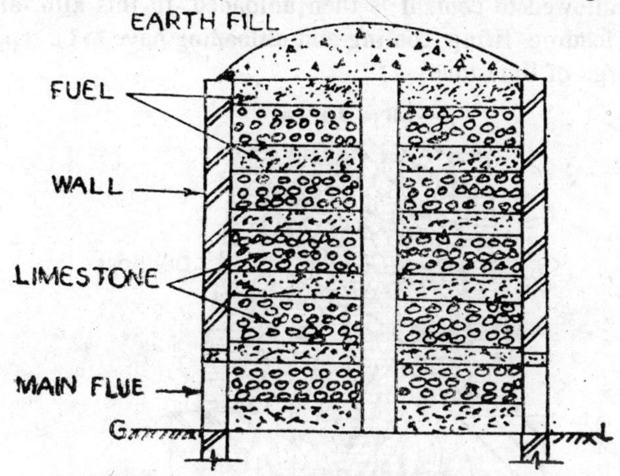

F.g. 4.3. Intermittent Flame Kiln.

(ii) Intermittent flare kiln. This is the intermittent kiln, in which fuel is not allowed to come in contact with the crushed limestone. This

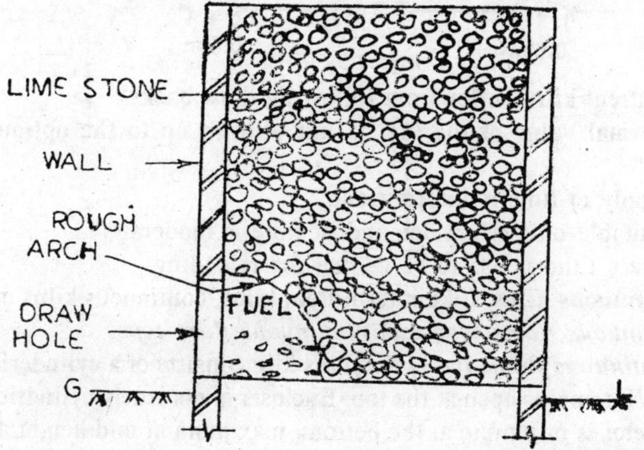

Fig. 4.4. Intermitent Flare Kiln

kiln also consists of an encloser lined by fire brick from inside and open at the top. Fuel holes or fire places, and draw holes are suitably provided in the encloser. While filling the charge of lime stone in the kiln, first of all an arch like structure is developed at the floor of the kiln by using selected larger pieces of unburnt limestone. After this the kiln is filled with crushed lime stone of smaller pieces. In this case, kiln is generally not covered from the top. Now fuel is burnt in the flue or space left below the rough arch and flame of the fire gets into the limestone charge and burnts it. The process of burning fire in the flue is continued til limestone charge is thoroughly burnt. Now burning of the fire is stopped and kiln in allowed to cool. It is then unloaded. In this kiln, all the processes of loading, firing, cooling and unloading have to be repeated for each charge of limestone.

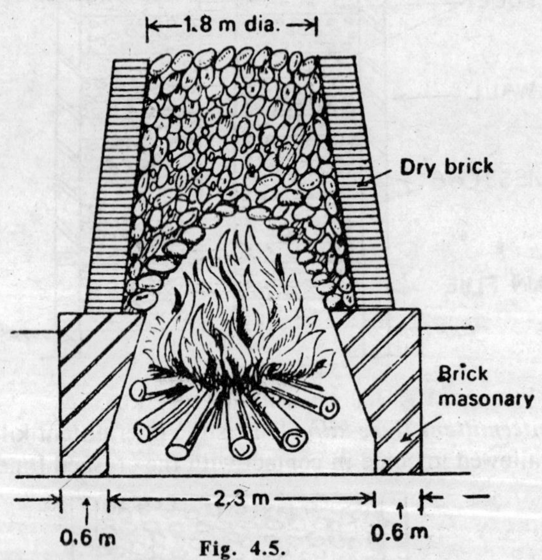

Fig. 4.5.

Intermittent kilns suffer from following draw backs :

(i) Thermal value of the fuel is not utilized up to the optimum extent.

(ii) Supply of lime is intermittent

(iii) Suitable only when demand of lime is moderate.

(iv) Every time it has to be cooled for reloading.

3. Continuous kilns. Like intermittent kilns, continuous kilns may also be *continuous flame type* and *continuous flare type*:

(i) Continuous flame type kiln. This kiln consists of a cylinderical encloser which remains open at the top. Encloser is not truely cylindrical, but the diameter is minimum at the bottom, maximum at mid height and

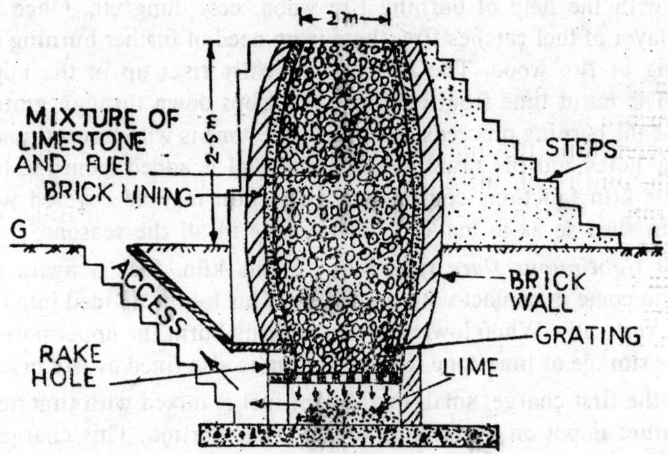

Fig. 4.6. Continuous Flame type kiln.

mid way, between maximum and minimum at the top. If diameter at bottbm is say 1.50 m; it will be about 2 m at the top and about 2.50 m at mid height. The kiln is lined by fire bricks, from inside and is provided with a grating at the bottom. Open space is left below the grating to collect the burnt limestone falling through the grating. Draw hole is also, provided to take out the burnt lime.

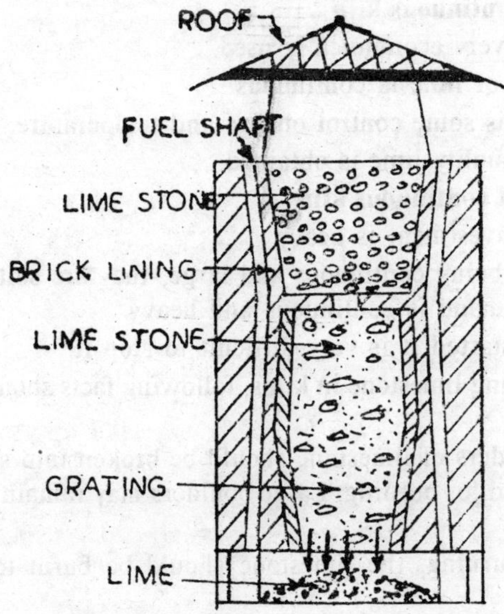

Fig. 4.7. Continuous Flalre type kiln

The kiln may be charged with alternate layers of fuel and limestone or by a mixture of limestone and charcoal. The kiln is ignited from bottom with the help of burning fire wood, cow dung etc. Once the bottom layer of fuel catches fire, there is no need of further burning the cow-dung or fire wood. The fire automatically rises up in the upper layers. The burnt lime from bottom layer drops down through grating holes. As the burning proceeds, the burnt limestone is withdrawn through the draw holes and the raw limestone and fuel is added from the top. Thus this kiln functions continuously. The kiln may be covered with rough tin shed so as to make it functionable in all the seasons.

(ii) Continuous flare type kiln. In this kiln, fuel is again not allowed to come in contact with lime stone. This kiln is divided into two sections vertically. When lower portion is being burnt the upper portion serves as storage of limestone. Lower poriton is also lined by fire bricks.

In the first charge, small quantity of fuel is mixed with limestone and mixture is put on the grating of the lower portion. This charge is fired. After this, fuel is not mixed with the limestone, but is fed through shafts built around the upper and lower sections of the kiln. As the limstone in the lower portion burns, the hot gases of combustion rise in the upper portion and thus, heat of waste gases is utilized for pre-heating the limestone. Burnt limestone is withdrawn through the grating holes, while feeding of crushed limestone is done from top. Thus the kiln functions without any interuption. The kiln may be covered from top by roof, so that, it may remain workakable througth out the year.

Advantages of continuous kiln

(i) Fuel is very economically used.

(ii) Supply of lime is continuous

(iii) There is some control on fire and temperature.

(iv) Good quality lime is obtained.

Disadvantages of continuous kiln

(i) Initial investment is heavy.

(ii) Supply being continuous and large, they are suitable only at places, where demand is continuous and heavy.

(iii) Once started it is very difficult to stop it.

While burning limestone in kilns, following facts should always be taken care of :

1. Big boulders of limestone should be broken into suitable size, before they are fed for burning. Large boulders may ramain under burnt and go waste.

2. While burning, the limestone should be burnt to bright red

colour. This colour of hot burnt limestone shows that burning of limestone is complete.

3. Temperature of burning should be so regulated that neither limestone remains under burnt nor it is over burnt.

4. Limestone should not be subjected to sudden vigorous fire. This may result in the blowing of stone to small pieces due to quick release of CO_2 and moisture.

5. Quantity of fuel should be strickly according to the requirements.

3. Slaking of burnt or calcined lime. It is a process by which the lime is made suitable for use in engineering works. It has already been stated earlier that quick lime obtained after burning the limestone has great affinity for moisture. When quick lime is exposed to atmosphere it starts getting moisture from air and thus starts slaking. This process of slaking is very slow as availability of moisture from atmospheric air is limited. The phenomenon of slaking quick lime by atmospheric air is known as *air slaking* or *natural slaking*. Slaking of quick lime is done with the help of water at construction sites. The slaking of lime with the help of water can be divided into two parts.

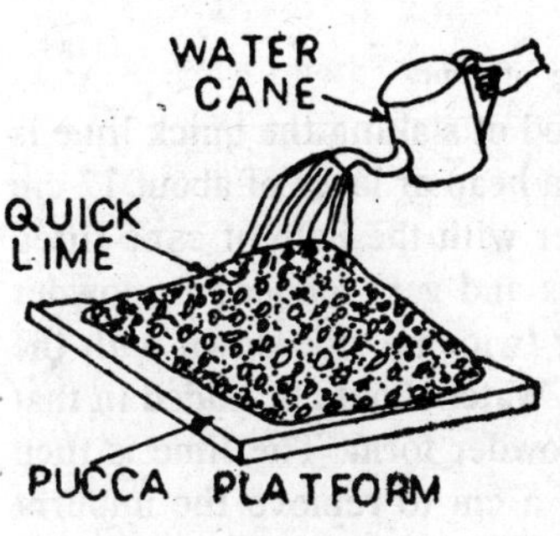

Fig. 4.8

(i) Slaking to paste.

(ii) Slaking to powder.

(i) Slaing to paste. In this process of slaking, quick lime is added in a tank containing sufficient quantity of water. Quantity of water should be 2 to 3 times the volume of quick lime to be slaked. While slaking no lump of quick lime should remain projecting above the surface of water. After putting quick lime into tank containing water, the mixture should be kept stirred for sometimes, so that no particle which can slake remains unslaked. In fact slaking to past of lime can be done with the help of a pair of tanks. One of the tanks is constructed at ground level. The second tank is constructed adjacent to the previous tank with one wall common, but its level is kept low in such a way that level of the lower tank remains lower than the bottom level of the upper tank. By this system the contents of upper tank can be poured into the lower tank. Both the tanks remain connected by a hole at bottom of the common wall. See Fig. 4.9.

Lime is first of all slaked in upper tank. During slaking the hole connecting both tanks, remains closed. Now the hole is opened and all the dssolved contents get poured into the lower tank leaving behind unslaked and bigger particles in the upper tank. The hole connecting the tanks may be fitted with a sieve to not to allow bigger particles flow into the lower tank. Water from lower tank is partly evaporated and partly percolated and in a matter of a day or two, the white solution of lime, which is also known as milk of lime, is converted into paste. This is known as slaking of the lime to paste.

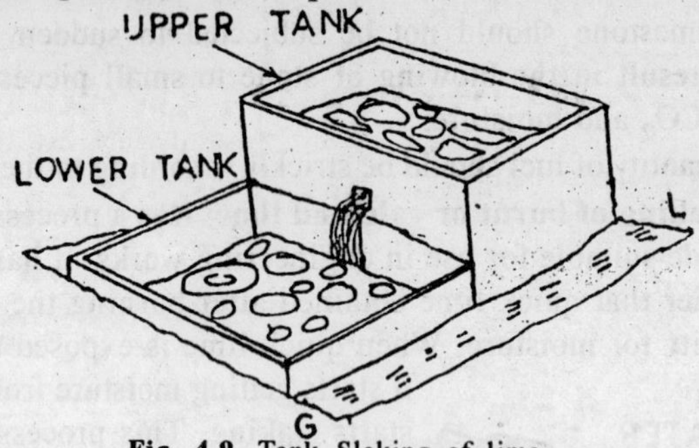

Fig. 4.9. Tank Slaking of lime.

(ii) Slaking to powder. In this method of slaking the quick lime is spread on a pucca cemented plateform in a heap or layer of about 12 cm thickness. Water is sprinkled on this layer with the help of cane fitted with a roce at its nozzle. The lime slakes and gets reduced to powder form. The heap of lime is turned once or twice up side down with the help of phaora during sprinkling of water. Water should be added in that much quantity only that slakes lime in powder form. The lime is then screened through a sieve of 3 meshes to a cm to remove the unburnt lumps and other foreign matter. Screened lime is used for making the mortars.

Slaking to powder form can be done by taking quick lime in baskets and baskets are immersed in water for few seconds and taken out and thrown on a masonry platform in a heap form. Quick lime crumbles and falls to powder form. Period of immersion of the basket in water is kept vary small.

4.12. Manufacture of Natural Hydraulic Lime

Natural hydraulic lime is manufactured by calcining kankar, which is an impure form of limestone. Kankar may be available in form of blocks or nodules. Nodules of kankar are found at the surface or slightly embedded in ground, where as kankar blocks are found at the river banks. Kankar is quarried with the help of crow bars and pick-axes. Quarried kankar is washed and crushed into suitable sized pebbles.

Calcination of kankar is done in the same way and in same kilns as has been explained for fat lime.

Slaking operation of hydraulic lime is very slow. Generally calcined kankar is first of all ground dry and then water is sprinkled over it. Following are some of the points of difference in slaking of fat lime and hydraulic lime.

Fat lime	Hydraulic lime
1. Comparatively large quantity of water is required	1. Comparativly smaller quantity of water is required.
2. Time of slaking is small (2-4 hrs).	2. Time of slaking is more (12-48 hrs).
3. Lot of heat is generated and slaking water starts boiling	3. Not much heat is generated.
4. Quick lime is added to the water filled in the tank.	4. Water in sprinkled gradually over the spread layer of calcined hydraulic lime.
5. It swells about 1.5 times in paste form and 2 times in powder form	5. In paste form it does not swell, but in powder form it may swell 1.5 times.

4.13. Manufacture of Artificical Hydraulic Lime

If natural raw material like kankar is not available, hydraulic lime can be manufactured by artificial means. In manufacturing artificial hydraulic lime, fat lime is converted into hydraulic lime by adding clay and other constituents which produce hydraulicity. Method of conversion of fat lime into artificial hydraulic lime depends upon the type of limestone. If limestone to be used is of very soft nature like chalk, it is first ground into fine powder. This powder is now mixied with appropriate proportion of clay and the mixture is burnt in the kiln. The resulting product is slaked by shrinkling water. The lime manufactured thus, has all the properties of hydraulic lime.

If limestone from which hydraulic lime is to be manufactured is of hard variety, it is first burnt and slaked like fat lime. To the slaked lime, required proportion of clay is added and the mixture is cast into suitable sized balls. The balls are allowed to dry and then burnt in kiln. The burnt balls are ground and slaked like natural hydraulic lime. The resulting product is an artificial variety of hydraulic lime. As this lime is produced, by twice burning in the kiln, it is also called *twice kilned lime.*

4.14. Storage of Lime

Quick lime obtained from kilns if not slaked, started deteriorating due to action of the atmospheric moisture. Hence, quick lime should be slaked immediately and slaked lime can be kept stored for 14 days in form of lime putty or paste. This putty must be used in this time, otherwise lime would lose all its useful properties. However, if storage of lime for longer periods is unavoidable, it should be done in closed, properly insulated stores, where moisture cannot penetrate.

4.15. Testing of Lime

1. Hydraulic lime mortar—lime : sand : : 1 : 3.
2. Adhesive strength (with bricks) after 7 days curing = 2.25 kg/cm^2.
3. Tensile strength (briquette test—1 sq. inch) after 21 days of curing = 6.3 kg/cm^2.
4. Compressive strength (5 to 7.5 cm cube test) after 21 days of curing = 35 kg/cm^2.

I.S.I. specifies the following tests for lime.

(i) Visual inspection. The lime sample is taken and examined for colour. If colour is milky white, it is fat or pure lime. If ordinary white it is fat lime,. but having certain amount of adultration. If colour is dirty or grey, it shows hydraulic lime having lot of coal ash, etc. If lime available consists of lumps, it shows either quick lime or unburnt lime.

(ii) Chemical analyses. This test is done to find out cementation value and also hydraulic properties of sample. For cementation value of lime, the following equation may be used.

$$\text{Cementation value} = \frac{2.8A + 1.1B + 0.7C}{D + 1.4E}$$

Significance of A, B, C, D, and E have already been given earlier.

(iii) Hydrochloric acid test. This test is carried out to classify the lime and also to assess the lime content.

Take small amount of powdered lime in a test tube and note the level of lime, after adding water to it. The tube is stirred with glass rod and left to rest for 24 hrs.

If there is lot of effervescene, it indicates high percentage of calcium crabonate. The residue left at the bottom of the test tube indicates the proportion of impurities or hydraulic properties of the lime. If thick jel is formed in the test tube which would not flow out even by turning the test tube up side down, it shows eminently hydraulic lime. If the jel formed is not very thick and tends to flow out on tilting the tube, it indicates feebly hydraulic lime. If there is no jel, it is fat lime.

(iv) Soundness test. This test is carried out by Le-chatelier apparatus. It consists of a brass cylinder mould attached with two long indicators and two glass plates. See Fig. 4.10

The mould is placed on glass plate filled with 1 : 3 : 12 mixture of cement hydrated lime and sand mortar. Mortar is prepared by adding water at the rate of 12% of the wt. of the mixture. The mould is covered from the top by second glass plate and left for one hour. The distance between the indicator needless is then measured. The mould is then placed in a damp air cup board for 48 hours and subjected to action of saturated steam for 3 hours (without immersing in boiling water.). The mould is allowed to cool and the distance between the ends of the two indicators is measured again. The increase in the indicator ends should not be more than 10 mm (allow 1 mm for expansion of added cement).

I.S. 1624-1960 gives popping and Pitting tests for fat lime. Pats are prepared by mixing 70 gm. of hydrated lime with 70 c.c. of water and 10 gm of plaster of paris. They are subjected to steam action and examined for disintegration, popping, and pitting Any of these occurrences is an indication of unsoundness of lime.

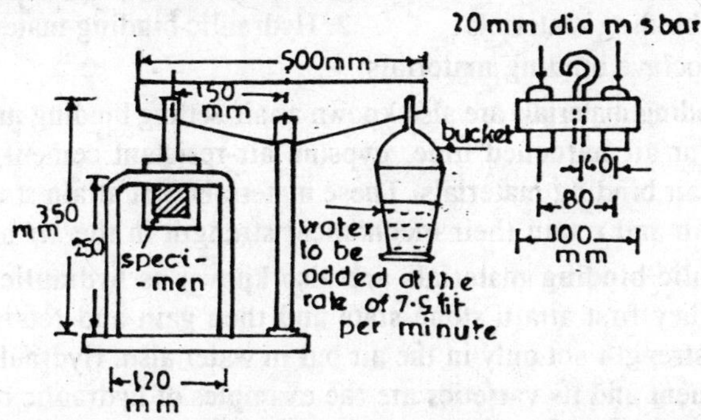

Fig. 4.10. Test for transverse strength.

(v) Test for workability. By this test, workability of the mortar is estimated. Take handfull of prepared mortar and dash it on the surface of the wall, where it is to be used. The area covered by the mortar in relation to its dashed amount gives an indication of suitability of various ingredients in the mortar.

(vi) Test for transverse strength. Prepare a test specimen 2.5 cm × 2.5 cm × 10 cm. The specimen is cured for 28 days at 90% humidity at a temperature of 24-30°C. These test specimen are immersed in water for half an hour and tested in the apparatus for transverse strength. The specimen is fixed in the machine and load is applied transversely with the help of a third roller placed at mid length of the specimen. The load is applied at the rate of 7.5 kg per minute till the specimen brakes in bending. Span of the specimen is kept 8 cm. See Fig. 4.10.

The modulus of rupture (m) of the test specimen is found out by following relationship.

$$m = \frac{3\,W\,S}{2b\,d^2}$$

where m = modulus of rupture in kg/cm^2

W = breaking load in kg.

S = span in cm. 8 cm.
b = breadth of the section = 2.5 cm.
d = depth of the section = 2.5 cm.

Substituting the value $$m = \frac{3W \times 8}{2 \times 2.5 \times (2.5)^2} = 0.768W$$

The value of m should be more than 10.5 kg./cm^2 for class A lime and more than 7 kg/cm^2 for class B lime.

4.16. Classification of binding materials

The binding materials can be classified under following three heads.

1. Air binding materials 2. Hydraulic binding materials
3. Autoclave binding materials.

Air binding materials are also known as air-setting binding materials, Quick lime or air hardened lime, gypsum air-resistant cement are the example, of air binding materials. These materials first attain stone state and then gain and retain their mechanical strength in the air only.

Hydraulic binding materials are also known as hydraulic-setting materials. They first attain stone state and then gain and retains their mechanical strength not only in the air but in water also. Hydraulic lime, portland cement and its varieties are the examples of hydraulic bindling materials.

Autoclave binding materials are also known as autoclave-setting substances. They set only when treated in autoclaves with saturated steam at pressure varying from 8 to 12 atmosphers and at temperatures between 170°C to 200°C. The lime-silica, sand portland cements, etc. are the examples of such binding materials.

4.17. Precautions to be taken in handling lime

Following precautions should be taken :

1. Contact with water. Quick lime should not be allowed to come in contact with water before slaking.

2. Facilities to workers. Lime dust in injurious to workers health. Hence workers handling lime should be provided with goggles and respirators. To avoid skin burns workers should also be given rubber gloves, gum boots, skin protective cream etc.

3. Fire hazard. The quick lime gives out lot of heat while slaking and all measures should be taken to avoid chances of fire hazards.

4. Instructions to workers. Workers should be instructed that as soon as they finish work in lime they should wash exposed parts of the body with fresh water. They should daily oil their skin to avoid skin burns.

QUESTIONS

1. **Define the following terms.**
   ***(i)* Fat lime *(ii)* Quick lime *(iii)* Hydraulic lime *(iv)* Calcination *(v)* Slaking of lime.**
2. **(*a*) Enumerate the properties of lime.**
   (*b*) Enumerate the uses of lime.
3. **Write down the properties and uses of fat lime and hydraulic lime.**
4. **What are the different kinds of lime available for use on works? Mention the uses of each variety. Indicate the chemical reactions taking place during the slaking and setting of lime.**
5. **Describe briefly how lime is prepared and explain the difference between quick lime, hydraulic lime, and fat lime.** (*A.M.I.E. May 1963*)
6. **(*a*) Describe briefly a method of burning lime stone for manufacture of lime.**
   (*b*) Explain the difference between quick-lime fat lime, and hydraulic lime. (*A.M.I.E. May 1966*)
7. **Explain the working of intermittent and continuous kilns for the manufacture of lime.**
8. **Describe various tests used to asses the suitability of the lime.**
9. **Give Indian standard specifications for limes.**

5

CEMENT

5.1. Introduction

Cement is a very important binding material, used in the construction industry. It may be natural cement or artifical cement. Natural cement is manufactured by burning and then crushing the natural cement stones. Natural cement stones are such stones which contain 20 to 40% of argillaceous matter *i.e.* clay, and remaining content mainly calcareous matter which is either calcium carbonate alone or mixture of calcium carbonate and magnesium carbonate. Natural cement resembles very closely eminent hydraulic lime.

Artificial cement is manufactures by burning appropriately proportioned mixture of calcareous and argillaceous materials at a very high temperature and then grinding the resulting burnt mixture to a fine powder. The burnt mixture of calcareous and argillaceous matter is known as *clinker*. In order to delay the setting action of cement, when mixed with water, a little percentage of *gypsum*, is also added in the clinkers before grinding them to fine powder. It may be natural cement or artifically manufactured cement, when water is mixed with it, a chemical reaction takes place, as a result of which the cement paste first sets and then hardens into a stone like mass. When cement is mixed with fine sand and water, *cement mortar* is produced and when it is mixed with fine sand, crushed stone aggregate and water, the resulting mixture is known as *cement concrete*. Cement is always used inform of mortar and concrete in construction works and never alone.

5.2. Point of Difference Between Cement and Lime

1. Colour of lime is always whitish. Colour of cement is generally grey, but it can be manufactured in other desired colours also.

2. Cement when mixed with water, starts setting in a matter of 10 to 30 minutes and acquires sufficient strength in a day or two. Lime does not start setting at such a small time and it takes quite a long period before hardening.

3. Cement is several times stronger binding material than lime.

4. Lime should not be allowed, to come in direct contact of iron

girders and other fitting, as lime eats away the iron. Cement on the other hand, protects iron and other metallic fitting from atmospheric action.

5. When water is added to quick lime, lot of heat is generated, but in case of cement, heat generated is unnoticeable.

6. Cement cannot be used for white washing the walls like lime.

5.3. Natural Cements

It has already been stated in article 5.1 that natural cements, are manufactured by burning and then crushing to powder, the natural cement stones. These stones contain 20 to 40% of argillaceous matter and the rest as calcareous matter. Argillaceous matter is nothing, but clay. Calcareous matter is either calcium carbonate alone or calcium cabonate mixed with the magnesium carbonate. Since chemical composition of natural cement stones vary considerably from place to place, the properties of natural cement also keep on varying. Even cement being manufactured in one factory may be varying in properties. The setting time of this cement varies from 5 minutes to as much as five hours. Hydraulic properites of this cement are entirely dependent upon the percentage of clayey material present . If percentage of clayey matter is high, quick setting cement is produced, but its ultimate strength may be low. On the other hand lower percentage of clay produces a slow setting cement, but its ultimate strength may be high. *Roman cement, Pozzolana cement* and *medina cement* are the common varitieis of natural cements.

1. Roman cement. It is one of the best varities of natural cements. It is also known as *Parker's cement*. It is produced from brown coloured nodulus clay known as London clay. This clay contains 30% to 40% clay and the remaining content as calcium carbonate alone or a mixture of $CaCO_3$ and $MgCO_3$. The crushed London clay is burnt at low temperature and then ground to fine powder to produce Roman cement. This cement sets almost immediately, when mixed with water, hence, its small quantity should be mixed with water and used immediately. This cement should be carefully stored, so as to avoid its being coming in direct contact of atmosphere. The strength of this cement is about 1/3 that of artificial cement.

2. Pozzolana cement. It is a volcanic clay which was first spotted at a place named Pozzuoli in Italy. This cement drives its name from the place, it was first obtained. This clay contains about 80% clay along with lime, magnesia, and iron oxide in varying proportion. Its colour is generally red or purple. Puzzolana itself does not have any cementing value, but when mixed with rich lime, it produces a sort of hydraulic cement which is more resistant to chemical reactions than ordinary portland cement. But its rate of hardening or gaining strength, is very slow. This cement is manufactured artificially on a big a way, because it is not easily attacked by chemical agencies and sea water. This cement evolves very small amount of heat and requires longer time for curing, since its rate of gaining strength is very small.

3. Medina Cement. This cement is manufactured from septaria clay occuring in England. It is quick-setting, and light brown in colour. It resembles more or less Roman cement, but it is stonger.

Natural cements were being used on large scale in old days, but with advent of artificial cement, natural cements have gone out of use. To-day they are absolet.

5.4. Artificial Cement

Artificial cement is manufactured by burning at high temperature an intimate mixture of argillaceous and calcareous substances and lastly crushing the resulting clinkers to a fine powder after adding a little gypsum to it. Gypsum is added to delay the setting action of the cement for some time, so that, it may be properly mixed, applied and finished. Without gypsum, setting action of cement starts, the moment the water is added to the cement, thus giving no time for mixing, placing and finishing. The setting time of artificial cements can be varied by suitably varying the percentage of gypsum. Artificial cements are used almost every where, because of following reasons.

(i) Artificial cements can be manufactured in any desired colour.

(ii) Their initial setting time can be easily regulated.

(iii) Their rate of hardening can be regulated.

(iv) Their rate of evolution of heat can be regulated.

(v) Their properties can be maintained always same by maintaining same composition of raw material.

(vi) They can be manufactured in very large quantities.

Common variety of artificial cement is known as *normal setting* cement or ordinary cement. This cement was first invented by a leeds mason named Joseph Aspdin of England in 1824. This cement resembles very closely to a sandstone, which is found in very large amounts at a place, Portland, in England and thus this cement is also some times referred as *Portland cement*. To-day, so many varieties of cements are available in the market. Before discussing each variety, let us study the composition, properties and manufacture of ordinary, portland or normal setting cement, as this is the basic artificial cement. All other cements are manufactured by varying its composition a little, this way or that way.

The manufacture of Portland cement was started in England around 1825. Soon the manufacture of this binding material started at other countries as follows.

Name of country	*Starts of manufacture of cement.*
England	1825
Germany	1855
Belgium	1855
U.S.A	1972
India	1904

The first cement factory in India was installed in Tamil Nadu in 1904 by South India Industry limited.

5.5. Composition of Ordinary Cement

The ordinary cement consists of three ingredients predominantly. They are clay or alumina, silica and lime. Besides, these ingredients most of the cements contain small amount of iron oxide, magnesium oxide, sulphur trioxide, alkalies and other materials. The typical percentages of these constituents in a good ordinary cement may be as follows.

Table 5.1

Name of constituent	*Typical percentage*	*Limit of %*
1. Alumina or clay (Al_2O_3)	5%	3—8%
2. Silica (SiO)	22%	17—25%
3. Lime (CaO)	62%	60—67%
4. Iron oxide	3.0%	0.5—6%
5. Magnesia (MgO)	2%	0.1—4%
6. Sulphur trioxide	1.0%	1—3%
7. Alkalies (Soda and Potash)	1%	0.2%—1%
8. Calcium sulphate ($CaSO_4$) (Gypsum)	4%	3—5%

Functions of each ingredient of the cement, are briefly given as follows.

1. Alumina or clay. Alumina is responsible for the setting action of the cement. Larger the amount of alumina present in the cement, quicker it will start setting. Excess quantity of aluma weakens the cement. Alumina forms complex aluminates with silica and calcium and imparts the setting property to the cement.

2. Silica (SiO_2). It also goes in to chemical combination with calcium and forms hard silicates which are responsible for imparting strength to the cement.

3. Lime (CaO). It is the most important ingredient of the cement and its bulk in cement is above 60% of the total contents. Its proportion should be carefully decided. If lime is added unnecessarily in excess quantity, some part of it, left in forms of free lime which causes expansion and disintegration of cement at the time of setting and hardening. Lesser than the required quantity will cause decrease in the strength of the cement, as then sufficient calcium silicates will not be formed, which are mainly responsible for the strength characteristics of the cement.

4. Iron oxide. This ingredient mainly imparts colour to the cement. Besides this, it also goes into chemical combination and helps increase strength and hardness of the cement.

5. Magnesium Oxide. (MgO). It also imparts strength and hardness to the cement, but only when present in small amount.

6. Sulphur Trioxide. Small percentage of sulphur renders cement sound. Excess amount of it may make it, unsound.

7. Alkalies Alkalies, present in the raw materials used for the manufacture of the cement are mostly driven out by the flue gases during burning. Still it may be present in the cement, but only in very small amount. Excess of alkalies, cause efflorescance in the cement and thus act as impurity.

8. Calcium Sulphate ($CaSO_4$) or (Gypsum). This ingredient is used to retard or prolong the initial setting action of the cement.

Harmful constituents of cement

Out of the above mentioned eight ingredients, Alkalies, which are oxides of Potassium and Sodium, and Magnesium oxide (MgO) are the predominent ingredients which adversely affect the quality of cement. If amount of alkalies exceeds 1% it causes unsoundness of the cement. If amount of MgO exceeds say 5% it causes cracks in hardened mortar or concrete. This cracking is due to the fact, that MgO burns at a temperature of about 1500°C and slakes very slowly when mixed with water.

Location of cement factory site – Location of the site for cement factory should be done considering the following points.

1. Climatic conditions at site should be favourable for the manufacture of the cement
2. Required labour should be available abundently and economically.
3. Local and nearby area should provide adequate market for sale.
4. Electric power should be available abundently, and economically and continuously.
5. Raw materials, should be available locally.

6. Transportation facilities should be adequately available

7. Gardens, parks, picnic spots and other recreation centres should be available.

5.6. Manufacturing the Cement

Cement can be manufactured by following two methods.

1. Dry process (Modern technology)
2. Wet process (Old technology)

Both the processes of manufacture of cement are more or less alike except for the difference that the raw materials are ground and mixed and fed into the burning kiln in dry state in dry process, where as they are in form of a slurry in case of wet process. It may be dry process or wet process of manufacturing the cement, the following three distinct operations have to be performed.

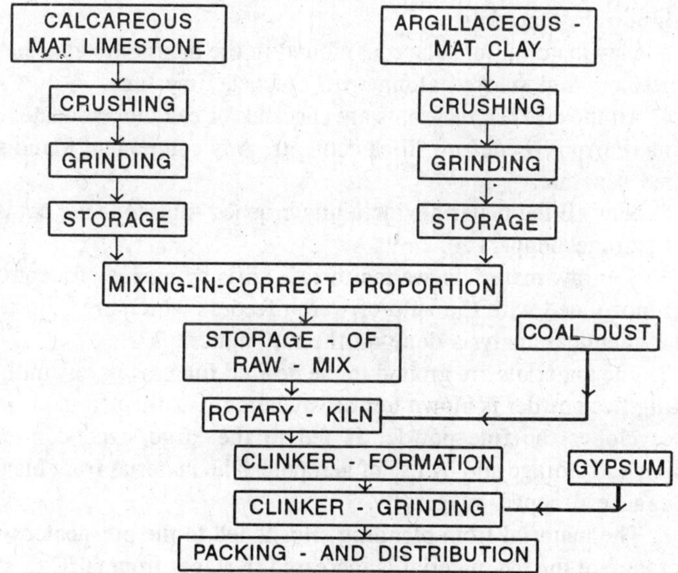

Fig. 5.1. Flow diagram of Dry process of cement manufacture

1. Mixing of raw materials.
2. Burning
3. Grinding

5.7. Mixing (in dry process)

Dry proces of mixing is adopted when raw material are very hard. All the involved materials are first of all broken in crushers in size of about 2.5 cm. separately. The crushed materials are then dried with the help of drought of dry air being passed over them. All the dried materials are then pulverized separately into fine powders with the help of ball mills and tube mills and stored separately in hoppers. All the pulverized materials are then mixed together thoroughly in appropriate proportions. The prepared dry mix is kept stored in silos, ready to be fed into the kiln for burning. Step by step is as follows.

1. Most of the cement factories are located close to the lime stone quarries. The limestone boulders are brought to the factory from quarries in dumpers and dumped in the hopper of the crusher.

2. Single stage hammer mill crushers are used to reduce big boulders of limestone to 75 mm size and this crushed limestone is moved from the crusher by a series of conveyors for stacking. In most of modern plants, the modern stacker-reclaimer system is used. The stacker helps in spreading the crushed materials in horizontal layers and the reclaimer restricts the variation of calcium carbonate in crushed limestone to less than 1%. Thereby reducing the chances of quality variation in the materials.

3. Clay material (argillaceous) found in the quarry are also dumped into crushers and stacked along with crushed limestone.

4. All the crushed materials are checked for calcium crbonate, lime, alumina, Ferrous oxide and silica contents. Any component found short is added separately.

5. Now all the materials including crushed limestone are conveyed to the storage hoppers.

6. The raw materials are fed to raw mills by means of a conveyor and proportioned with the help of weigh feeders which are adjusted as per the chemical analysis done on the raw materials.

7. The materials are ground to the desired fineness in raw mill. The resulting fire powder is blown upwards where it is collected in cyclones. From cyclones the fine powder is fed to the large sized continuous blending and storage silo by use of aeropole. The material from blending silos can be dropped by gravity.

8. The material from blending silos is led to the pre-heater where temperature of the fed material is increased in stages from 60°C to 850°C with the help of hot gas having temperature of 1000°C. The pre-heator is a sloped kiln in which well proportional raw material in fed from top. There being slope the material automatically comes at the lower end of the pre-heater.

9. The material from the bottom of the pre-heater is fed to the rotary kiln where clinkers are formed due to multi-stage pre-heaters. Because of multi-storage pre-heaters the length of the rotary kiln is considerably reduced.

10. Clinkers coming out of rotary kiln are ground and gypsum is added and cement in ready for packing and distribution.

5.8. Wet Process

This process of mixing is usually adopted when raw material are quite soft. Chalk or limestone is crushed is ball or roller mills, and stored in silos. Clay or argillaceous materials are mixed with water in containers, known as wash mills. This washed clay is stored in basins. Now crushed dry limestone or chalk from silos, and wet clay from basins, are allowed to fall in a channel in correct proportion. The channel leads the mix to grinding mills, where both the materials are intimately mixed. Some water may be added if the resulting mix is quite thick. This mix is known as *slurry* The slurry thus prepared is stored in tanks where it is kept constantly stirred. The chemical composition of the slurry is checked here, and if it needs any correction it is done. The corrected slurry is kept stored in storage tanks and kept ready for feeding into the rotary kiln for burning.

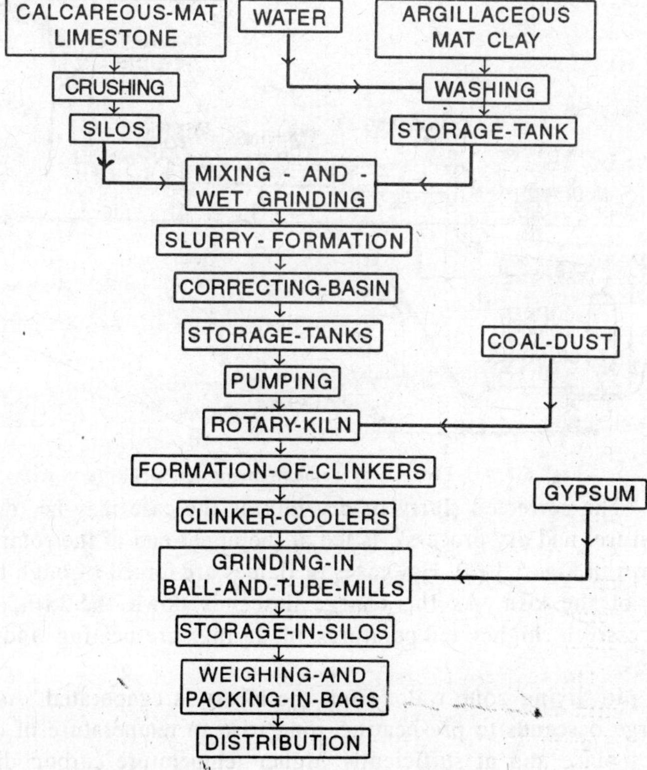

Fig. 5.2. Flow diagram of wet process for cement manufacture

It is thus clear that raw mix is dry, in dry process of mixing, where as it is in slurry state in case of wet process. Dry process of cement manufacturing is not advocated as this process is slow, more costly and above all, the quality of cement produced is of inferior and non-uniform quality. The remaining two operations *i.e.* burning and grinding are same in both the processes of manufacture of cement.

The dry mixture or wet slurry, prepared in the process of mixing is sent for burning in a long inclined slowly rotating kiln. This kiln is commonly known as rotary kiln. It keeps on rotating about its inclined longitudinal axis at the rate of about one revolution per minute. The kiln consists of a mild steel cylinder having a diameter varying from about 2.5 m to 3.0 m. The length of the cylinder varies from 30 m to about 75 m. The cylinder is lined from in side, by means of refractory bricks. The cylinder is supported on rollers and its longitudinal axis is kept inclined at 1 in 20 to 1 in 30 slope. The slope of the kiln is developed by constructing the supports of continuously decreasing height.

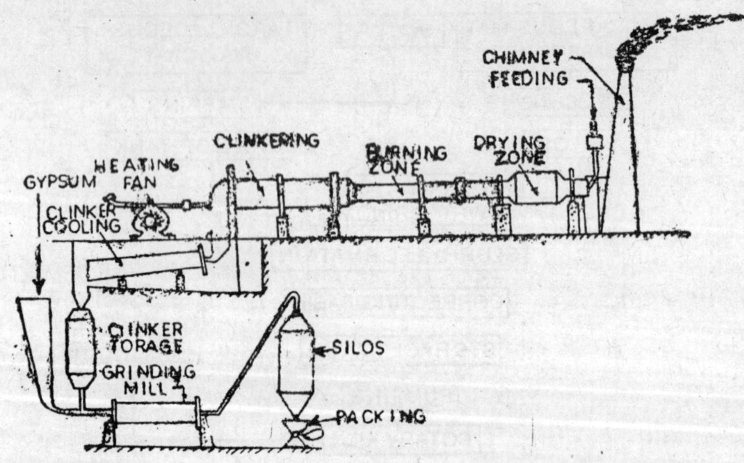

Fig. 5.3 *(a)* Process of cement manufacture (Rotary Kiln)

The corrected slurry or dry mix as the case may be (depending upon wet and dry process), is fed at the upper end of the rotary kiln as shown in Fig. 5.3 (*a*). Hot gases or flames are forced through the lower end of the kiln. As the charge descends down the kiln, it meets successively higher temperatures in drying, pre-heating and burning zones.

In drying zone water from the slurry is evaporated. As the dry charge descends to pre-heating zone, rise in temperature of dry mass takes place and at sufficiently higher temperature carbon dioxide is librated and the mass turns into small sized lumps known as nodules.

The nodules then enter the next zone called burning zone. Temperature in burning zone is kept about 1500°C to 1700°C (2800°F.). Nodules get burnt up in burning zone and are converted into white hot clinkers varying in size from 5 mm to 10 mm. The clinkers are very hot as they come out of burning zone.

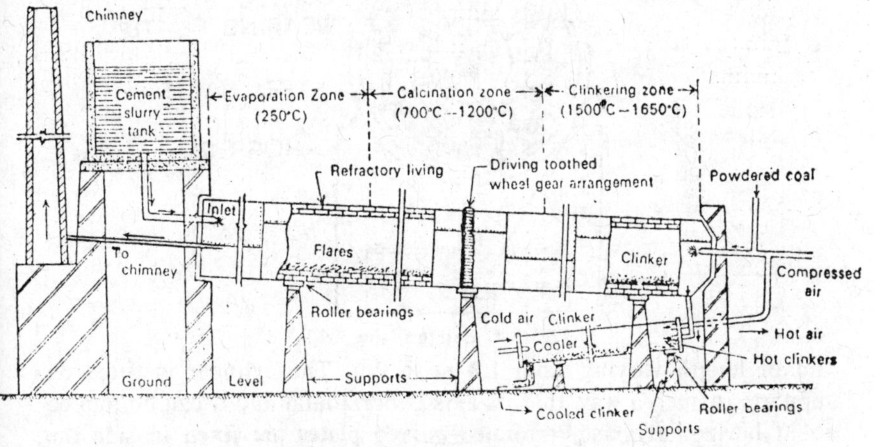

Fig. 5.3 *(b)*

They are then fed into another rotary kiln of small size which is also laid inclined. The hot clinkers are subjected to cooling here and cooled clinkers are conveyed to clinker storage bins by means of conveyor belt. Chemical fusion of lime and clay takes place in the burning zone only.

5.9. Grinding.

Cooled clinkers are fed into ball millls and tube mills for grinding to fine powder. During grinding, a small quantity of gypsum varying from 2 to 4% is added. Gypsum is added to control the intial setting time of the cement. Had gypsum not been added, the cement would have set the moment the water is added to it, without giving time for mixing, placing and finishing. Gypsum acts as a retarder. The ground cement, as it comes out from grinding mills, is forced by compressed air into the silos or bins for storage. The cement from silos is packed into bags by packing machine automatically. Each bag of cement contains 50 kg of cement whose volume is taken at 35 litres. Flow diagram of burning and grinding of cement is shown in Fig. 5.3.

Ball Mills and Tube Mills

Ball mills. Ball mills are used for grinding the clinkers, rather course. The ball mills consists of 2 m to 2.5 m diameter steel cylinder

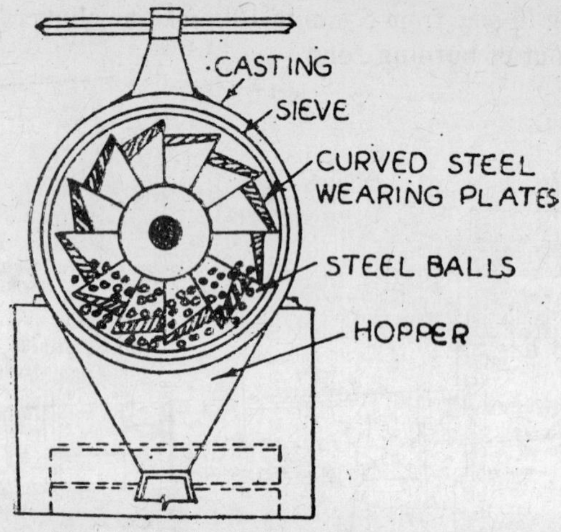

Fig. 5.4. Ball grinding will

and of length varying from 1.8 m to 2m. The cylinder is fitted on supports in such a way, that its axis is horizontal and it can be rotated about horizontal axis. Perforated curved plates are fixed in side the cylinder, in such a way that their ends remain slightly overlapping each other. The cylinder is charged with steel balls varying from 5 cm to 12 cm diameter. The clinkers to be ground are fed into the cylinder and cylinder is rotated about its horizontal axis. While rotating, the steel balls strike on the clinkers and carry out their pulverization. The pulverized material gets sieved through perforations of the curved plates, and fine crushed material, is collected from the out let at the bottom of outer casing of the mill.

Tube mills. Basic concept of tube mill is the same as that of ball mill. In tube mill the size of the steel balls is smaller than in balls mills. Tube mill consists of a tube like, long horizontal steel cylinder supported on supports fixed with ball bearings. Diameter of the cylinder of tube mill is about 1.5 m, but its length may be as much as 10 m. The cylinder of the tube is charged by steel balls, varying in size from 2 cm to 2.5 cm. A worm wheel device is fitted at the inlet end to feed the crushed clinkers from ball mills. No perforated curved plates are fitted in the tube. As tube mill is rotated, the charge of crushed clinkers from ball mill gets ground finer and finer as it slowly proceeds from inlet end of the tube mill towards the out let end. Pulverized or very finely ground material. is collected at the out let end. In case of very large scale production, air separators may be used to separate finely ground particles. In this case current of air is used to carry away the pulverized particles.

Compartment mill. It is nothing, but a combination of ball as well as tube mills. This mill consists of different chambers in which steel balls of varying sizes are placed. The first compartment consists of largest sized steel balls and that last one of smallest sized steel balls. Size of the balls goes on decreasing successively. The clinkers are fed into first chamber having largest sized steel balls. The grinding of clinkers into smaller and smaller sized particles goes on in successive chambers and ultimately finely pulverized cement, comes out of the outlet. Compartment mills are mostly used in big installations.

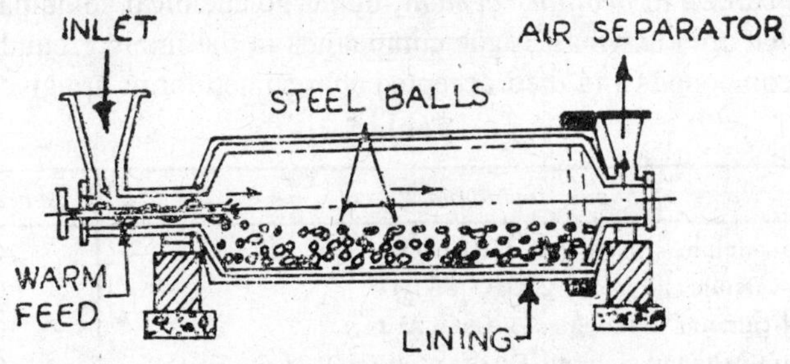

Fig. 5.5. Tube grinding mill

Packing of cement

Cement was conventionally used to be packed in jute bags. But these bags had following draw backs.

1. Jute bags when emptied retain some cement which is wasted.

2. Because of wastage in jute bags full quantity of cement did not reach the concrete mixtures.

3. The handling of jute bags proves harmful to the health of labourer as they inhale a considerable amount of cement-during loading and unloading.

4. The quality of cement in affected due to entry of moisture from the atmosphere.

To over come the above mentioned shortcomings, the "National Council of Cement and Building Materials" has developed an improved jute bag having close-knit design. The packing of cement has been made compulsory in these bags by the Govt. of India. The manufacturers now offer variety of packing bags.

In advanced countries the cement is packed in multi-wall polypropylene paper laminated bags. These bags are made of polypropylene woaven fabrics and internally laminated with craft paper. These bags have become very popular in India also. Following are their advantages.

1. The quality and quantity of cement is assured.
2. The bags are attractive, simple hygienic and easy to handle.
3. They are light and water resistant
4. They have very good resale value once torn or disfigured they can be used as tar Paulene, covers of roofs of the poor's hutments during rains.
5. Being leak-proof the wastage of cement is 100% eliminated.

5.10. Setting and Hardening of Cement

During burning and fusion in rotary kiln, all the ingredients given in *composition of ordinary cement*, under go chemical combination and form what are known as Bogue compounds in the finely ground cement. Bogue compounds and their accepted abbreviated forms are given below:

Table 5.2

	Name of bogue compound	*Abbreviation*
1.	Tri-calcium silicate (3 CaO SiO_2)	C_3S
2.	Di-calcium silicate (2 CaO SiO_2)	C_2S
3.	Tri-calcium aluminate (3 CaO Al_2O_3)	C_3A
4.	Tetra-calcium alumino Ferrite (4 CaO Al_2O_3 Fe_2O_3)	C_4AF

The proportion of bogue compounds vary is various types of cements. Tri-calcium silicate (C_3S) and di-calcium silicate (C_2S) are the compounds mostly responsible for the strength characteristics of the cement.

After addition of water in cement, tri-calcium aluminate (C_3A) is the first compound which starts hydrating and is responsible for early setting of the cement. Hydration of C_3A generates considerable heat, which may be responsible for undesirable properties of the concrete. C_3A does not contribute any strength to the concrete. But it is mainly responsible for setting action of the cement.

After C_3A, hydration of tri-calcium silicate (C_3S) starts. It is C_3S, whose hydration is responsible for the initial strength of the cement. The strength acquired during first 7 days is mostly due to hydration of C_3S.

Di-calcium silicate (C_2S) reacts with water at a very slow rate and hence, strength of the concrete, after 7 days, is mainly due to hydration of C_2S. C_2S starts contributing strength after 7 days of its placement and continues for about one year, though rate of getting strength from this compound goes on decreasing with passage of time.

Tetra-Calcium-alumino ferrite is more or less inactive compound and does not play any significant role in setting and hardening properties of the cement.

Although the processes of setting and hardening of cement take place simultaneously, yet there is difference between the two. Setting of the cement, is changing plastic state of cement to stiff solid, state, which is not strong enough and has a very small compressive strength. Hardening of the cement is the rate of gain of strength. With the passage of time as the hydration proceeds, the compressive strength of the product goes on increasing.

In short it can be said, that the rapidity of initial setting of the cement is controlled by amount of tri-calcium aluminate, where as high early strength by that of tri-calcium silicate. Strength of cement developing after 7 or 8 days of its placement is dependent on the amount of Di-calcium silicate. Percentage contents of Bogue compounds and composition of some of the important cements are given in Table 5.3 and 5.4.

Table 5.3. Composition of Some Important Cement

Analysis percent	*Rapid hardening cement*	*Normal cement*	*Low heat cement*	*Sulphate resisting cement*
Lime	64.5	63.1	60	64
Silica	20.7	20.6	22.5	24.4
Alumina	5.2	6.3	5.2	3.7
Iron oxide	2.9	3.6	4.6	3.0

Table 5.4. Percentage of Bogue Compounds

Name of compound	*Rapid hardening cement*	*Normal cement*	*Low heat cement*	*Sulphate resisting cement*
Tri-calcium aluminate (C_3A)	9	11	6	5
Tri-calcium silicate (C_3S)	50	40	25	40
Di-calcium silicate (C_2S)	21	30	45	40
Tetra-calcium alumina Ferrite (C_4AF)	9	11	14	9

During manufacture of cement, if there is free lime left in the cement due to under-burning of clinkers, the amount of this uncombined lime (CaO) in the finished cement may cause considerable expansion and disruption.

Tri-calcium aluminate (C_3A) and Tetra-calcium alumino-ferrite (C_4AF) are known 'Celit', Tri-calcium silicate (C_3S) as alit and Di-calcium silicate (C_2S) as belit compounds.

Based upon the minerological composition of clinker the percentage of C_3A, C_4AF, C_3S and C_2S compounds should be as follows.

1. High-alit containing C_3S more than 60%.

2. Alit, containting C_3S more than 50 to 60%.
3. Belit containing C_2S more than 35%.
4. Celit.

(i) Aluminate containing C_3A more than 12%.

(ii) Alumino ferrite containing C_3A less than 2% and C_4AF more than 18%.

5.11. Physical Properties of Portland Cement

The physical properties of Portland cement are: (*i*) The fineness of grading, (*ii*) The setting time, (*iii*) The strength, (*iv*) The soundness and (*v*) Head of hydration.

All these properties have been given in I.S. 269-1975 and are being briefly discussed here.

(i) Fineness. Rate of chemical reaction depends largely upon the fineness of the cement. Finer the grading, the greater is the rate of reaction, which hastens the early development of strength. Coarser cement particles also settle down in concrete, which cause bleading. Too much fineness is also undesirable as it will generate greater heat and the concrete is likely to develop cracks. Fineness is measured either in term of percentage of weight retained after sieving or surface area in cm^2 per gram of cement.

(ii) Setting time. In order that the cement concrete may be placed in position of its use, before its setting starts, it is essential to keep suitable initial setting time for the cement. Similarly after concrete has been paced in position, it should harden as early as possible, so that the structure is put to use at the earlist. The initial setting is a stage in the process of hardening. that after this, any crack in the concrete will not reunite.

Final setting time is the stage in the process of hardening of cement, when concrete acquires sufficient strength. Initial setting time and final setting times for important varieties of cement are given in table 5.5.

(iii) Compressive strength. The quality of cement is judged from the compressive strength of the cement and sand mortar 1:3. The compressive strength at the time of failure for ordinary cement should be not less than the following values.

After 3 days 160 kg/cm^2 (16 N/mm^2)
After 7 days 220 kg/cm^2 (22 N/mm^2)

(iv) Tensile Strength. For assessing tensile strength of the cement, six standard briquettes are made from cement mortar. All these briquettes are fractured after 1, 3 and 7 days of curing. The average stength of briquettes should be as follows.

Time of curing	ordinary cement	Rapid hardening cement.
After 1 day	—	20 kg/cm^2 (2 N/mm^2)
After 3 days	20 kg/cm^2 (2 N/mm^2)	30 kg/cm^2 (3 N/mm^2)
After 7 days	25 kg/cm^2 (2.5 N/mm^2)	—

(v) Soundness. Presence of excess quantities of free lime and magnesia in the cement, cause unsoundness of the cement. These substances slake very slowly and cause, volumetric expansion of the concrete, which may result in the disintegration of the concrete. Soundness of cement is measured either by Le-chateliar method or by autoclave method. Sound cement should not show expansion of more than 10 mm by Le-chateliar method and 0.5% by autoclave method.

(vi) Heat of hydration. Chemical reaction, between water and cement compounds is known as *hydration*. During hydration of the cement, sufficient heat is generated. The process of heat generation is quite rapid in the initial phase of the setting, but its rate diminishes with the passage of time. Special care has to be taken to dissipate this heat, otherwise mass concrete works are likely to develop cracks. For mass concrete works low heat cement should be used. Heat of hydration for low heat cement should be as given below as per I.S. 4031-1968.

After 7 days	not more than 65 caloris/gm
After 28 days	not more than 75 caloris/gm

All the physical properties of some important cements are given in Table 5.5 as per I.S. 269-1967,

Table 5.5. (Physical properties of cement I.S. 269-1967)

Physical properties	*Ordinary cement*	*Rapid hardening cement*	*Low heat cement*
1. Setting time			
(*i*) Initial setting time not less than	30 mts	30 mts	60 mts
(*ii*) Final setting time not more than	10 hrs	10 hrs	10 hrs
2. Compressive strength with I.S. 650-1966 sand.			
(*i*) After 1 day ± 30 mts not less than	—	160 kg/cm^2 (16 N/mm)	—
(*ii*) After 3 days ± 1 hrs not less than	160 kg/cm^2 (16 N/mm^2)	275 kg/cm^2 (27.5 N/mm^2)	100 kg/cm^2 (10 N/mm^2)
(*iii*) After 7 days ± 2 hrs not less than	220 kg/cm^2 (22 N/mm^2)	—	160 kg/cm^2 (16 N/mm^2)
(*iv*) After 28 days ± 4 hrs not less than	—	—	350 kg/cm^2 (35 N/mm^2)

3. Tensile strength			
After 1 day .	—	2 N/mm^2	—
After 3 days	2 N/mm^2	3.0 N/mm^2	—
After 7 days	2.5 N/mm^2	—	—
4. Fineness.			
(*i*) By I.S. 90 micron sieve-residue by weight should not exceed %	10	5	—
(*ii*) Specific surface by air permeability method not less than cm^2/gm	2250	3250	3200
5. Heat of Hydration			
(*i*) At 7 days not more than	—	—	65 cal/gm
(*ii*) At 28 days not more than	—	—	75 cal/gm
6. Soundness			
(*i*) By Le-chatelier method expansion not more than	10 mm	10 mm	10 mm
(*ii*) By autoclave method specimen shall not have expansion of more than	0.5%	0.5%	0.5%

5.12. Chemical Properties of Cement

Chemical properties of ordinary and rapid hardening cements when tested according to I.S. 4032-1968 should be as follows.

1. Ratio of percentage of lime to percentage of silica alumina and iron oxide when calculated by formula

$$\frac{CaO - 0.7\, SO_3}{2.8\, SiO_2 + 1.2\, Al_2\, O_3 + 0.65\, Fe_2O_3}$$

Should lie between 0.66 and 1.02 limits.

2. Weight of insoluble residuce - not more than 2 %.

3. Weight of magnesia - not more than 6%.

4. Ratio of percentage of alumina to that of iron oxide - not less than 0.66.

5. Total sulphur content inform of SO_3 - not more than 2.75%.

6. Total loss in weight on ignition - not more than 4%.

In the case of low heat cement, the percentage of lime after deduction of that necessary to combine with sulphuric anhydride (SO_3) present in cement, shall be as follows.

Not more than 2.4 SiO_2 + 1.2 Al_2O_3 + 0.65 Fe_2O_3.

Not less than 1.9 SiO_2 + 1.2 Al_2O_3 + 0.65 Fe_2O_3.

In all other chemical properties low heat cement shall comply the requirements specified in 2, 3, 4, 5 and 6 above in this article.

5.13. Types of Cements

Most commonly used cement in structures is the ordinary Portland cement. But for use under specific conditions, number of special types of cements have been developed. Following are some of the cements in most common use, under ordinary, as well as specific conditions.

1. Ordinary Portland cement.
2. Rapid hardening cement.
3. Low heat cement.
4. Blast furnace slag cement.
5. Sulphate resistant cement.
6. Air entraining cement.
7. White and coloured cement.
8. High alumina cement.
9. Pozzuolanic cement.
10. Oil well cement.
11. Super sulphate cement.
12. Expansive cement.
13. Quick setting cement.
14. Water repellent cement.
15. Water proofing cement.

1. Ordinary Portland Cement. This cement is also known as *normal setting cement* and is recommended for adoption for all types of structures. It is used in pavements, R.C.C. works and at all such structures, where heat of hydration will not cause any defect. This cement has low resistance to sulphate reaction. Its rate of gaining strength, heat of hydration, drying, shrinkage and resistance to cracking are moderate. Its initial setting time is not less than 30 mts and final setting not more than 10 hrs.

2. Rapid hardening cement. This cement is also known by the name of *high-early-strength Portland cement.* Manufacturing process of this cement is the same as that of ordinary Portland cement but it differs in chemical composition, degree of clinkering temperature and fineness of grinding. The property of high early strength is achieved by high degree of fineness in grinding. clinkering at higher temperature and adding increased lime content in the composition. Strength attained by this cement in 3 days and 7 days, is almost the same as that attained by ordinary cement in 7 days, and 28 days, respectively. The main advantage of this cement is that, it attains high strength in less time and thus enables removal of form-work at the earliest. This cement is used for high-way slabs, which is to be opened to the traffic at the earliest possible moment. It is also used for the manufacture of precast elements. This cement is also useful for cold weather concreting, because its rapid rate of strength development and consequent, high rate of heat evolution, protects concrete against freezing.

3. Low heat cement. In the case of mass concrete structures such as dams, retaining walls, bridge abutment, rate of loss of heat of hydration from the surface is much lower than that generated. This causes, rise in temperature inside the mass of concrete and may develop thermal and shrinkage cracks if proper precautions are not taken. Under such circumstances low heat cement can be advantageously used. This cement is proportioned is such a way, that C_3A and C_3S are formed in lesser amount, but C_2S is formed in increased amount. By this measure the rate of evolution of heat of hydration is considerably reduced. Low heat cement has not only slower rate of heat generation, but also greater resistance to cracking. In the initial stage of setting and hardening, rate of heat evolution is small as rate of chemical reaction is slow. But in the latter stage rate of setting and hardening is faster, than ordinary cement. The ultimate strength attained by this cement is practically the same as that attained by an ordinary cement. The heat generated by ordinary cement in three days is nearly 80 calories/gm of cement, where as for low heat cement it is of the order of 50 calories per gm of cement. This cement is manufactured only to special order and its intial setting time should not be less that 60 mts. This cement offers greater sulphate resistance due to decreased amount of C_3S. This cement is however, not suitable for ordinary structures.

4. **Blast furnace slag cement**. It is a cement, manufactured by grinding specially proportioned amounts of ordinary cement clinkers, with granulated blast furnace slag of selected quality. When Portland cement and slag are ground together, the resulting cement is known by the name *Portland-slag-cement*. When lime and slag are ground together, it is called lime-slag-cement. The percentage of slag in portland slag cement varies from 40% to 70% where as it varies from 70% to 90% in the case of lime slag cement. Lime slag cement is not very good resistant of air and frost and hence, its use is restricted to damp situations only. Portland slag cement offers good resistance to corrosion and good bond with steel. This cement is extensively used in the manufacture of pre-fabricated reinforced concrete units. There is one more cement in which slag is used. It is a *sulphate-slag-cement*. In this cement slag varies from 80% to 90%. It also contains about 5% Portland cement clinkers. This cement is highly resistant to sulphate actoin and hence, recommended to be used in marine works and other underground works.

5. **Sulphate Resistant Cement**. Ordinary portland cement does not resist the sulphatic action to a large extent. Disintegration due to sulphatic action is due to the presence of C_3A, which reacts with sulphates and forms sulpho-aluminates and causes swelling and disintegration. To make cement more sulphate resistant, percentage of C_3A is reduced and

that of C_2S increased. Rate of hardening of this cement is slow and requires longer period for curing. To offset the slower rate of hardening due to changed chemical composition, sulphate resistant cements are ground a little finer than ordinary cements.

6. Air entraining cement. It is just the ordinary cement in which 0.01 to 0.05% by weight air entraining agents have been added. Air entraining agents are foaming agents such as vinsol, resin, and darex. Air entraining Foaming agenets are added during the process of grinding the clinkers. Concrete made with such a cement contains minute, well distributed air bubbles, through out the concrete mass. Due to air bubbles strength of this concrete gets reduced by 10 to 15%. Air content in the form of small bubbles should not be more than 3 to 4% of the volume of the concrete. Such a cement is resistant to severe frost action and is immune to surface scaling due to application of common salt or calcium chloride, used for De-icing purposes of the concrete pavements. Concrete made from this cement is more plastic and workable, and develops less segregation.

7. White and coloured cement. It is ordinary cement having pure white colour. It is very costly since lot of precautions have to be taken in its manufacture. It is used for terrazzo flooring, face plasters, traffic curbs, airodrome markings and other ornamental works. Snow-crete, silvi-crete, Atlas, etc. are the patented forms of white cement. Strength of this cement is slightly lesser than that of ordinary cement, but it is 4 to 5 times costlier.

Grey colour of the cement is due to the presence of iron oxide. In the manufacture of white cement, iron oxide is limited to less than 1%. Also superior raw materials such as china clay and pure lime stone are chosen in its manufacture. For clinkering or kiln process, oil is used in place of powdered coal to avoid adulteration by coal ash. In the absence of iron oxide sodium aluminium fluoride (cryolite) is added to act as a fluxing agent.

Coloured cements are produced by adding suitable mineral pigment to ordinary or white cement. Pigment, free from soluble salts are added to the cement, during grinding. Following pigments are commonly used.

Iron oxide	Red, Yellow, Brown, Black.
Manganese oxide	Black, Brown.
Chromium dioxide	Green.
Cobalt blue, ultra marine blue	Blue.
Carbon pigments	Black.

Coloured cements are sold in the market, under the patented names of colour-crete, rainbow, snowcem, etc. They are mostly used for giving decorative finished, to building, swimming-pools, floors, fountains etc.

8. High alumina cement. This cement is also known as aluminous cement. It contains as high as 35 to 45% of aluminates. This cement is manufactured from Bauxite and chalk or lime stone. Bauxite and chalk or lime stone are first of all mixed dry and then heated until molten mass is obtained, which is later casted into pigs. The pigs are broken up and ground to required fineness. The fineness of grinding of this cement is 8 to 10% higher than that of ordinary cement. This cement is very dark in colour, almost black powder. In this cement, setting time is controlled by the rate of cooling of the fused product and not by adding gypsum. Following are the special characteristics of this cement.

(i) Its initial setting time is 3 to 6 hours and final setting takes place within 2 hrs, of the initial setting.

(ii) Due to high percentage of aluminates being present, this cement develops strength very fast. In 24 hours, it develops as much strength, as an ordinary cement acquires in 28 days.

(iii) This cement is very much resistant to sea water attack.

IV. Its compressive strength is nearly double of that of ordinary cement.

(v) There is no trace of free lime and hence, this cement is more sound than ordinary cement.

(vi) It is highly resistant to sulphate bearing waters and sea waters, and is used for the construction near sea shores and also under water.

(vii) It is also used for making refractory and heat resistant concrete.

(viii) It is used for sealing rocks or concreting against internal water flow.

(ix) It is not used for mass concrete works as it generates rapid heat of hydration.

The cement is also called *cement Fondu* in France, 'Lightening' in England and 'Lumnite' in united states. While using, this cement must not be mixed with any other cement, as heat evolved during setting is greater than any other cement.

9. Pozzuolanic cement. This cement is produced by grinding together a mixture of 60 to 80% of Portland cement and 40 to 20% of Pozzuolana. Pozzoulana may be a natural active material such as volcanic ash or pumice or an artificial product such as burnt clay or shale containing silicious and aluminous mineral substances. The rate of development of strength is lower than that of normal Portland cement, especially at low temperature.

Pozzuolana in optimum proportion with cement (20 to 30%) improves the quality of concrete. It increases the workability. lowers heat of hydration and increases the water tightness. This cement has got greater resistance against sulphatic action and sea waters. More over it decreases the cost and is useful in the mass concrete works.

10. Oil well cement. This cement is used for cementing oil wells, which are very deep. Ordinary cement, if used at such depth will harden, before it, could reach its place of use. Oil well cement should be capable of being pumped for about 3 hrs, when subjected to high pressure and temperature. Thus cement to be used for this purpsoe should have the property of slow setting and must harden quickly after setting. This is accomplished by adjusting the composition of cement or by adding retarders to the ordinary cement. This is possible by adjusting the proportion of iron oxide, so that all the alumina is converted to tetra-calcium alumina ferrite (C_4AF). The proportion of tri-calcium aluminate (C_3A) formed is therefore, very small and setting time of cement is increased.

The function of cement in oil well is to fill the space between the steel lining tube and wall of the well and also to grout porous strata to prevent water or gas from gaining access to the oil bearing strata, oil well cements besides preventing water from infilterating the oil bearing strata also protect the oil well casting from corrosion. It also helps support the oil well casting and thus reduces the tensions in the steel pipe.

11. Super-sulphate cement. This cement is made by grinding a mixture of well granulated blast furnace slag (80 to 85%), calcium sulphate (10 to 15%) and ordinary cement (1 to 2%). This cement is ground finer than the ordinary portland cement. One of the significant properties of this cements is its low total heat of hydration. It is therefore, very useful for mass concrete works. This cement is highly resistant to chemical attack. Concrete made fom this type of cement expands, if cured under water and shrinks if cured in air.

12. Expansion cement. This cement has a property of expanding, while hardening, whereas other cements shrink. Shrinkage cracks of ordinary cements may be eliminated by adding suitable proportion of expansion cement in it. In repair work also, this cement is quite useful. Opened up joints can be repaired with this cement to make them water tight.

13. Quick setting cement. When concrete has to be laid under water, quick setting cement can be advantageously used. The setting action of this cement starts within 5 minutes and it becomes stone-hard is less than one hour. This property of cement is developed by adding small percentage of aluminium sulphate and also by grinding this cement much finer than the ordinary cement.

14. Water repellent cement. This cement is used, where water tight conditions are predominent. This cement is nothing, but an ordinary cement mixed with small perentage of water proofing compounds. This cement is manufactured under trade name of *Aqua-crete*.

15. Water-proofing cement. It is an ordinary cement mixed with small percentage of some metal (Al and Ca) stearate, at the time of grinding. Concrete made with such a cement is more resistant to water penetration and is used for the construction of water retaining structures like tanks, reservoirs, swimming pools, dams, bridge piers, retaining walls, etc. This concrete is also more resistant to the corrosive action of acids and alkalies, which are mostly found in industrial waters.

5.14. Storage of Cement

Cement has to be stored in factories,where it is manufactured and also at the field construction sites, where it is to be used. Moisturte is the greatest enemy of cement. Cement has great affinity for moisture and it should be stored in such a way, that moisture may not reach it. If some how moisture happens to reach cement, it gets set, in form of lumps. If lumps formed are so hard that they cannot be pressed to powder between the fingers, it should be taken for granted that cement has been rendered useless. Hence, cement should be stored in specially constructed stores having damp proof floors, water proof walls and leak proof roofs. Cement stakes should be raised leaving a clear distance of 30 cm from the wall of the store room. Height of the stake should not exceed the height of 15 bags. Width of the stake should be limited to 3 m. Stocks received in the stores should be properly tagged with bin cards. The stocks received first should be issued first. All the doors, windows and ventilators should be effectively sealed to prevent ingress of moisture in store.

5.15. Laboratory Tests for Portland Cement

The quality of cement is verified by conducting various exhaustive tests. Following are the standard tests for cement.

1. Chemical composition test.
2. Fineness test.
3. Compressive strength test.
4. Tensile strength test.
5. Consistency test.
6. Setting time test and
7. Soundness test.

1. Chemical composition test. For this, detailed chemical analyssis of cement is conducted. Chemical composition requirements of an ordinary and low heat portland cements have been given earlier in this chapter, under heading chemical composition.

2. Fineness test. This test is done to verify the standard of grinding of cement. We know that rate of hydration and hydrolysis of cement, depend, upon its fineness and thus testing of the fineness of the cement is an essential feature. Fineness of cements can be determined either by *sieve test* or by *air permeability test.*

In sieve test, the cement sample weighing 100 gms in taken and is sieved through I.S. Sieve No. 1 for 15 minutes. The residue left over the sieve should not be more than 10% of the original weight.

In air permeability test, the specific surface of cement particle is calculated. Specific surface acts as a measure of the frequency of particle of average size. Specific surface of ordinary rapid hardening cement and low heat cement as recommend by I.S.I. have been given in this chapter earlier, under heading physical properties of cement.

3. Compressive strength test. This test is carried out to determine the compressive strength of the cement. For this test, cement and standard sand are taken in ratio of 1:3 and a paste is prepared by adding water at the rate P/4 + 2.5. Here P is the percentage of water required

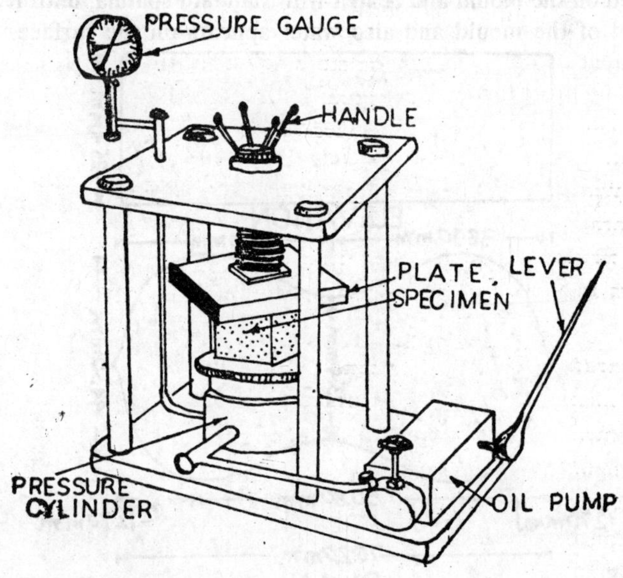

Fig. 5.6. Compression testing machine

to produce a paste of standard consistency. The paste so prepared is filled in 76 mm. cube mould and vibrated on vibrating machine for 2 minutes. Twelve such cubes are moulded. The freshly moulded cubes are first kep in a damp cabin for 24 hrs. and then shifted to water bath for curing. The cubes are then tested under a compression testing machine after 1, 3, 7 and 28 days of immersion. At each period interval three cubes should be tested and average compressive strength of the three should be taken as the compressive strength. The average compressive strength for ordinary, rapid hardening and low heat cements should be as given *under physical properties.*

4. Tensile strength test. This test is carried out as follows

(i) Prepare a test cement mortar by taking cement and standard sand in ratio of 1:3 and then mixing water. The percentage of water to be mixed is determined by formula P/5 + 2.5, where P is the percentage of water required to produce a paste of standard consistency. The percentage of water comes out to about 8% by weight of cement and sand.

(ii) Take a standard briquette and clean its internal suface properly. Small amount of greese or oil may also be applied to facilitate extrusion of the moulded sample.

(iii) The mould is placed on a non-porous plate and filled with previously prepared mortar. After filling the mould some additional mortar is heaped on the mould and beaten with standard spatula, until it acuires the level of the mould and also water appears on the surface.

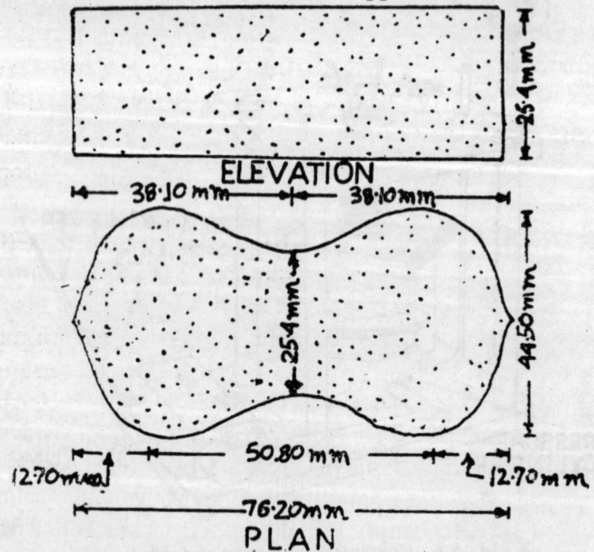

Fig. 5.7. Briquette for tensile test of cement

(iv) The mould is turned up side down on the same non-porous plateform and again some more additional mortar is heaped and beaten with standard spatula till water appears, on the surface and level of the mortar acquires level of the briquette mould. The briquette in the mould is finished by smoothening the surface with blade of a trowel. Twelve such briquettes are prepared. Quantity of cement may be about 600 gm. for one dozen briquettes.

(v) The briquettes are kept in damp (90% humidity) atmosphere at a temperature of 27° ∓ 2° for 24 hrs.

(vi) The briquettes are now carefully removed from the mould and kept submerged in clean fresh water, having temperature of about 27° ± 2°C. The briquettes are held is water just prior to testing.

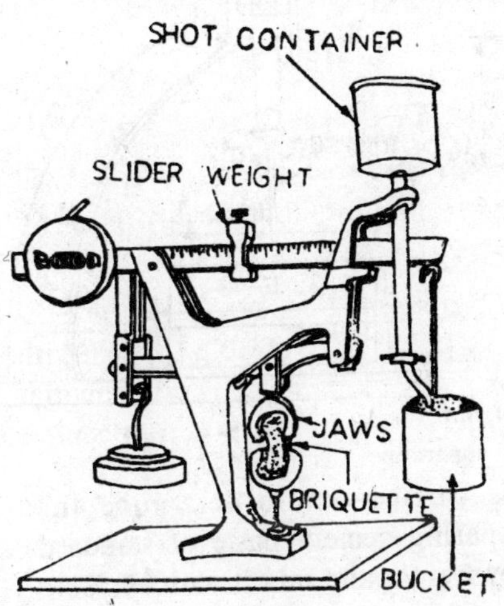

Fig. 5.8. Trensile test machine.

(vii) The briquettes are held in the metallic jaws of tensile testing machine one by one and loaded with the help of lead shots. Load is applied at the rate of 35 kg/cm^2.

(viii) The briquettes are tested at the end of 1 day, 3 days and 7 days. At least 3 to 6 briquettes should be tested at one period interval and average strength should be taken as the tensile strength of the cement, for that particular interval.

(ix) Results obtained should comply with the results given by I.S.I. under physical properties of portland cement.

5. Consistency test, Initial setting time test, Final setting time test. In order to carry out tests for standard consistency, initial setting time, and fiinal setting time. Vicate's apparatus is used. This apparatus consists of a frame to which a movable rod is attached. An indicator is attached to the movable rod with the help of which penetration of the needle can be measured. There is a cylindrical mould which can be split into two halves as and when required. The mould is always used by keeping it on non-porous plate. Vicates apparatus consists of three attachments-square needle, plunger, and needle with annular collar. Square needle is used for determining initial setting time. Needle with annular collar is used for final setting time and plunger for normal or standard consistency test.

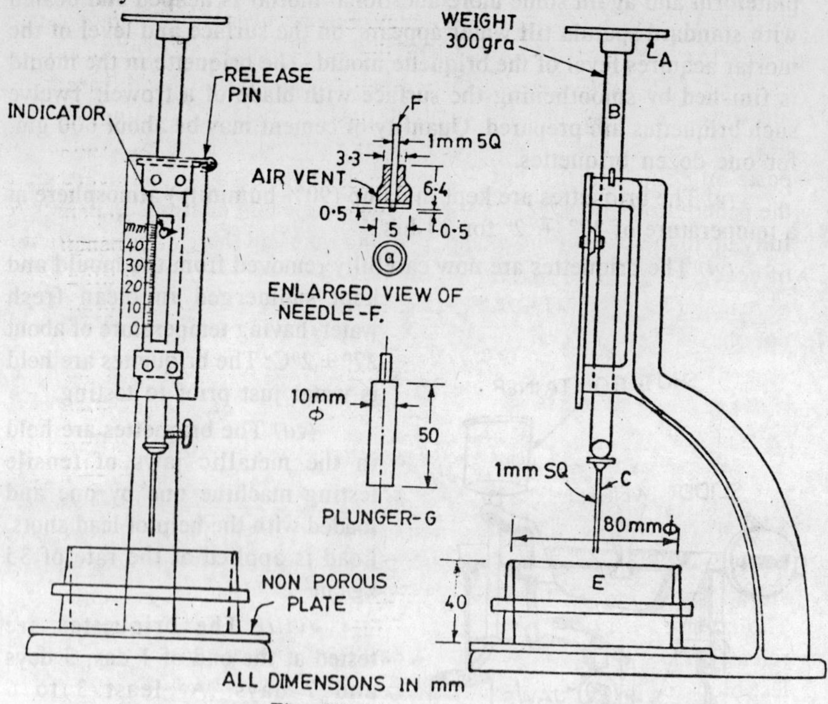

Fig. 5.9. Vicat apparatus.

Consistency test. This test is carried out to determine the percentage of water required for preparing cement paste of standard consistency. Take 300 gm of cement by weight and mix it with 30 % *i.e* 90 gm of water. The mixing of cement and water is done in a non-porous plate, so that no water is lost during mixing. Fill the vicat's mould with this paste and level its sufrace with the help of trowel blade.

Now plunger is attached to the movable rod of vicate's appartus. The plunger is brought in contact of the paste filled in the mould and gently left to penetrate by itself under the load of rod only. Penetration of the plunger is noted. Now the mould is filled again with cement paste, but by varying moisture content a little and penetration of the plunger is noted again. The trails are continued till penetration of the plunger is such that it remains only 5 mm to 7 mm from the base of the mould. The consistency of cement paste corresponding to the penetration of 5 to 7 mm from the bottom of the mould is known as standard or normal constistency.

The time interval, between additon of water to the commencement of filling the mould is known as *gauging time* and this should not be more than 3 to 5 minutes.

Initial setting time. For this test, the vicat's mould is filled with cement paste of standard consistency. Square needle of 1 mm × 1 mm is attached to the movable rod of the vicat apparatus. The needle is gently brought in contact of the cement paste and quickly released and alloweed to penetrtate the cement paste. In the beginning, needle penetrates completely. The process of bringing needle in contact of paste and quick release, is repeated at suitable interval and every time the penetration of needle is noticed. The needle will continue to penetrate fully up to the base of the mould for some time and there after penetration of needle will go on decreasing. The process is kept repeating till a stage is reached, when needle penetrates up to about 5 mm measured from bottom of the mould.

The interval between the addition of water to cement and the stage, when needle ceases to penetrate 5 mm layer of paste measured from the bottom, is known as initial setting time of the cement. Initial setting times for various types of cements have been given earlier in physical proeperties.

Final setting time. In this case also cement paste of standared consistency is prepared and filled in the vicat mould. Needle with annular collar is fixed at the bottom end of the movable rod of vicat apparatus. The needle is brought in contact of the paste in the mould and gently released. The time upto which the needle makes an impression on the test block of paste, but collar fails to make an impression is noted. The time interval between the moment water was added to cement and the moment, the stage is reached, when needle makes impression, but collar fails, is known was final setting time of the cement. This time is about 10 hours for ordinary cement.

Both initial and final setting time tests are used to detect the deterioration of cement due to storage. It may however be noted that this is purely a conventional type of test and it has no relation with the setting or hardening of actual concrete.

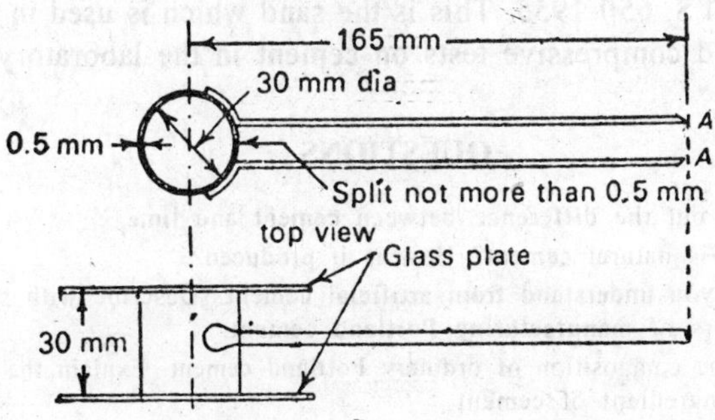

Fig.5.10. Le-chatlier's apparatus.

6. Soundness test. This test is carried out to detect the presence of uncombined lime in cement. Due to presence of free lime and magnesia, cement under goes volume change after setting. This is because both these materials in uncombined state slake very slowly. This volume change causes unsoundness of the cement concrete. The soundness test is performed with the help of Le-chatelier apparatus. It consists of a cylindrical brass mould 30 mm inside diamter and 30 mm height. The mould is split and split does not exceed 0.5 mm. Two indicators with pointed ends are attached to the mould, one indicator being on either side of the split of the mould. Thickness of mould is 5 mm.

The mould is placed on a glass plate and filled with prepared cement paste as stated in consistency test. Another glass plate is placed on the top of the filled mould and whole assembly is submerged in water for 24 hours. The temperature of water is kept varying from 27° to 35°C. After 24 hours, the assembly is taken out of water and distance between the points of indicators is noted. The mould is again placed is water and water is heated slolwy in such a way that boiling of water is achieved in about half an hour. The boiling of water is continued for three hours, after which mould is taken out and allowed to cool down. The distance between the indicator end points, is again measured. The difference between the two measurements represents the expansion of cement. The expansion exhibited by the Le-chatelier mould should not exceed 10 mm for any type of portland cement.

5.16. Indian Standard Sand

This sand is obtained from Ennore, a place in Tamilnadu state. Its colour may be grey or whitish. Its grains are angular (approximately spherical) and made mostly of broken quartz. This sand may contain very small percentage of elongated or flattened grains, but must be totally free from silt and organic impurities. Its grading is such that it passes entirely through I.S. Sieve 85 and when sieved over I.S. Sieve 60 not more than 10% by weight should pass through the sieve. For other details refers I.S. 650-1955. This is the sand which is used in carrying out tensile and compressive tests on cement in the laboratory..

QUESTIONS

1. (*a*) Point out the difference between cement and lime.
   (*b*) What is natural cement? How is it produced?
2. What do you understand from artificial cement? Describe with sketch the dry process of manufacturing Portland cement.
3. Explain the composition of ordinary Portland cement. Explain the functions of each ingredient of cement.

4. How does cement set? What are the functions of four principle or Bogue compounds of cement?
5. Explain with the help of neat sketch, the wet process of manufacturing the ordinary cement.
6. What are the physical and chemical properties of cements? Explain them in brief.
7. Enumerate the laboratory tests for cement and describe any three of them.
8. Prepare a list of types of cements and explain the properties of following cements.

   (i) Rapid hardening cement. *(ii)* Quick setting cement. *(iii)* Low heat cement. *(iv)* Puzzolana cement.
9. *(a)* What are the harmful constituents of cement?

   (b) What are the precautions, which are to taken for storage of cement.

6

MORTARS

6.1. Definitions

The mortar is a paste like substance prepared by adding required amount of water to a dry mixture of sand or fine aggregate with some binding material like, clay lime or cement.

When clay is used as a binding material, the resulting mortar is known as *mud mortar*. If, it is lime, the resulting mortar is *lime mortar*. Similarly, if cement is the binding material it is known as *cement mortar*.

Before properties and uses of different types of mortars are explained, let us gain some knowledge about the fine aggregate which is commonly known as sand. Sand is mostly used as inert material in mortars and concretes.

6.2. Sand

It is a form of silica (SiO_2) which may be siliceous, argillaceous, according to composition. Sand particles consists of small grains of silica. It is formed by the decomposition of sand stone due to various weathering effects. It is mostly obtained from pits, shores, river beds and sea beds. Sand may be classified into three categories as follows.

1. Pit sand
2. River sand.
3. Sea sand.

A brief description of each type of sand has been given.

1. Pit sand. This sand is obtained by forming pits into the soil. It is sharp, angular, porous and free from harmful salts. Clay and other impurities should be washed and screened. Fine pit sand, when rubbed between fingers should not leave any stain on it. From strength point of view coarse grained sand is prefered than fine grained sand. Clean pit sand is used for most of the mortars.

2. River sand. It is found at river banks and beds. River sand is fine, round and polished due to rubbing action of water currents. Its interlocking value is less as its grains are rounded due to rolling at river bed. It is almost white in colour. Its grains are smaller than pit sand and hence, it is more suitable for plastering work. It is normally available in pure condition. It can be used in all the types of works.

3. Sea sand. This sand is obtained from sea shores. It is also fine, rounded and polished due rubbing action of water. Its colour is light brown. This sand is the worst of the three, as it contains lot of salts. These salts absorb moisture from atmosphere and cause permanent dampness and efflorescence in the structure. Such structures may ultimately collapse. Sea sand also retards the setting action of cement. Hence, this sand should as far as possible be discarded.

6.3. Classification Based on Fineness

The sand may be divided into three categories-fine sand, coarse sand, and gravelly sand, depending upon its fineness. The sand passing through screen having openings of 1.5875 mm is known as fine sand. Similarly sands passing through sieve having clear openings of 3.175 mm, and 7.62 mm are respectively known as coarse sand and gravelly sand. Fine sand is mostly used for plaster work, coarse sand for masonry work and gravelly sand for concrete works. Sand is used as a fine aggregate in concretes and mortars. The aggregate is said to be fine aggregate, when its particles pass through 4.75 mm mesh sieve. The fine aggregate should be completely retained on 0.07 mm mesh. Particles finer than 0.06 mm come under silts and clays and are considered as harmful constituents.

6.4. Bulking of Sand

Bulking of sand means increase in its volume. Fine aggregates or sands, increase in volume when they possess some moisture. Bulking is due to formation of a thin film of water around the fine aggregate or sand particles. Thickness of water film goes on increasing with more and more moisture and consequently, increase in volume continues. But after certain percentage of water, volume of sand starts decreasing with

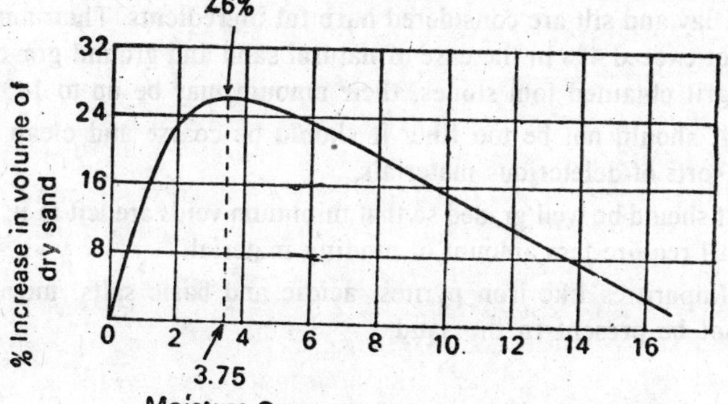

Fig. 6.1. Bulking of sand.

increasing amount of water. At certain percentage of water, increase in volume completely vanishes and volume occupied by sand becomes equal to the volume of dry sand. Percentage moisture content and percentage bulking of sand is shown in Fig. 6.1.

To compensate the bulking effect, extra sand has to be added in the mix of mortars and concretes, so that its amount may be as per specified ratio. Finer sands exhibit greater percentage of bulking than the coarser one. Increase is volume may vary from 25 to 40% depending upon the fineness of sand, when moisture content varies from 5 to 8% by weight. A simple test as described may be conducted to ascertain the percentage of bulking of sand.

Take graduated container or cylinder and fill it to the known height by the sand, whose bulking percentage is to be ascertained. Let height of sand at this moment be h_1 cm. The container is empited from sand and refilled with water. During empyting, care should be taken that no sand is lost during this transaction. Now sand which has been taken out of the container, is slowly dropped in the container and stirred throughly. The sand is allowed to settle. The height of settled sand is measured. Let this height be h_2 cm. The h_2 height of the sand is equal to the actual dry height of the sand. Percentage bulking of sand may be found out as follows.

$$\text{Percentage bulking of sand} = \left(\frac{h_1 - h_2}{h_2}\right) 100\%.$$

6.5. Desirable Properties of Sand

Following are the desirable properties of good sand.

1. It should be inert completely.

2. Its grains should be sharp, strong, and angular.

3. It should not contain salts which attract atmospheric moisture.

4. Clay and silt are considered harmful ingredients. Their amount should not exceed 4% in the case of natural sand and ground gravel. In sand or grit obtained fom stones, their amount may be up to 10%.

5. It should not be too fine. It should be coarse and clean, free from all sorts of deleterious materials.

6. It should be well graded so that minimum voids are left in it. This aspect will require less amount of binding material.

7. Impurities like iron pyrites, acidic and basic salts, mica etc. should not be present in the sand.

6.6. Function of Sand in Mortars

Sand is mixed with binding material for following purposes.

1. **Bulk**. It increase the volume of the mortar and consequently makes mortar more economical.

2. Sand prevents excessive shrinkage of the mortar. This aspect avoids cracking of the mortar during setting.

3. It helps in the setting action of fat lime mortars. Atmospheric air containing carbon dioxide can reach lime through voids of sand and cause its setting.

4. Strength of the mortar or concrete can be adjusted by addition of larger or smaller amounts of sand.

5. Since sand is an inert material, it renders structure more resistant against atmospheric agencies.

6.7. Fineness Modulus of Sand

Fineness modulus (F.M.) is an index which gives an idea, about the fineness or coarseness of aggregate. It is defined as the cumulative percentage of residue retained on a set of sieves and dividing the sum by 100. I.S. Sieve No. 480, 240, 120, 60, 30 and 15 are used as a set of sieves for finding F.M. of fine aggregate. An example of F.M. of sand is given here. Sample is taken as 1 kg or 1000 gm.

Table 6.1

I.S. Sieve size and No.	*Wt. retained in gm.*	*Cumulative wt. retained in gm.*	*Cumulative % wt. retained in gm.*	*Cumulative % passing gm*
10 mm	0	0	0	100
4.75 mm. (480)	20	20	2	98
2.36 mm. (240)	100	120	12	88
1.18 mm. ((120)	100	220	22	78
600 micron (60)	190	410	41	59
300 micron (30)	350	760	76	24
150 micron (15)	240	1000	93	7
	1000 gm		246	

$$\text{Fineness Modulus (F.M.)} = \frac{246}{100} = 2.46$$

Very fine and coarse sands, both are objectionable. Fine sands are uneconomical whereas coarse sands give harsh and less workable mixes. Lesser value of F.M. oives an indication of larger amounts of finer part. whareas larger values show coarser sand. It is recommended by I.S.I.

that the F.M. of sand should lie, between 2.5 and 3.0. I.S.I. has given following F.M. ranges for various types of sands.

Fine sand	F.M.	2.20 to 2.60
Medium sand	F.M.	2.60 to 2.90.
Coarse sand	F.M.	2.90 to 3.20.

6.8. Tests for Sand

To ascertain the properties of sand, following tests may be performed.

1. Take a smaller amount of sand and rub it between finger tips. If clayey spots are left on the fineger, tips, it is an indication that sand contains considerable amount of clay impurities.

2. Sand may be tested by actually putting it in the mouth. The taste of the sand will reflect the presence of any salt.

3. Take a glass of water and put some quantity of sand in it. The glass is stirred and allowed to settle for some time. If clay is present in the sand, its layer will be formed at the top of sand.

4. Take a small quantity of caustic soda solution of 3% concentration in a bottle nicely stoppered. Put some sand in the solution and stopper the bottle again. The bottle is vigorously shaken and allowed to stand for 24 hours. If colour of the solution changes to brown, it indicates the presence of organic matter.

5. *Void test.* Fill a container of known capacity with wet sand. Add water slowly into the container containing wet sand till water rises to the top of the container. The amount of water added in the container are the voids in the sand.

6.9. Selection of Sand for Use

Sand normally does not require elaborate testing, if it were to be used in usual works. It may be washed with water and used. But in case of important works, sand is throughly tested to justify its use. The test for sand have already been given Art 6.8.

1. Sieve analysis may be done to know the fineness and grading of the sand. If sand is either too fine or too coarse, it may be improved by adding suitable quantity of deficient constituent.

2. Test may be made to find out the voids in the sand.

3. Presence of salts may be detected either by tasting or tests.

4. Sand is washed and then again tested to see whether adultrated sand can be used after washing or not.

5. Sand may be tested in tensile tests.

Keeping results of all the above stated tests inview the sand may be accepted or rejected.

6.10. Substitutes for Sand

If good sand is not available at or near the site, other materials like stone screenings, burnt clay or surukhi; cinders or coal ash; coke dust etc. may be used as substitutes.

Stone screenings. It is fine particle material obtained by screenings crushed stones. Its grains are sharp which impart more of strength to the mortar.

Surkhi. It is very popular subsitute for sand. It is obtained by finely powdering burnt clay. It may be obtained by grinding slightly under burnt or pila bricks. It should be clean and free from all sorts of impurities. When sieved through I.S. sieve No. 9 the residue left over it, should not exceed 10% by weight. Clays also differ in quality and as such different qualities of surkhi are obtained from them. All the clays require diffferent temperatures of burning, so as to get best quality of surkhi. Surkhi performs following functions.

(i) It performs all the functions of sand stated earlier.
(ii) It imiparts more of strength to the mortar.
(iii) It improves hydraulic properties of the mortar.

Since it disintegrates under the action of air and humidity, mortar with surkhi should not be used for external surfaces.

6.11. Types of Mortars

The mortars may be classified into four categories as follows.

1. Mud mortar. 2. Lime mortar.
3. Cement mortar. 4. Gauged mortar.

1. Mud mortar. Mud mortar is prepared from a mixture, of puddle mud and water. In this., clay is pugged or puddled with water, until it acquires the required consistency. It is also called Gara. It is mostly used in masonries of Kuchha bricks in villages. It may be used even for pucca masonry works if the work is not very important. Single or double storeyed pucca houses can be made by using mud mortar for masonries, but these houses have to be plastered or pointed with cement mortar. Masonry in good mud mortar can stand a safe pressure of about $16t/m^2$. It can be used for plastering kuchha huts also.

2. Lime mortar. In this type of mortar, lime which may be fat lime or hydraulic lime, is used as a binding material. During setting, lime shrinks considerably and hence, 2 to 3 times its vume of sand is added to limit the shrinkage. If fat lime were to be used in the mortar it should be slaked before use. Fat lime mortar is unsuitable for water-logged and damp situations.

In case hydraulic lime, proportion of lime to sand by volume is about 1:2 or so. This mortar should be used within one hour after mixing. This mortar can withstand damp conditions and is stronger than fat lime mortar. 1:2 or 1:3 lime sand mortor is considered suitable for normal brick work construction. For making lime mortar for lime concrete in foundation the proportions may be 1 lime : 2 sand, or 1 lime : 1 surkhi : 1 sand.

Preparation of lime mortar. Lime mortar can be prepared by following methods:-

1. Manual mixing or pounding method.
2. Mortar mill mixing or grinding.

1. Manual mixing or pounding method. In this method, mixing of moratr may be done on a water tight plateform or in a shallow pucca tank called '*hudie*'. Lime and sand are first mixed in dry state and then water is added. The mortar is worked with powrahs to a fine workable consistency. The mortar is turned up and down two three times. This method of preparing lime mortar is very crude method and is adopted only on small works. The mortar prepared by this method may not be perfectly homogeneous.

2. Mortar mill mixing or grinding. In this method, lime and sand are first of all mixed in dry state, on dry impervious plateform. The dry mix is then fed into the mortar mill and water in required amount is added. After this, the mix is ground till a uniform consistency mortar is obtained. All the thick particles of unslaked lime get ground and become slaked. When one such charge becomes ready, it is taken out of the mill and new charge added.

The grinding mills may be classified into two categories.

1. Bullock-driven grinding mill. 2. Power-driven grinding mill.

1. Bullock-driven grinding mill. It consists of a circular trench of diameter varying from 5 m. to 8 m. The width and depth of the trench is about 40 cm each. Width of the trench is decided depening upon the thickness of the grinding wheel of stone. Stone grinding wheel remains attached to a wooden shaft at its one end. The other end of the shaft, is pivoted at the centre point of the circular trench. Bullocks are used to cause rotation of the stone wheel, in the circular trench. It is the stone wheel which causes grinding of the mortar in the mill. For details see Fig. 6.2. This mill is also known as Ghani.

2. Powder-driven grinding mill. Basic concept of this mill is same as that of bullock driven grinding mill except that power is used to cause rotation of stone wheels in place of pair of bullocks. In this system a pair of stone wheels are used which remain attached at both the end of a common shaft. Shaft carrying stone wheels, is placed in a pan. In this mill, stone wheels remain static or fixed and pan containing mortar mix, to be ground, is rotated around them. Fig. 6.3 shows the sketch of a power drive grinding mill.

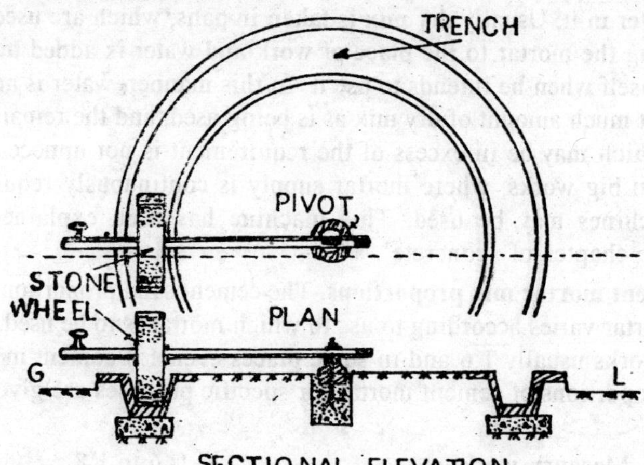

Fig. 6.2. Bullock driven grinding mill.

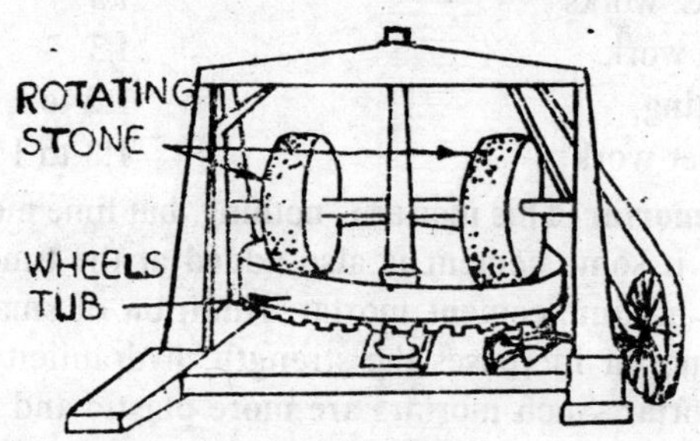

Fig. 6.3. Power drive mortar grinding mill.

3. Cement mortar.. Cement mortar consists of a mixture of cement, sand and water in suitable prorportion. The prorportion of cement to sand by volume varies from 1:2 to 1:6 or even more. This mortar is stronger, than all other mortars and as such is commonly used in the construction of load bearing walls pillars, columns etc. Being impervious, it is advantageously used for external, walls, exposed situations, and below ground level. Cement is measurd in bags. One cement bag is 50 kg in weight and 35 liters in volume. Sand is used by volume. But in doing so, allowance for moisture in sand, is also taken into account.

Mixing the cement mortar. Cement mortar does not require grinding like lime mortar. Cement and sand are mixed in required proportion in dry state on an impervious plateform. Sometimes, steel troughs are also used for mixing the dry contents. The contents of the mix are mixed two or three times, so that mixture shows a uniform colour. Now dry mix is taken only that much in a container, as can be used within half an hour, from adding water in it. Usually dry mix is taken in pans, which are used for transporting the mortar to the place of work and water is added by the mason himself when he intends to use it. In this manner, water is added to only that much amount of dry mix as is being used, and the remaining dry mix which may be in excess of the requirement is not unnecessary spoiled. On big works, where mortar supply is continuously required, mixer machines may be used. This machine has been explained in subsequent chapter of 'concrete'.

Cement mortar mix proportions. The cement sand proportion in a cement mortar varies according to use to which mortar is to be used. For masonry works usually 1:6 and in some places even 1:8 cement mortar is used. Proportions of cement mortar for specific purposes are given as follows.

(i)	Masonry work	1: 6 to 1:8
(ii)	Foundation concrete	1:3 to 1:4
(iii)	R.C.C. works	1:3
(iv)	Arch work.	1:3
(v)	Pointing.	1:2 to 1:3
(vi)	Plaster work	1:3 to 1:4

4. Gauged mortar. This mortar is nothing, but lime mortar prepared as before, but in it some cement is also added at the time of using it. It is also known as lime-cement mortar. Addition of small amount of cement in lime mortar increases the strength, hydraulicity, and rate of setting, of the mortar. Such mortars are more plastic and workable. As hydraulic lime itself has got sufficient strength characteristic, no useful purpose is served by adding cement to it. Cement is mostly added to lime mortars having fat lime.

Gauged mortar forms an excellent mortar for bcick or stone masonry in Foundation, plinth and super structure. In rubble stone masonry it is considered as very good mortar.

6.12. Special Mortars

These are the mortars which are used under specific conditions. Some such mortars are.

1. Light weight mortar.
2. Fire-resistant mortar.
3. Packing mortar
4. Sound absorbing mortar
5. X-ray shield mortar.

1. Light weight mortar. This mortar is obtained by adding materials, such as asbestos fibres, jute fibres, wood powder, saw dust etc. to ordinary cement or lime mortars. The mortar is very much used in heat-proof and sound proof structures. The mortars having bulk density of less than 1500 kg/m^3 are termed as light weight mortars.

2. Fire-resistant mortar. This mortar is obtained by mixing powder of fire-bricks or fire clays with aluminous cement. The usual proportion being one part aluminous cement and two parts powdered fire clay. This mortar can withstand the effects of very high temperatures and as such is used for lining of furnaces, fire places and ovens etc.

3. Packing mortars. In order to pack oil wells packing mortars are used. These are special mortars having the properties of high homogenety, water resistance, predetermined setting time, ability to form solid water proof plug in cracks and voids of rocks, resistance to subsoil water pressure etc. The packing mortars include cement - sand, cement - loam and cement - sand - loam. The composition of packing mortars is fixed depending upon the hydrogeologic conditions, packing methods and type of timbering.

4. Sound absorbing mortars. Its main purpose is to reduce noise level. The bulk density of such a mortar varies from 600 to 1200 kg/m^3. The composition of these mortars consists of cement, lime, gypsum slag etc. The aggregates are taken from light weight porous materials such as cinders, pumice etc.

5. X-ray shielding mortars. These plasters are used to cover walls and celing of X-ray cabinets. It is heavy type of mortar having bulk density over 2700 kg/m^3.

6.13. Properties of Good Mortar

1. Its should be cheap and durable
2. It should be easily workable
3. It should have good adhesion with bricks, stones etc.
4. It should not adversely affect the building units on which, it is to be used.
5. It should be in position to develop the desired stresses in it.
6. It should set and harden quickly, so that speed of construction work may be maintained.
7. It should offer good resistance to the penetration of rain water.
8. It should not crack in joints and it should be in position to maintain, its original appearance for sufficiently long periods.

6.14. Test for Mortars

Following tests may be performed to ascertain the properties of mortars :-

1. Tensile strength test.
2. Crushing strength test.
3. Adhesiveness test.

1. Tensile strength test. For this test briquettes are moulded from the mortar to be tested.

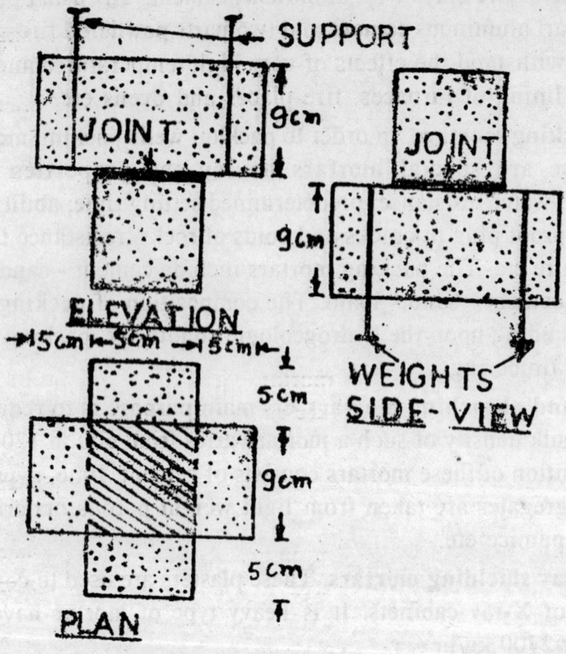

Fig. 6.4. Adhesiveness test.

Cross-sectional area at the weakest section of the briquettes is 38 mm × 38 mm. Ultimate tensile stress per cm^2 is obtained by dividing falling load with 14.44

2. Crushing strength test. For this test, a specimen brick work is done with the mortar under test. This work is then gradually loaded till failure occurs due to crushing. Ultimate crushig strength is obtained by dividing maximum load, with cross sectional area.

3. Adhesiveness test. Two bricks are placed one above the other, each at right angles to the other, Mortar is placed at the common meeting surfaces of the two bricks. If size of the bricks is 19 cm × 9 cm × 9 cm the area of the common meeting surfaces of the two bricks would be 9 cm × 9 cm = 81 cm^2. The cross formed by two bricks is suspended from the upper brick and weights are atached to the lower bricks. The weights are gradually increased till both the bricks split from each other. Ultimate adhesive strength of the mortar is obtained by dividing maximum load by 81.

6.15. Precautions in using Mortar

1. Bricks or stones to be jointed by mortar should be used by soaking them in water for at least 12 hours. This will avoid soaking of water by the building units from the mortar and thus strength of the mortar will not be affected.

2. After preparation mortar should be used at its destined place as early as possible. Cement mortar should be used within 30 minutes of adding water to it. Lime mortar should be consumed within 36 hours, after its preparation. During 36 hours, it should be kept wet or damp. Ganged mortars should be used within 2 hrs of the addition of cement.

3. The mortars should be used as stiff as possible without affecting, its convenience in use. In other words, mortar should be stiff, but workable.

4. The works made from mortar should be kept wet for a weak or two. Exposed external surfaces are sometimes, covered to protect them from wind and sun.

5. The mortar which has set, and which has been lying unattended, should not be used.

6. Setting action of mortar is affected by the presence of frost. Hence, it is advisable either to stop work in frosty weather or use such cement, which will set before it starts freezing.

7. Salt water is good for lime mortar as it prevents, its quick drying. But, it is injurious to pure lime mortar and surkhi mortar, as it causes efflloresence and dampness.

8. Fat lime mortar is very weak in strength. It may however be improved by adding pozzuolana and other substances.

Lean mortar. This term reflects that mortar which has very small proportion of cementing material.

Rich mortar. The mortar having larger proportion of cementing material is known as *rich mortar*.

QUESTIONS

1. Define mortar. What are the type of mortars? Explain utility of each type of mortar.
2. (*a*) What are the desirable properties of good sand?
   (*b*) State the function of sand in mortar.
3. Write short notes on:-
   (*a*) Classification of sand.
   (*b*) Gauged mortar.
   (*c*) Lean mortar.
   (*d*) Substitutes for sand.
   (*e*) Fineness modulus of sand.
4. (*a*) Describe the method of preparing lime mortar and cement mortar.
   (*b*) Give the proportion in which the ingredients of different types of mortars are mixed under different conditions of use.
5. (*a*) Enumerate the good properties of mortar.
   (*b*) What is surkhi? How is it manufactured? Explain its uses.
6. What do you understand by bulking of sand? What importance this aspect has got in relation to mortars?
7. Explain the tests for sand and mortar.

7

CONCRETES

7.1. Introduction

Concrete is an artificial material, obtained by mixing together cementing material, coarse aggregate, fine aggregte and water. If cement is used as cementing material in the mix, it is known as *plain cement concrete*. If steel rods are embedded in the plain cement concrete, it is then called reinforced cement concrete, abbreviated as R.C.C. If instead of cement, lime is used as cementing material in the mix, the resulting mass in termed as *lime concrete*. Lime concrete cannot be made reinforced like cement concrete, as lime eats away the steel in due course of time. Lime concrete is used for foundation blocks or as under coats in case of flat roofs and floors. Cement concrete is the concrete which is universally used. There is no structural element which cannot be made from cement concrete or R.C.C.

All the ingredients of the cement concrete when freshly mixed, produce a plastic mass which can be poured into suitable forms or moulds, to give desired shape to the resulting solid mass. Plastic mass gets converted into solid stone like hard mass with passage of time, due to chemical action taking place between cement and water. Aggregates (both coarse as well as fine), which are mineral materials like sand, gravel, crushed stone etc. do not under go any chemical change. They simply provide mass or volume to the concrete and reduce shrinkage effects in it. Hardened cement concrete resembles stone in weight, strength, and hardness.

7.2. Classification of Concretes

Like mortars, concretes can also be classisifed into following categories.

1. Mud concrete. 2. Lime concrete.
3. Cement concrete.

1. Mud concrete. This concrete does not carry any importance. It is prepared by mixing brick bats in mud mortar. Brick bats may be made from kuchha or pucca bricks. Sometimes, even crushed stone may be mixed with mud mortar to form mud concrete.

Mud concrete is used for preparing hard base, over which lime concrete may be laid and then permanent flooring may be spread. During construction of ground floor of buildings, filling of earth is first of all consolidated by sprinkling sufficient amout of water. During consolidation process broken brick bats or crushed stone pebbles, lying waste at the site, are also apread and rammed into the fillings by rammers. Earth filling added with water and broken brick or stone bats, forms mud concrete which on setting develops a hard sufrace, over which permanent flooring of any form may be laid. The same processes of consolidation with mud concrete may be carried out during preparation of foundation bases.

The coarse aggregate used in mud concrete is usually of broken bricks of size 4 cm 100 m^3 brick ballast is mixed with 40 m^3 of prepared mud mortar.

2. Lime concrete. This concrete carries lot of importance. It is extensively used in foundations of the buildings, two to three storied heights. Besides this, it is very much used in the preparation of hard base for floors. It is also used over roof slabs. This concrete is cheaper than cement concrete and hence is within the purchasing reach of an average citizen.

Hydraulic lime is always used in this concrete. Fine sand or finely ground surkhi is used as fine aggregate. The sand used should pass completely through I.S. 30 sieve, but 10% should be retained on I.S. 15 sieve. 4 cm size coarse aggregate is mostly used in mass concrrete works. Concrete to be used for diffferent purposes has different proportions. Concrete to be used in foundations and floors is prepared by mixing 40 m^3 lime mortar of 1:1 ratio with 100 m^3 coarse aggregate 4 cm size. If lime concrete is to be used over roof, 100 m^3 of 2 cm coarse aggregate is mixed with 47 m^3 of lime mortar 1:3 ratio.

Wet mixing of lime concrete. First of all lime and sand or surkhi are mixed together by adding suitable amount of water on a pucca impervious plate form. If conditiions warrant the mortar may be prepared in circular grinding mill.

Coarse aggregate is stacked in a uniform layer on a pucca plate form and lime mortar as prepared above is spread over it, in uniform layer in suitable quantity depending upon the proportion of the ingredients to be adopted in the concrete. The stack thus prepared is mixed by manual labour using pawrahs. The stack is cut from one side and throughly mixed by adding water. The whole stack is thus mixed.

Sometimes, in case of small works lime mortar as described above is not prepared before hand. A stack is prepared by spreading layers of coarse aggregate, fine aggregate and powdered lime one above the other on a pucca plateform. Coarse aggregate layer is spread at the bottom and powder lime at the top. The stack thus prepared is first mixed dry and then by adding suitable amount of water. The concrete prepared is transported to the place of its use,. by filling in steel pans. The concrete is spread in thin layers in foundations, and each subsequent layer is laid only after the previously laid layer gets throughly compacted. Compaction of the layers is done by rammers in case of foundations and ground floors, but by wooden. Thapies or beaters in case of roofs. Masonry work should not start for at least 7 days on the freshly laid lime concrete. The surface prepared from lime concrete should be cured for at least 10 days.

3. Cement concrete. Cement concrete is prepared by mixing together cement, sand, crushed rock and water. Cement cocrete is a very important structural material and hence, it should be carefully designed, mixed, placed and cured. Properties of various types of cements and that of fine aggregate have been discussed in chapters 5 and 6 respectively. Before going ahead with the task of designing and using of cement concrete we will first of all discuss requirements of remaining undiscussed elements of cement concrete.

7.3. Water

It is added to cement concrete to bring about the hydration of the cement and lubricate the aggregate particles. Water which is suitable for drinking is usually considered safe for concreting purposes also. Water having acids, alkalies and decayed vegetable matter, reduces the strength of the concrete and hence should not be used. Sea water is also unsuitable for use in concrete. It has been noticed that strength of the concrete made from sea water is 10 to 20% less than that when fresh water is used. At location, where fresh water is not available, stale and impure water can be used. Maximum permitted concentrations of various harmful elements as suggested by I.S.I. are given below.

1. To neutralize 200 ml of water sample it should not require more than 2 ml of 0.1 normal NaOH.

2. To neutralize 200 ml sample, it should not require more than 10 ml of 0.1 normal HCl.

3. Percentage of solids should not exceed the following percentages.

Organic solids	0.02%
Inorganic solids	0.30%

Sulphates 0.05%

Alkali chlorides 0.10%

In case of any doubt, the engineer in charge may actually conduct compressive strengh test on concrete. Compressive strength exhibited by concrete should not be less than 90% of the strength expected from a concrete made with the distilled water.

7.4. Coarse Aggregate

It is the aggregate whose particles completely pass through 7.5 cm mesh sieve and which are entirely retained on 4.75 mm sieve. Aggregate having particles greater than 7.5 cm is known as *cyclopean aggregate*.

Characteristics of Aggregates A good aggregate should not contain any deleterious material which may cause physical and chemical changes in the concrete. An aggregate should have clean, uncoated, properly shaped particles of strong, dense, durable mineral and rock materials. Some of the improtant characteristics of aggegate are given here, which may affect the performance of concrete.

1. Shape of particles. As per I.S. 383-1963 shape of the particles of the aggregate may be round, regular, angular and flaky. Rounded, irregular, and angular particles of aggregate show percentage voids of 35%, 37% and 41% respectively. Rounded particles do not have good interlocking, where as irregular and angular particles exhibit very good interlocking effect. Flat, elongated or flaky particles are considered weak aggregates.

2. Surface texture. Surface texture greatly affects the bond between particles and cement paste. An aggregate with rough surface has better bond than smooth surfaced particles. Similarly an aggregate with smooth surface, but having surface pores is considered good for bond.

3. Porosity and absorption. The aggregate should have smaller porosity and absorption.

4. Increase in volume. Fine aggregates or sands increase in volume due to moisture. This has been explained in chapter 6. Coarse aggregates do not increase in volume because of moisture. But amount of moisture in coarse aggregate should be considered while determining the amount of water for the concrete.

5. Deleterious materials. Iron pyrites, coal, mica, shale, clay, alkali, organic impurities, are some of the materials, whose presence in the aggregate is viewed as harmful. These materials, should not be present in such quantity that may affect the strength and durability of the concrete. Deleterious materials cause following effects.

(i) They interfere with the hydration of cement.

(ii) They affect bond between cement paste and aggregate.

(iii) They reduce the strength and durabilty of cement concrete.

(iv) They modify the setting action and contribute to efflorescence.

As a thumb rule, the total amount of deleterious materials in aggregate shoulds not exceed 5%.

7.5. Grading of Aggregate

Grading of aggregate means particle size distribution of the aggregate. If all the particle of an aggregate were of one size, more voids will be left in the aggregate mass. On the other hand an aggregate having particles of varying sizes will exhibit smaller voids. Principle of grading is that the smaller size particle fill up the voids left in larger size particles. By adopting proper percentages, of various sized aggregates, composite aggregate mix can be developed which will be thoroughly graded. Properly graded aggregate produces dense concrete and needs smaller quantities of fine aggregate and cement. The grading of aggregate is expressed in terms of percentages by weight retained on a series of sieves, 80 mm, 40 mm, 20 mm, 10 mm, 4.75 mm sieves are used for grading of coarse aggregate, where as 10 mm, 4.75 mm, 2.36 mm, 1.18 mm 600 micro, 300 mic and 150 mic are used for fine aggregate.

Grading determines the workability of the mix, which controls segregation, bleeding, water-cement ratio, handling, placing and other characteristics of the mix. These factors, also affect economy, strength, volume change, and durabilty of hardened concrete.

There is no universal ideal grading for the aggregate. However, I.S.I. has specified certain limits within which a grading must lie to produce a satisfactory concrete. But these limits depend upon the shape, surface texture, type of aggregate and amount of flaky or elongated material. Variation in grading of sand, causes a large variation in workability, strength, and other properties. But the variation in the grading of coarse aggregate does not effect, these properties to the extent of fine aggregtate.

Coarse aggregates are supplied in nominal sizes. Coarse aggregates and their grading as suggested by I.S.I. are given below.

Table 7.1. Coarse Aggregate Grading

I.S. Sieve	*Percentage passing of graded aggregate of nominal size by weight*			
	50 mm	*20 mm*	*16 mm*	*12.5mm*
80 mm	100	-	-	-
63 mm	-	-	-	-
40 mm	95-100	100	-	-
20 mm	30-70	95-100	100	100
16 mm	-	-	95-100	-
12.5 mm	-	-	-	95-100
10.0 mm	10-35	25-55	30-70	40-85
4.75 mm	0-5	0-10	0-10	0-10
2.36 mm	-	-	-	-

Grading limits of fine aggregate as specified by I.S. 2386-1965 are given below. I.S.I. has specified fine aggregate grading into four zones, namely zone I, II, III and IV.

Table 7.2. Grading Limits of Fine Aggregate

I.S. Sieve	*Percentage passing by weight*			
	Grading Zone I	*Grading Zone II*	*Grading Zone III*	*Grading Zone IV*
10 mm	100	100	100	100
4.75 mm	90-100	90-100	90-100	95-100
2.36 mm	60-95	75-100	85-100	95-100
1.18 mm	30-70	55-90	75-100	90-100
600 mic	15-34	35-59	60-80	80-100
300 mic	5-20	8-30	12-40	15-50
150 mic	0-10	0-10	0-10	0-15

7.6. Proportioning of Fine Aggregate to Coarse Aggregate

Zone I, fine aggregate is the coarst and Zone IV the finest. Zone II is finer, than Zone I sand and Zone III sand is finer than zone II sand. As the fine aggregate grading progressively becomes finer, the ratio of fine aggregate to coarse aggregate should progressively be reduced. Coarse to fine aggregate proportions by weight are given as follows.

Table 7.3. Proportion by Weight of Coarse to Fine Aggregate

Maximum size of coarse aggregate	*Fine to coarse aggregate ratio for sands*			
	Zone I	*Zone II*	*Zone III*	*Zone IV*
10 mm	1 : 1	1 : $1\frac{1}{2}$	1 : 2	1 : 3
20 „	1 : $2\frac{1}{2}$	1 : 2	1 : 3	1 : $3\frac{1}{2}$
40 „	1 : 2	1 : 3	1 : $3\frac{1}{2}$	-

7.7. Maximum Size of the Aggregate

For same workability and strength, concrete having larger sized aggregate, requires less amount of cement, than in concrete having smaller sized aggregate. In large bulk works, larger sized aggregate is preferred, because it envolves lesser consumption of cement. Lesser cement reduces the heat of hydration and consequently thermal stresses and shrinkage cracks. But there are other considerations also which control the size of the aggregate. Large sized aggregate presents smaller surface area to be wetted per unit weight and hence, with same W/C ratio, workability of concrete having comparatively large sized aggregates is more. Small sized aggregate, has poor bond with cement paste and hence, its strength is lower than that having large sized aggregate. The maximum size of the aggregate is governed by following factors also.

(i) It should be 3/4th of clear spacing between reinforcing bars or betwen reinforcing bars and forms.

(ii) It should be 1/3rd of the depth of plane concrete slab.

(iii) 40 mm, 20 mm, and 10 mm sized aggregates are most commonly adopted in concrete works. For structures like abutments, piers, retaining walls, 40 mm sized aggregate should be used. For flooring works normally 10 mm sized aggregate is used. For normal R.C.C. works 20 mm sized aggreate is used.

7.8. Measurement of Cement Concrete Ingredients

Cement. It is always measured by weight. It is mostly used in terms of number of bags. One bag of cement weights 50 kg and has a volume of 35 litres.

Fine aggregate. For high class works, it should be used by weight. However, for ordinary works, it can be measured by volume. If it is taken by volume, allowance must be made for its bulking.

Coarse aggregate. This aggregate does not suffer any bulking due to moisture. Hence, coarse aggregate may be measured either by weight or by volume. However, the weight of a given volume of aggregate is affeeted by grading of the aggregate.

Water. It is always measured by volume and specified as, so many litres per bag of cement. For a given quantity of water to be mixed in concrete. adjustment should be made for the amount of moisture already present in sand and aggregate.

Significance of Bulking of Sand

The phenomena of bulking of sand has been discussed in chapter 6. The importance of bulking of sand in reflected from the following facts.

1. Dry sand and completely flooded sand with water have practically the same volume.

2. Coarse aggregate is not affected by moisture content.

3. One of the reasons of adopting proportioning by weight is the bulking of sand as proportioning by weight avoids the difficulty due to bulking of sand.

4. Bulking of sand assumes great importance when volumetric proportioning of the aggregates is adopted. If the bulking of sand is not considered the concretes produced on volumetric proportioning method will be deficient in fine aggregate and the concrete quality will be affected. Moreover less volume of concrete will be produced thus increasing the cost of concrete.

7.9. Water Cement Ratio (W/C Ratio)

It is the ratio of water to cement in a concrete mixture. Water and cement both are taken by volume. Strength and workability of the concrete greatly depend upon the amount of water. For a particular propotion of materials, there is a specific amount of water which gives the optimum strength to the concrete. Amount of water more or less than specified amount, causes decrease in the strenght of the concrete.

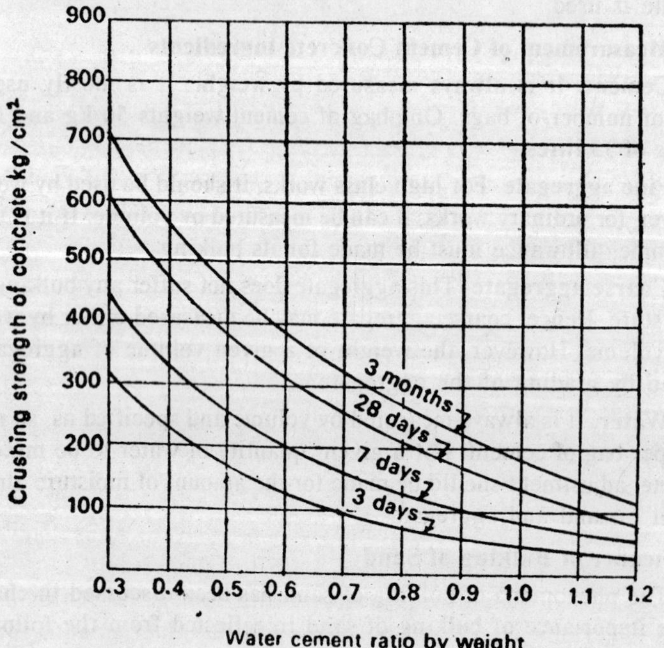

Fig. 7.1. Water cement ratio by weight.

It was Mr. Duff Abrahm, who in 1918 stated that the strength of the concrete is dependent only upon W/C ratio, provided concrete mix is workable. Lesser the W/C ratio in a workable concrete mix, greater will be its strength.

Later Mr. Power proved that cement does not combine chemically with more than half the quantity of water in the mix. Cement requires about 1/8th to 1/4th of its own weight of water to become completely hydrated. This suggests that if W/C ratio is less than 0.4 to 0.5, complete hydration of the cement can be secured.

W/C ratio also depends upon the method adopted to secure compaction of concrete. If compaction is to be done by vibrators, less W/C ratio is required. Addition of plasticising agents in the concrete mix, also increase the workability and reduce the W/C ratio.

Duff Abraham's law is valid only provided that concrete is of workable plasticity and the concrete to be tested is cured under standard conditions of temperature and weather.

7.10. Proportioning of Concrete Mixes

The concept behind the proportioning of concrete mixes is that the resulting concrete is densest, strongest and requires least amount of cement. Following are the methods of proportioning concrete.

1. Arbitrary standard method
2. Minimum voids method.
3. Fineness modulus method.
4. Maximum density method.
5. W/C Law.

1. Arbitrary standards method. This method is based upon the concept that fine aggregate should be sufficient to fill voids of coarse aggregate, and cement to fill the voids of fine aggregate. By experience, it is seen that ratio of fine aggregate and coarse aggregate to develop a dense mix lies betwen 1 : 1.5 and 1 : 2.5. This ratio is taken as 1 : 2. Similarly amount of cement required to fill the voids of fine aggregate is ascertained. Based on experiments and experience, it has been possible to find arbitrary ratio of cement, fine aggregate (F.A.) and coarse aggregate (C.A.) in form of 1:*n* : 2*n*. These ratios are by volume. According to this method, if *n* parts of F.A. are to be added to one part of cement, 2*n* parts of C.A. will have to be added irrespective of the actual requirements. Based on this method 1 : 1 : 2 , 1 : 1.5 : 3, 1 : 2 : 4, 1 : 3 : 6, 1 : 4 : 8 ratio of concrete have been fixed.

2. Minimum voids method. In this method, voids in F.A. and C.A. are found out by carrying out actual experiments. After this amount of F.A. and cement are fixed in such a way that their amount are slightly in excess of the voids in C.A. and F.A. respectively. The mix so proportioned is considered to be having minimum voids and thus the densest and strongest.

3. Fineness modulus method. Definition of Fineness modulus (F.M.) and how is it found out has been explained in previous chapter of 'mortars'. If F.M. of C.A. and F.A. are separately known, a mix of desired F.M. and giving highest strength can be developed as follows:

$$W = \left(\frac{F_2 - F}{F - F_1}\right) \times 100$$

where W = percent proportion of F.A. to be added to 100 parts of C.A.

F = Desired F.M. of the mix

F_1 = F.M. of F.A.

F_2 = F.M. of C.A.

4. Maximum density method. In this method, several boxes of same volume are used. All the boxes are filled with varying proportions of F.A. and C.A. and weighed. The proportion, giving highest weight is adopted for use as it will give the most densest concrete mix. This method was later improved by Mr. Fuller. He gave following expression for obtaining the grading of materials which will give highest density.

$$M = 100\left(\frac{d}{D}\right)^{1/2}$$

where D = Maximum size of C.A.

d = Maximum size of F.A.

M = % by weight of material finer than diameter d

5. W/C Law. As already stated earlier that the strength of well compacted concrete with good workability is dependent only on W/C ratio. According to Mr. Abrahm the strength of rich concrete is more not, because it contains more cement, but due to decrease in W/C ratio. He gave the following formula establishing relationship between strength and W/C ratio for the concrete.

$$S_{28} = \frac{984}{4x}$$

where S_{28} = cylindrical crushing strength of concrete in kg/cm^2 after 28 days of curing.

x = W/C ratio by volume.

7.11. Cube Strength of Concrete

The cube strength of the concrete may be defined as the strength of the concrete in kg/cm^2 on 15 cm concrete cube with a constant W/C ratio and cured in water at 27 ± 2°C for 28 days. When cubes are prepared on field site, they are called the *works cube* and the strength of these cubes is called the *works cube strength*. Now-a-days, cement concrete mixes are not classified by the ratio of their ingredients, but by the cube strengths tested after 28 days of curing M_{100}, M_{150}, M_{200} etc. are the concretes having cube strengths respectively of 100, 150, and 200 kg/cm^2 after 28 days of curing in field conditions.

Now the system of representing stresses has changed to S.I. system. According to S.I. system force is represented by newtons (N) and area in millimetre square. Accordingly the IS 456-1978 has represented the concrete mixes by M_{10}, M_{15}, M_{20}, M_{25}. Here M represents the mix and subscript 10, 15, 20 represent the cube strength of the mix in New tons/ per millimeter square (N/mm^2) corresponding to M_{100}, M_{150}, M_{200}, M_{250}, M_{300}, M_{350} concrete mixes in M.K.S. system they are M_{10}, M_{15}, M_{20}, M_{25}, M_{30}, and M_{35} in S.I. system. In order to convert stress from kg/ cm^2 to N/mm^2 divide stress in kg/cm^2 by 10. Concrete mixes and their corresponding cube stresses are given in table below.

Concrete mix in M.K.S.		*Concrete mix in S.I. system*	
Mix	*Cube strength in kg/cm²*	*Mix*	*Cube strength in N/mm²*
M_{100}	100	M_{10}	10
M_{150}	150	M_{15}	15
M_{200}	200	M_{20}	20
M_{250}	250	M_{25}	25
M_{300}	300	M_{30}	30
M_{350}	350	M_{35}	35
M_{400}	400	M_{40}	40

7.12. Properties of Cement Concrete

Properties of cement concrete may be classified under following two categories.

1. Properties of concrete in plastic stage.
2. Properties of hardened concrete.

1. Properties of concrete in plastic stage. The properties pertaining to plastic stage of concrte are the following:

(i) Workability. It is a measure of ease with which concrete can be handled from the mixer stage to its final fully compacted stage.

The proportion and properties of water, cement and aggregates, influence the workability of the concrete. According to I.S.I. "the workability is that property of concrete which determines the amount of internal work necessary to produce full compaction" Elements that affect workability can be listed as follows.

(a) Quantity of water in the mix. Increased amount of water, increases the workability.

(b) Proper grading of the aggregate mix. If. F.A. as well as C.A. are properly graded, workability is increased.

(c) Increased amount of cement will also increase workability as more water will have to be added to maintain constant W/C ratio.

(d) Ratio of F.A. and C.A. If proportion of C.A. is reduced in relation to F.A. workability can be improved.

(e) If aggregates with rounded grains are used, the wokability is improved.

(f) By adding admixturs workability can be increased.

(g) Maximum size of C.A. also affects workability.

(h) Method of compaction of concrete also affects workability. In case concrete is to be compacted by vibrators rather stiff or less workable concret can be used.

Workability of concrete is measured by slump test. The test has been explained ahead.

(ii) Segregation. Tendency of separation of C.A. grains from the concrete mass is called *segregation*. It increases when concrete mixture is lean, and too wet. It also increases when rather larger and rough textured aggregate is used. Segregation is harmful to concrete properties. Phenomenon of segregation can be avoided as follows.

(a) Addition of little air entraining agents in the mix.

(b) Restricting the amount of water to smallest possible amount.

(c) All the operations like handling, placing and consolidation are carefully conducted.

(d) Concrete should not be allowed to fall from larger heights.

(iii) Bleeding. The tendency of water to rise to the surface of freshly laid concrete is known as *bleeding*. The water rising to the surface carries with it, particles of sand and cement, which on hardening form a scum layer popularly known as *laitance* Concrete bleeding can be checked by adopting following measures.

(a) By adding more cement.

(b) By using more finely ground cement.

(c) By properly designing the mix and using minimum quantity of water.

(d) By using little air entraining agent.

(e) By increasing finer part of fine aggregate.

2. Properties of hardened concrete. Compressive strength tensile stength, bond strength, impermeability, resistance to wear, weather and chemical attackes, shrinkage, creep, thermal expansion, and elasticity are the several properties of hardened concrete. Good concrete has high compressive and tensill strengths. It also has good bond together with good resistance to wearing, weathering and chemical attachs. It is also impermeable, but concrete having high strength is generally more shrinkable. Tensile strength and bond strengths of concrete are generally 10% of the compressive strength of the concrete.

Concrete is not truely an elastic material, but it behaves as an elastic material within the range of usual working stresses. The value of elasticity varies from 14 t/cm^2 to 30 t/cm^2.

Sustained loads applied to concrete cause permanent deformation which is called 'creep'. This is also sometimes, known as plastic flow or time yield phenomenon. Creep is always more than the elastic deformation. Creep is desirable in case of R.C.C. structures as it causes distribution of stresses.

Like other materials, concrete also expands or contracts with rise or fall of temperature. The average value of thermal exapanion is 3×10^{-6} which is nearly same as that for steel. Thermal ėxpansion is more in the case of rich mixes.

Permissible stresses in various grades of concrete as suggested by I.S. 456-1978 are given as follows permissible shear stress is however dependent upon percentage of reinforcement steel in concrete.

Table 7.4

Concrete grade	*Permissible compressive stress N/mm^2*		*Permissible shear stress N/mm^2*	*Permissible bond stress*		*Permissible bearing pressure on full area*
	Bending	*Direct*		*Average*	*Local*	
M 10	3.0	2.5	0.3	0.4	0.7	2.0
M 15	5.0	4.0	0.5	0.6	1.0	3.0
M 20	7.0	5.0	0.7	0.8	1.3	4.0
M 25	8.5	6.0	0.8	0.9	1.5	5.0
M 30	10.0	8.0	0.9	1.0	1.7	6.0
M 35	11.5	9.0	1.0	1.1	1.8	7.0
M 40	13.0	10.0	1.1	1.20	1.9	8.0

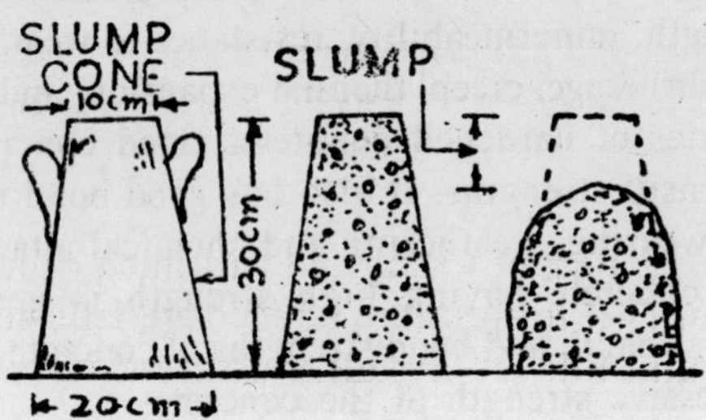

Fig. 7.2. Slump test.

7.13. Slump Test

This test is conducted to find out the workability of the concrete. It is performed with the help of a vessel, shaped in form of a frustum of a cone open at both the ends. Diameter of top end is 10 cm, while it is 20 cm at the bottom end. Height of the vessel is 30 cm. 16 mm diameter and 60 cm long steel rod having pointed end is used for temping purpose.

The vessel is placed on a flat non-absorbant suface and is then filled with specimen concrete in four layers of equal thickness . While filling, each layer should be tamped, 25 times by tamping rod, before the next layer is filled. After filling, the concrete is struck off level with the top of the mould. After filling, the mould is lifted up vertically leaving concrete mass on the impervious surface. The concrete mass is allowed to subside under its own weight and this subsidence is noted which is nothing, but slump of the concrete. The values of slumps based on ACI's recommendations are given as follows.

Table 7.5. Recommended values of slumps for different purposes

	Type of construction	*Slump range in mm*
1.	Heavy mass construction	25-50
2.	Pavements	25-50
3.	Unreinforced footing, caissons, and substructure walls.	25-75
4.	Bridge deck	25-75
5.	R.C.C. Foundations, walls etc.	50-100
6.	R.C.C. slabs, beams, walls.	50-125
7.	Building columns.	75-125
8.	Vibrated concrete	12-25

7.14. Factors Affecting Proportions of Concrete

1. W/C ratio. Strength, elasticity, durability and impermeability of concrete is increased with decrease in W/C ratio, provided the concrete is workable. Shrinkage increases with larger W/C ratio.

2. Cement content. With increase in cement content, W/C ratio is decreased and consequently strength, elasticity, durability and impermeability is increased. More cement, improved workability increase shrinkage..

3. Temperature. Rate of setting and hardening of concrete is high at higher temperature. If temperature of concrete falls below 0°C, free water in concrete turns into ice crystals and expands in volume and the concrete is disrupted. Such concrete on thawing will have no strength.

4. Age of concrete. Strength of concrete goes on increasing with age, though the rate of increase becomes very slow as time goes on passing.

5. Aggregate. Size, shape, and grading of the aggregate, control the concrete properties to a large extent. Rounded aggregates give better workability than flaky and angular aggregates. Larger the size of the aggregate greater will be the strength, provided mix is workable. Properly graded aggregates give better workability and strength than poorly graded mixes.

6. Curing. Curing is the process of keeping the setting concrete damp, so that complete hydration of cement is brought about. Besides strength, curing affects following qualities also.

(a) It improves wear resisting and weather resistant qualities.

(b) It reduces shrinkage.

(c) It increases impermeability and durability of concrete.

7. Frost. It causes disintegration of concrete. Resistance to frost action depends upon the structure of the pores in the concrete.

8. Entrained air. The entrained air in concrete is due to incomplete compaction. It has the effect of reducing the strength of concrete. With 1% of entrained air the strength of concrete is reduced by 5%. It also increases permeability of concrete.

7.15. Strength of Concrete

Strength of the concrete is considered as its compressive strength. All other strength characteristics of the concrete are relaterd to the compressive strength. It depends upon the W/C ratio, grading of aggregate, shape and size of the aggregate and above all, the controls exercised during various operations, right from mixing of water, to the end of curing of the concrete. As per I.S. 456-1978 various concrete mixes should exhibit following maximum compressive strengths where cubes of 15 cm made out of specimen concrete, are tested after 28 days of curing.

Table 7.6

Concrete grade	Compressive strength at preliminary test		Compressive strength at works test in	
	kg/cm²	N/mm²	kg/cm²	N/mm²
M 10	135	13.5	100	10
M 15	200	20.0	150	15
M 20	260	26.0	200	20
M 25	320	32.0	250	25
M 30	380	38.0	300	30
M 35	440	44.0	350	35
M 40	500	50.0	400	40

Works test compressive strength is calculated on field concrete mix on 15 cm cubes. Sometimes, instead of cubes, 15 cm diameter and 30 cm high cylinders are used. In that case minimum cylinder compressive strength required is taken as 0.8 times the compressive strength computed for 15 cm cube. If instead of 15 cm cube, 10 cm cube is used for test, the results obtained on 10 cm cubes should be reduced by 10% to determined its equivalent strength for 15 cm cubes. Where cubes larger than 15 cm are used,. generally no modification is necessary unless otherwise specified.

7.16. Mixing of Concrete

The process of mixing cement, water, F.A. and C.A. in suitable proportion is known as *mixing of concrete*. This process should ensure uniform colour, consistency, and homogenity of the concrete. Segregation should not take place during process of mixing. The mixing methods may be hand mixing or machine mixing.

Hand Mixing. Hand mixing is used, where quantity of concrete is very small. It can also be used where machines for mixing are not available or where noise is not desirable.

Cement and sand are first of all mixed dry on a clean, hard and impermeable platform. Dry mixing is continued until the mix attains uniform colour. Now this mix is spread on the measured stock of coarse aggregate in required amont and they are mixed dry again to have uniform colour. Shovels are used for this mixing purpose.

Make hollow in the middle of the mixed pile and add about 75% of the required quantity of water. Now mixing is done and the remaining quantity of water is added to acquire the uniform workability. In this method of mixing, about 10% more cement is used to make good the cement lost due to possible water flowing out of the mix and also to make good. strength characteristics due to inferior results of hand mixing.

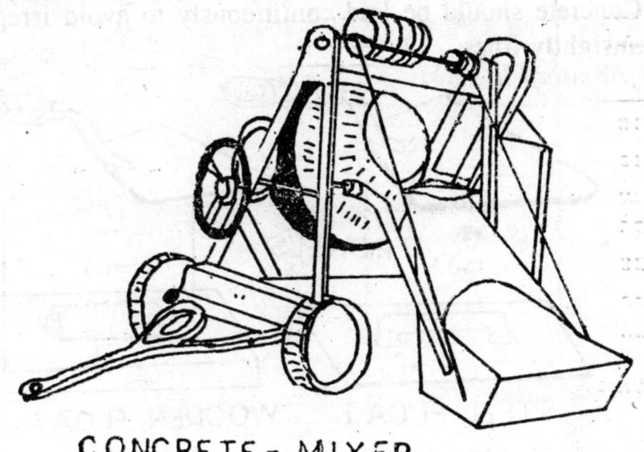

Fig. 7.3.

Machine Mixing. On large works, machine mixing proves economical and convenient. Concrete produced by machine mixing is more homogeneous, and can be prepared with comparatively lesser W/C ratio.

The concrete mixers may either be batch type or continuous type. Batch mixers, mix and discharge each load of materials separately, where as continuous mixers produce steady stream of concrete so long as it is in operation. Latter type mixers are not in common use. Batch type mixers are mostly adopted. These may be rotary or non-tilting type or tilting type.

7.17. Transporting the Concrete

Concrete prepared either by hand mixing or machine mixing has to be transported to its place of use, before hydration of cement starts.

During transportation, efforts should be made to prevent segregation or less of any of the ingredients. The method of transportation of concrete depends upon the quantity of concrete and work site situation. Transportation of concrete is done by pans, wheel barrows, truck mixers, belt conveyors and pumps. Mostly concrete mixing is done near the site of the work. In such circumstances, pans and wheel borrows prove most economical and convenient. If mixer site is far off from the site of the work, truck mixers may be used. Where large quantity of concrete is to be put at very congested site, pumps may be used for the purpose. Belt conveyors are used when concrete is to be transported continuously and to a higher level.

7.18. Placing of Concrete

The concrete should be placed and compacted before its setting starts. Following precautions should be taken while placing the concrete.

(i) Concrete should be laid continuously to avoid irregular and unsightly lines.

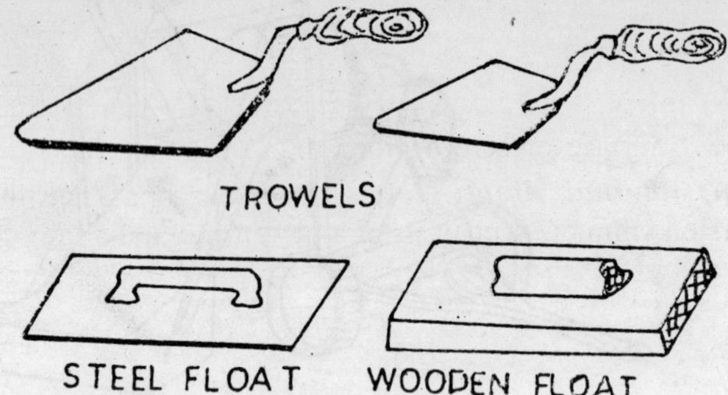

Fig. 7.4. Trowels and Floats.

(ii) To avoid sticking of concrete, form work should be oiled before concreting.

(iii) While placing concrete, the position of form-work and reinforcement should not be disturbed

(iv) To avoid segregration, concrete should not be dropped from height more than 1 m.

(v) Concrete should not be placed in rains.

(vi) Thickness of concrete layer should not be more than 30-45 cm, in case of mass concrete and 15-30 cm in case of R.C.C. works.

(vii) Walking on freshly laid concrete should be avoided.

(viii) It should be placed as near to its final position as practicable.

7.19. Consolidation or Compaction of Concrete

Consolidation of plastic concrete is termed as compaction of concrete. In this process, efforts are only directed to reduce the voids in the compacted concrete. Compaction of concrete can be done either manually or mechanically. When it is done manually, it is called hand compaction or tamping and in second case, it is termed as machine compaction.

Hand compaction. It is done with the help of steel tamping rods or timber screeds. Narrow and deep members are compacted with tamping rods. Thin slabs and floors are tamped with the help of screeds. Compaction should done in layer of 30 cm for mass concrete and 15cm for R.C.C. Compaction should be carried out for such a time that a layer of mortar starts appearing at the compacted surface. Excessive and under compaction of concrete, both are harmful.

Machine Compaction. Machine or mechanical compaction of concrete is done with the help of vibrators. Vibrators produce vibrations which when transmitted to plastic concrete make, it to flow and affect compaction. Over vibration should not be allowed as otherwise C.A. particles will get concentrated at the lower layers and only mortar will be left at the top surface. There are three types of vibrators in most common use.

(i) Internal vibrators *(ii)* Form vibrators and
(iii) Surface or screed vibrators

(i) Internal vibrators. It is also known as needle, poker, or immersion vibrator, It consists of a power unit and a long flexible tube at the end of which a vibrating head is attached. whenever compaction is to be done, the vibrating head is inserted in concrete. This vibrator is very useful for compaction of mass concrete.

(ii) Form vibrator. This vibrator is used by clamping to the form-work. It parts vibrations to the concrete through formwork. This vibrator is used only, if the use of internal vibrator is not practicable as in the case of thin and congested situations. It is also called external vibrator.

(iii) Surface vibrator. It is also named as screed or pan vibrator. It is clamped to the screed. It imparts vibrations to the concrete from the surface when screeding operation of the concrete is carreid out. It is effective only for depth of about 20 cm and hence useful for thin horizontal surfaces such as pavements.

7.20. Finishing

Finishing means, giving desired smoothness or finishing to the surface of compacted concrete. For achieving good finishing, slump of the concrete should not be more than 5 cm. Screeding, floating and trowelling are the usual operations, envolved in finishing.

7.21. Curing of Concrete

Curing is the operation by which moist conditions are maintained on finished concrete surface, to promote continued hydration of cement. If proper curing is not done, complete hydration of cement will not take place, with the result that concrete will not acquire its full intended strength. More over shrinkage cracks will develop in the concrete. Curing also brings about improvement in durability, impermeability, wear and weather resisting qualities. There are several methods of curing. Adoption of specific method depends upon the nature of work and the climatic conditions. Various methods of curing are the following

(i) Shading. **This method has limited application. The object of shading the concrete is to prevent evaporation of water from the surface. It also helps, protect concrete surface from heat, direct sun, and wind.**

In cold, shading helps in preserving heat of hydration of cement for preventing freezing of concrete.

(ii) Covering the surface with hessian or gunny bags.

(iii) Sprinkling water. In this method, water is sprinkled on the surface from time to time.

(iv) Ponding of water. In this method, water is filled in kiaries which are formed on the surface by sand or mud. The method is used for curing horizontal surfaces.

(v) Membrane curing. In this method, surface of concrete is covered by a water proof membrane which is kept in contact with concrete. The membrane prevents evaporation of water from concrete. Wax, emulsion, bitumen emulsion, bituminized water proof paper, and plastic films, are the common membrane materials.

(vi) Steam curing. This method is adopted in the case of precast members. By this method hydration of cement is brought about within very short time.

Admixtures Sometimes ingredients other than conventional have to be added in concrete to improve some of its qualities. These ingredients and known as admixtures. The addition of an admixture may improve the concrete with respect to its strength, hardness, workability, water-resisting power etc.

Alum, aluminium sulphate, borium oxide, bitumen, calcium chloride coal ash, common salt, lime, iron oxide, mineral oils, organic oils, potassium chloride, silicate of soda, tar products, zinc chromate, volcanic ashes are the commonly used admixtures. It is always necessary to know the complete detail of any admixtures before it is recommended. Depending upon their respective activities they can be classified in the following form.

1. Accelerators.
2. Air entraining admixtures
3. Plasticisers
4. Retarders.

It may be noted that some admixtures may have the combined effect of the above individual activities. The use of admixture in concrete is increasing rapidly becasue of the following advantages.

1. Quantity of cement in reduced.
2. W/C ratio can be reduced.
3. Durability of concrete gets increased
4. Permeability of concrete may be increased or decreased as desired.
5. Time in saved in repairs and maintenance.
6. Final setting time of concrete can be adjusted.

7. Higher early and ultimate strengths are achieved.
8. Higher slumps and self levelling concretes are obtained.

7.22. Removal of Form Work

The hardening of concrete depends upon the temperature of atmosphere and type of cement used. Hence, removal of form work will have to be decided according to temperature and type of cement used in the concrete. Form-work removal times are given in Table 7.7. These timings are for atmospheric temperature of 20°C.

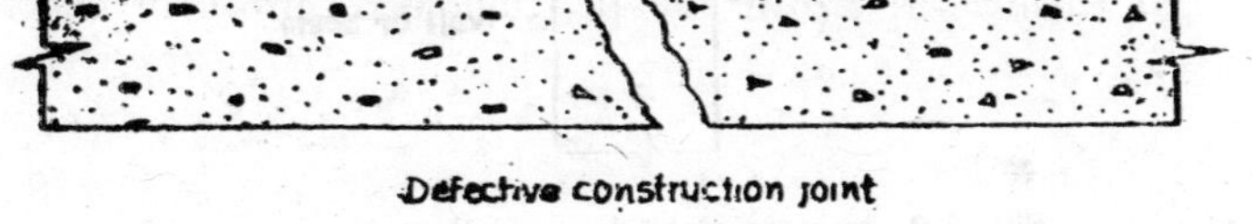

Fig. 7.5. Construction joint.

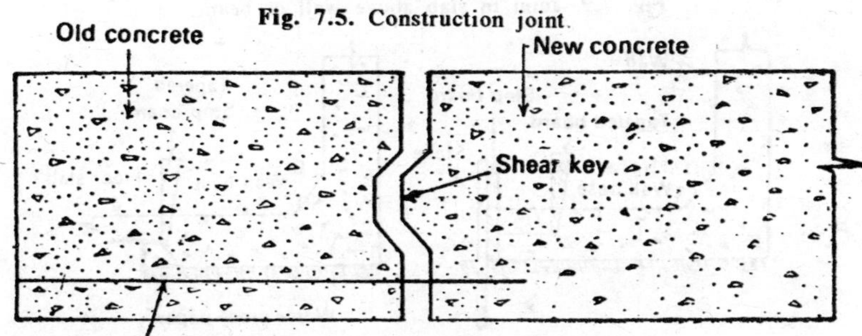

Fig. 7.6. Joint with reinforcing steel bar.

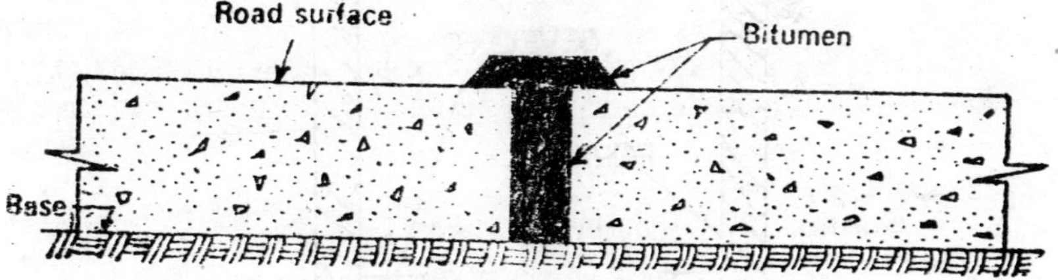

Fig. 7.7. Expansion joint.

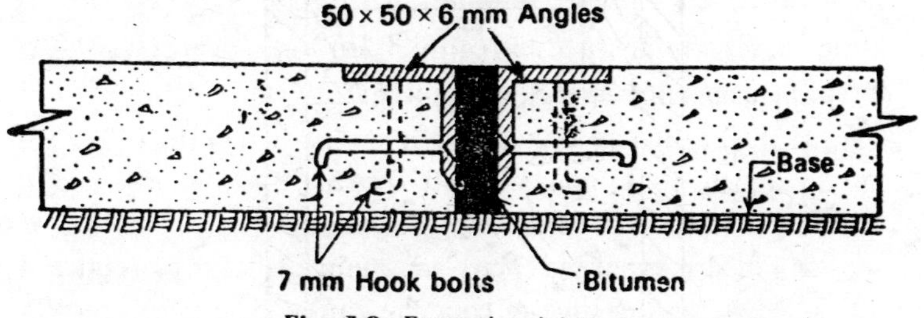

Fig. 7.8. Expansion joint.

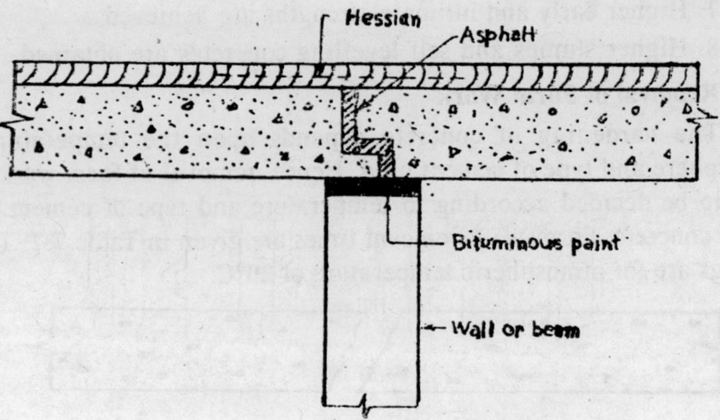

Fig. 7.9. Joint in slab above wall or beam.

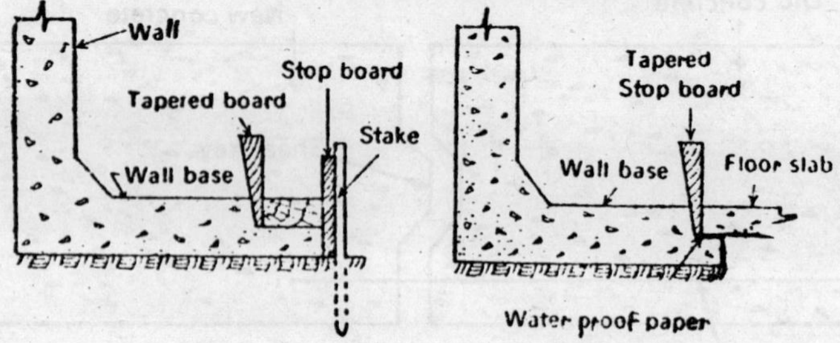

Fig. 7.10. Joint at base of water tank.

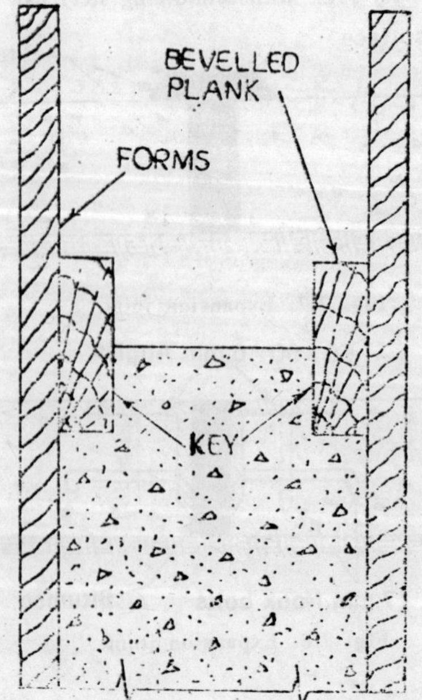

Fig 7.11. Joint in vertical column

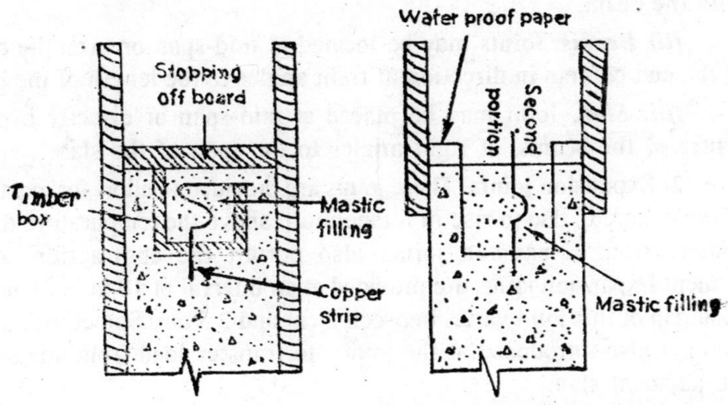

Fig. 7.12 Another type of joint in column.

Table 7.7. Form-work removal timings (I.S. 456-1964)

	Description	*Time in day*
1.	Columns, walls, vertical sides of beams and slabs.	1-2 days
2.	Slabs when props are left in position	3 days
3.	Beam soffits, when props are left in position	7 days
4.	For slabs spanning up to 4.5 m, removal of props may be after	7days
5.	For slabs spanning more than 4.5 m, props may be removed after	14 days
6.	For beams up to 6 m span props may be removed after.	14 days
7.	For beams more than 6 m span, props can be removed after.	21 days

7.23. Joints in Concrete

Except in small jobs, it is not possible to place concrete in one continuous operartion. Joints are also required for functional consideration of the structure. The joints can be classified under following catefories:

1. Construction joints.
2. Expansion joints.
3. Contraction joints.
4. Working joints.

1. Consruction joints. These joints are provided. where there is break in the construction programme. Location of construction joints should be such that it interferes minimum with the functional characteristics of the structure. Best location may be as follows:

(i) Columns. Joints should be located a few cms below its junction with the beam.

(ii) Beams. Joints may be located at mid-span or over the centre of the end column in direction at right angles to the length of the beam.

(iii) Slab. Joint may be placed at mid-span or directly over the centre of the beams, at right angles to the span of the slab.

2. Expansion joints. These joints are provided to allow for expansion of the concrete, due to rise in temperature above the temperature during construction. Expansion joints also permit the contraction of the element.Expansion joints are provided at an interval of 18 m to 21 m. The open gap of this joint varies between 2 cm and 2.5 cm. Sometimes, dowel bars are also introduced at the joints to transfer load from one slab to the adjacent slab.

3. Contraction joint. These joint are provided to permit contraction of the concrete elements. These joints are spaced closer than the expansion joints. These joints are made tongued and grooved, so as to maintain proper interlocking of the adjoining slabs.

4. Warping joints. These joints are provided to relieve stresses induced due to warping effects. They are also known as *hinged joints.*

The gap of all the joints should be filled with joint filler. The usual joint fillers are built in strips of metal, bitumen-treated felt, cane fibre board, rock bound with rubber or resin, soft wood, natural cork etc.

Guniting. It is a process by which inferior or damaged concrete work can be effectively repaired. It is also used for providing an impervious layer.

Gunite is a mixture of cement and sand, usually in proportion of 1:3. A special equipment known as cement gun is used to deposit this mixture on the concrete surface under a pressure of about 2 to 3 kg/cm^2.

The surface to be treated is cleaned and washed. The nozzle of the gun is generally kept at a distance of about 80 cm from the surface to be treated. Velocity of flow through the nozzle is from 120 to 160 m/sec. This process carries following advantages.

(i) High impermeability is achieved.

(ii) The repairs can be carried out in any situation in a very short time.

(iii) High compressive strength say 500 to 700 N/mm^2 at 28 day can be obtained

7.24. Some other Types of Cement Concretes

There are several types of cement concretes which can be developed to suit the specific requirements. Such concretes are develoepd either by varying the proportions of usual cement concrete elements or by adding some additional constituents.

1. Plum concrete. It is ordinary cement concrete. The only difference being the comparatively large sized C.A., is used in it. It is used in the construction of gravity dams, heavy bridge piers, etc. The size of C.A. in this concrete may be as large as 20 cm. But the proportion of such large sized C.A. should not be more than 20% of the total amount of C.A.

2. Light weight concrete. It is again an ordinary cement concrete with only difference that special light weight C.A. is used in place of usual crushed stone C.A. Light weight concrete can also be obtained by adding such reagents which either develop gas or foam, during the process of mixing of concrete, Such concrete develops porous cellular structure of concrete, after setting and this structure is far lighter than the usual cement concrete.

3. Air entrained concrete. This concrete is develoed by either using air-entraining cement or other such agent. This cement concrete can resist very successfully the effects of frozen water, sulphate action and stresses developed during seting of concrete.

This concrete is more workable, plastic and adhesive than ordinary concrete. It is more impermeable and does not suffer from the difficulty of segregation. In it W/C ratio and amount of F.A. both are less than ordinary concrete.

4. No fines concrete. This cement concrete does not have any F.A. It is a mixture of cement, C.A., and water only. Such concrete can be adopted for castin-site external load bearing walls of houses, small retaining walls, damp-proofing sub-base material etc.

The following are the advantages of no-fines concrete.

1. Drying shrinkage of no-fies concrete is relatively low.

2. Sand being absent there is no transmission of water by capillary action.

3. It has all the advantages of light weight concrete.

4. Because of the presence of large voids its insulating properties are better.

5.There is savings of fine aggregate then proves economical.

6. Pressure on form work is about 2/3 rd as it is a light weight concrete.

7. There is no problems of any segregation.

The limitations of this mortar are.

1. It does not much cohesion in fresh state and hence requires longer time for removal of forms.

2. It is highly permeable.

3. The compressive, bond and flexural strengths are considerably low. It is not used for R.C.C. works.

5. Vaccum Concrete. We know that only about half of the water added in concrete goes into chemical combination and the remaining water is used to make concrete workable. This concrete is prepared and laid as an ordinary concrete. But after laying water which has making concreting workable is extracted by a special method known as *vaccum method*. Thus water left in this concrete is only that which is to go in chemical combination and hence resulting concrete becomes very strong.

6. Water proof concrete. This concrete is prepared by adding some water-proofing or water-repellant compound in the concrete. This concrete is used for rendering structures water proof.

7. Reinforced cement concrete. Ordinary cement concrete is very weak in tension, but very strong in compression. Steel rods may be embedded on the tension side of the member. Such concrete in which steel rods are embedded, is called reinforced cement concrete, abreviated as R.C.C.

8. Pre-stressed-concrete. It is also reinforced cement concrete, but steel rods are pre-stressed before embedding in the concrete. These rods remain pre-stressed even after the concrete has fully set. Elements of this concrete, when subjected to bending, do not develop cracks. Pre-stressed concrete saves as much as 5% of concrete.

9. Cellular or aerated concrete. In it, concrete is made light by introducing air bubbles throughout the mass. It is useful for roof slab and precast units in partitions. It is made by adding aluminium powder to a rather wet mix of cement, sand, lime and water. The mass begins to rise due to the hydrogen bubbles evolved by the chemical action and there by sells are formed in the concrete.

10. Foamed concrete. It is also a light weight concrete prepared by mixing blast furnace slag with the concrete.

11. Pre-cast concrete. Concrete may be classified as precast and cast-in-situ. Cast-in-situ concrete is ordinary cement concrete which is prepared at the site of its actual use.

Pre-cast concrete is also an ordinary cement concrete, but prepared not at the site of use, but in factory, where precast units of concrete are produced on a very large scale. It is possible to prepare well-made precast products by keeping a high standard of finishing. Pre-cast concrete units help very much in keeping the pace of the work as they do not require any casting and curing at the site.

Estimating yield of concrete The volume of concrete resulting from a concrete mix depends upon factors such as W/C ratio, size of aggregate, compaction etc.

The approximate volume of resulting concrete can be found out by adopting the following Thumb rule.

If the proportion of concrete is a:b:c, the resulting concrete will have a volume of $\frac{2}{3}$ (a + b+ c)

when a = parts of cement

b = parts of sand

c = parts of coarse aggregate

Accurate volume of concrete can be determined by considering the absolute volumes of various components of concrete plus the volume of entrapped air. In well compacted concreted, the volume of entrapped air in less than 1% and therefore, it can be rejected.

Let w, a, b, and c be absolute volumes of water, cement, fine aggregate, and coarse aggregate respectively. Then

$w + a + b + c = 1$

The absolute volume can be obtained af follows

$$\text{Absolute volume} = \frac{\text{weight of the material}}{\text{apparent S.G} \times \text{unit wt. of water}}$$

Assume the following values for calculations of absolute volume

1. Cement. = S.G. = 3.15 and weight of each bag 50 kg.

2. Sand. = S.G. = 2.65 and unit weight 1600 kg/m^3 when dry.

3. Coarse aggregate = S.G. 2.80 and unit weight 1500 kg/m^3 when dry.

4. Unit weight of water = 1000 kg/m^3

5. W/C ratio = 0.6 tonnes weight of cement

Example : Estimate the yield of concrete per bag of cement for concrete mix of proportion 1:3:6.

***(i)* As per Thumb-rule**

One bag of cement = 0.035 m^3

yield (approx) $= \frac{2}{3}\{0.035+3\times0.035+6\times0.035\}$

$= \frac{2}{3}$ (0.035 + 0.105 + 0.210) = 0.233 m^3

By absolute volume method

(i) Absolute volume of cement $= \dfrac{50}{3.15 \times 1000} = 0.02 \text{ m}^3$

(ii) Absolute volume of sand $= \dfrac{3 \times 0.035 \times 1600}{2.65 \times 1000} = 0.063$

(iii) Absolute volume of coarse aggregate $= \dfrac{6 \times 0.035 \times 1500}{2.80 \times 1000}$

$= 0.1175$

Absolute volume of water $= \dfrac{0.60 \times 50}{1 \times 1000} = 0.03 \text{ m}^3$

Total $= 0.226 \text{ m}^3$

On comparison it can be easily seen that results obtained by thumb rule are almost the same as obtained by absolute volume method.

Quality control of concrete. In engineering maintenance of quality control is very essential so that sub-standard constructions are avoided. Adherance to specification provided in contract document is known as quality control. Building, dams and other important structures build by cement concrete last for many decades and hence quality control of concrete during the construction of such important structures is a must.

The concrete as such is a heterogeneous material and hence it would assume a wide range of properties if produced without excersing nay control.

The concrete produced at site should be stronge dense, worakble and economical. To achieve this following general requirements are required to be observed.

1. There should be no air bubbles left in the concrete. For this consolidation of the concrete should be perfect.

2. Cement used should be finely ground.

3. W/C ratio should be kept low.

4. In order to achieve good inter locking, aggregates of cubical particle should be used.

5. Curing of concrete should be perfect.

The quality control of concrete demands a high degree of carefulness among the personnel connected with the production of concrete. Extreme care is to be exercised at every stagte so as to obtain the desired results. All suitable precautions must be taken to insure proper inspection of the ingredients, batching, mixing, transporting and placing.

7.25. Form Work

The temporary encloser which is used to contain the plastic concrete till it soldifies and acquires sufficient strength is known as form-work, centering, or shuttering. The form work is removed when concrete element casted in it, acquires sufficient strength. Following points should be considered is the design of form work.

(i) It should be such which can be easily fixed and then removed.

(ii) It should be rigid and strong to sustain the load of the concrete element and also the laod due to impact and vibrations etc.

(iii) It's inside surface should be oiled so that concrete may not stick to it.

QUESTIONS

1. Define concrete. How concrete can be classified according to building materials used?
2. Does mud concrete carry any significance in engineering structures? If not where it is mostly used. What should be its proportion?
3. How lime concrete is prepared? For what purposes it is mostly used?
4. What do you understand by term grading of the aggregate? What importance this term carries as far as design of concrete mix is concerned :
5. *(a)* How various ingredients of cement concrete measured?

   (b) What are the characteristics of coarse aggregate?
6. Explain water cement ratio for cement concrete. Why it is so important to exercise full control on it, while mixing cement concrete?
7. What are various methods of proportioning concrete mixes? Explain each method briefly.
8. What are the properties of a cement concrete?

   (i) When concrete is in plastic state.

   (ii) When concrete is in hardened state.
9. *(a)* What are the factors which affect properties of cement concrete? Explain each factor in brief.

   (b) Explain slump test.
10. How mixing of cement concrete is carried out? Explain the methods in details.
11. Explain the following operations in respect of cement concrete.

    (i) Transportation of concrete.

    (ii) Placing of concrete.

    (iii) Consolidation or compaction of concrete.

    (iv) Finishing of concrete.

    (v) Curving of concrete.
12. Why joints are essential in cement concrete structures? What are different types of joints? Explain each joints in brief.

13. Explain the terms.
    (i) Form-work
    (ii) Pre-cast concrete.
    (iii) Reinforced cement concrete.
    (iv) Light weight concrete.
    (v) Guniting.

8

TIMBER

8.1. General

Timber is obtained from trees. Timber denotes structural wood. A standing living tree is known as *standing timber*. When tree has been cut and its stem and branches are roughly converted into pieces of suitable lengths. It is known as *rough timber*. When roughly converted timber is further sawn and converted into commercial *size the planks, logs, battens, posts, beams, etc. it is called converted timber*

Timber has been in very common use for engineering purposes since ancient times. Even to-day there are certain works, where timber is considered as the most ideal material. To-day although materials like steel, cement, stone bricks etc. have occupied lot of field, where timber was predominently used, still timber continues to be an important structural material.

There is difference between terms *timber* and *wood*. Wood includes all types of wood which may be burning wood, structural wood, furniture wood etc. *But wood suitable for use as a structural material is called timber.*

8.2. Advantages of Timber

Advantages of timber are given in brief.

(i) It is easily available every where.

(ii) Its salvage value is high.

(iii) It can be easily transported by converting large pieces into smaller pieces.

(iv) Working on timber is easy. Timber constructions can be easily repaired. Additions and alterations to timber structures can be easily done.

(v) It can be easily jointed.

(vi) In marine works, timber is considered as an ideal material as it does not corrode. Cement and iron structures corrode in sea water, if they are not protected with special preservative.

(vii) Being light in weight, it is preferred for building works in earth quake prone regions.

(viii) It is an excellent material for decorative and general use furnitures. Lot of other internal decorations can be carried out with it.

(ix) It can with stand, shocks better than iron and concrete.

(x) It is good insulator of electricity and heat.

(xi) It is good sound absorbing material.

(xii) Timber can be easily strengthened by attaching steel or other material with it.

8.3. Use of Timber

Uses of timber are numerous. Some of its important uses are given as follows:

(i) It is very much used for railway track sleepers.

(ii) It can be used inform of piles, vertical posts, beams, lintels, doors and windows.

(iii) It can also be used as members of roofing trusses.

(iv) It is an important material for furniture-making

(v) It is used for floors, ceiling , partition walls.

(vi) It is used as form-work for cement concrete structures.

(vii) It is very much used in making sports goods, musical instruments, well curbs, agricultural implements, etc.

(viii) Packing cases are mostly made from soft timber.

(ix) It is very much used for timbering the deep trenches.

(x) Railway coaches and wagons, are also made from high class timber.

It can be said that there is no Engineering field, where timber is not used one way or the other.

8.4. Classification of Trees

The trees may be classified into two categories depending upon their mode of growth.

1. Exogeneous trees. 2. Endogeneous trees.

1. Exogeneous trees. The growth of these trees is out wards. The section of such trees shows distinct consecutive rings. These rings are known as *annual rings*. Every year a new ring is added to the tree section. Number of annual rings show the age of the tree at the time of its felling. Structural timber or timber mostly used for engineering purposes is obtained from this category of trees. Exogeneous tree may be further sub-divided into two groups.

(*a*) Conifers or evergreen trees and (*b*) Deciduous trees.

(*a*) *Conifer trees.* These trees have pointed needle like or scale-like leaves. They bear cone-shaped fruits. They are generally ever-green trees. They ylield soft wood. Deodar, kail, chir, fir pine, spruce, cedar and cypress trees are typical examples of such trees.

(*b*) *Diciduous trees.* These trees have flat broad leaves. The leaves of these trees fall in autumn and new leaves appear in spring, every year. They yield hard wood. Typical examples of trees in this groups are oak, mahogany, teak, shisham, wall nut, Ash, beach etc. Timber for structural purposes is mostly derived from this category of trees.

Soft Wood and Hard Wood

Soft wood. It is obtained from ever-green group of trees. The cellular structure of soft wood is simple and shows fairly distinct annual rings. They have light colour, uniform texture and straight grains. They possess lot of resinous matter and are light in weight. Most of the woods, used for constructional purposes belong to this class. Soft wood is relatively cheap, easily workable, and sufficiently strong.

Hard wood. It is obtained from broad-leaved group of exogeneous trees. Hard wook has complex cellular structure and its annual rings are not distinctly visible. This would generally be non-resinous, heavy, and dark coloured. Hard wood is mainly used for decorative purposes like veneering, panelling, furniture making etc.

It should be noted that the terms soft wood and hard wood have commercial importance only. It is quite likely that some varieties of soft wood may be stronger than some varities of hard wood. Soft wood and hard wood, may be compared as follows.

	Description	*Soft woods*	*Hard woods*
1.	Weight	Light	Heavy
2.	Colour	Light	Dark
3.	Annual rings	Distinct	Indistinct
4.	Fire resistance	Poor	Good
5.	Medullary rays	Indistinct	Distinct
6.	Structure	Resinous	Non-resinous
7.	Strength	Less strong	More strong

2. *Endogenous trees.* Growth of such trees is inwords. They show fibrous mass along longitudinal direction. Timber obtained from these trees has limited application in engineering works. Bambmoo, cane, palm etc. are the typical examples of such trees.

8.5. Growth of Tree

The tree sucks its food from soil through its roots in forms of sap.

The sap is then raised by cells and fed to the brances and leaves of the tree. The sap consists of moisture and minerals like phosphates and nitrates. In addition to sap, trees also require some organic foods in form of proteins, fats and carbohydrates. The sap losses moisture through leaves and absorbs carbon dioxide from air and gets denser. The process is called photo synthesis. The thickened sap desends in autumn and gets deposited under the bark in form of a thin layer known as *cambium layer*. Cambium layer hardens with time and thus adds a new annual ring to the section of the tree stem.

8.6. Tree Structure

Fig. 8.1 shows the cross-section of an exogeneous tree. The timber tree consists of a mass of fibres which run parallel to the length of its stem and branches. The fibres, also known as cells are in form of hollow tubes which are arranged in an irregular manner round the centre of the tree. The function of these cells is to strengthen the wood and to conduct sap from the roots to the brachches and leaves. Following are different components of the cross-section of the tree.

1. Pith. It is the inner most central core of the tree. It is sometimes known as *heart* also. The size and shape of pith varies for different types of trees. It consists entirely of cellular tissues and it nourishes the plant in its young age. When the plant becomes old, the pith dries up and decays. The sap is then transmitted by wooden fibres deposited round the pith.

2. Heart wood It is dark coloured portion of the tree surrounding the pith. It is almost dead portion of the tree and does not take active part in its growth. It is this portion of tree which provides strongest and durable timber for various engineering purposes.

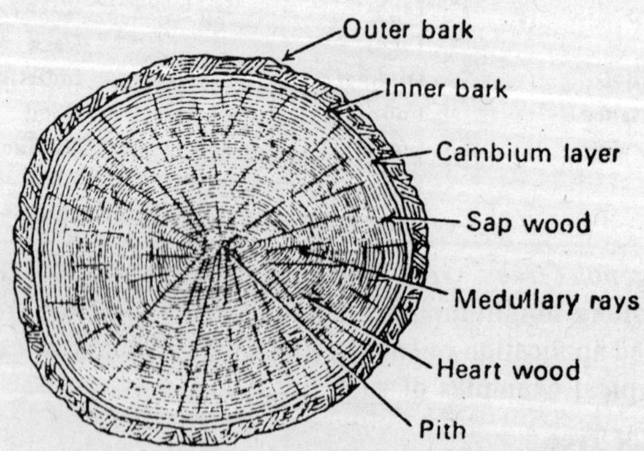

Fig. 8.1. Cross Section of a Tree.

3. Sap wood. The portion of light coloured wood lying between heart wood and cambium layer is knwon as *sap wood.* This wood is comparatively light in weight. The wood is of recent growth and thus contains lot of sap. This is the active part of the wood and thus helps in growth of the tree. It is this wood through which sap moves in an upward direction. This wood is also called as *albur.* A annular rings in this wood are less sharply defined than those of heart wood.

4. Cambium layer. A thin layer of sap lying between sap wood and inner bark is known as '*Cambium layer*'. It is a sap which has yet not been converted into sap wood. If the bark is removed the cambium layer gets exposed and the cells stop to be active which results in the death of tree.

5. Inner bark. The thin layer, covering the cambium layer, is known as '*inner bark*, This layer protects cambium layer from out side injuries.

6. Out bark. It is the outer most protective layer which may have fissures and cracks. It is also called *cortex*. It consists of cells of wood fibre.

7. Medullary rays. These are thin radial fibres, éxtending from cambium layer right upto pith. These rays help in holding together annular rings of both heart as well as sap wood. They may be continuous, but mostly they are broken. In some varieties of trees they are not very distinct.

Micro-structure of tree. The structure of wood when studied under a microscope, it reveals that wood consists of living and dead cells of various sizes and shapes. The cells are of three types.

1. Conductive cells. These cells transmit nutrients from roots to branches and leaves of the tree.

2. Mechanical cells. These are thick walled elongated cells. They impart strength to the wood.

3. Storage cells. They store and transmit nutrients to living cells in the horizontal direction. They are located in Medullary rays.

8.7. Felling of trees

Cutting of trees to get timber from them, is called *felling of trees.* Following facts should be carefully considered while cutting the trees.

(i) Season of felling the trees. Trees should be cut only when sap is not active. The seasons when sap is least active are generally mid-summer and mid-winter. However, the reason for felling the trees is dependent upon the climatic conditions of the locality and the type of tree. In autumn and spring, sap is in vigorous motion and hence felling of trees in these seasons should be avoided. For hilly areas, mid-summer and for plain areas mid-winter, are the proper seasons for felling trees.

(ii) Age of trees. The trees should be felled only when it has just attained maturity. Under aged tress would yield more of sap wood. Over matured trees develop certain defects in heart wood and thus quality of timber is affected.

(iii) Method of felling trees. The task of felling trees should be entrusted to an experienced person only. Before felling, the slope of the tree is accessed and cut is given to the stem on the side of the slope of the tree, as near to the ground as possible. Now cut is made on the opposite side of the slope and trees is felled. If tree is to be felled against the direction of the slope, ropes are tied to the tree and pulled to the direction of felling by giving suitable cut to the stem.

8.8. Conversion of Timber

The process by which timer is cut and sawn into suitable marketable sizes is known as *conversion of timber*. After felling tree's stem, and major branches are cut into logs of suitable lengths. These logs are then transported to a saw machine and converted into marketable sections. Following facts should be kept in view while carrying out conversion of timber. Conversion of timber is done at the saw mills.

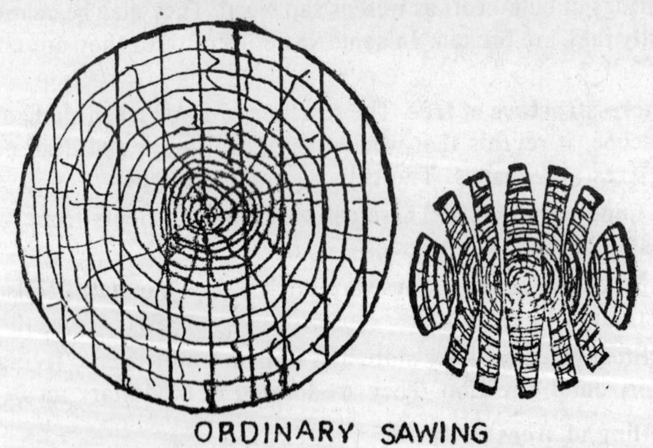

Fig. 8.2.

(i) Conversion or sawing of the timber should be done by an experienced person. Wastage of timber during sawing should be kept minimum.

(ii) Suitable allowance should be kept for squaring, planing and shrinkage while fixing the position of the cuts. This allowance may vary from about 3 mm to 6 mm.

(iii) In order to obtain strong timber pieces, the sawing should be

done practically tangential to annual rings and parallel to the medullary rays.

(iv) Wooden beams should be sawn in such a manner that they do not contain pith in their cross-section. To achieve this, the timber is first sawn through pith into two halves.

(v) Conversion of timber is done by sawing in following manner:

1. Ordinary sawing. It is also known as flat, slab, or Bastered sawing. The saw cuts are almost tangential to the rings. The cuts go right through the cross-section of the timber piece. The method is most easy, method of sawing. The wastage of timber in this case is minimum. In this case sap wood shrinks much more than the central part of the heart wood. This makes wooden planks thin at the edges and thick in the middle. Warped timber planks are also shown in Fig. 8.2 itself.

2. Quarter sawing. This type of sawing is shown in Fig. 8.3 (A). Saw cuts are given at right angles to each other. This method also envolves least wastage of the useful timber.

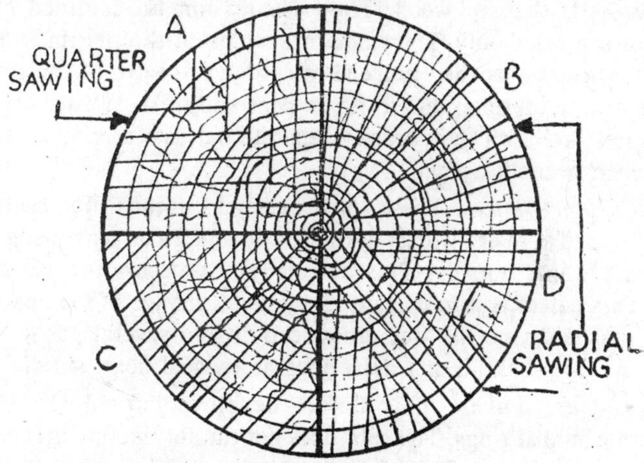

Fig. 8.3. Quarter and Radial sawing.

3. Tangenial sawing. In this sawing saw cuts are given tangental to annual rings and at rightangles to medullary rays. All the cuts meet each other at right angles. Due to the cutting of the medullary rays, the timber cut sections become weaker.

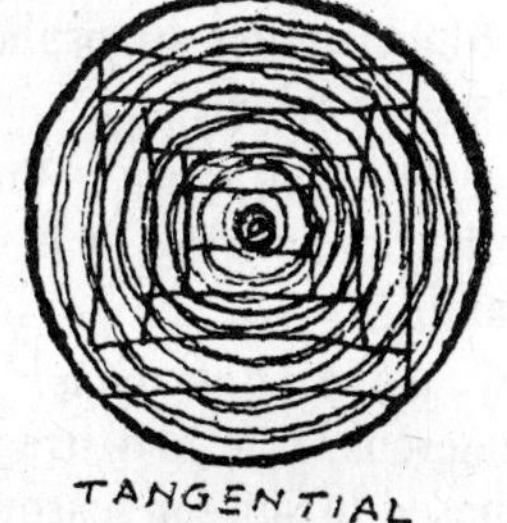

Fig. 8.4.

4. Radial sawing. The saw cuts are given parallel to medullary rays and perpendicular to the annullar rings. The sections obtained by this method of sawing shrink at a uniform rate and hence warping tendency is less. The method is used for conversion of hard timber. This method is quite difficult to adopt.

8.9. Defects in Timber

The defects that usually occur in the timber may be classified into two categories as follows:

1. Defects that develop during growth of the tree.
2. Defects that develop after felling the tree.

1. Defects that develop during growth of tree The defects that come under this category have been briefly discussed as follows:

(i) Shakes. This is most serious type of defect in timber. These are sort of cracks which partly or completely separate the fibres of wood. A shake is nothing, but separation of the timber along the grains. Shakes may be of several types.

(*a*) *Star shakes.* These are radial cracks or splits that extend from bark towards the sap wood. They usually ramain confined upto the plane of sap wood only. The cracks are widest at the circumference and go on narrowing as they proceed towards the centre of the tree. Star shakes usually develop due to fierce heat and frost. When logs having this defect are sawn they usually separate out into a number of pieces and hence become useless.

(*b*) *Heart shakes.* These splits or cracks occur in the central part of the trees. There are widest at the centre and go on narrowing as they proceed towards outside. This defect usually occurs in over-matured trees. This defect is usually caused due to shrinkage of the heart wood. Heart shakes divide the tree cross-section into several parts. Straight running heart shake is not as serious as twisted heart shake.

(*c*) *Cup shakes.* This defect develops curved slit between successive annual rings. The split does not run for the full circumference of the annual rings. This defect usuaully develops due to unequal growth. Another possible reason for their development may be contraction of timber under atmospheric changes together with the twisting action of strong winds.

(*d*) *Ring shakes.* When cup shake defect runs for full circumference of the annual ring, it is called *ring shake*. It is more serious than cup shake.

(*e*) *Radial shakes.* They are similar to star shakes. They are numerous, fine and irregular. They usually occur when felled tree is exposed to sun for seasoning. The cracks run for a short distance from bark to-wards the centre and then follows the course of an annual ring and ultimately goes towards the pith.

(ii) Rind-galls. It is a curved swelling found on the body of the tree. They are usually caused by the growth of layers over the wounds left after the branches have been cut off in an irregular and improper manner See Fig. 8.5.

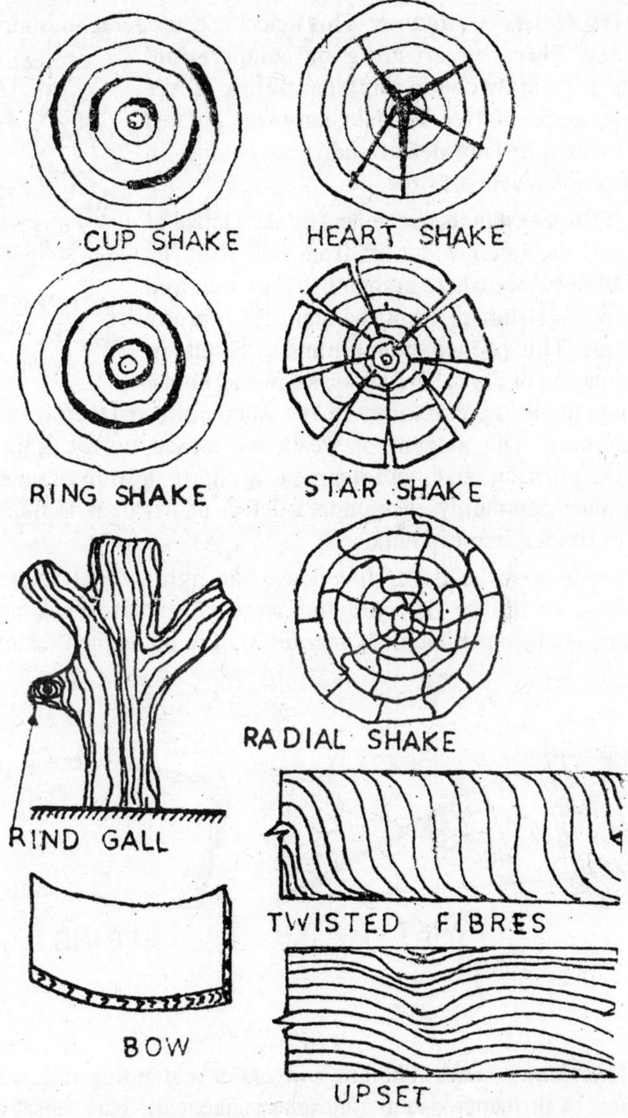

Fig. 8.5. Various defects in timbers.

(iii) Twisted fibres. They are caused by twisting of young trees constantly in one direction under the action of strong prevalent winds. Timber with twisted fibres is unsuitable for sawing. The timber having this defect is mostly used for posts and poles in an unsawn condition.

(vi) Upsets or ruptures. This defect is caused due to injury suffered by wood fibres by crushing or compression. Upsets are mainly due to improper felling of tree and exposure of tree in its young age to fast blowing wind. This defect indicates change in direction of wooden fibres.

Fig. 8.6. Timber defect.

(v) Knots. Knots are generally developed at the bases of branches cut off from the tree. The wood fibres, from where branch has been removed receives nourishment from the stem for a pretty long time. This phenomenon ultimately results in the formation of dark, hard rings, known as knots. As knots break the continuity of the wooden fibres, they form a source of weakness. The amount of weakness caused by the knot depends upon the position, size, and degree of grain distortion around it. Knot is the most commonly encountered defect of wood. It is impossible to procure timber free of knots.

Knots may be dead, live loose, or tight. Tight knots are not objectionable unless they are too large. Their presence on tension members is objectionable. It is very difficult to plane the timber at knots.

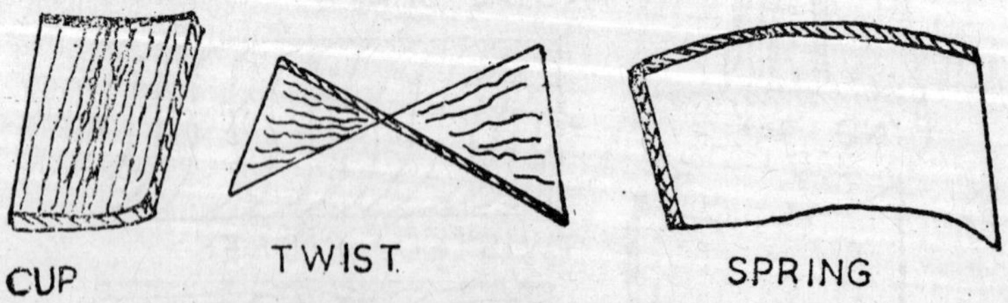

Fig. 8.7.

(vi) Wind cracks. The outer layers of a standing tree suffer from the effect of shrinkage due to atmospheric agencies. This causes cracks on the outer surface only. These cracks are known as *wind cracks*. See. Fig. 8.6.

(vii) Burls. This defect is developed, when a tree receives shock or injury in its young age. Irregular projections appear on the surface of the tree which are knwon as *Burls*.

(viii) Callus. The soft tissue or skin which covers the wounds of a tree is called *callus*.

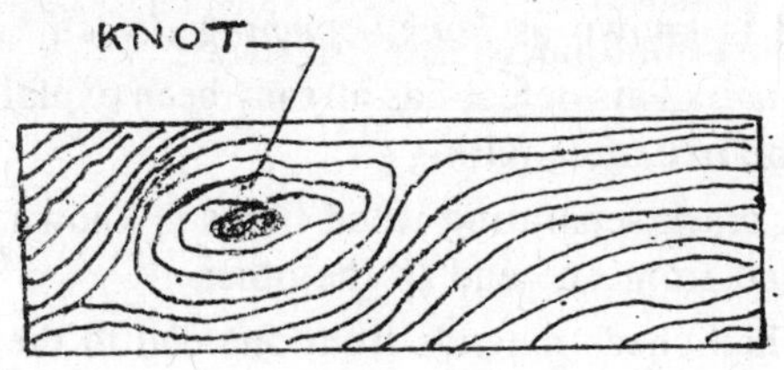

Fig. 8.8. Knot.

(ix) Coarse grain. The tree growing very fast have their annual rings quite widened. The timber having widened annual rings is known as *coarse grained timber*. Such timbers possess less strength.

(x) Dead wood. The timber obtained from dead standing trees contains dead wood. Dead wood is indicated by its reddish colour, and light weight.

(xi) Druxiness. This is the defect in which white decayed spots of timber remain concealed under healthy wood. This defect is probably caused due to access of fungi.

(xii) Foxiness. This defect is caused either due to poor ventilation during storage or due to over-maturity of the tree. This defect is indicated by red or yellow tinge in wood.

2. Defects that develop after felling the trees. Conversion of timber is done almost immediately after felling the tree. The defects that may develop after felling the tree and also during conversion and seasoning are the following.

(i) Bow. When planks of converted timber shrink and bend in curved form, in the direction of length, the defect so indicated is called, *Bow*. See Fig. 8.5.

(ii) Cup. This defect is indicated when wooden planks bend in curved form in transverse direction.

(iii) Twist. A plank which has distorted spirally along its length, the defect so formed is called *twist*. See Fig. 8.7.

(iv) Case Hardening. The upper exposed surface of timber dries at a very fast rate and as such it shrinks and is subjected to compressive stresses. The interior surface of timber, not being exposed, dries very

slowly and thus is under tension. This defect in which timber is subjected to stresses and strains due to unequal shrinkage of internal and external surfaces is known as *case hardening*

(v) Honey combing defect. Various radial as well as circular cracks develop in the internal portion of the timber due to stresses developed during drying. The timber thus assumes honey-combed texture and the defect so developed is known as *honey-combing defect.*

(vi) Radial shakes. This defect has already been explained. Radial cracks develop in the tree after felling.

(vii) Check. A crack separating wood fibres is known as a *check.* Checks do not extend from one end to the other.

(viii) Split. When check extends from one end to the other, it is known as a *split.*

(ix) Wane. This defect is denoted by the presence of original rounded surface on the prepared piece of timber.

(x) Diagonal grains. This defect may occur, if timber has been improperly sawn. This defect is indicated by diagonal marks on straight grained surface of the timber.

8.10. Stains in Timber

Some times light colured spots develop on the surface of the timber. These spots are termed as stains in timber. These spots develop very soon on light coloured timber. Timber strains may be divided into following categories.

1. Stains developed by trouble some fungi like Mould fungus and sap stain fungus.

2. Stains developed by fungus can cause decay of timber. The effect developed by such fungi is called *dote*.

3. Stains develop during growth of tree. These stains develop due to soil and frost action.

4. Stains developed due to chemical contamination.

5. Stains developed due to oxidation of wooden cells. These stains become dark due to exposure to direct sun.

Different types of stains have been briefly discussed here.

1. Mould fungi. Fungi are minute microscopic plant organisms. They attack timber only when the following two conditions are simultaneously satisfied.

(i) The moisture content of timber is above 20%

(ii) There is presence of air and warmth for the growth of fungi.

Mould fungi lives on food of tree. They do not attack wooden cells, nor they try to break them. Hence, these stains do not affect the strength characteristics of timber. These stains are generally green, brown and sometimes, even white in colour. These spots can be rubbed off by planning, brushing or sand papering.

2. Sap stain fungi. These stains develop on timber having moisture content of 27% to 30%. On soft wood, they develop blue coloured spots, but on hard wood, they develop grey coloured spots. This fungi also does not attack the timber.

3. Dote. These spots may be brown, red or grey in colour. If these spots develop due to lack of ventilation and excessive moisture content, they affect the strength of timber very badly.

4. Mineral stains. These stains mostly occur on hard type of timbers. Their colour may be brown or grey. They can be removed by bleaching action. They also do not affect strength of the timber.

5. Chemical contamination stains. These stains develop on tables used in chemical laboratories. Acidic chemicals cause red or rose coloured spots, where as Basic chemicals develop green or blue stains.

6. Iron stains. They develop by a special type of chemical contamination. These spots develop due to presence of tanin in the timber. But very few timbers have this material in sufficient amount, so as to cause iron stains.

8.11. Decay or Deases of timber

Decay of timber does not occur either due to any chemical action or due to fermenation of sap, but due to fungal action. Hence, if timber is kept away from fungi, insects, and marine borers the age of the timber can be prolonged indefinitely. The main causes of timber decay are the following.

(i) Alternate dry and wet conditions.

(ii) Defective seasoning of the timber

(iii) Fungi which is responsible for developing diseases in timber such as various type of stains and rots.

(iv) Insects such as marine bores, beetles, termites etc.

(v) Lack of ventilation.

(vi) Dark and damp conditions.

Timber rot is a sort of timber decay. During rot, disintegration of timber takes place and gases like hydrogen sulphide and carbon dioxide are generated. Timber rot may be primarily classified into two categories as follows.

(*i*) Dry rot. (*ii*) Wet rot.

(i) **Dry rot**. It is disintegration of converted timber by the harmful effects of certain fungi. This fungi feeds on wood and converts it into dry fine powder. Dry rot attack occurs, when timber is imperfectly seasoned and also when it is subjected to warm moist conditions. The confined, atmospheric conditions where there is no free circulation of fresh air, also promote dry rot. This fungi when exposed to air and sunlight dies immediately. If some timber is affected by dry rot the best remedy is to cut the affected protion and the remaining unaffected portion may be preserved by painting with copper sulphate solution. Dry rot may also set in if unseasoned timber is tarred, charred, or painted. Dry rot may be prevented by using well seasoned timber, free from sap.

Detection of Dry rot. A timber log may have been completely damged by dry rot, but still it may not show the visible signs of its being affected. It can be detected by tapping or scratching at one end and placing the ear at the other end of the log. If tapping sound is distinctly heard the log is supposed to be intact. If Dull sound is heard it is the indication of internal decay. During drilling if dry fine powder is extracted, it is also an indication of log being affected by dry dot.

Prevention of dry rot

1. Dry rot may be prevented by using well-seasoned timber free from sap.
2. The timber should be adequately ventilated by fresh air.

(*ii*) **Wet rot**. It is the decomposition of the timber caused by moisture. It is caused, if alternate wet and dry conditons prevail around the timber. This decay of timber is not caused by fungal attack. When unseasoned timbers are exposed to rain and wind, they are liable to be attacked by wet rot. The timber affected by wet rot, gets converted into greyish brown powder. Wet rot can be prevented by using well seasoned timber in exposed or under ground conditions. The exposed timber if covered with tar or paint, also helps preserve timber against moisture.

Attack of insects on timber. Decomposition of timber may be caused by certain insects also. Following are such insects.

1. Beetles.
2. Marine borers.
3. Termites or white ant.

Brief description of each type of insects has been given.

1. Beetles. These insects are also known as *borer beetles*. They make pin holes and tunnels in the timber without affecting the outer shell or cover. Timber attached by beetles may look sound till it suddenly collapses. They are very small insects and bring about the decay of the timber at a very fast rate. These insects attack sap wood of all species of hard wood.

2. Marine borers. Marine borers are generally found in hot salty sea waters. The body of these insects is very soft. They are crawling animals. Their length may very from some centimeters to as much as three meters. Teredo Navalish, Banksia and Martesia are its principle varieties. Marine borers do not eat wood, but they make holes and tunnels in timber for taking shelter. The holes bored by these insects may be as large as 2 cm diameter and depth may very from 50 mm to 80 mm. The timber which has been attacked by marine borers becomes very weak. No timber, how hard, it may be, is immune to the attack of marine borers.

3. Termites. These insects are found in very large amount in tropical and sub-tropical countries. They are popularly known as *white ants*. They do not disturb the outer cover of the timber, but they develop tunnels inside the timber in different directions. Hence, like other insects the timber pieces affected by termites may look sound, but may fail without any pre-warning. These insects do not live in exposed conditions. They form colonies in the wood. While forming colonies, they eat away the timber. Soft timbers like Mango timber, is easily attacked by these insects. Hard timbers like teak, sal, are not easily affected because they have certain chemicals in their composition the smell of which prevents attack of termites.

Methods of stacking. Before seasoning, the timber should be stacked in yards so as to protect the timber from direct sun.

Ends of logs should be protected against splitting by applying anti-splitting compositions and stacked on foundations in closed stacks in one or more layers.

***(i)* One and nine method of stacking**. This method of stacking timber is most suitable for moderately heavy coniferous sleepers in hot climates and for heavy timbers in moist climates. For reference see Fig, 8.9.

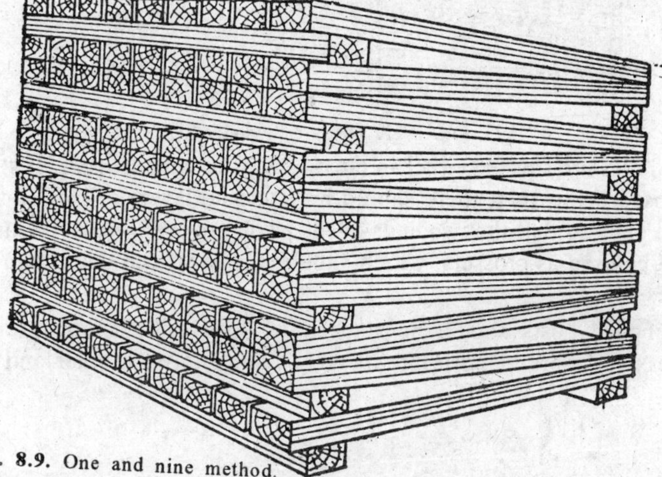

Fig. 8.9. One and nine method.

(ii) **Close crib method**. This method of stacking timber is shown in Fig. 8.10. This method allows reduced air circulations and thus slows down the pace of seasoning. This method is recommended for stacking heavy structural timbers like sal in hot and dry localities.

(iii) **Open crib method**. It is just a little modification of close crib method as provision is made to allow more air circulations. Its is more akin to the one and nine method in its effects. Stacks of not more than 100 sleepers are recommended.

Fig. 8.10. Close crib method.

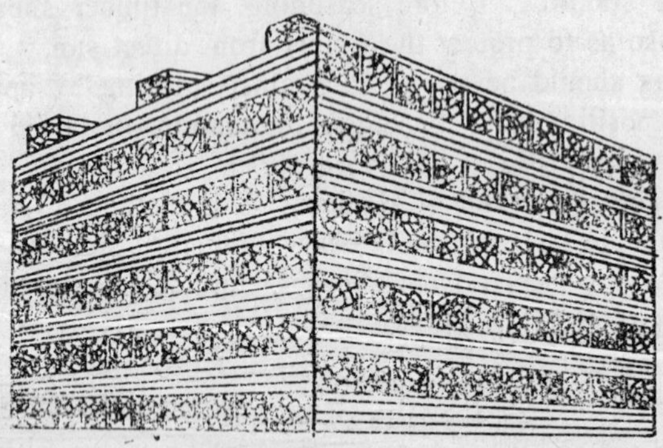

Fig. 8.11. Open crib method.

Poles are stocked either in closed, heaps or with crossers. If stacked in closed heaps then there should be alternate layers of batt ends and of top ends so that the two ends of the stock are level. Poles themselves could be used as crossers, which should not be spaced more than three metres.

Fence Posts should be stacked in open crib fashion in which successive layers of posts are at right angles to each other and there

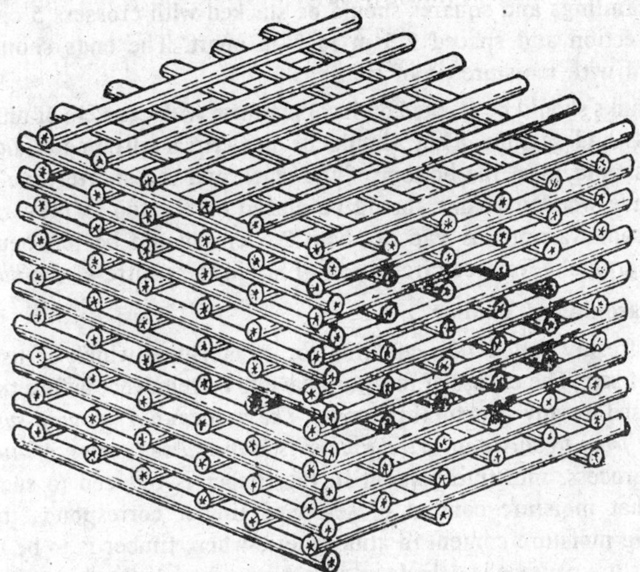

Fig. 8.12. Stocking with crossers.

is a gap of about 8 cm between adjacent posts in the same layer, c/c distance between crossers should not exceed 1.5 m and the height of stack should not exceed 3 m.

Horizontal stacking of sawn timber is done on vertical pillars of treated timber, brick masonry or cement concrete 30 cm square and 30 cm to 45 cm high pillars. The pillars are spaced 1.2 m c/c both along length and breadth of the stack. Long beams made of strong timbers of 10 cm × 10 cm cross-section are placed on Foundation pillars to form a frame work for stacking timber.

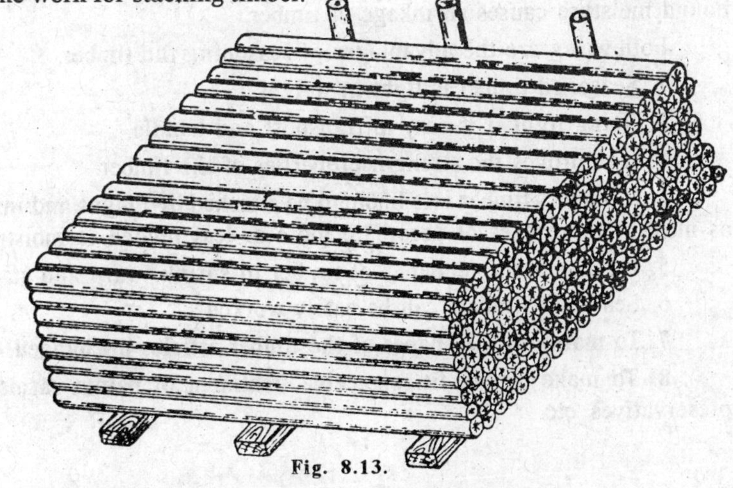

Fig. 8.13.

Scantlings and squares should be stacked with crossers 5 cm × 4 cm in section and spaced 2.5 m to 3 m apart. The ends should be protected with moisture proof coatings.

Planks should be stacked on level platform with crossers of uniform thickness and section. They should be in vertical alignment. Longer planks should form the bottom of the stack and the shorter one's the top. Heavy wooden beams should be placed on the top to prevent top layers from warping. A gap of about 2.5 cm should be left between adjoining planks for free circulation of air in the centre of the stock.

8.12. Seasoning of Timber

A freshly felled tree contains lot of moisture which is usually inform of sap. The excess of moisture have to be removed, before timber can be used for any structural purposes. *The process of removing surplus moisture from freshly converted timber is known a seasoning of timber.* In this process, moisture content in the timber is reduced to such an extent that moisture content of seasoned timber corresponds to the prevailing moisture content in atmosphere, where timber is to be used. The moisture content is calculated as a percentage of the dry weight of the wood. If timber is having moisture content less than the moisture content in the environment, it will absorb moisture from air. Seasoned timber should be protected from exposure to rain and excessively high humid conditions.

Moisture in timber can be present either in the cell cavities or in the cell walls. The former moisture is known as free moisture and latter one as bound moisture. When timber containing moisture is exposed to atmosphere, free moisture is lost first. When free moisture is completely removed, it is known as *fibre saturation point.* After this any loss of bound moisture causes shrinkage of timber.

Followiing are the advantages of seasoning the timber.

1. Seasoned timber is light in weight.
2. Being light it is easy to transport and handle.
3. It improves the strength properties of the timber.
4. It renders timber less liable to be attacked by fungus and insects as most of the causes of decay are more or less related to moisture.
5. It reduces the tendency of timber to shrink, warp and stack.
6. Seasoned timbers can be easily worked.
7. To maintain the shapes of the timber articles unchanged.
8. To make timber fit to receive treatment of paints varnishes, preservatives etc.

Methods of seasoning the timber

Methods of seasoning timber may be divided into two categories.

1. Natural seasoning. 2. Artificial seasoning.

1. Natural seasoning. In this method timber logs are sawn into planks or other marketable sizes immediately after felling the tree. The sawn timber is stacked under covered shed. Sawn timber is stacked in such a way that sufficient space is left around each sawn piece, so that free circulation of air may take place without any difficulty. Timber pieces may be stacked horizontally or vertically. *But horizontal stacking arrangement is the most common method.* The plateform, where stacks is to be erected should be raised from the adjoining ground by at least about 30 cm. The stack is prepared by laying layers of sawn pieces in cross-wise direction in alternate layers. Length of the stack is equal to length of timber pieces. *Width and height of the stack are restricted to about 1.5 m and 3 m respectively.*

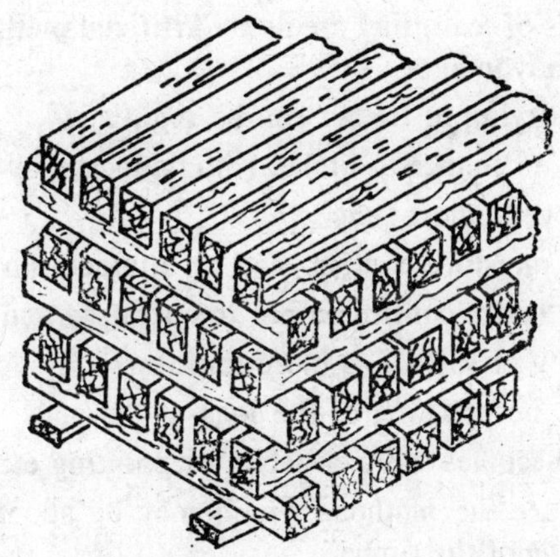

Fig. 8.14. Stock of Sawn Timber.

A number of such stacks may be constructed under the same shed. Minimum distance between adjacenet stacks should be kept about 60 cm. This method of seasoning is also called air seasoning. Natural air remains circulating around each piece of the stack and in due coarse of time, which depends upon the climatic conditions and the type and size of the timber, seasoning is brought about.

Advantages of Natural seasoning

1. No skilled supervision is necessary.
2. It is simple and cheap method of seasoning the timber.

3. Thick timber sections can be successfully seasoned only by air seasoning.

Disadvantages of Natural seasoning

1. As process depends upon natural air, no control can be exercised over it.
2. It is very slow as it may take months time depending upon climatic conditions and also on size and type of timber.
3. Seasoning may not be uniform and even.
4. Since ends dry rapidly, the timbers seasoned by this method may have ends split.
5. Moisture conetnt may not be brought to the desired level.
6. If proper precautions are not taken, the timber may be attacked by fungi and insects, during the process of seasoning.
7. It requires very large space.

Artificial seasoning

To over come the short comings of natural method of seasoning, artificial methods of seasoning are used. Artificial methods of seasoning have following advantages.

1. Rate of drying of timber can be regulated.
2. There is no chance to timber being attacked by fungi or insects.
3. It takes very short time.
4. Desired moisture content may be attained during seasonings.
5. There is better control on air, temperature and humidity.
6. Seasoning of surface is more uniform.
7. There is no splitting of the logs at the ends.
8. Timber becomes more suitable for painting etc.

Following are the methods which may be adopted to carry out artificial seasoning of the timber.

1. Water seasoning.
2. Boiling.
3. Kiln seasoning.
4. Chemical seasoning.
5. Electrical seasoning.

Brief description of each artificial method has been given here.

1. Water seasoning. In this method of seasoning, logs of timber to be seasoned are kept wholy immersed in water. It is preferable to immerse the logs is running water. Care should be taken to see that timber logs do not remain partly immersed. Thicker or larger ends of the logs are kept pointing towards the up-stream side. It is claimed that sap, sugar, gum etc. are leached out of wood. If timber logs are maintained in water for a period of about 2 to 4 weaks. Now timber is taken out of water and allowed to dry in free air. This method is comparatively quick and renders timber less liable to warp and shrink. Any organic material contained in the sap is also removed. This method however weakens the timber and makes it brittle.

2. Boiling seasoning. In this method, the timber is immersed in water and water is then boiled. After 3 to 4 hours of boiling the timber is taken out and allowed to dry slowly in free air. In this method timber may be exposed to steam in stead of boiling water. This method although proves costly, but period of seasoning is considerably reduced.

3. Kiln seasoning. This method of seasoning is carried out in air-tight chambers or ovens. Converted timber pieces are stacked inside the chamber such that spaces are left for free circulation of air. Now air, fully saturated with moisture and heated to about 40°C is forced inside the chamber. The circulating air of controlled humidity takes up the moisture from the timber and seasons it. Saturated circulating air prevents evaporation from the surfaces of timber pieces. Heated air, gradually enters the inside of the timber pieces and moisture content a gradually reduced. If required, the temperature may be further raised and maintained till the desired degree of moisture content is reached.

Kiln used for seasoning may be of two types namely *stationary kiln* and *progressive kiln*.

Stationary kiln consists of only one compartment which contains all the fitments which are essential for exercising close control on humidity and temperature. Stacks of converted timber are constructed in the chamber and after seasoning, they have to be dismentaled and seasoned timber taken out of chamber.

In progressive kiln, individual timber logs or stacks of timber to be seasoned are made to move or travel from one end of the kiln to the other and in doing so the timber gets seasoned. This kiln consists of various zones of temperature and humidity. As the timber stacks move from one end of the kiln to the other they are subjected to various temperatures and humidity conditions, most commensurate for the seasoning of timber. This kiln seasoning is adopted only when seasoning has to be done on a very large scale. If proper control on this kiln is not maintained, seasoning of timber may not take place, up to the desired degree of moisture content.

In kiln seasoning effective control on circulating air, temperatture and relative humidity, is very important.

4. Chemical seasoning. In this method, the timber to be seasoned in first immersed in salt solution and then seasoned in the ordinary way.

In this method the interior surface of timber dries in advance of exterior surface and hence, chances of development of external cracks are greately reduced. This methods of seasoning is also known as *salt seasoning*.

5. Electrical seasoning. This is the most quick method of seasoning. High frequency A.C. current is used in this method. When current is passed through green timber, it experiences very little resistances. This resistance to electrical current increases as timber dries. Increased resistance also leads to increase in temperature and thus seasoning of timber is carried out. This method is not commercially adopted as, it is very costly.

8.13. Preservation of Timber

In order to protect the timber structure from attacks of fungi and insects their preservation is essential. Preservation prolongs the life and durability of timber structures. Preservation of timber consists of some sort of treatment given to the surface of the timber. A good preservative should posses the following properties.

(i) It should be cheap, durable, unaffected by light and heat, non-inflammable and easily available.

(ii) Its smell should not be very objectionable and its covering capacity should be large.

(iii) It should be safe for the persons and should not affect strength characteristic of the timber.

(iv) It should be quite effective in killing fungi, insects etc.

(v) It should offer high resistance to moisture.

(vi) Its penetrating power into the wood fibres should be high.

(vii) It should not disfigure the surface of the timber.

Coaltar, oil paints, creosote oil, certain chemicals and Ascu treatment are the usual preservatives most commonly used.

Methods of preservation of timber. The methods which are commonly used for the preservation of timber are the following:

1. Charring.
2. Tarring.
3. Painting.
4. Creosoting.
5. Wolman's salt
6. Ascu-treatment.
7. Vacuum-Pressure process.
8. Hot and cold process.
9. Seasoning of the timber.

1. Charring. It is a rather very old and crude method of preservation of timber. No preservative is used in it. The timber to be charred is firstly kept wet for 1/2 to 1 hours and then burnt to a depth of about 15 mm and cooled with water. This process is called the *charring*. Due to burning, a coal layer is formed on the surface and it is this layer which performs preservative function. This layer is not affected by moisture, fungi, or white ants. This method may be adopted for preserving lower ends of posts of timber.

2. Tarring. This method consists of applying a layer of hot tar on the surface. This treatment is generally given to embedded ends of the posts or surfaces of timber coming directly in contact with lime concrete and masonry. This treatment is not given on the exposed surfaces as it spoils the appearance.

3. Painting. Paint as applied to the timber not only makes it beautiful to look, but also acts as a preservative. Paints like solignm paints prevent any white ant attack, on the timber.

4. Crosoting. Creosote is an oil obtained by distillation of Tar. The process of applying, creosote oil to the timber surface, is known as *creosoting. The method of preservation is mostly adopted in case of poles, piles, railway sleepers etc.*. Creosoting is generally done under pressure.

5. Wolman's salts. Mixture of *creosote oil* and *sodium Fluoride is known as Wolman's salt*. It is soluble in water. It does not contain any sulphur and as such does not leave any stains on the treated timber. This treatment can eliminate certain type of fungi. The timber can be immediately painted or varnished after the application of Wolman's salt. Treatment of timber with zinc chlorite, sodium Fluoride, magnesium, sileo Flouride or copper sulphate renders the timber immune from attacks of Fungi.

6. Ascu-treatment. This treatment was first developed by *Forest Research Institute Dehradun (India)*. It is available in powder form. Its composition is as follows.

1. Hydrated arsenic pentoxide ($As_2 O_5 2H_2O$) 1 part
2. Copper sulphate ($CuSO_4. 5H_2O$) 3 parts
3. Pottassium Dichromate ($K_2Cr_2O_7. 2H_2O$) 4 parts

Ascu solution is prepared by mixing six parts of this powder to 100 parts of water by weight. The solution thus prepared is sprayed on the timber surface to be preserved. This treatment gives very effective protection against white ants. The surface treated by this solution can be waxed, varnished, polished and painted. Timber to be treated, may even be immersed in the Ascu-solution. But timber should be allowed to dry for 3 weaks to 6 weaks before it is used. This solution is colourless.

7. Vaccum-pressure process. It is considered one of the best preservative treatment. This method is adopted, when maximum absoprtion of the preservative is to be achieved.

This process may be further subdivided into following two categories :

(i) Bethel or full cell process and

(ii) Empty cell or Rueping process.

(i) Bethal process. In this method a closed cylinder having a tight door is used. Timber to be treated with preservative is put in the cylinder and at least 56 cm. of mercury vaccum is created in the cylinder after closing its door, tight. During this, air and moisture get removed from the timber cells. Now after a lapse of about half an hour since vaccum was created, preservative is added in the cylinder with the help of vaccum pump. Now vaccum pump is stopped and 3.5 to 12.5 kg/cm^2 anti-siphonic pressure is created. The preservative gets injected deep into the timber because of this pressure. The pressure is finally released and a vaccum of 38 to 56 cm again developed and maintained for about 15 minutes. This vaccum is created to with draw the excessive creosote from the timber.

(ii) Rueping process. In this case, timber to be treated with preservative is stacked in a closed strong cylinder and subjected to an air pressure of 1.75 to 5.0 kg/cm^2 depending upon the sap content of the timber. Now preservation solution is introduced in the cylinder and pressure in the cylinder is maintained varying from 5 kg/cm^2 to 12.5 kg/cm^2. The pressure is lastly released. This causes considerable amount of preservative to expel out from the cells of the timber. This process is comparatively cheaper than Bethel's process. This method is also known as *Empty cell process.*

8. Hot and Cold process. In this process the timber is stacked, in the tank and cold preservative solution, usually creosote, is run into the tank, till timber stacks get completely submerged. The preservative is now heated to a temperature of about 90°C and maintained at this temperature for some time. The preservative and timber are then allowed to cool. During heating, air in timber cells expands and gets expelled. While cooling, the residual air in cells contracts and causes partial vacuum which causes the preservative to be sucked in to the tinber. It is also known as *open tank process.*

9. Seasoning of the timber. Proper seasoning of the timber is the best preservative. If timber is not properly seasoned no preservative will be able to protect the timber from attacks of certain insects or fungi. Improperly seasoned timber if covered with some paint of preservative would confine the moisture in the timber which will cause decay or decomposition of timber. Hence, all the preservatives described above prove successful only, if they are used on properly seasoned timber.

Indian timbers can be classified as non-refractory timbers, moderately refractory timbers and highly refractory timbers depending upon the ease with which they can be seasoned. Seasoning may be natural or artificial. It is said that perfect seasoning is the most effective means of preservation. Proper damp proofing and providing free circulation of air around the built in portions of Timber are essential for the preservation of timber used.

8.14. Qualities of Good Timber

Following are the qualities of good timber.

1. A good timber should be hard and durable.
2. It should be capable of resisting the actions of fungi, chemicals and physical agencies.
3. The fibres of the timber should be straight and compact.
4. The timber should be free from knots, twists, upsets, burls shakes, flaws etc.
5. Its colour should be dark. It should be obtained preferably from heart wood. Colour should be uniform.
6. It should be properly seasoned.
7. Its freshly cut surface should smell sweet.
8. Its weight should be heavy.
9. It should be easily workable. It should not clog the teeth of saw and should be capable of being easily planned.
10. Timber should be tough *i.e.*, it should be capable of resisting shocks.
11. It should be able to withstand the weathering affects.
12. It should be strong enough to withstand bending, direct and shear effects efficienctly.
13. A clear ringing sound should be emitted by the timber when struck. Heavy dull sound indicates decayed timber.
14. It should offer adequate fire resistance.
15. It should be elastic.

8.15. Fire-resistance of Timber

During fires, structural elements made of timber get ignited and get rapidly destroyed. They even add to the intensity of fire. But timber used in heavy sections may provide sufficient fire-resistance, because timber is bad conductor of heat.

The timbers may be classified as refractory timbers and non-refractory timbers. Non-resinous timbers do not easily catch fire and as such, are termed as refractory timbers. Teak and sal are the examples of such timbers. Timbers containing resinous substances readily catch fire and hence are termed as non-refractory timbers. Deodar, chir, fir etc., are the examples of such timbers.

Timbers may be rendered more fire resistant by adopting following methods.

(i) Sir ABEL'S Method. The surface of timber to be treated is cleaned and coated with a dilute solution of sodium silicate. Above it a cream like paste of slaked fat lime is applied and finally a coat of concentrated solution of silicate of soda is applied. This process has been quite successful for making the timbers fire-resistant.

(ii) Application of chemicals. In this method certain chemical solutions are used for coating the timber. Two coats of 2% solution of borax or sodium arsenate are found to be quite effective in rendering the timbers fire-resistant. Besides, this, Ammonium sulphate, Ammonium chloride, Ammonium phosphate, Zine chloride, Sodium silicate, Pottasium silicate are the other chemicals which may be used in spray form to render timber fire-resistant.

8.16. Market Forms of Timber

After felling the tree, the timber is converted into commercial marketable sizes. Market forms of timber may be following :

1. Battens. These are small sectioned timber pieces. No cross-sectional dimension exceeds 5 cm in battens.

2. Logs. Trunk of trees left after removing all the branches is known as *log*.

3. Baulk. It is roughly squared swan log. One of the cross-sectional dimensions exceeds 5 cm while the others exceeds 20 cm.

4. Planks. It is a timber piece, having parallel sides. Its thickness is always less than 5 cm and width always more than 5 cm.

5. Board. It is a timber pieces with parallel sides, whose thickness is always less than 5 cm and width always more than 15 cm.

6. Deal. It is again a parallel sided pieces, whose thickness varies from 5 cm to 10 cm and width does not exceed 23 cm.

7. Scantlings. These are timber pieces, whose breadth and thickness are always more than 5 cm, but their length is always less than 20 cm. These are miscellaneous cut stuff.

8. Pole. It is a log having its diameter not more than 20 cm. It is also known as *spar*.

8.17. Veneers

Veneers are thin sheets of timber of very superior quality. They are obtained by rotating wooden logs of very high quality timber against a

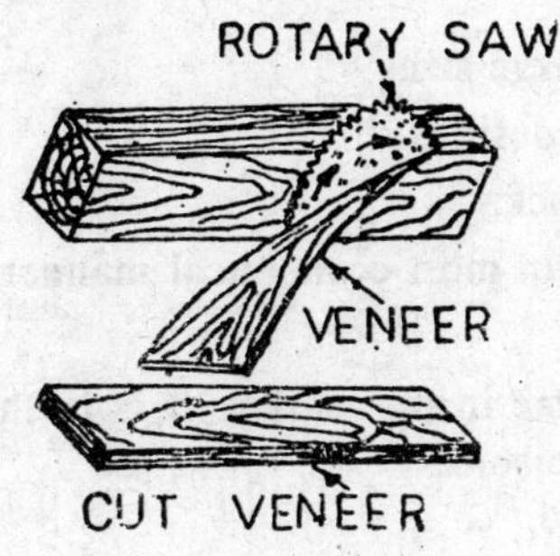

Fig. 8.15.

sharp knife of rotary cutter. Thickness of veneer may very from 0.4 mm to as much as 6 mm. or even more. After removing from parent logs, the veneers are dried in kilns to remove moisture from them. See Fig. 8.15.

Veneers are used in the manufacture of plywood batten boards and lamin boards. Veneers are peeled off from timbers like teak, sissoo, rosewood, oak, mahogany etc. The process of preparing a sheet of veneers is known as *veneering*. It may also include glueing of veneer sheets of superior quality over a base of wood of inferior quality. This process is the least expensive method of forming a decorative surface on inferior quality timbers.

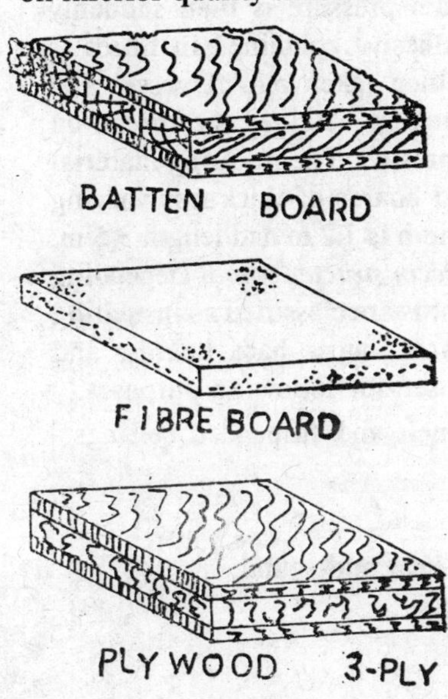

Fig. 8.16.

8.18. Plywood

Ply means thin layer. Plywood is in form of boards prepared from thin layers of wood or veneers. Veneers in plywood are taken in odd numbers. Veneers are placed one above the other with the direction of grains of successive layers at right angles to each other. All the veneers are held together with the help of adhesives. The direction of grains at right angles in successive veneers, increase the strength of the plywood both in longitudinal and transverse directions. While glueing the various veneers, pressure may also be used. The face of the plywood which has bettter finishing, is known as face and other exposed face as back of the plywood. The plywood is generally manufactured in three ply 5 ply, five ply seven ply, and so on. Thickness of three ply sheet varies from 3 mm to 5 mm. Plywood sheets are manufactured in size varying from 90 cm × 90 cm to 240 × 120 cm.

Advantages of Plywoods

1. They suffer very little expansion or shrinkage, due to variation in moisture-content.

2. They are light and available in large sizes.
3. They are available in decorative designs.
4. They are not liable to split or crack.
5. They make use of costly timbers in most economical manner.
6. They are very easy to work with.

Now a new refined plywood has come in the market. It is in the name of kitply. Kitply is not affect by moisture.

8.19. Fibre Boards

Fibre boards are manufactured from wood or other vegetable fibres. The pieces of wood, cane, or other vegetable fibres are heated in a hot water boiler. Due to boiling, wood fibres get separated. These fibers, are put in a vessel and steam is admitted in it under a pressure. The steam pressure is then suddenly increased to about 70 kg/cm^2 and this pressure is maintained for few seconds. The steam pressure is then suddenly released and in doing so, the natural adhesive contained in fibres is separated completely. These fibres are then taken out of vessel and cleaned of all superfluous gums. The fibres so obtained are spread on wire screen in forum of loose sheets and pressed. The resulting material is called the fibre board. These are rigid boards of thickness varying from 6 mm to as much as 25 mm. Their width is 1.2 m and length 3.5 m. They are also known as *pressed wood* or *reconstructed wood*. Depending upon their form and composition fibre-boards are classified as insulating boards, medium hard boards. Hard boards, super hard boards, and laminated boards. Fibre-boards may be used for following purposes.

(i) For the construction of wall panels and suspended ceilings.
(ii) To construct partitions.
(iii) In form of form works.
(iv) As insulating material against heat and sound.
(v) As table tops and for flush doors.

8.20. Impreg Timbers

Sunmica, Formica, Sungloss etc. are the examples of impreg timber. Impreg timber is nothing, but timber fully or partly covered with resin. Phenol formaldehyde is the resin most commonly used. Thin strips of wood or veneers are taken and immersed in resin. The resin fills the space between wood cells and by chemical reaction, a consolidated mass is developed. This mass is then cured at a temperature of about 150°C to 160°C.

Impreg timbers are strong, durable, good looking, and are not affected by moisture and weather conditions. They resist acidic effects and are electrically insulated.

8.21. Compreg Timbers

They are just impreg timbers except, that they are cured under pressure. Compreg timbers are more strong and durable as compared to impreg timbers.

8.22. Lamin Boards

They consists of core, made of narrow sawn timber strips 3 to 7 mm wide. Core is covered at both the faces by veneers or ply boards. Lamin boards are manufacturedin large range of sizes. Thickness of these boards varies from 10 mm to 20 mm. These boards are available up-

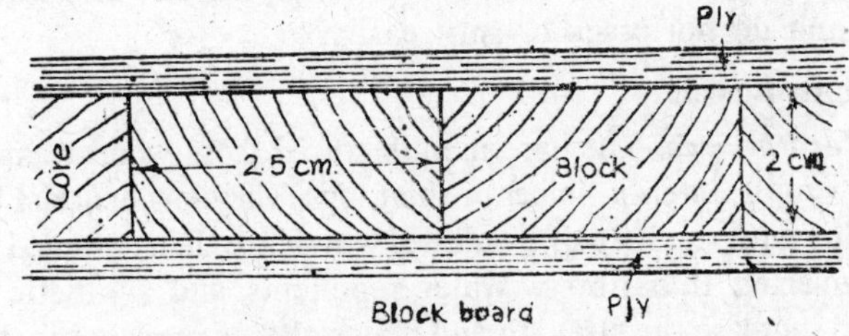

Fig. 8.17. Block board.

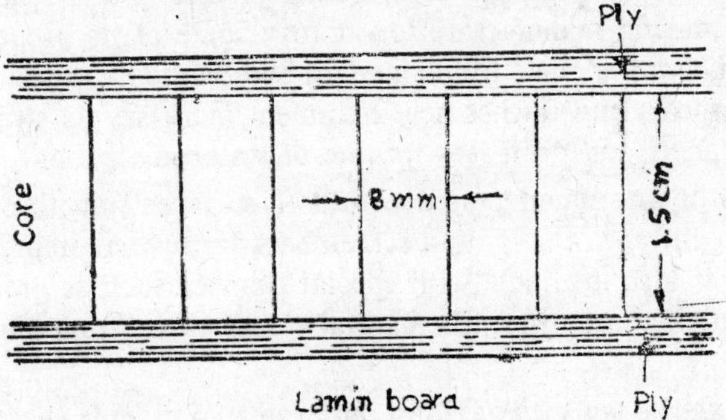

Fig. 8.18. Lamin board.

to 1.5 m in width and 2.5 m to 3 m in length. They are light and strong and do not crack or split easily. They are used for partitions ceilings, and door etc. See Fig. 8.18.

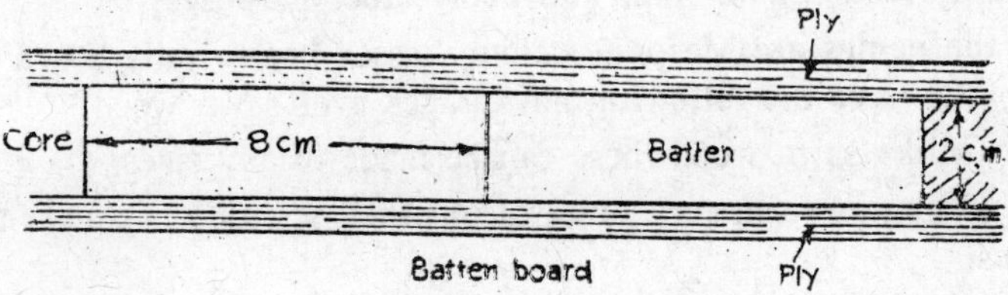

Fig 8.19. Batten board.

8.23. Block Board

They consist of core made of small timber blocks up to 25 mm thickness glued together edge to edge. Both the faces are lastly covered by ply wood of 3 mm thickness. Direction of grains of the core is at right angles to that of outer plies. These are cheaper than Lamin boards and are used for partitions and doors etc. Usual thicknesses are 12 mm to 50 mm lengths vary from 1.2 m to 2.4 m and width from 90 cm to 1.2 m.

8.24. Batten Boards

These are just like Lamin boards and block boards in construction except that core is made from timber blocks of width up to 8 cm and 2 to 3 cm thick. These boards are used for door panels table tops and other large flat surfaces. Direction of the grains of the core battens is at right angles to that of the adjacent out ply sheets. These are light and strong and do not crack or split easily.

8.25. Hard-Boards

Hard boards. They are manufactured from wood wastes obtained from saw mills, inferior timber or short logs. They raw material is converted into chips with the help of machines which are then softened with steam and converted into fibres. Water repellents and synthetic resins are added to increase the strength and material thus prepared is then pressed into boards of unifom thickness in hydraulic presses. Other materials may be added during manufacture to improve some of its properties. *Tempered hard board* is made from standard hard board by the addition of certain chemicals and further heat treatment increases its strength, abrasion resistance, and decreases its rate of water absoprtion.

Hard boards are manufactured with both surfaces smooth or one surface smooth and the other with a screen back, or reverse impression of a screen. It is also available with special finishes such as grooved, embossed, or marked into tiles. The natural colour varies from blond to dark brown.

Width of sheets is usually 1.25 m but even 1.75 m wide sheets too are available. The maximum length is 4.75 m and thickness varies from 2 mm to 20 mm.

Hard board is used for interior and exterior wall panels, ceilings, siding, table and counter tops and many other purposes.

Trade names are Masonite celotex, essex board, jolly board etc. Hard boards have the following advantages over sawn wood.

(*i*) Unlike sawn wood these can be made of any sizes.

(*ii*) Being uniform and homogeneous their strength is equal in all directions.

(*iii*) They are free from defects like shakes and knots.

(*iv*) As per requirements they can be obtained with suitable finishes like embossed perforated, wood grained, plastic faced, veneer finished or enamelled etc.

8.26. Properties of some important timbers

Properties and uses of certain important timbers have been given here.

1. Babul. It is a throny tree which has very small conical leaves. Its flowers are yellow. It is found almost in all parts of India. It can develop in sandy tracks, where available moisture for growth is usually very small. Its properties are:

(i) Its timber is strong, hard, and tough.

(vii) It is durable, but difficult to work.

(iii) Its texture is quite strong.

(iv) It is not available in large lengths.

(v) Its colour is whitish red which turns into red-brown due to exposure.

(vi) Its weight is 880 kg/m^3.

(vii) It can take very good polish.

It is used for the construction of bullock carts, tool handles, well curbs, and agriculture implements etc.

Chir. It is found in Himalyans at heights varying from 500 m to 2500 m. It is very much used in temporary wooden and low class wood works. Its properties are :

(i) It is light in weight (560 kg/m^3)

(ii) It is very easy to work and season.

(iii) Its colour is red, brown or yellow.

(iv) It is very soft and its strength properties are very weak.

3. Deodar or Diar. The trees of this timber are straight and long and have conical leaves. It is found in Himalyans at heights varying from 1000 to 3000 m. It is an important timber. It is used for railway sleepers, piles, other construction works, cheap furnitures and railway carriages. It is found in Punjab, U.P. and Himalayas. Its properties are:

(i) It weighs 560 kg/m^2

(ii) It is compact, hard durable and strong.

(iii) Its colour is yellow which becomes more and more dark due to exposure.

(iv) It is easily worked.

(v) It gives sweet smell and its timber is such as, if it has been soaked in oil.

(vi) It can be finished very smooth.

(vii) It receives varish very easily.

Sal. It is found in A.P., Maharashtra, U.P., Bihar, M.P., and Orissa. It is very good variety of timber and can be used for any purpose. Its surface can not be finished smooth and as such, it cannot be used for decorative types of works. It is mostly used for tent pegs, doors and window frames, and as wooden piles, bullies etc. Its properties are :

(i) Its colour is either light brown or yellow.

(ii) It is hard, compact and heavy type of timber (800 kg/m^3)

(iii) It is durable and strong.

(iv) It cannot be worked easily and hence, it cannot be finely polished.

(v) Its seasoning is very slow.

5. Teak. This timber is mostly found is M.P. and South India. Its leaves are broad and it is used for ship building, railway sleepers, furniture, and railway carriages. It can be used for any structural or decorative purpose. It a costly timber and hence used for costly and specilized works. Its properties are :

(i) It can be seasoned easily.

(ii) It shrinks very small.

(iii) It weighs 770 kg/m^3

(iv) Its colour is yellow to dark brown.

(v) It can be worked easily and it can be finely varnished.

(vi) Its fibres are straight.

(vii) It does not warp due to shrinkage.

(viii) It contains such resinous materials which prevent any disease from developing in this timber.

(ix) It is fire-resistant, acidic action resistant, and also white ant. resistant.

6. Shisham, Tali or Sissue. It is one of the most useful and high class timbers. It is found in Punjab, M.P. Karnataka, U.P. and Maharashtra. It is used for furnitures, ply wood, sports goods, Railway sleepers bridge piles etc. Its properties are:

(i) Its colour is dark brown, containing golden and drak brown coloured linings. Colour further darkens on exposure.

(ii) It is a heavy timber (880 kg/m^3)

(iii) It can be seasoned easily.

(iv) It can receive very high class polish.

(v) It is difficult to work.

7. Aini. It is found in A.P., Madras, Kerala, and Maharashtra. It is used for general building works, furniture, pavings etc. Its colour is yellowish brown. It is close grained and strong timber weighing about 600 kg/m^3. It can be used under water and it takes fine polish.

8. Arjun. It is mostly found in M.P. Its main use is in the form of posts, rafters, beams etc. It is dark brown, heavy timber. It weigh 870 kg/m^3. It is also a strong, durable timber.

9. Bakul. It is close-grained tough wood. Its colour is reddish brown. It is used most in the making of cabinets. It is mostly found in North India and weighs 880 kg/m^3.

10. Benteak. It is found in Maharashtra, Madras and Kerala. It is a strong timber which can be given a smooth finish. It weights 675 kg/m^3. It is used for building construction, furnitures and boat construction, etc.

11. Banyan. It is found all over India. It weights 580 kg/m^3. Its colour is brown. It is strong and durable only under water. It is mostly used for well curbs, tent poles, etc.

12. Bamboo. It is also found in most parts of this country, but its abundance is in Asam and Bengal. It is an endogenous tree. It is used for scaffolding, thatch roofs, etc.

13. Jack. It is found in coastal areas of Madras and Maharashtra. It is used for furnitures, well curbs, door panels, cabinet making. Boat construction etc. It is a compact, even grained, moderately strong, and easily workable timber. It takes good polish. It weighs 595 kg/m^3. Its colour is yellow when fresh, but darkens with age. It maintains its shape well.

14. Irul. It is found in Kerala, A.P., Maharashtra Orissa and Tamil Nadu. It is used for Railway sleepers agricultural implements, paving blocks etc. It is a hard, heavy and durable timber. It weight 835 kg/m^3. It is difficult to work and season.

15. Jarul. It is found in Assam, Bengal and Maharashtra. It is a light reddish grey coloured timber. It is durable and hard. It can be easily worked. It can be given fine finishing. It weighs 640 kg/m^3. It is used for boat building, railway carriages, scaffolding, cart making etc.

16. Kathal. It is found in A.P., Kerala, Tamil Nadu and Maharashtra. It is used for piles, doors and windows, etc. It is not attacked by white ants. It varies in colour from yellow to deep brown. It is quite heavy and hard timber. It cracks readily when exposed to sun. It is durable under water and damp conditions.

17. Laurel. It is found in A.P., Bihar, Orissa, H.P., Kerala and Madras. It is used for house construction, boat construction, structural work and railway sleepers. It is dark brown in colour. It is hard tough and strong type of timber. It is likely to crack and resists attack of dry rot. It is immune to white ant. It weighs 880 kg/m^3 and it can be given smooth finish.

18. Mahogany. It is used for furniture, pattern making, cabinet work etc. It is found at Western Ghats. It is reddish brown in colour. It is easily worked. It takes good polish; it is durable under water. It weighs 720 kg/m^3 after seasoning. It is hard and tough timber. It contains resinous oil to save itself from insect attack.

19. Mango. This tree is found in practically all over India. It is used for cheap furniture, packing boxes, cabinet work, panels for doors and windows, etc. Its colour is deep grey; it is easy to work. It is moderately strong and weighs 655 kg/m^3.

20. Mulberry. It is found in Punjab. It is used for baskets, hockey sticks, sports, and furniture. It is brown in colour. It is tough, elastic and strong. It can be easily seasoned. It takes up clean finish. It can be easily turned and carved. It weighs 650 kg/m^3.

21. Oak. It is used most for sports goods. Its colour is yellowish brown. It is strong and durable timber. It weighs 865 kg/m^3. It possesses straight silvery grains.

22. Palm. It is found all over India. It is used for furniture, roof covering, rafters, joists etc. It is strong durable and fibrous timber. It weighs 1040 kg/m^3. It contains ripe timber in the outer crust. The colour of ripened timber is dark brown.

23. Pine. White pine is soft, while other coloured pines are quite hard and tough. It decays easily when comes in contact with soil. It is heavy and coarse grained timber. White pine is light and straight grained. It is used for pattern making, frames for doors and windows, paving material, etc. White pine is used in the manufacture of matches.

24. Samul. It is also found all over India. It is used for packing cases, match industry, well curbs and cheap furnitures. It is loose grained, inferior quality wood, which is white in colour. It weighs 450 kg/m^3.

25. Toon. It is found maximum in Assam. It is used for furniture, packing boxes, cabinet making, etc. Its colour is reddish brown. It can be easily worked. It weights 530 kg/m^3.

26. Tamarind. It is also found all over India. It is used of well curbs, sugar mills, carts, brick burning, agricultural implements, etc. It is a fruit giving tree. Its colour is dark brown. It is very knotty and durable timber. It is beautiful tree for avenues and gardens. It develops very slowly. It weight 1280 kg/m^3.

27. Sundri. It is mostly found in Bengal. It is used for boat making, piles, poles, tool handles, carriage shafts etc. It is dark red in colour. It is hard, tough, difficult to work and season. It weighs 960 kg/m^3. It is elastic, strong, durable and close-grained timber.

28. Spruce. It is immune to marine borers attack. It also resists decay. It can warp, twist and shrink. It weighs 480 kg/m^3. It is used for piles under water, aeroplanes, etc.

29. Siris. It is very much found in North India. It is used for well curbs in salty water, beams, posts, furnitures etc. It weighs 1040 kg/m^3. It is dark brown in colour. It is hard, durable and difficult to work.

30. Haldu. It is broad leaved tree. It is used for furnitures and agricultural implements. Its can be used for making cabinets and other decorative works. Its colour is yellow which turns grey with age. It is hard durable and easily seasonable timber. It weighs 670 kg/m^3. Its fibres are symmetrical and it is easily workable timber.

31. Kail. It is found in Himalyans right from Bhutan to Afganisthan at height varying from 2000 m to 4000 m. Its trees remain ever green. It is used for railway sleepers, construction of houses, match sticks. Its colour is light brown. It can be easily seasoned, and its fibrès are well bound.

QUESTIONS

1. Draw a cross-section of an exogeneous tree and show its various parts. Give brief description of each shown part.
2. (*a*) Explain the advantages and uses of Timber.
   (*b*) How trees can be classified?
3. How a matured tree is felled? How felled tree is converted into marketable sizes?
4. (*a*) Explain the various defects in Timber.
   (*b*) Enumerate the characteristic of a good timber.
5. Explain the term seasoning of timber. Explain various methods of timber seasoning?
6. What are the common defects in timber? How would you find whether an apparently sound log of timber is hollow inside?
7. (*a*) Describe the various methods for the preservation of timber.
   (*b*) What are the common uses of timber in building industry?
8. (*a*) Explain dry rot and wet rot. How can they be prevented?
   (*b*) What is ply wood. How is it manufactured?

9. (*a*) Name the marketable sizes of the timber. Also give the limiting dimensions of each size.

   (*b*) Sketch Heart shake, cup shake, warp, Rindgall, Knot, in the timber.

10. (*a*) What are fibre-boards? How are they manufactured? What are their uses?

    (*b*) Describe the process of conversion of timber

    (*c*) What are Knots? How are they classified?

9

PAINTS, VARNISHES, WHITE WASH,. AND DISTEMPERS

9.1. Object of paints

Paint performs following functions:

1. It protect wood from decaying.

2. It prevents corrosion of metals.

3. It protects the surface from harmful effects of atmospheric agencies.

4. It gives decorative and attractive appearance to the surfaces.

5. It renders surface hygienically safe and clean.

9.2. Characteristics of an Ideal Paint.

1. The paint should be cheap.

2. It should have good covering power. In other words it should be able to cover maximum area of the surface with minimum quantities of the paint.

3. It should be easy and harmless to the user.

4. The painted surface should dry neither too slowly nor too rapidly.

5. It should retain its original colour for along time.

6. When applied, the paint should form a thin uniform film on painted surface.

7. Atmospheric agencies should not be able to affect the painted surface.

8. The paint should form a hard and durable coat on the painted surface.

9. The painted surface should posses attractive and decorative pleasing appearance.

10. The paint should not peel off from painted surface.

11. The painted surface should not show any cracks.

12. It should be good fire and moisture resistant.

9.3. Constituents of an Oil Paint or Oil borne paints

An oil paint essentially consists of the following ingredients

1. A base.
2. An inert extender or filler.
3. A vehicle or carrier.
4. A drier.
5. A solvent or thinner.
6. A colouring pigment.

Each of the ingredient has been explain as follows:

1. Base. It is a solid substance, in a fine state of division. It forms the bulk of a paint. Its main function is to provide an opaque coating which would hide the surface to be painted. It makes the coating film of paint, resistant against abrasion and prevents formation of shrinkage cracks in the film. White lead, red lead, zinc white, iron oxide, titanium white, aluminium powder and lithophone are the most commonly used bases. Properties and conditions of each type of base have been discussed ahead.

2. An inert extender or filler. Barium sulphate (Baryte) silica, lithophone, whiting, charcoal, gypsum silicate of magnesia or alumina etc. are the usual inert extenders. They are added in the paint to reduce the cost and also to modify some of the properties of the paints. They reduce weight of the paint and render paint more durable. They should not be used in excess amount as other wise paint may lose its original character and may become weak.

3. Vehicle or carriers. They are liquid substances which hold solid ingredients of the paint like bases extenders, colouring pigments in liquid suspension. They help in spreading the paint evenly on the surface and act as binders for the other paint ingredients to adhere to the surface being painted. Refined linseed oil is most commonly used as a vehicle in oil paints. Besides linseed oil, tung oil, poppy oil, nut oil may also be used, but under specific circumstances only. Properties and uses of various vehicles have been discussed ahead.

4. Driers These are metallic compounds which when added to the paint in small quantities accelerate the process of drying of the paint. Driers absorb oxygen from atmosphere and transfer, to the linseed oil vehicle, and accelerate the process of drying. Litharge, Manganese dioxide, lead acetate and cobalt are the usual driers, out of which litharge is most commonly used. Driver have a tendency to affect the colour of the paint and also to destroy the elasticity of the paint. Hence, they should not be used in excess amount. They are not used at all in final finishing coat of the paint.

Red lead may also be used as a drier, but it is less effective than litharge. It is used only when its addition does not effect the tint of the paint.

Manganese sulphate is also used as a drier, but its use is advocated with zinc paints only, so as to avoid the risk of discolouration of a lead drier. Manganese sulphate should be mixed very carefully, otherwise, spots will be formed on the painted surface. Various patented driers are also available in the market in form of soluble driers or paste driers. The soluble driers are compounds of metals such as lead, cobalt, manganese etc. dissolved in linseed oil or some other volatile liquid. Paste driers are also compounds of lead, cobalt, manganese etc., but mixed with inert fillers such as whiting, barytes etc. and ground in linseed oil.

5. Solvents or thinners. The function of a thinner is to reduce the consistency of the paint, so that it can be easily applied on the surface. It evaporates after the paint has been applied to the surface. It also helps the paint in, its penetration into the surface to be painted. Turpentine oil is the most commonly used solvent or thinner. Petroleum spirits and naphtha, are also very good solvents, but they are used under specific circumstances only. As turpentine oil is very easily affected by whether, it should not be used and if it has to be used, it should be used in minimum amount for exterior works.

6. Colouring pigments. These are colouring agents which are used to develop desired shade of the paint. For white, black and other very dark shades, the base itself of the paint is chosen in such a way that, it will develop the colour of the paint through base itself. In case of other shades, colouring pigments of desired shade are mixed with the paint. In order to obtain the desired colour of the paint, two or more pigments may have to be used in combination also. Colouring pigments may be divided into following five divisions.

(i) Precipitates. Prussian blue, chrome green, chrome yellow etc.

(ii) Natural earth. Umbers, ochres, iron oxide etc.

(iii) Calcined colours. Lamp black, carbon black, red lead, Indian red etc.

(iv) Lake colours. These are prepared by discolouring China clay, barytes, suitable dyes, etc.

(v) Metallic powders. Aluminium powder, bronze powder, copper powder, zinc powder etc.

Various colouring pigments to develop a particular colour are as follows:

Blue. Indigo, prussion blue, cobalt blue, ultramarine blue.

Brown. Burnt umber, raw umber, burnt sienna.

Black. Lamp black, ivory black, graphite, vegetable black.

Green. Chrome green, copper sulphate, emerald green, green earth.

Yellow. Chrome yellow, raw sienna, yellow ochre, zinc chromate, barium chromate.

Red. Carmine, red lead, Indian red, vermillion red, venetian red.

9.4. Various types of bases for paints

1. White lead. Out of all the bases of paints, it is the cheapest base and is thus in most common use for ordinary painting works. It is available in market both in powder form and stiff paste form. Paste is made by mixing white lead with linseed oil. It is dense, permanent and water proof. It possesses good spreading and binding power. It is very poisonous when exposed to atmosphere, contaminated with sulpher. It is blackened. It is most suitable for wooden surfaces and not used for iron surfaces as, it does not offer protection against rusting.

2. Red lead. It is lead oxide and is available in market either inform of powder or stiff paste ground in linseed oil. It is quite suitable for painting iron surfaces and for providing a priming coat to wood surfaces. As it solidifies in a short time with linsed oil, it can be used as a drier.

Lead based paints are excellent moisture resisting and have good bond with the surface. These paints fade mostly by checking and cracking of the paint film.

3. Zinc white or zinc oxide. Zine white is an oxide of zinc and forms the base of all the zinc paints. It is available in powder as well as in paste form, made by grinding with linseed oil. This paint has good hiding and spreading power. This paint is not poisonous and neither, it is affected by sulpher vapour charged atmosphere. It is costlier than lead white paint and is less durable and workable than it. Its film is very hard and brittle and has tendency to develop surface cracks.

4. Iron oxide. Iron oxide forms the base of all the iron paints. It is exclusively used for the priming coat on iron or structural steel. The tint of paint varies from yellowish brown to black. It mixes readily with the vehicle oil and is quite cheap and durable. It is effective in preventing rusting of iron surfaces.

5. Titanium white. This material possesses intense opacity. It is chemically inert and not affected by heat or light. It is used as under coat, in case of enamel paints. It is non-poisonous and provides a thin transparent film.

6. Antimony white. It is very nearly similar to titanium white.

7. Lithophone. Lithophone is a mixture of barytes and zinc sulphide obtained by the process of precipitation under carefully controlled conditions. It is cheap and can be easily applied on the surface. When exposed to day light it changes colour and as such it should not be allowed to come in contact of water.

8. Aluminium powder. It is the base of all the aluminium paints. This paint is generally used for a priming coat of new work. It prevents working and cracking of wood. It is imperveous and maintains same moisture content in the wood, if painted with it.

9.5. Vehicles

They are the liquid substances which hold solid ingredients of the paint, in liquid suspension. Various types of vehicles commonly used under varying conditions, have been described as follows:

1. Linseed oil. This is the vehicle, most commonly used in paints. It is extracted from flax seeds. Linseed oil is clear, transparent, pale and sweet to the taste. It is almost colourless. Drying process of linseed oil is not dependent on evaporation, but on oxidation. It is used in various grades as follows:

(*a*) *Raw linseed oil*. It is clear, transparent, pale and practically colourless. Its rate of drying is slow and as such it is mostly used for interior works of very delicate nature. Its rate of drying can be enhanced by adding about 10% of white lead by weight to the oil and then allowing the mixture to settle for a period of about a week.

(*b*) *Boiled linseed oil*. It is prepared by mixing some amount of drier such as litharge or red lead, about 10% by weight to the raw oil and boiling the mixture. The boiled oil is thicker and darkly coloured than raw oil. It dries quite rapidly, As far as elasticity and power of penetration are concerned boiled linseed oil is inferior to raw linseed oil. It cannot be used for internal delicate works. It is mostly used for exterior surfaces. Being dark in colour, it is not found suitable for light coloured paints or white paints.

(*c*) *Full boiled linseed oil*. This is just like boiled linseed oil except that it does not possess a dark colour. It can be used for white or light coloured paints also. The vehicle is found more suitable for painting plastered surfaces.

(*d*) *Double boiled linseed oil*. It has quick drying qualities. It is suitable for external painting work. But is quite thick and requires turpentine as thinning agent. It can also be used for painting plastered surfaces. It smells slightly different from raw linseed oil.

(*e*) *Stand oil*. Previously this oil was used to be prepared by exposing raw linseed oil to open sun till, it thickened like honey. But now a days this process is brought about by heat treatment. This oil dries quite slowly and provides a clear durable, shining finish.

2. Tung oil. This oil is far superior than linseed oil, and, as such used for preparing paints of superior quality.

3. Poppy oil. It is extracted from poppy seeds. It is very costly and used for internal painting of light shades. It dries slowly. Its colours do not disfigure easily and hence, it is used for making paints of delicate colours. Its raw quality is not suitable for paints. Hence it has to be processed with some other material before, it can be used as a good vehicle.

4. Nut oil. It is obtained by pressing walnut seeds. It is practically colourless and dries rapidly. It is a cheap vehicle and is used for painting ordinary works of temporary nature. It may be used for white and light coloured paints.

9.6. Preparation of Oil Paints

Mostly white lead is used as base, in all the light coloured oil paints. The base *i.e.* white lead is either obtained in form of paste directly from market or white lead is ground in linseed oil to the paste like consistency. White lead paste is broken further by adding a linseed oil and stirring the mixture with the help of wooden stick. Drier if to be used is also ground in little linseed oil and separate paste of it is prepared. If some specific colour is to be developed in the paint the colouring pigment is also mixed with linseed oil and a third separate paste is prepared. Now all the three pastes *i.e.* white lead paste in linseed oil, colouring pigment paste in linseed oil, and drier paste in linseed oil, are mixed together and stirred. If the resulting mixture is very thick, it should be thinned into consistency of cream by adding more of linseed oil and stirring it well. The mixture thus prepared is screened through fine sieve or convass. The screened mixture is an oil paint ready for use. The paint may be further thinned to desired consistency simply by adding more of linseed oil or turpentine or both, just before its actual use.

The paint once prepared should be used at the earliest. If prepared paint has to be kept unused for some time, it should be kept covered with a thin film of water, so that paint may not dry off or spoiled by skinning. Now a days, ready mixed paints of various composition and colours are available in the market. Shalimar paints, Solignum paints, Holes paints, etc. are some of the patented trade names of ready-mixed paints in India. Ready mixed paints are usually very thick and not fit for direct application on the surface. As such ready mixed paints are required to be thinned to the desired consistency, before use by adding suitable thinners and stirring them well.

9.7. Types of Paints

1. Aluminium Paint The paint is prepared by holding very finely ground aluminium in suspension either in quick drying spirit varnish or slow drying oil varnish as per the requirements of the surface to be painted. The suspension liquid *i.e.* spirit or oil, evaporates and a thin metallic film of aluminium is left on the surface. This paint is used for painting wood work and metal surfaces. It is widely used for painting hot water pipes, gas tanks, marine piers, oil storage tanks, radiators, etc. Following are the advantages of aluminium paints.

(i) It has very good weather-resisting and water-proofing properties.

(ii) It is visible in darkness also because of its silver shinning colour.

(iii) It has high electrical resistance.

(iv) It protects the surfaces of iron and steel against corrossion, better than any other paint.

(v) It possesses a very large capacity. For instance one litre of this pain may cover an area of about 200 m^2.

(vi) It is highly heat reflective

(vii) It can withstand the effect of atmosphere contaminated with acidic fumes, and also effects of sea water.

2, Anti-corrosive paints. As their name suggests, these paints are used mainly to protect the surface of metallic structural steel work, against the negative effects of acids, corrosive chemicals fumes, etc. There are several paints which exhibit these properties. These paints essentially consist of the linseed oil as vehicle and red lead, zinc oxide, iron oxide, zinc dust, zinc chromate etc, as their base. In order to modify the characteristics of the paints, driers and inert fillers are also sometimes, added. These paints are cheap durable and are usually black in colour.

3. Asbestos paint. This paint is used for stopping leakage of metal roofs and painting gutters, spouts, flashings etc. to prevent their rusting. This paint is also used as damp-proof coat to cover the outer face of the basement walls. This paint can withstand the effects of acidic gases and steam.

4. Bituminous paint. This paint consists of asphalt, bitumen or pitches, dissolves in any type of oil or petroleum. The paint is always black in colour but its colour, can be modified by mixing certain pigment like red oxide etc. in it. This paint is used mostly for painting iron-works under water. These paints deteriorate when exposed to direct sun. It is also used for water proofing.

5. **Bronze paints**. These paints are prepared by disbursing aluminium bronze or copper bronze in nitro-cellulose lacquer as vehicle. They produce a very reflective type of surface and hence very useful for being applied on radiators. These paints are equally effective for painting interior or exterior metallic surfaces.

6. **Cellulose paint**. This type of paint is prepared from cellulose sheets, nitro-cotton and photographic films. This paint dries very quickly and provides a flexiable, hard, and smooth surface. The paint does not harden by oxidation but by evaporation of thinning agent. The surface of this paint can be easily washed and cleaned. It remains unafffected by hot water, smoky or acidic atmosphere. This paint is used for painting cars aero planes, etc.

7. **Casein paint**. Casein is a product extracted from milk curd. This when mixed with base like whiting, titanium, lithophone, etc. forms the paint which is usually available in powder or paste form. This paint has high capacity and can be applied on new plaster work. It is usually used on walls, ceilings wall-boards, cement block construction etc. to increase the appearance of the surface. When this paint is to be used on external surface, a little amount of linseed oil or varnish, should be added to the paint to make it capable to withstand the exposure effects.

8. **Cement paint**. This paint is available in powder form. It consists of white or coloured cement as its base and water acts as vehicle. No oil or varnish is added to it. This paint is available in variety of shades. It is durable and water-proof. This paint proves to be useful for surfaces which are damp at the time of painting and are also likely to remain damp after painting. Water is mixed with the powdered paint immediately, before it is to be applied to the surface. It is preferable to provide cement paint on rough surface, as adhesion of paint on smooth surface is poor. For painting surface of corrugated iron sheets, cement paint may be mixed with boiled linseed oil. The paint should be constantly stirred during use.

9. **Enamel paint**. This paint is prepared by adding base like white lead or zinc white to a vehicle which is a varnish. To obtain the desired colour, colouring pigments may also be added. This paint dries slowly and forms a hard, durable, smooth gloosy solid thin film. Different types of enamel paints are being manufactured in a variety of colours. Surfaces of this paint are not affected by atmosphere. Enamel paints can be used both for interior as well as exterior painting. In order to obtain better appearance, an under coat of titanium white in pale linseed oil may be applied, before enamel paint is applied over it.

10. Emulsion paint. This paint consists of synthetic resin like poly vinyl acetate. It can be applied easily. It retains its colour for a very long time. The surface of the paint is tough and can be cleaned by washing with water. This paint has excellent resistance against action of alkali. It dries very quickly in about one to two hours. For prolonged service, emulsion paint should be applied in two coats. For painting over rough cement plastered surface, a thin cost of cement paint should be applied, before applying emulsion paint over it.

11. Graphite paint. It is black in colour. It is used over the surface which come in contact with ammonia, chlorine, sulphur gases, etc. It is very much used in under ground railways.

12. Plastic paints. This paint contains a variety of plastics in suspension and is available in the market under different trade names. This paint is available in very attractive and pleasing shades. It is mostly used in show rooms, display rooms, and auditorium etc. It can be applied by spray or by brush.

13. Silicate paint. It is prepared by mixing calcium and finely ground silica with resinous materials. It forms a very hard and durable film on painted surface. It can be directly applied on brick, concrete or plastered surface, but only after wetting them. This paint does not require any priming coat and surface can be finished in two or three coats. This paint should not be applied on hot surfaces.

14. Luminous paint. This paint is prepared by mixing calcium sulphide with varnish. This paint shines in darkness like radium dials of watches. This paint should be applied on surface which have been rendered free from corrosion or lead paints in particular.

15. Inodorous paint. This paint consists of white lead or zinc white mixed with methylated spirit. No turpentine is used in this paint. White lead or zinc white is ground in oil. Shellac with some quantity of linseed oil and castor oil, is dissolved in methylated spirit and this mixture is mixed with lead or zinc white paste prepared in linseed oil. This paint dries quickly, but is not durable. The spirit in the paint gets evaporated immediately and a film of shellac and white zinc or lead remains deposited on the surface.

16. Rubber paint. This paint is prepared by treating rubber with chlorine gas (chlorinated rubber) and then dissolving it in suitable solvent. This paint can be used on new concrete and lime plastered surfaces. This paint dries quickly. It is little affected by weather and sunlight. It is resistant against chemical actions, water, etc. It can be applied on fresh concrete surface *i.e.*, surfaces which are not completely dry.

9.8. Painting Brush

Good brushes should only be used for painting work. Old brushes do not apply paint uniformly on the surface. The brushes having good bristles only should be used Horse haired brushes are not suitable for this job. Bristle brushes are elastic and have good paint-holding capacity. Bristles of brushes are split at their free ends which is not possible with horse hair brushes. Bristle brush should be kept soaked in water for about 2 hours and then allowed to dry before use. While painting, the bristles of brush should be immersed in paint only for about 1/3rd length of the bristles and soaked bristles should be gently pressed against the edge of the pot containing the paint, before brush is carried to paint the surface. After completing the work, brushes should be cleaned thoroughly with kerosene oil.

9.9. Knotting Process

It is the process by which knots on the surface of wood-work are killed by applying certain substances over the knots. The substances applied over the knots prevent exudation of wood resin from the knots and thus can not destroy the film of paint by way of craking, pealing, or discoloration. There are three methods which are commonly used for knotting:

(i) Patent knotting. In this method of knotting two coats of varnish prepared by dissolving shellac in methylated spirit are used one after the other over the knots.

(ii) Ordinary or size knotting. In this method, two coats are applied. Ingredients of first coat consist of red lead ground in water, to which a strong glue size has been mixed. The solution so prepared is applied hot on the knots.

Second coat ingredients consists of red lead ground in oil to which boiled oil and turpentine have been added as thinners. It is applied on knots soon after the first coat has dried.

(iii) Lime knotting. In this method, the knots are covered by hot lime for about 24 hours. After this, the surface in scrapped off and knots are treated by ordinary or size knotting.

9.10. Priming

This is actually first coat of the paint, whose main function is to fill the pores of wooden surface by penetrating into the surface. It also acts as the foundation for subsequent coats of the paint. Primers have definite role to perform and their choice depends on the paint to be used and conditions of surface of timber. In general the constituents of the priming coat should be kept same as those of subsequent coats, but their proportion may vary. The priming coat is generally applied, before fixing wood-work in position.

9.11. Stopping

This process consists of filling up all the nail holes, cracks open joints, dents and other depression on the surface by putty. *Putty is prepared by kneading white chalk powder or whiting into linseed oil.* Putty should be given same colour, that will match the shade of the finishing coat, by adding suitable colouring agent to it. After primer coat, applied on the surface has dried and putty in the open joints, nail holes, had been filled up, the surface of the wood is rubbed by means of pumices-stone or glass paper. At places of joints, depressions, nail holes etc. surface is first rubbed, before applying putty. Putty is allowed to dry, before it is rubbed.

9.12. Coats of Paints

The paints is applied on the surface in two, three or four coats. The first coat is known as priming coat and last one as finishing coat. All the intervening coats are known as under coats.

Prime coat forms a thin film which helps in adhesion of the paint with the surface. It also protects the surface from weathering action. Materials for priming coat should be selected keeping in view the nature of the surface to be painted.

Under coats serve as foundation to the finishing coat. These coats fill all the irregularities of the surface.

Finishing coat is lastly applied as per the requirements.

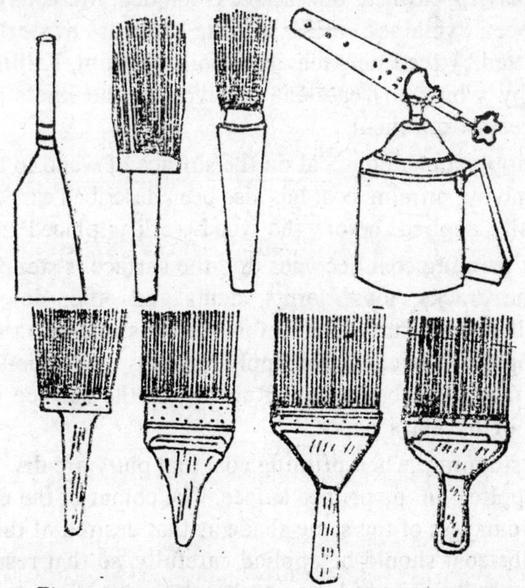

Fig. 9.1. (Painting brushes and painting gun)

9.13. Spray Painting

It is the modern method of applying the paint on the surface. For this, spary gun or pistol is used. The pistol works under compressed air and throws a spray of paint over the surface to be painted. Spary painting is far superior than brush painting. The advantages of the spray painting may be the following :

(i) Speed of painting is considerably more than brush painting.

(ii) Nature of work is far superior than that with the brush.

(iii) An expert painter can develop artistic patterns on the surface.

(iv) It is economical in labour and material both. Only two coats of spray painting are considered sufficient where as brush painting would require three to four coats.

(v) To maintain uniformity of the ingredients the paint is kept continuously stirred by mechanical stirring equipment.

9.14. Painting the surface of a new-wood work

New wood work requires at least four coats of painting. The process of painting may be carried out in the following stages:

1. Before painting is done it should be ensured that wood work to be painted is properly seasoned. At the time of painting, it should not contain more than 15% of the moisture. The surface of the wood-work should be perfectly cleaned from dust and all the nail heads should be punched to a depth of about 3 mm from the surface.

2. After having cleaned, the surface is knotted. Methods of knotting have already been explained earlier. All the knots are properly killed so that resin emitted by the knots may not spoil the paint. Killing of knots is a process by which a treatment is given to the knots to prevent exudation of resin from them.

3. Now apply a priming coat on the surface of wood to be painted. Methods of applying priming coat has also been described earlier. Priming coat is generally applied, before the wood-work is placed in position.

4. When priming coat becomes dry, the surface is stopped. In this process all the cracks, loose joints, dents and other defects in the surface are filled with putty. But before putty is applied, these places should be properly rubbed. After applying putty and when putty has dried, the surface is rubbed again. Rubbing of the surface is done by pumice stone or by glass paper.

5. After stopping, when priming coat and putty are dry, the under-coatings are applied on the primed suface. The colour of the under-coats should be more or less of the same shade as that desired of the finishing coat. The under-coat should be applied carefully, so that resulting film is thin, opaque and does not bear any brush marks. Sometimes, under

coats, may be two or three depending upon the desired finish. The final appearance, and durability of the paint depend very much on the quality of under-coats. Each coat should be applied when the coat applied previously has sufficiently dried. For superior works each coat is rubbed, before applying the next coat.

6. When under-coats are perfectly dry, the finishing coat of paint is applied. This coat should be applied very carefully, so that finished surface is free from patches and brush marks.

9.15. Painting Iron and Steel Surfaces

1. The surface to be painted is rubbed with wire bruses to remove any rust or scale from the surface.

2. The surface should be washed with caustic soda or lime water to remove grease spots, if any. Petrol, benzine may also be used for washing the surface.

3. A priming coat of iron oxide paint or red lead paint should be applied on the cleaned surface. Red lead is considered as the best primer.

4. Now two or more coats of desired paint are applied over primed surface with the help of a brush or spray gun. Each coat of paint should be applied only after the coat applied earlier has dried completely.

Repainting old wood work

If the surface of old paint has become greasy, it should be cleaned by rubbing with pumice stone or sand-paper. On the other hand if old paint has developed blisters and has badly cracked then it has to be completely removed. The old paint can be removed by using following solutions :

1. Make a solution by dissolving 200 gm of caustic soda in one litre of water. When old surface of old paint is washed with this solution, it dissolves the old paint and surface becomes paintless.

2. Make a solution of one part of soft soap and two parts of potash. To this solution add one part of quicklime and mixture is applied on the surface of old paint in hot state and allowed to stay for 24 hours. The surface in then washed with hot water.

3. Prepare a mixture consisting of equal parts of washing soda and quicklime. This mixture in brought to a paste form by adding required quantity of water. This paste is applied on the surface of old paint and kept for about an hour. The surface in then washed with water.

After removing the old paint from the surfaces, the wood work is painted as in case of painting on new wood work.

Repainting old iron work

The old surface should be cleaned by washing with soap water. If surface is greasy it should be removed by washing the surface with lime and water. If old paint is to be removed it should be done by burning with blow lamp and then surface scraped off. After this painting is done as for new surface.

9.16. Painting Galvanized Iron Work

The surface of galvanized iron work is very difficult to paint. As the paint will not adhere to the surface, some treatment is required, before a priming coat is applied. As far as possible, it should be tried to expose the galvanized surface to wheather for about a year. During this period of weathering, zinc coating on galvanized surface gets oxidized and forms a thin film of zinc oxide on the surface to which paint can easily adhere. However, if it is necessary to paint new G.I. work immediately, either of the following two solutions may be used to treat the new surface.

1. Solutions consists of 100 gm of copper acetate in 2 ½ litres of water.

2. Solution prepared by mixing 13 gms of each of muriatic acid, copper chloride, copper nitrate and sel-ammoniac to a litre of soft water. This much solutions will cover a surface of nearly 250 m^2.

Either of these solutions when applied on the new G.I,. work, the surface is turned black in a period of about 12 hours and ensures proper adhesion of the paint. Now a priming coat consisting of red lead mixed with linseed oil and turpentine in equal proportions is applied on the treated surface. The surface can be painted with desired paint after preming coat has perfectly dried.

Alternatively, the surface of G.I. is given a wash of soda or zinc sulphate and when it dries, a priming coat of red lead mixed with linseed oil and turpentine may be applied. Desired painting is done after drying of the priming coat.

9.17. Painting a Plastered Surface

For painting a plastered surface following factors should be considered.

1. As far as possible fresh plastered surfaces should not be painted. At least 6 months to 12 months time should be given to the plastered surface to dry completely.

2. Fresh plaster is alkaline in nature, because lime is liberated during the hydration of cement. Oil based paints and distempers are

prone to alkali attack in the presence of moisture. Hence, if freshly plastered surface is to be painted, an alkali resistant primer paint should be applied or alternatively, paints not containing any oil should be used

3. Spots of plastered surface showing efflorescence should be brushed off. If spots appear again, they should again the brushed off and painting should be postponed till such spots cases to appear.

If new plastered surface has to be painted, it should be given a wash of dilute solution of zinc sulphate to neutralize the free lime before a primer is applied. Primer for plaster work is prepared by mixing equal parts of white and red lead in boiled linseed oil. If necessary, depressions, holes, etc. in the plastered surfaces should be filled up with plaster of paris and surface rubbed smooth before primer coat is applied. Lastly two or three coats of desired paint may be applied as usual after the primed surface has dried completely. Oil paints, cement paints, silicate paints, and emulsion paints are mostly used for plastered surface. Now-a-days emulsion paints have come in the market. These paints have good alkali-resistance and sealing properties. Emulsion paints are permeable and hence can be applied on wet surfaces.

9.18. Painting Concrete Surfaces

For painting concrete surfaces, cement paints are used. They are available in powder form. They are used by mixing with water. Prepared paint should be consumed with in 2 hrs. of its preparation. Two coats should be applied at an interval of 24 hrs. The painted surface should be cured by sprinkling water at intervals.

9.19. Painting Damp Walls

For painting damp walls, a paint prepared as follows is applied in one or two coats with the help of brushes. On drying the painting coat forms a dry hard film on the painted surface.

Take 6.4 kg of pale resin, 11 litres of paraffin and 9 litres of benzoline, mix them together and stir thoroughly so that resin gets thoroughly dissolved. To this mixture add 11 kg of whiting and grind it well. The mixture thus formed is a paint which may be used on the damp wall surface.

Painting floor surfaces

The enamels are used for painting floor surfaces. The selected enamel should be strong to resist abrasion, moisture and alkali action It should also be of shining nature and quick drying type.

9.20. Defects in Painting

Following defects may occurs in painted surface:

1. Fading. The paint may lose some of its colour due to effects of sun rays on colouring pigments.

2. Flaking. Due to poor adhesion, paint may peel off from the surface.

3. Grinning. If the opacity of the final coat is insufficient the back ground of the painted surface is clearly visible. This defect is known as *grinning*.

4. Bloom. Due to bad ventilation or defective paint, dull patches are developed on the painted surface.

5. Flashing. This is opposite of bloom. In this defect gloosy patches are developed on the painted surface. The reasons of this defect may be cheap paint, weather reaction, or poor workmanship.

6. Blistering. This defect occurs due to trapped moisture behind the painted surface.

7. Running. This defect occurs when surface to be painted is very smooth. In this defect small areas of the surface are left uncovered with paint.

8. Sagging. Thickness of painting should not be excessive. If too much thick coat of paint is applied, the defect is known as *sagging*.

9. Wrinkling. This defect occurs in thickly painted surfaces.

10. Saponification. Defect of formation of soap patches on the painted surface is known as *saponification*. This defect occurs due to chemical action of the alkalies.

Failure of Paint - When paint applied on the surface does not perform its purposes it is called failure of the paint. Painting is an easy job but also has its own peculiarities. The following are the main causes of failure of paint.

1. Bad workmanship - Painters generally are in habit of thinning the paint too much so that he may save paint and labour both. This leads to bad workmanship and it is possible that paint may be absent for portions of surface.

2. Wrong choice of paint - Choice of paint in done based upon climatic conditions, nature of surface to be painted and so many other factors affecting the performance of the paint. Low quality paints are cheap but their durability is very poor.

3. Surface preparation - If the surface to be painted has not been prepared well to receive the paint, it may lead to failure of the paint.

4. Moisture - Leakage of moisture on any painted surface accelerates the process of separating the paint layer from the surface.

5. Salts and alkalies - The movement of moisture can also transport salts from either internal volume of masonry or new deposits. Such salts and alkalies saponify the oil paints.

6. Conditions for painting - The painting should be done when atmospheric conditions are favourable Dirt, Dust and moisture must not get entrapped during the process of painting.

9.21. Varnish

Varnish is a solution of some resinous substance in alcohol, oil or turpentine. The process of covering the surface with varnish is known as *varnishing*. Varnishing is done only on wooden surface. Varnish performs following functions.

(i) It brings about brilliance to the painted surface.

(ii) It protects the surface against adverse effects of the atmosphere.

(iii) It increases the durability of the paint film.

(iv) It beautifies the surface without hiding the beautiful grains of the wood.

Varnish plays an important part in finishing wooden surfaces of doors, windows, floors, furniture, etc.

9.22. Properties of Good Varnish

1. Varnish should not shrink or show cracks after drying.

2. The thin film of varnish developed after drying on the surface should be tough, hard and durable.

3. The natural colour of the varnish should not fade away when varnished surface is exposed to atmospheric action.

4. It should make the surface glossy.

5. It should dry rapidly.

6. It should impart the finished surface uniform colour and pleasing appearance.

7. It should not hide the natural grains of the surface.

9.23. Constituents of the Varnish

A varnish has usually three elements: 1. Resins or resinous material 2. Driers and 3. Solvents.

1. Resinous materials. Copal, lac, or shellac, amber and rosin are the commonly used resins for varnishes.

2. Driers. Driers are used to accelerate the process of drying of the varnish. Litharge, lead, acetate, and white copper are the various types of driers, out of which litharge is mostly used.

3. Solvents. Selection of solvent is made depending upon the type of resin. For amber and copal resins boiled linseed oil is used as solvent. For lac or shellac, methylated spirit is used. Turpentine is used for dissolving rosin, gum dammar and Mastic and Nephtha are used as a solvents for cheap varieties of resins.

9.24. Type of Varnishes

The varnishes can be classified into following categories depending upon the solvent used.

1. Oil Varnish. This type of varnish is manufactured by dissolving hard resins such as amber and copal in linseed oil. Turpentine may be used in small quantity to thin the varnish, and also to render it workable. Oil varnishes form a hard and durable film, but they dry slowly.

2. Spirit varnish. This type of varnish is prepared by dissolving resins such as lac or shellac in methylated spirit. This varnish dries very quickly and gets easily affected by weather action. This varnish is mostly used for wood furniture. Suitable pigment may be added to give required shade to the varnished surface.

3. Turpentine varnish. In this type of varnish, gum, dammar, Mastic, and rosin like resins are dissolved in turpentine. These varnishes are light in colour and dry quickly. They are not as tough and hard as oil varnishes.

4. Water varnish. This varnish is prepared by dissolving shellac in hot water. Shellac does not dissolve readily in water and as such to accelerate the process of dissolving shellac in water either ammonia or potash, or soda or borax is added. This vanish is used for painting pictures, posters and maps.

5. Asphalt Varnish. This varnish is obtained by dissolving melted asphalt in linseed oil. The varnish may be thinned by adding suitable amount of either turpentine or petroleum spirit. This varnish is used for varnishing fabricated iron and steel products.

6. Spar varnish. This varnish drives its name from its use. It is mostly used on spars and other exposed parts of the ships. It is very good weather resistant. It should not be used indoor.

7. Flat varnish. This is an ordinary varnish to which material such as wax, finely divided silica and metallic soaps are added, to reduce the gloss of the varnished surface. This varnish presents a dull appearance.

9.25. Process of Varnishing

While varnishing a wooden surface, following operations are required to be carried out.

1. Preparation of surface. The surface to be varnished should be thoroughly rubbed smooth by means of sand paper and thoroughly cleaned from dust and dirt.

2. Knotting. This process is similar as has been explained in painting. All the knots should be covered with a hot preparation of red lead or glue size.

3. Stopping. After knotting, the surface of wood-work is stopped. This is done by means of hot weak glue size. This coat fills all the pores of the surface. Only glue will form about 10 litres of glue size. If glue is not available, two coats of boiled linseed oil can be used as an alternative. After stopping when surface becomes dry, it is rubbed again with sand paper.

4. Applying varnish coats. After stopping process, varnish is applied on the surface in very thin coats. Next coat is applied only when previously applied coat has dried. For varnishing, fine brittle varnishing brush should be used.

9.26. French Polish

It is just a spirit polish. It is prepared by dissolving 150 gms of pure shellac in one litre of methylated spirit. The solution thus prepared is screened through a fine cloth. If any specific shade is desired in the varnish, it can be obtained by adding suitable pigment in it. This varnish is used for varnishing very high class wooden furniture.

Method of applying French Polish

1. Clean the surface of wood work for all sorts of dirt and dust.

2. Rub the surface of wood work with sand paper to smoothen all unevennesses of the surface.

3. Cover all the knots on the surface by a hot preparation of red lead and glue size as is done in knotting process.

4. Fill all the holes and indentations with glazier's putty.

5. After applying glaziers, putty, the surface is given a coat of mixture made from whiting and methylated spirit. 1.5 kg whiting is mixed with one litre of spirit to prepare this mixture. The surface is again rubbed by sand paper and whipped clean after surface has dried completely.

6. On the prepared surface French polish is applied with a pad of woollen cloth covered by a fine cloth. The paid is moistened with French polish and rubbed hard on the surface. Several coats of polish have to be applied as per desired finishing.

9.27. Furniture Polish

The polish is generally prepared by the carpenters at home. Typical composition of a furniture polish may be as follows:

Methylated spirit	1 litre
Copal varnish	0.5 "
Linseed oil	9.0 "
Turpentine	0.5 "
Muriatic acid	30 "
Venegar	0.5 "

In preparation of this varnish, linseed oil is heated first and then all other ingredients added into it and mixed up well.

9.28. Wax Polishing

Wax polishing is a treatment given to the varnished surface to modify its elegance and obtain a highly pleasing lustrous surface. It also protects the under coats. Wax polish is mostly used for polishing mosaic floors, terrazzo floors and concrete surfaces.

Preparation of wax polish. It consists of bee wax, linseed oil, turpentine and varnish. Varnish, turpentine, linseed oil and bee wax are respectively, taken in ratio of 1:2:3:4 by weight. First of all bee wax and linseed oil are mixed together and heated on mild fire. After sometimes, bee wax gets dissolved in the oil and mixture is allowed to cool down slightly. Now turpentine and varnish are also added to the mixture and stirred. Wax polish is ready for use.

This polish is applied in the similar manner as French polish. Wax-polish is applied on the prepared cleaned surface with the help of soft pad of cotton cloth, and kept continuously rubbed for about 30 minutes. Second coat is applied after the first coat has dried. Similarly several coats of wax polish are applied till desired surface finish is obtained.

9.29. Lacquer

Lacquers are sort of varnishes, having very low solid contents. To acquire a desired film, several coats of lacquers are required to be applied. They dry very fast and on drying they give a tough and durable finish which can be easily rubbed. They can be used on surfaces of furniture, floors, linoleum etc. They are available in a variety of colours. They can be applied by brush or by spray gun.

9.30. Stains

it is a sort of liquid preparation. It is used to change the colours of cheap quality timber to those of high quality timber. Aniline, a derivative of coaltar is mostly used as a base and water, alcohol, oil etc. are used as vehicle. Stains are named after the name of vehicle used in its preparation. Water stains, oil stains, spirit stains respectively have water, oil and alcohol as the vehicle. Water stains make surface of the timber rough and hence not desirable. Spirit stains dry very fast and hence require an expert painter to use them. Oil stains are considered most suitable for coating hard timber surfaces. Oil stains are obtained by mixing chrome yellow burnt sienna, amber etc. with linseed oil. Some amount of turpentine and a drier can also be used to control its properties.

9.31. Oiling of Timber Work

In order to make timber more durable and good looking they are sometimes oiled. The oiling mixture is prepared as follows.

Take double-boiled linseed oil three parts and bee wax one part and heat their mixture on a slow fire till wax is melted. The mixture is then cooled and turpentine oil is further added and stirred well. The oil mixture is ready for application. The mixture is freely applied on the wooden surfaces with the help of brushes till surface becomes saturated.

Sometimes, a mixture of country sweet oil, vinegar, and turpentine in equal proportion can be used for oiling the timber work.

9.32. Coal Tarring

Wood or iron work to be coated is first cleaned of all dust, rust, scales etc. in the similar fashion as is essentially done, before painting. The mixture is prepared and applied as described below.

The mixture consists of 1 kg of unslaked lime and about 5 litres of tar. The tar is heated till it starts boiling. The hot mixture is thinned by adding about 0.4 litres of country spirit. The mixture is best applied while it is hot.

9.33. Distempering

It is also a process of applying wash or coating like white washing or colour washing on the surface. But finished surfaces obtained by distempering are far superior than those obtained by white washing or colour washing. Distempers are available in ready made form in the market under different trade names.

Compositions of distempers. Any distemper consists of a base, a carrier, colouring agent, and size. Whiting (powdered chalk) is used as base and water as the carrier. Colouring agents or pigments are added only, if specific shade is to be obtained. Glue is mostly used as size. Distemper may also be termed as a water paint, having whiting as base and water as the carrier.

Distempers are available in powder form or paste form. They are to be mixed with hot water before use. There is a variety of oil bound distempers also, in which the drying oil is so treated that it mixes with water readily. Oil bound distempers are available in paste form in different shades in sealed tins. Before use, water is mixed with the distemper to thin it, to the required consistency. After application on the surface, the oil content of the distemper hardens and forms a durable coating. Distempers are applied on the surface with the help of distemper brushes which are about 10 cm wide. All the manufactures of readymade distempers supply complete directions as to how to use their product. These directions should be strictly followed to achieve the best results.

Process of distempering

(i) Preparation of the surface. Surface to be distempered should be absolutely dry. Dampness in the surface spoils the distemper coat. New plastered surface should be left for at least 2-3 months, so that it may dry out completely. Holes, patches, cracks, efflorescence spots etc. should be thoroughly cleaned and filled with gypsum or lime putty. If the surface is to be redistempered the old coating should be washed with water and allowed to dry. The surface in the last should be thoroughly rubber with sand paper and cleaned.

(ii) Applying prime coat. After preparation of the surface it should be primed by applying a coat of whiting in water or only of milk. Priming coat helps in developing a good bond of distemper with the surface. Normally manufactures recommend the use of material for priming coat for their product. The priming coat should be allowed to dry completely, before distemper coat is applied over it. Sometimes, cement wash is also given on the surface to act as prime coat.

3. Distempering. After having applied the priming coat, first coat of distemper is applied on the surface. The first coat should be of a light tint and applied with great care. Second coat is applied after the first coat has dried and become hard. Distempering costs are applied with the help of broad stiff distemper brushes. Now a days distempers can be applied with the help of spray pistols also. Sometimes, if application of prime coat is not felt necessary, a coating of warm glue should be applied prior to the application of distemper.

Colouring the exterior surfaces. Colour wash to be used on cement concrete, stucco and brick surfaces, are manufactured with weather resistant ingredients during the process of manufacturing of the colour wash. Snowcem, silacrete, colour create are nothing, but trade names of different types of cement based colour washes. They are very good for external exposed situations. The base materials for external washes are nothing but cement.

Properties of distempers

1. Distempers generally shrink on drying. Hence of surface to receive distemper is weak, it may lead to cracking and flaking of the distempers.

2. Distempers are available in powder form and also in paste form. Powdered distempers are known as dry distempers, where as paste form distermpers are known as oil bound distempers. Oil bound distempers are superior than dry distempers. Distempered surfaces with oil-bound distempers are washable.

3. Coatings of distempers are comparatively thick and are more brittle than other water paints.

4. Distemper film is generally porous in nature and it allows water vapour to pass through it. Hence it allows new walls to dry out with out damaging the distemper film.

5. They are less durable than oil paints.

6. Distempers are generally light in colour and provide a good reflective coating.

7. They can be applied on cement plastered surface, lime plastered surface, brick-work, insulating boards, etc.

Wall paper - The wall papers have come in a big way. They are used to give decorative finishing to the interior of walls and ceilings. They are made exclusively from paper or combined with other materials. They may be primed, unprimed, embossed metal coated etc. They are available in single colour or multi-colour patterns printed on the face surface.

The surface of the wall on which wall paper is to be used is dried, levelled, and made free from chalk or lime solution. All the cracks and holes are filled up with lime-gypsum solution. The surface is then pasted with wrapping paper or newspapers by applying suitable paste. The wall paper which is available is rolls in then hanged very carefully on the surface. The continuity of the pattern or design on wall paper is maintained.

The wall paper is available in so many varieties, colours and patterns.

The varnished wall paper can be polished after hanging over the wall. Some wall paper varieties are washable and they can be painted with oil paint. The wall paper with sound-absorbing properties is also available. The metal-coated wall papers are also available. They remain coated with a primer of metallic powder.

9.34. White Washing and Colour Washing

White washing is a process of giving wash covering to the plastered surface. For white washing, a wash of slaked lime is prepared with water. Some other agents like gum, rice water, common salt etc. are also added to the wash, to develop desired adhesion with the surface to be white washed. If wash prepared is added with some colouring agent to develop desired colour, it is known as colour washing. White washing or colour washing is done on the prepared surface with the help of Moonz brush.

The base material of the white wash or colour wash is fat lime or shell lime. Lime is slaked in a larger drum by adding bulk of water to it. After 24 hours, solutions of slaked lime is taken, screened and dissolved gum in hot water added to it. The resulting solution is white wash solution. If this solution is added with some colouring agent the resulting solution is known as colour wash.

White wash or colour wash should be applied on the surface after cleaning and drying. Second coat should be applied only after the first coat has completely dried.

Plastering. In order to obtain an even, smooth, regular and clean surface of ceilings and walls, a thin covering of plastic mortars is applied on the surfaces. This thin covering is known as plastering. The process of applying this covering on the surfaces is known as 'plastering'. Plastering the external exposed surfaces is known as rendering. The object of rendering is to safe guard the exposed surfaces against penetration of rain water and also against adverse effects of other atmospheric agencies.

Plastering is done by the mortars. The mortars have already been discussed earlier. If mud mortar is used for plastering, it is known as mud plaster. Similarly plasters done by using lime, mortar and cement mortar are, respectively, known as lime plaster and cement plaster. Mortars used for lime plaster is usually 1:2 or 1:3 and that for cement plaster 1:3 to even 1:5 depending upon the desired strength of the plaster.

Pointing. In pointing, only joints of masonry walls are treated and filled with lime or cement mortar. In plastering whole of the surface is covered with mortar, but in pointing only point are filled with mortar. The joints are first raked for about 13 mm depth with the help of wire brushes and cleaned by sprinkling water in the joints. This is done to ensure proper bond of the pointing mortar into the raked joints. If lime mortar is used for pointing, ratio of lime and sand is taken as 1:1. In case of cement mortar pointing ratio of mortar may be 1:2: or 1:3. In order to improve the appearance of the pointed surface, pointing may be done of several types. Beaded pointing. Flush pointing, recessed, pointing,

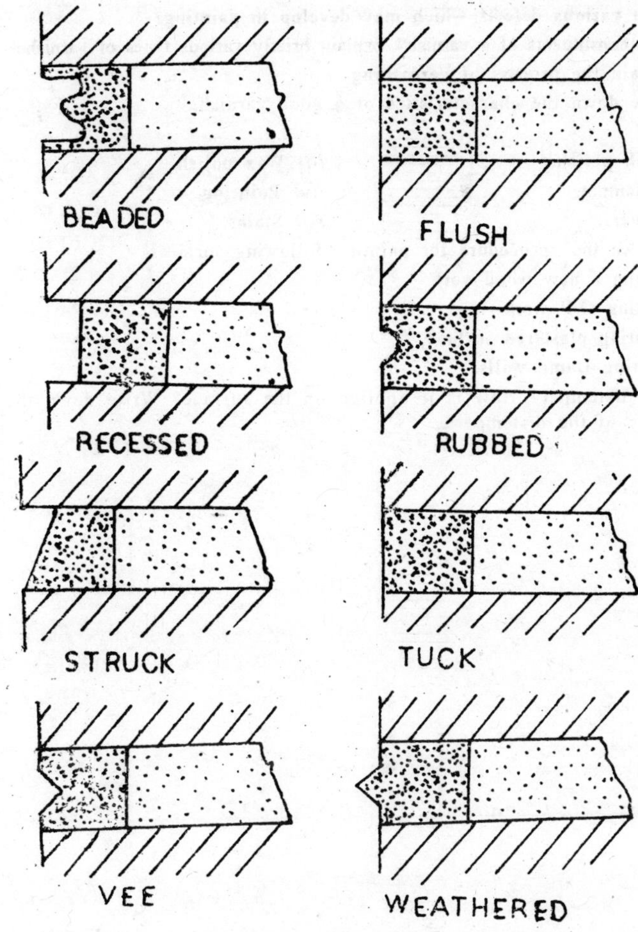

Fig. 9.2. Various types of pointings..

keyed rubbed or grooved pointing, struck pointing, tuck pointing, vee-pointing and weathered pointing are some of the types of pointings, See Fig. 9.2.

QUESTIONS

1. Mention the functions of painting and point out the characteristics of an ideal paint.
2. What are the chief ingredients of an oil paint? Describe the functions of each ingredient.
3. Enumerate various types of vehicles used in paints. Give a brief description of each base.

4. Enumerate various types of vehicles used in paints. Give briefly the properties of each vehicle.
5. What are various defects which may develop in painting?
6. What are constituents of a varnish? Explain briefly various types of varnishes.
7. (*a*) Explain the process of varnishing.
   (*b*) Write down the characteristics of a good varnish.
8. Explain:
   (i) French polish. *(ii)* Wax polish.
   (iii) Distemper. *(iv)* Pointing.
   (v) Lacquers. *(vi)* Stains.
9. Write down the procedure for painting following surfaces.
   (i) Painting a new wood-work.
   (ii) Painting G.I. work.
   (iii) Painting plastered surface.
   (iv) Painting Damp walls.
10. What is distemper? How is it applied on the surface? Write down the properties of the distempers.

10
PIG IRON

10.1. Introduction

Metals are very much used for various engineering purposes. They are used as structural materials like doors, windows, pipes, roofing materials. There is no field in existence, where some metal is not used in one way or the other. Out of all the metals iron is most popular metal. Moreover, this metal is also available is abundance. It is also a life substance. It is found in green plants and also in the blood cells. Iron metals are also called ferrous metals. For the purposes of study, different metals may be grouped under two headings.

1. Ferrous metals. 2. Non-ferrous metals.

The former metals contains iron as the main ingredient, where as non-ferrous metals do not contain iron. Ferrous metals may be divided into three categories namely, cast iron, wrought iron and steel. All these three irons and non-ferrous metals have been discussed in subsequent chapters. In this chapter only pig iron has been discussed. Pig iron is the basic material for the production of cast iron (C.I.), wrought iron (W.R.), and steel.

10.2. Iron Ores

Ore is a solid naturally occuring mineral from which one or more constituents are obtained by certain treatment. Iron is also obtained from naturally occuring mineral called *iron ores*. Iron is present in iron ores inform of oxides. The amount of iron oxide varies indifferent iron ores. Iron ores also contain impurities like silica (SiO_2) Alumina (AlO_3), calcium carbonate (C_aCO_3), magnesia, manganese oxide, sulfur and phosphorus which are considered to be very harmful. Some of these impurities which are of no value are called *gangue*. The more the amount of gangue is present in the ore the lesser is the amount of iron present. Such ores also consume more fuel and flux in their extraction. Following are some of the important varieties of iron ores, which are used for the extraction of iron.

1. Haematite (Fe_2O_4) The colour of this ore may vary from deep red to grey-black. It is rich iron ore and contains about 65 to 70% of iron. Its S.G. varies from 4.5 to 5.3. It does not contain any combined water and has low contents of sulphur and phosphorous. It is non-magnetic. It is mined at Mysore and Madhya Pradesh. It is also mined in very large amount in Brazil, Spain. U.S.S.R., U.S.A., Africa, France, and Germany.

2. Magnetite (Fe_3O_4). Its colour is black or grey. It is the richest iron ore and contains iron about 70 to 73%. Its S.G. varies from 4.9 to 5.2. It is very hard and strongly magnetic in nature. Being very hard, it is mined by using drills and explosives. This ore is available at Madras but it has not been exploited as yet as coal fields are not located near by. Sweden, U.S.S.R., U.S.A., Canada, Ireland, Norway are the other countries where it is predominently found.

3. Pyrites (FeS_2). It is iron sulphide. It contains 45 to 47% of iron content. Its S.G. varies from 4.8 to 5.1. Its colour may be pale brass, yellow or bronze yellow. This ore is found almost in all parts of the world, but is not used for extraction of iron as it contains sulphur which renders the resulting iron brittle.

4. Limonite. It is also known as *hydrated haematite* ($2Fe_2O_3\ 3H_2O$). Its colour varies from pale yellow to black. It contains about 60% iron with 14.5% of combined water. Its S.G. varies from 3.6 to 4.0. In India, this ore is available at Jamshedpur. It is also available in Germany, Spain, England, and U.S.A.

5. Siderite. Chemically it is the carbonate of iron ($FeCO_3$). Iron content in this ore may vary from 40 to 48%. Its S.G. varies from 3.7 to 3.9. Its colour may be pale yellow, brownish black or brownish red. In India, this ore is available at Raniganj in Bengal. It is also available in England and U.S.S.R. It usually occurs in the form of nodules or in discontinuous beds.

10.3. Pig Iron

It is the crude impure iron obtained from iron ore. Pig iron forms the basic material for the manufacture of cast iron, wrought iron and steel. It contain 92 to 95% iron, 3 to 4% of carbon and remainder as the impurities like Sulphur, manganese, phosphorous etc. Pig iron as such is a weak and brittle material and can not be used for structural purposes. In this chapter manufacture and classification of pig iron will be studied.

10.4. Manufacture of Pig Iron

Manufacture of pig iron involves following three distinct stages:

1. Dressing of iron ores. 2. Calcination and Roasting of ores.

3. Smelting or melting of ores.

All these three operations have been briefly described.

1. Dressing of iron ores. The iron ores obtained from mines may be in the form of big boulders. Hence, the ore are first of all broken up and crushed to pieces of size about 2.5 cm. For this operation rock crushers may be used. After crushing, the ores are generally washed in a stream of water so as to remove impurities like clay, loam and other materials called *gangue materials*. Perforated trays may be kept in water to remove sand and pebbles. Magnetic separators may also be used to remove the impurities contained in the iron ores, but they are used only in dry conditions.

2. Calcination and roasting. The operation is done on the dressed iron ores. Dressed ores are heated in the presence of air. This preliminary heating is called calcination and it is done to oxidize the iron ores. Water and carbon dioxide are driven out by this process. Dressed ores may be roasted, so as to make them hot dry. Roasting drives away sulphur and or volatile materials from the ores. If iron ore is an oxide, roasting operation may, be avoided.

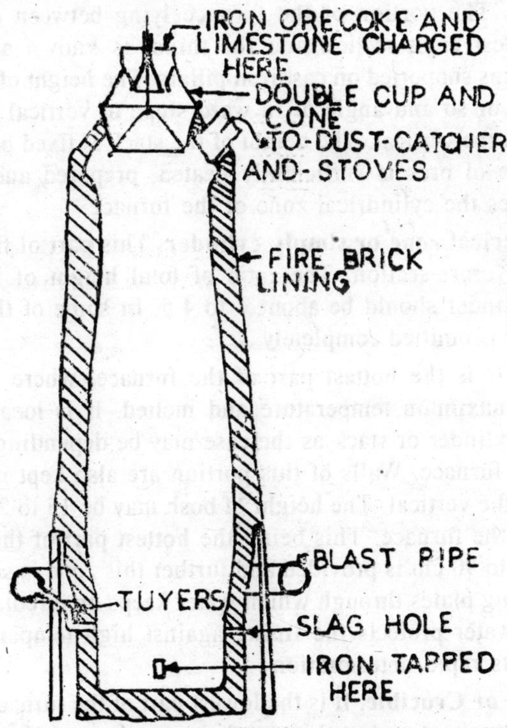

Fig. 10.1. Blast furnace.

3. Smelting. In this operation dressed and calcined ores are melted

is a furnace known as *blast furnace*. The metal is separated by melting from ores. The process of melting the dressed ores in the blast furnace is known as *smelting*.

Blast furnace. It is a tall irregularly shaped vertical steel cylinder. The outer shell of the furnace is of steel plate 30 to 40 mm thick. The inside surface of the cylinder is covered with a lining of fire bricks. The height of the furnace may be about 30 m and diameter between 6 m and 10 m. The dimensions of blast furnace are actually fixed depending upon the desired out put from it. Fig. 10.1. shows different parts and usual shape of the blast furnace. The working of various parts has been discussed in brief.

1. Throat. It is actually the mouth of the blast furnace. It is located in a vertical wall near the top of the furnace. Its function is to allow dust and gases to escape to the atmosphere.

2. Feeding system. The charge for the blast furnace is admitted in to the furnace from the top. The feeding device consists of a double cup and cone arrangement which prevents the escape of gases while charging the furnace.

3. Stack. The portion of the furnace lying between cylindrical portion of widest cross-section and the throat is known as *stack*. It generally remains supported on cast iron pillars. The height of stack may be about 18 m or so and angle of in ward slope of vertical walls may be 3° to 5° with the vertical. The height of the stack is fixed on the basis that the charge of ores is sufficiently heated, prepared and reduced, before it reaches the cylindrical zone of the furnace.

4. Cylindrical zone or simply cylinder. This part of the furnace has the widest cross-section. The ratio of total height of furnace to diameter of cylinder should be about 4 to 4.5. In some of the designs cylindrical part is omitted completely.

5. Bosh. It is the hottest part of the furnace, where charge, is heated to the maximum temperature and melted. It is located at the bottom of the cylinder or stack as the case may be depending upon the design of blast furnace. Walls of this portion are also kept inclined at 10 to 14° with the vertical. The height of bosh may be 15 to 20% of the total height of the furnace. This being the hottest part of the furnace, thick lining 60 to 90 cm is provided and further this zone is surrounded with bosh cooling plates through which water keeps on circulating. The circulation of water protects the lining against high temperature and thus prevents its rapid deterioration.

6. Hearth or Crucible. It is the lowest part of the furnace. Molten iron and slag remain stored in this part between the periods of tapping them out. This part of the furnace may be 2m to 3m high.

7. Tuyeres. The tuyeres are nothing, but blast air nozzles. A number of tuyeres are located in the bosh portion of the furnace. All the tuyeres are connected to tuyer pipe which runs round the furnace and supplies air to the tuyer nozzles. The diameters of tuyer pipe and nozzles depend on the quantity of air required in unit time to carry out the burning or smelting of the charge adequately.

8. Other miscellaneous attachments. In addition to the parts mentioned above the blast furnace is also provided with following attachments.

(i) Hot blast stoves. They are provided to make use of hot gases of blast furnace. They are usually in form of steel cylinders lined by fire bricks from inside. They are filled by fire bricks in criss-cross manner. The air or gases are made to circulate through them. The heat of gases is stored in the fire bricks, which is supplied to the cool air for heating, before it is forced into the blast furnace.

(ii) Blowers. Sufficient numbers of blowers should be installed to supply adequate quantity of air to the tuyer pipe and then to the tuyer nozzles.

(iii) The surplus hot gases coming out of blast furnace can be used for firing or heating the other furnaces or for raising the temperature of materials or water.

Working of blast Furnace. Mixture of dressed iron ores, fluxing material and fuel is prepared is required proportion and it is then fed into the blast furnace through double cup and cone arrangement. Some times dressed ores, fluxing material and coke are fed in alternate fashion. The mixture fed from top of the furnace is made to descend through throat portion of the furnace. The blast of hot air is forced through tuyeres under a pressure of about 2 kg/cm^2 near the bottom of the furnace. The hot air blast promotes the combustion of the coke and help carry the gases upwards. The oxygen in the hot air blast, combines with the carbon in the coke (fuel) to form carbon dioxide (CO_2) which under intense heat gets further reduced to carbon monoxide (CO). Both carbon and carbon monoxide (CO) act as reducing agents and reduce iron ore to metallic state. The operation of reduction of the ore to metallic iron starts almost immediately below the top of the furnace. As the charge descends-further reduction is continued as temperature in the furnace goes on increasing. By the time charge reaches bosh zone, the reduction of iron ore is almost completed. The following are the reactions that place inside the furnace.

$$3Fe_2O_3 + C \rightarrow 2Fe_3O_4 + CO$$
$$Fe_3O_4 + 4C \rightarrow 3Fe + 4CO$$
$$3Fe_2O_3 + CO \rightarrow 2Fe_3O_4 + CO_2$$
$$Fe_3O_4 + 4CO \rightarrow 3Fe + 4CO_2$$

At the bottom of the furnace *i.e.* in bosh portion, a temperature of about 1500°C is maintained. The charge fed from the top gets completely reduced by the time, it reaches the bosh and molten iron gets collected at the bottom of the furnace. Slag which is formed during reduction also collects over the molten metal at the bottom of the furnace. As slag is lighter than molten metal, it always remains floating. Slag is a material which is formed by reactions between fluxing material and impurities in ore.

Lime stone is the material which is used as fluxing material and coke is widely used as fuel in these furnaces. Fluxing material is the material which can be easily fused. It mixes with the impurities in the iron ore and forms fusible material called *slag.*

The slag is taken out of furnace through a hole known as *cinder notch,* which is provided just below the ring of tuyeres at an interval of 2 to 3 hours. Molten iron is tapped off through another hole known as *iron notch,* provided near the bottom of the hearth at an interval varying from 4 hours of 6 hours.

If blast furnace is located very near to the other steel works, the molten pig iron as obtained from blast furnace may be directly used for further purification and preparing other types of steels. Alternatively, the molten pig iron is filled in to suitable moulds and allowed to cool and solidify. In one such method the molten iron is run into sand moulds prepared near the blast furnace. The iron blocks as obtained from sand moulds which are known as *pigs* or *sows*

Pig iron contains about 93 to 95% of iron about 4 to 5% of carbon and remaining being impurities like sulphur, silicon, manganese, phosphorus etc.

Slag obtained from blast furnace contains about 45% lime, 35% silica, 12% alumina and the remaining being impurities like magnesia, $CaSO_4$, manganese oxide etc. This slag may be thrown as a waste or may be used for following useful purposes.

1. Manufacture of slag cement.
2. As coarse aggregate in cement concrete, railway blast etc.

10.5. Other methods of Pig-iron manufacture

Alternative methods for the manufacture of pig iron have been tried in different countries. These methods are :

1. Electric-reduction process. This method may be adopted at places where electricity is cheaply and amply available. The furnace in this case is heated by means of electrodes.

2. Low shaft blast furnace. In this method, blast of enriched oxygen is used instead of usual hot air. In this case, reduction of iron ores is achieved in comparatively short period. It also enable reduction of stack height of the furnace.

3. Sponge iron process. In this method, iron is directly obtained from ore. The ore is reduced at a temperature below the melting point. The product thus obtained is called *sponge iron*, which is a porous mass of reduced iron with some amount of slag in it. This process is very much used in Germany and Japan.

10.6. Classification of Pig Iron

Pig iron is classified mainly according to the percentage of carbon present in it. The carbon present in the pig iron is in the form of combined carbon as well free carbon. Combined carbon makes the metal hard and gives it a fine crystalline structure. Free carbon which is also termed as graphite, or uncombined carbon makes the metal soft and gives, it a coarse grained structure. Depending upon the proportions of combined and uncombined carbon, pig iron may be classified into six categories.

No. 1 Pig iron. It contains almost enterely free carbon varying from 3 to 3.5%. It is very soft, dark grey in colour, and its fracture exhibits large lustrous flakes of graphite. This iron is very weak, but very much used for making very fine and sharp castings.

No. 2. Pig iron. It is also like No. 1 pig iron except that it contains about 0.4% combined carbon and flakes of graphite are less distinct than No. 1 pig iron. It is less fluid when melted.

No. 3. Pig iron. It contains combined carbon as 0.6%, but total carbon content is less than that for No. 1 and No. 2 pig irons. Its fractured surface shows comparatively smooth and regular compact surface with very little graphite flakes. It is much harder than No. 1 and 2 pig irons. It is extensively used in foundry works.

No. 4 Pig iron. This iron contains combined carbon up to 0.9%. It is lighter in colour and has finer grains. On account of its greater hardness it can be used for rough castings. This iron may also be classified as No. 4 foundry and No. 4 forge. No. 4 forge is white in colour and on account of its intense hardness is solely used for the manufacture of wrought iron in the puddling furnace. It can be combined with other lower grade pig irons and can be used for foundry works.

All the above mentioned, form No. 1 to No 4 type pig irons, may be called by a single name grey pig irons, and are most extensively used for foundry works.

No. 5 Pig iron. It is also known as *mottled pig iron*. It contains about equal proportions of combined and uncombined carbon. The fracture of this pig is mottled. It is used for heavy foundry castings. It is a very strong type of pig iron.

No. 6. Pig iron. This iron is obtained when furnace is not provided with sufficient fuel or when ore or fuel contains a higher percentage of sulphur or when raw materials are burnt at low temperature. It has almost entire carbon in combined state. It is therefore, extremely hard and brittle. On melting it does not become fluid enough for casting and as such it cannot be used in the foundry work. It is hard and strong and can be melted easily. It is mostly used in the manufacture of wrought-iron. It is also called white pig.

Bessemer pig. It is obtained from haematite ores. It should be free from sulphur, copper and phosphorous. The presence of manganese and silicon in small % improves the quality of pig iron. This pig is used in the manufacture of steel by Bessemer or acid open-heart process.

QUESTIONS

1. Define ore. Discuss important varities of iron ores.
2. Describe the manufacturing process of pig-iron by blast furnace
3. Draw a neat sketch of a blast furnace and explain its working in details.
4. Discuss the various classifications of pig iron.
5. (*a*) Why fluxing agent is essentially added in the mixture to be fed into a blast furnace?

   (*b*) What are the uses of blast furnace slag?

11

CAST-IRON

11.1. Introduction

As its name suggests, this iron is used only for making castings and as such is known as *cast iron*. It is obtained from pig iron, already discussed in chapter 10. The pig iron is remelted to secure proper grade and carbon content and is casted, or moulded into desired shaped castings.

11.2. Manufacture of Cast Iron

A furnace named cupola furnace is used in the manufacture of cast-iron. Cupola furnace is very similar to blast furnace, but is comparatively smaller in size. It consists of a cylinderical shell, made of thick iron plate. It is lined from inside by refractory bricks. The inside diameter, of the cylinder is about 1 m and height varying from 4 m to 7 m. Diagram of a typical cupola furnace is shown in Fig. 11.1. This furnace does not work continuously. A charge is put in the furnace which is melted and discharged into moulds. This completes one cycle of operation in a

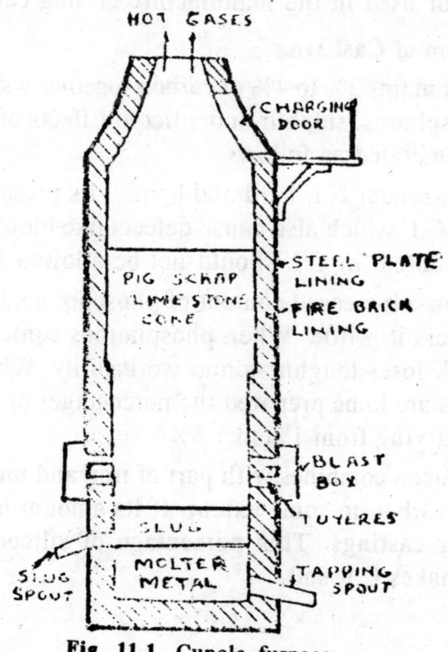

Fig. 11.1. Cupola furnace.

cupola furnace. The furnace is again cleaned thoroughly, before a new charge is admitted in it. Tuyers for blowing air into the charge are, located at regular intervals alround the furnace near its bottom. This furnace is open at the top. It is provided with side door near the top for admitting the fresh charge in the furnace. Separate tapping holes are provided at suitable heights for draining out the slag and molten iron from bottom of the furnace. The fuel used in mostly coke.

The furnace is filled either with an intimate mixture of pig iron, scrap iron, lime stone and coke or in form of alternate layers of coke and mixture of pig iron and scrap iron with lime stone. Lime stone is used as a fluxing agent. Scrap iron is added to improve the quality of the resulting cast iron and also to bring about economy in the cost of production.

Once the furnace is charged, it is fired and blast air is blown through tuyers under pressure. In this case air is not preheated and the impurities in pig iron are removed by oxidation. The cold air gets heated in the furnace as combustion of coke is taking place in the furnace. High temperature causes pig iron to melt. Lime stone acts as a flux to combine with the impurities in the pig iron, fuel ash: and separates them in form of the slag which floats above the molten iron. The impurities of pig iron are removed to some extent and relatively pure iron is obtained in molten stage from the bottom of the furnace. Molten iron is led into moulds and cast iron castings are obtained, after its solidification. Slag is also drained from the top of molten C.I. at regular intervals and disposed off either as waste or used in the manufacture of slag cement.

11.3. Composition of Cast Iron

Cast iron contains 2% to 4% of carbon together with impurities like mangenese, phosphorus, sulphur and silicon. Effects of impurities have been briefly enumerated as follows :

Sulphur. It render C.I. hard and brittle. Its presence causes rapid solidification of C.I. which also cause defects like blow-holes and sand-holes. Sulphur content in C.I. should not be allowed to exceed 0.1%

Phosphorous. Increased content of phosphorous increases fluidity of C.I. and renders it brittle. When phosphorous content exceeds 0.3% the resulting C.I. loses toughness and workability. When very delicate and thin castings are to be prepared the percentages of this content may be maintained varying from 1% to 1.5%.

Silicon. Silicon combines with part of iron and forms a solid mass. It also removes carbon to some extent. If its amount is less than 2.5% it ensures better castings. This percentage of silicon also decreases shrinkage and makes C.I. soft.

Manganese. It renders C.I. hard and brittle. Its amount should be restricted to less than 0.75% or so.

11.4. Properties of Cast iron

Following are the properties of C.I.

1. It is hard and easily fusible.
2. It is brittle and as such it cannot resist the effects of impacts and shocks.
3. Its melting temperature is 1250°C.
4. It does not rust.
5. It becomes soft when placed in soft water.
6. It cannot be magnetised.
7. It cannot be tempered, but it can be hardened by heating and sudden cooling.
8. It shrinks on cooling. An allowance to this fact is always considered while sizing the patterns or moulds for foundry work.
9. It is strong in compression, but weak in tension. Average quality C.I. has compressive and tensile strengths as 6000 kg/cm^2 and 500 kg/cm^2 respectively.
10. It cannot be rivetted or welded. Two pieces of C.I. can only be connected by nuts and bolts.

11.5. Uses of C.I.

C.I. is extensively used for structural as well as other purposes. Important uses have been enumerated as follows :

1. For making C.I. pipes. These pipes can withstand very high pressure heads.
2. It is used for man hole covers, flushing cisterns, and other sanitary fittings.
3. As compression members or struts in trusses.
4. For all sorts of castings. Thus field of C.I. is very wide as lot of machine parts, machine blocks, are always casted in standard shapes and sizes.
5. For manufacturing carriage wheels, rail chairs etc.
6. It is also used in form of bracket, gates, lamp posts etc.

11.6. Types of Cast-Iron

Cast-iron may be classified into the following categories :

1. Grey cast iron
2. White cast iron
3. Mottled cast iron
4. Chilled cast iron

5. Malleable cast iron 6. Ductile cast iron
7. Toughened cast iron 8. Alloyed cast iron

Brief description of each type has been given here.

1. Grey cast iron. Fractured surface of this iron shows grey colour, which is due to the presence of free carbon in the form of graphite. Carbon content in the C.I., varies from 2.5 to 3.75%. Strength of this iron can be improved by exercising control over its composition and rate of cooling. It is soft and melts easily. It has coarse crystalline structure. It has good rigidity, and high compressive strength. But it is weak in tension and impact absorbing characteristics. It is extensively used for making castings.

2. White cast iron. This type of C.I. is developed when carbon and silicon are kept low and there is no free carbon in it. This C.I. is very hard, brittle and wear resistent. Its colour is silvery white and can take good polish. The carbon content in it varies between 2.8% to 3.5%. It cannot be used for delicate castings.

3. Mottled cast iron. It is an intermediate variety between grey C.I. and white C.I. Its fracture shows mottled appearance. This C.I. is used in situations where abrasion resistance is important.

4. Chilled cast iron. This C.I. iron is hard for certain depth from the exterior surface and soft for the rest of the depth. Exterior hard surface is indicated by white iron and interior soft portion of the body is indicative of Grey C.I. It is used to provide wear resistant surfaces to castings. This C.I. is just greay cast iron which is produced by casting against chills. Running surface to a C.I. railway wheel is chilled and covered with a hard skin of white iron, but the other parts of the wheels are of tough grey iron.

5. Malleable cast iron. This C.I. is produced by extracting a portion of carbon from white cast iron. This is done by embedding white C.I. in powdered red haematite and raising temperature to a bright red heat in an annealing oven. This C.I. is malleable. It is stronger, tougher and more ductle than ordinary C.I. It can be easily bent, forged, and welded. This C.I. is largely used for intricate forms such as toothed wheel, pokers, tongs. etc.

6. Ductile cast iron. This C.I. is produced by additing small quantity of magnesium to the molten grey cast iron. Magnesium changes the shape of the graphite particles of C.I. and this results in the formation of ductile cast iron. This C.I. has properties intermediate between C.I. and cast iron steel. The structure of ductile C.I. can be further modified by heat treatment. This C.I. has higher fluidity, strength, toughness, machineability; than malleable C.I. It is also considered, better in wear resistance, shock resistance, weld ability, and castability than, Malleable C.I.

7. Toughened cast iron. This type of C.I. is obtained by melting C.I. with wrought iron scrap. The proportions of wrought iron scrap is about 1/4 to 1/17th of the weight of cast iron.

8. Alloyed cast iron. This cast iron is produced by adding some alloying element in the cast iron. This is done to bring about desirable changes in the properties of C.I., without affecting its casting characteristics. Nickel, chromium, molydenum, vanadium and copper are some of the elements which are used for alloying purpose with cast iron.

11.7. Castings

Casting is the term used to indicate the formation of products of the desired shapes from the molten cast iron. Necessary shape to the products is given using moulds or dies. The moulds used for the castings may be made from sand or metal. The material used for the preparation of mould appreciably affects the speed of moulding, rate of cooling of the molten metal, surface of casting, mechanical strength of casting, and the cost of the finished products.

Sand casting. A pattern exactly of the shape and size of the product to be casted is prepared. The pattern is generally made from hard wood. The surface of the patterns is smoothly finished and waxed, so that the product casted with the help of this pattern has smooth surface. If very few number of products are to be casted, the pattern is generally made from hard wood. If pattern is to be used several times, it may be made from aluminium, brass or even cast iron. The dimensions of the pattern are kept slightly more to allow for the shrinkage.

The pattern is generally made in two halves. The upper half and the lower half. Each half is kept in a rectangular frame called *flask*. The empty space between flask and pattern is filled with green (wetted) sand or loam. Vertical holes are developed at places in the sand, so as to serve as vent pipes. When sand acquires sufficient hardness, the pattern is slowly and carefully withdrawn. The mould for the product to be casted is ready for casting. The mould so preapred should be throughly cleaned and repaired, before molten metal is poured in it. Now the two halves of mould are placed one above the other and melted metal is poured in it. After some time the metal solidifies and casting is taken out of the mould. Irregularities left on the surface of casting are chipped off or rubbed out carefully.

Types of casting. Casting is a very specialized job and can be handled by experienced persons only. Here some fundamentals of casting have been given.

1. Centrifugal casting. In this method, molten metal is poured in to a rotating mould. Because of rotations, the molten metal spreads uniformly by centrifugal force. This method is used for casting C.I. pipes.

2. Chilled casting. Chilling is a process in which surface in its contact is subjected to sudden cooling, and this renders surface hard. In this method of casting, the outer surface of casting is made to cool suddenly, where as inner body is allowed to cool slowly. This renders outer surface of casting hard and inner surface rather soft. The mould used in this method may be made of metal or lined with metal. The hot molten metal is suddently cooled or chilled as it comes in contact with metallic surface of the mould. This type of casting is made use of in development of wear resistant surfaces, as in case of axle holes in railway carriage wheels etc.

3. Sand casting. It has already been discussed.

4. Die-casting. In this method of casting, molten metal is forced into the metal moulds under pressure. These castings are cheap, smooth, and compact. They require just removal of surplus metal and no other finishing treatment.

5. Hollow casting. In this method, a mould is made as usual and a solid core is placed in the middle. The molten metal is poured into the annualar space left between core and the mould. When metal has cooled, mould and core both are withdrawn. This casting is used for making hollow columns, pillars, pipes etc.

6. Vertifical sand casting. In this method sand mould and solid core are held in vertical position.

Requirements of a good casting

1. It should be free from cracks, air bubbles etc.
2. Its corners, edges, etc, should be clean, sharp and perfect.
3. Outer surface should be smooth.
4. Fractured surface should show fine grained uniform structure.
5. It should be capable of being chiselled or drilled.
6. It should be uniform and true to size and shape.

Casting defects. If proper care is not taken during casting, following defects may occur in the castings.

1. Cold short. The defect occurs, where two streams of molten metal do not unit properly.

2. Holes. This defect occurs, if vent holes are not adequately provided. This results in entrapping of air and gases which ultimately cause porous casting with holes.

3. Drawing. This defect is developed when molten metal solidifies, before the mould is completely filled up. This defect may be due to insufficient fluidity of molten metal, or due to inadequate space for entry of molten metal into the mould.

4. Lifts and shifts. These defects are only at the outer surface. They may develop due to movement in mould or core during casting.

5. Honey combing. This defect in the casting is due to fusing of surface sand on the casting.

6. Scabbing. This defect develops when mould sand is very heavy and sticks to casting. In this defect, scales are seen on the casting surface.

7. Swelling. This defect in castings may develop due to improper ramming of moulds.

QUESTIONS

1. Draw a new sketch of a cupola furnace and explain its working.
2. (*a*) Enumerate the properties of cast-iron.
   (*b*) State important uses of cast iron.
3. Discuss various types of cast iron.
4. How sand casting is done? Describe various types of castings.
5. (*a*) What are the defects in castings?
   (*b*) What are the qualities of good casting?

12
WROUGHT-IRON

12.1. Composition of Wrought Iron

It is considered as one of the purest forms of iron. Its composition is as follows :

Carbon	0.05% to 0.15%
Silica	0.15% to 0.2%
Phosphorous	0.12% to 0.16%
Sulphur	0.02% to 0.03%
Manganese	0.03% to 0.1%
Slag	2%

In this iron, slag remains distributed inform of a fine thread like filament. The slag acts as a barrier and prevents corrosion and fatigue cracks.

12.2. Manufacture of Wrought-iron

The process for manufacture of wrought iron is very laborious and tedious. The manufacture of this iron, involves following operations :

1. Refining of pig iron.
2. Puddling
3. Shingling or squeezing
4. Rolling

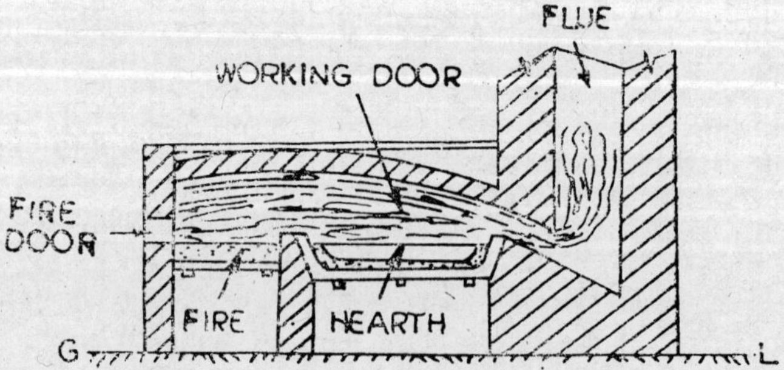

Fig. 12.1. Pudding furnace.

1. Refining of pig iron. No. 4 forge pig iron, which is white in colour, is used in the manufacture of wrought iron. The pig iron is melted in a furnace and a strong air current is made to pass over it. The melted iron being agitated, gets thoroughly oxidized. The oxidized mass is then cast into moulds and cooled suddenly to make is brittle. The resulting iron is known as *refined pig-iron*.

2. Puddling. Refined pig iron from refining stage is directly transferred into a furnace known as puddling kiln, reverberatory kiln or open hearth kiln. In modern methods, refining of pig iron stage as described above is usually, eliminated and manufacture of wrought iron is started from puddling stage only. Hence, it may be refined pig iron as obtained above or ordinary pig iron, it is charged into reverberatory furnace. Some amount of crushed lime stone is also added into the charge to act as fluxing agent. Oxidizing substances such as haematite ore, or oxide of iron, is also added to the charge. The charge is heated with the help of hot gases. The charge gets melted at about 2600°F within half an hour. Once the charge melts it is kept stirred continuously with the help of long handle rakes. Vigorous stirring is very essential in order to convert all the impurities to slag form. Iron oxide added in the charge oxidizes most of the impurities and results in the formation of carbon monoxide. This reaction causes the molten mass to boil-up and ultimately all the impurities are turned into slag form. The slag formed is removed through opening provided for this purpose.

The purified iron turns into thick pasty molten metal. This metal is converted into the balls varying in weight from 50 to 70 kg. These balls are also known as *puddle balls*.

The furnace used for puddling operation is shown in Fig. 12.1. It may be called puddling furnace, open hearth furnace, or reverberatory furnace. It consists of a source-shaped hearth which is lined by an oxidizing material like heamatite ore. This lining helps in eliminating the impurities in the iron. The combustion chamber and the chimney are situated on opposite ends of the hearth. Hearth is supported on steel plate which in turn is supported on dwarf brick walls. Water jacks are provided around the hearth to bring about cooling of the hearth by circulating water. The roof is given a peculiar shape so as to concentrate hot gases more on the hearth. Doors for feeding fuel, working, and slag removal etc. are also provided as per the requirements.

3. Shingling or squeezing. By this method, slag, which is contained in puddle balls is removed. This object may be achieved either by forging puddle balls under power hammers or by passing the balls through squeezing machine. The resulting material from this process is known as *bloom*.

4. Rolling. The squeezed balls (or bloom) are then passed through the grooved rollers in a rolling mill and bars known as muck bars are obtained. Muck bars still contain some slag and as such they are cut into pieces of about 90 cm length. These pieces are piled in cross-wise layers and heated to a welding heat in a furnace and rerolled. This removes slag further and refined iron is obtained. The bars produced at this stage are known as *merchant bars*. If these bars are again cut, stacked, heated in furnace and rerolled, the material gets still more purified and the resulting bars at this stage are known as *best bars*. In order to get wrought-iron of desired purity, this process may have to be repeated several times. Puddling process of manufacturing wrought iron is very expensive and as such not much used these days.

2. Astone's process of manufacturing wrought iron. This process of manufacturing wrought iron was developed by the James Aston of America in 1925. It is much quicker and cheaper method for manufacturing wrought iron in relation to puddling method.

Method. Pig iron containing low percentage of phosphorus is melted in cupola furnace. This molten iron is given soda ash treatment to remove any sulphur from the molten mass. The desulphized mass is transferred to bessemer convertor, where its temperature is raised to 1500°C. Slag is taken in a separate vessel and heated to 1200°C.

The molten metal from Bessemer convertor is pourd in the vessel containing comparatively cool slag. Molten metal contains large amounts of dissolved gases which are liberated when it strikes the slag. When molten steel comes in contact with slag which is comparatively at lower temperature, explosion take place and molten steel is converted into spongy mass having a temperature of about 1370°C. This spongy mass is given treatment of squeezing and rolling just like puddling method and ultimately, wrought-iron is obtained.

12.3. Properties of Wrought-Iron

1. It is ductile, tough and malleable material.
2. It can be easily forged and welded.
3. It cannot be used for castings as it fuses with difficulty.
4. It is corrosion resistant.
5. Its melting temperature is about 1535°C.
6. Its S.G. varies from 7.7 to 7.9.
7. Its ultimate tensile strength is about 4000 kg/cm^2 and compressive strength is about 2000 kg/cm^2.
8. It cannot be hardened or tempered.
9. It is the purest form of iron.
10. Fresh fracture shows clear bluish colour with a high silky lustre and fibrous appearance.

12.4. Defects in Wrought-Iron

Impurities like sulphur, phosphrous, silica and manganese are present in wrough-iron to some extent. Presence of these materials beyond certain limit, cause defects in any steel. The most common defects may be as follows :

1. Cold shortness. This defect is due to excessive presence of phosphrous (more than 0.6%) in the iron. Such wrought iron can be worked at high temperature, but not in cold condition as it is very brittle in that condition. Such as wrought iron cracks when bent cold or at low temperature.

2. Red shortness. This defect is caused, if sulphur is present in wrought iron more than 0.1% or so. Such a wrought iron possesses sufficient Tenacity, when cold, but it cracks when bent or finished at red heat. It is useless for welding purposes. This iron can be worked when cold, without cracking. Hence, this defect is entirely opposite in nature to cold shortness.

3. Blisters. This defect is caused when chemical reactions between carbon and iron oxide persists even after the manufacture of the article. This defect may even lead to corrosion of wrought iron.

4. Shelliness. This defect indicates the presence of loose textured areas in the metal. This defect is caused by defective manufacture of the article.

12.5. Use of Wrought-Iron

The use of wrought-iron has been replaced to a very large extent by mild steel. It is used only where tough material is required. Presently it is used, for rivets, railway couplings, water and steam pipes, bolts and nuts, horse shoes, bars, hand rails, straps for timber roof truses, chains etc. It can be used easily, worked hot or cold and as such it is used for fabricating Archetechtural works. It is also used in the manufacture of hard steel.

QUESTIONS

1. Draw a next sketch of reverberatory furnace and explain its working in details.
2. (*a*) What is difference between pig iron, cast iron, and wrought iron.

   (*b*) Describe the 'Asten's process of manufacturing wrought iron.
3. Explain the manufacture of wrought iron by puddling method. What is function of lime stone and iron oxide in the charge in reveberatory furnace?
4. (*a*) Explain defects and uses of wrought-iron.

   (*b*) What are the properties of wrought-iron?

13

STEEL AND ITS ALLOYS

13.1. Introduction

Steel is an intermediate form between cast iron and wrought iron. Cast iron contains the maximum amount of carbon, where as wrought iron contains the least. Cast iron is very good to take up compressive force and as such its use is limited to compressive members only. On the other hand wrought iron is a fibrous metal and is suitable for tensile forces only. Steel is the material which can be used both for compressive as well as tensile purposes. Steel is the most important basic material of this country. It has its application in practically all the spheres of Engineering. Steel is an alloy of iron and carbon. Pure iron without any carbon content is not very strong but when alloyed with carbon its strength can be increased remarkably. Iron when alloyed with carbon is known as steel, but when it is alloyed with other non-ferrous metals the resulting products are called *steel alloys*.

13.2. Mild Steel, Medium Steel and High Carbon Steel

As already discussed in earlier chapters that iron containing carbon varying from 2% to 4% is known as cast iron and that containing carbon from 0.25 to 1.5% is known as steel. By varying the carbon content various type of steels can be produced.

1. Low carbon steel or mild steel. This steel contains carbon upto 0.25%.

2. Medium carbon steel. This steel contains carbon varying from 0.25% to 0.7%.

3. High carbon steel. This steel contains carbon varying from 0.7% to 1.5%.

The properties like ductility, hardness, tensile strength etc., can be greatly improved by giving suitable heat treatment to the steel.

13.3. Manufacture of Steel

There are seven processes or methods by which manufacture of steel can be carried out. Brief description of each method has been given. The methods are:

1. Bessemer process. 2. Open hearth process.

3. Cementation process.
4. Crucible process.
5. Duplex process.
6. L.D. process.
7. Electrical process.

1. Bessemer process. This method is named according to the furnace used. Bessemer converter shown in Fig. 13.1. is used in this method. This process may be acidic or basic depending upon the nature of lining material of the converter. In acidic process the lining may be made of clay, quartz etc. Acidic lining is used when pig-iron used for the extraction, either does not contain or contains very small percentage of sulphur and phosphrous. In basic process, lining used is made of basic material such as manganese, lime etc. This lining is used for the pig iron containing any type of impurities. Basic processs is commonly used in this method as it is suitable for any type of impurities in the pig iron charge.

The converter consists of a steel vessel wide at the bottom, but narrowed at the top. It is mounted on horizontal axis in such a way, that it can be tilted at suitable angle in vertical plane. Tuyeres are provided at the bottom to allow the passage of air from air ducts.

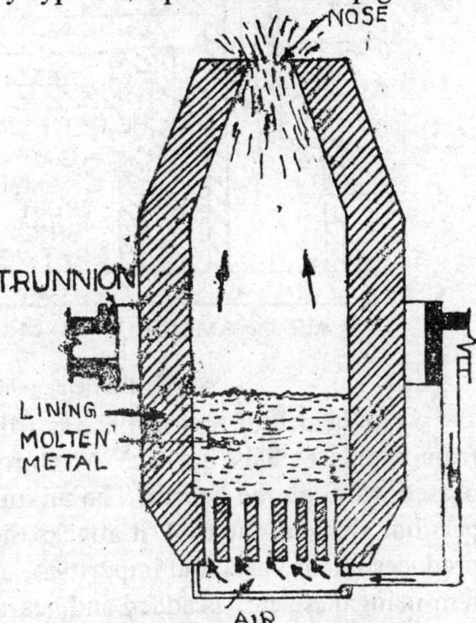

Fig. 13.1. Bessemer converter.

The converter is tilted and charged with molten pig-iron being received from cupola furnace. Some times molten pig-iron may be admitted directly from blast furnace also. The converter is brought to the upright position and a blast of hot air is forced through tuyeres provided at the bottom. Air blast while passsing through molten pig-rion oxidizes impurities of pig-iron. A brilliant reddish yellow flame is seen at the mouth of the converter and a loud roaring sound in the converter indicates the continuance of oxiation of impurities in the converter.. All the impurities get oxidized within 10 to 15 minutes and at this stage, intensity of flame at the mouth of the converter is reduced considerably. Silicon is oxidized first, then carbon, manganese, sulphur in the same order and lastly the phosphorous.

When oxidation is achieved, blast of air is shut off and ferro-manganese, spiegeleisen etc. is added in the required amount to obtain the steel of desired quality.

Blast of air is restarted for five minutes and the molten mass is now ready for discharge from the converter. The conveter is tilted and molten mass is poured into containers or moulds. On solidification, solid mass is take out of moulds. This solid mass is known as *ingot*. These ingots are then furnace treated to obtain steel in commercial forms.

2. Open hearth process. Like Bessemer process, this process may also be basic or acidic. Basic open hearth process is mostly used. The open hearth furnace is show in Fig 13.2. Construction of furnace can be easily understood from the diagram itself. It almost resembles the reverberatory furnace used in the manufacture of wrought iron.

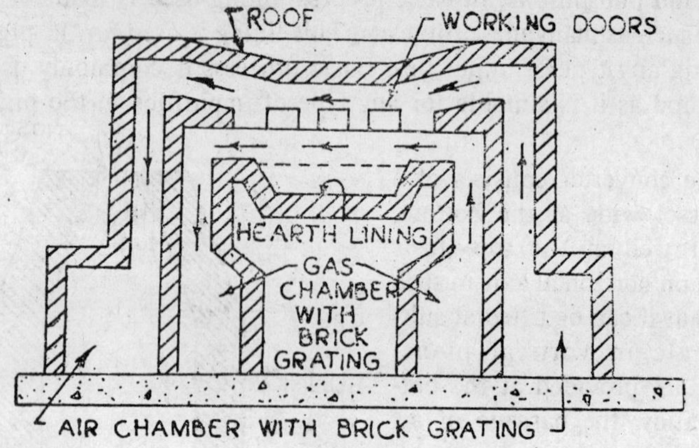

Fig. 13.2. Open hearth furnace.

The hearth of this furnace is filled with molten pig-iron received from cupola or blast furnace. Mixture of coal gas and preheated air is passed, through the hearth. The mixture catches fire and because of the peculiar shape of the roof, it attacks the molten mass of the hearth. This produces intense heat and impurities get oxidized. After this spiegeleisen, fero-manganese etc., is added and hearth is again heated for few minutes. The molten mass in the hearth is ready to be taken out which is filled is moulds and obtained inform of ingots. Ingots are latter further treated to obtain the commercial steel.

This method is very much used in the manufacture of steel because of following advantages:

(*i*) It gives out basic slag which can be used as a very good fertilizer.

(*ii*) The operation of this furnace is simple

(*iii*) It consumes very little time in oxidation of impurities.

(*iv*) Steel obtained by this process is of more uniform character.

(*v*) Scrap is used in form of spiegeleisen and as such, it is converted to a useful steel.

(*vi*) Hot gases can be regenerated and recirculated for heating the hearth. This aspect causes a great economy in fuel consumption.

3. Cementation process. This process is not used now a days. This process consists, first converting pig-iron to almost pure wrought iron and then adjusting the carbon content, to obtain the steel of desired quality. In this process dome shaped cementation furnace is used. In the furnace pure wrought iron bars are taken and put between layers of powdered charçoal and furnaces. Intense heat is maintained for a period, varying from 5 days to 15 days as per the desired quality of the steel. During this process carbon from charcoal combines with wrought iron and steel of desired composition is formed. This steel is covered with blisters or thin bubbles and hence, it is known as *blister steel*.

4. Crucible process. It is used to manufacture high carbon steel. Fragments of blister steel or bars of pure wrough iron are mixed with charcoal and heated in fire-clay crucibles. The molten steel is poured in to moulds to prepare ingots. Steel thus prepared is also known as *cast steel*. This steel is used for making surgical instruments, files, and superior quality cutlery. This steel is hard and of homogeneous quality.

5. Duplex process. This process is combination of acid Bessemer process and Basic open-hearth process. Molten pig-iron is first treated in acid lined Bessemer converter to remove impurities like carbon, silica, and manganese. The charge is then transferred to basic-lined open-hearth furnace and impurities, such as sulphur and phosphorus are removed.

In order to improve the quality of steel further. Duplex process may be extended to Triplex process. The molten steel as obtained from basic lined open hearth furnace is further treated in electric furnace.

6. L.D. process. In this process, pure oxygen is used in place of blast of air. The charge is put in L.D. converter and a jet of oxygen is brown through the molten metal. High temperature in the converter burns away the impurities and pure low carbon steel is prepared. This process has following disadvantages.

(i) A separate oxygen plant has to be established.

(ii) It is difficult to exercise control over the temperature.

(iii) It cannot handle all grades of pig-iron.

7. Electric process. The basic difference in the process and Bessemer or open hearth process is the use of electricity for melting and heating purposes. It consists of a vessel made steel plates and lined with basic refractory lining material. The vessel is tiltable. Electrode are fitted in the vessel and electric arcs are developed, which produce intense heat and cause charge in the vessels to melt. This method can not be used for manufacture of steel on large scale as its capacity is only about 10 to 15 tonnes. It is, however, useful for the manufacture of special steel on smalls scale. This method has the following advantages :

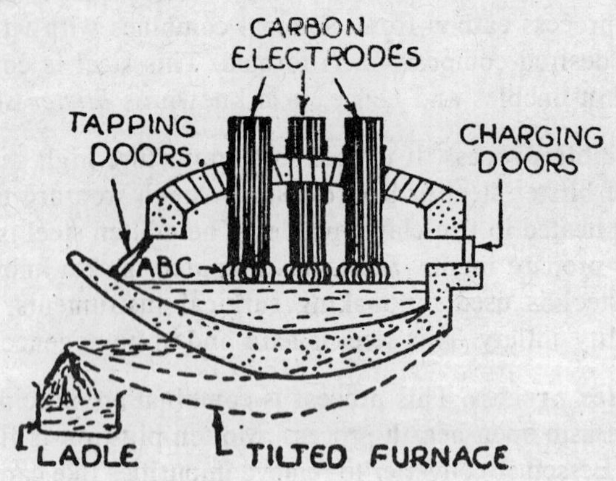

Fig. 13.3. Electric furnace.

(i) There is no smoke, ash, and as such neat the clean operation.

(ii) Temperature can be easily controlled.

(iii) Amount of slag formed is small.

(iv) It is very quick process.

13.4. Uses of Steel

The uses of steel containing different percentage of carbon have been given in Table 13.1.

Table 13.1. Use of Steel

Percentage of carbon	*Uses*
0.05 to 0.10	Pipes, wire, nails, tubes, welding stock, soft sheets motor body, tin plates.
0.10 to 0.20	Rivets, screws, pipes, tubes, bars, wires, machine fittings subjected to light stresses.
0.2 to 0.30	Gears, boiler plates, shafts, machine fitting, structural shapes, bars, pipes
0.3 to 0.40	Gears, keys, axles, connecting rods, forged and cold worked machine, spindles.
0.4 to 0.5	Heavily stressed machine parts, gears, axles, shafts, spring wire.
0.6 to 0.7	Rails, screw drivers, locomotive parts.
0.7 to 0.8	Springs, hammers, clutch plates, pick axes, chisels.
0.8 to 0.9	Chisels, dies, hand tools, punches, blades for hot shearing tools etc.
0.9 to 1.0	Drills, cutters, axes, dies, springs, large turning tools.
1.0 to 1.1	Planers, lathe, springs, drills, sharpner tools, axes, cutlery.
1.1 to 1.2	Thread cutting dies, carpenter's tool, small cutters, lathe tools.
1.2 to 0.3	Files, tools for planing extra hard wood, slotting tools, knives, razors, drills etc.
1.3 to 1.4.	Razor blades, turning tools, stone cutting tools, drills, files, wire drawing dies etc.

Steel having carbon content less than 0.1% is known as *deed steel* or *very low carbon steel*. Steel with carbon content up to 0.25% is termed as mild steel, upto 0.7% medium carbon steel and from 0.7 to 1.4 or 1.5% is known as *high carbon steel* or *hard steel*.

13.5. Factors Affecting Physical Properties of Steel

Strength, elasticity, ductility etc. are the physical properties of steel. The properties, get largely affected by following factors.

1. Carbon content.
2. Presence of impurities like sulphur, phosphorus, silicon etc.
3. Heat-treatment processes.

1. Carbon content. Steels of varying grades are produced by varying the carbon content. Higher the carbon content, more is the hardness and strength, but there is consequent decreases is ductility.

Effects of varying carbon content and use of such steel is shown in Table 13.1. Mild steel is very widely used for structural works.

2. Presence of impurities. The usual impurities of steel are sulphur, phosphorus, silicon and manganese. Effects of each impurity are as follows:

Sulphur. Upto 0.1%, sulphur does not affect the strength or ductility of the steel appreciably. Malleability and weldability is however, decreased in hot condition. Excessive amount of sulphur causes decrease in ductility and strength of the steel.

Phosphorus. It increases the fluidity of steel in molten state otherwise, its effect is always deterimental on the properties of steel. Its content in steel should preferably be kept less than 0.12%. Excessive amount of phosphorus decreases strength, ductility, and shock resistance.

Silicon. Up to 0.2% it does not affect the physical properties of steel. If its content is raised say up to 0.4% elasticity and strength are considerably increased without affecting ductility of steel seriously.

Mangnese. Upto 1% it rather improves the strength properties of steel. But when its amount exceeds 1.5% or so, steel becomes very brittle, and hence not much useful for structural purposes.

3. Heat treatment. Properties of steel can be altered to suit to our conditions by heating and cooling steel under controlled conditions. There are a number of heat treatment processes and as such they have been discussed ahead in this chapter under separate head.

13.6. Magnetic Properties of Steel

Since steel is very much used in electrical machinery to develop magnetic fields, its magnetic properties have to be studied. Magnetic properties can be altered by altering chemical composition of the steel. To achieve best magnetic properties proportions of various elements in steel should be as follows:

(i) Carbon. Lesser the carbon contant the better it is for magnetic properties. It should not be allowed to exceed 0.1%.

(ii) Silicon. Its content is deterimental as far as magnetic properties are concerned. It should not be maintained as low as possible.

(iii) Sulphur and Phosphorus. Increased amount of these elements decrease the magnetic properties. The combined percentage of these elements should not be allowed to exceed about 0.3%.

(iv) Manganese. Its amount also should not be allowed to exceed 0.3%.

13.7. Defects in Steel

Common defects in steel may be the following ones:

1. Cold shortness. This defect is due to excess amount of phosphorus being present in the steel. When steel is worked in cold state it cracks.

2. Red shortness. This defect is due to excess amount of sulphur. Such a steel cracks when worked in hot state.

3. Segregation. This defect is caused by differential solidification of constituents of the steel. Some constituents solidify earlier than the others and thus get separated. This defect is prominent on the top surface of ingots or castings.

4. Blow holes or cavities. The defect is caused when gas remains confined in the molten metal. On solidification, these gas bubbles come out and form blow-holes or cavities in the steel mass.

5. Internal cracks. These cracks are developed due to internal stresses developed during solidification of liquid mass. They may also develop during reheating the ingots.

6. Scabs. They are formed on the surface of an ingot, when molten steel is poured in the ingot mould. When liquid metal is poured into the ingot mould, it splashes and some of the splashes stick to the walls of the ingot and get solidified. When liquid steel rises to that level in the mould, it fails to forge with already solidified splashes and they remain on the surface of the steel ingot inform of scabs. This defect can be removed by chipping the ingot surface.

7. Pipes. These are irregularly shapped shrinkage cavities formed in the upper central portion of the solidified steel ingots. Since the liquid steel which solidifies in the last is contained in the upper central region of the ingot, the liquid metal leaves a pipe or cavity as it contracts during solidification.

13.8. Mechanical Treatment of Steel

Mechanical treatment is given to steel ingots, so as to convert them into market forms. The main object of the mechanical treatment is to improve the quality of the metal by forcing its particles closer. This treatment may be hot working or cold working. In cold working the steel is shaped at room temperature. In hot working the metal is heated to a temperature above its recrystallization temperature and than shaped. Hot working is the most common method of working the steel. Following operations are involved in mechanical treatment of steel.

1. Drawing
2. Forging
3. Pressing
4. Rolling
5. Extrusion.

1. Drawing. This method is used for the manufacture of wires and cylinderical rods. The metal is drawn through dies or other specially shaped tools. Dies are usually made up of hard steel or tungsten steel.

2. Forging. In this process the metal is heated above the prescribed temperature. Heated steel is put on anvil and beaten under the blows of hammer. The process improves the grain size of the metal and also increases the density of the steel. Forging may be done by hammer blows as described above or with the help of forging machine.

3. Pressing. This process is carried out in an equipment known as press. The metal to be shaped is placed on the die and it is subjected to slowly applied continued pressure till the steel gets completely filled up in the die. The metal thus pressed between the die and press takes the desired shape. This process is useful, when large number of similar articles are to be manufactured. The steel plates for tanks, thick hollow cylinders, boiler heads, are generally prepared by this method.

4. Rolling. In this method a set of specially prepared rolling mills is used. Ingots or blooms, while still is red hot condition are made to pass through different rollers, in succession till the articles of desired shapes are obtained. All the structural members of steel such as angles, channels, flats, joists, rails, bars, etc. are all obtained by the process of rolling. It is possible to manufacture even jointless pipe by this process.

5. Extrusion. In this process, the heated metal is forced under very high pressure through an opening or die. High pressure is applied either by mechanical press or hydraulic press. Rods, pipes, tubes, etc., can be manufactured by this method.

13.9. Heat Treatment Processes of Steel

Properties of steel can be largely controlled and altered by heating and cooling steel under controlled conditions. Following are the purposes of heat treatment.

(i) To suitably adjust the magnetic properties of steel.

(ii) To alter the structure of steel.

(iii) To increase the hardness of the surface.

(iv) To render the steel easily workable.

(v) To increase the resistance against corrosion and heat.

Heat treatment is an operation or a combination of operations involving the heating and cooling of the metal for the purpose of obtaining desirable properties in metal. This treatment consists of heating the metal above the critical temperature maintained for some definite time and finally cooling the metal in some medium which may be oil, air, water, brine or molten salts. The principle processes involved in heat treatment of steel are as follows:

1. Quenching or hardening 2. Annealing

3. Case hardening 4. Tempering
5. Normalizing.

1. Quenching or hardening. This treatment is given to make steel hard. It consists of *putting heated metal into a bath of oil, water or brine*. Structural changes caused during heating of the metal are permanently trapped by this method. Bath of oil, water or brine is known as *quenching medium*. Quenching medium is selected according to the degree of hardness required to be achieved. Following are the usual quenching mediums for different types of steels.

I. Ordinary carbon steel.	1 clear water
2. To obtain increased degree of hardness	1 brine
3. To ensure uniform hardness, toughness and warpage.	1 oil

Quenching is nothing, but cooling of the heated article at controlled rate.

2. Annealing. This process is adopted to make the steel soft, so that it may be easily worked. In this process, the steel is heated to about 50°C to 55°C above its critical temperature range. The metal is held at this temperature for specified period and then allowed to cool slowly in the furnace in which it was heated. Annealing temperatures are given as follows.

Carbon content in steel	*Range of annealine temp. in degrees C*
up to 0.12%	870 to 925°C
0.13 to 0.29%	840 to 870°C
0.30 to 0.49%	815 to 840°C
0.50 to 1.00%	790 to 815°C

Annealing brings about the following changes in steel.

(i) The grains of metal are refined without affecting the ductility seriously.

(ii) To remove the internal stresses developed during various operations.

(iii) To remove the entrapped gases from the metal.

(iv) To soften the metal and improve machining qualities.

(v) To obtained desired toughness, ductility and malleability.

(vi) To bring about the change in physical, magnetic and electrical properties of the metal.

3. Case hardening. In this treatment, the core of the metal remains unchanged, but its surface is rendered hard. This change in the surface is brought about by increasing the carbon content at the surface.

The metal to be given this treatment is held in the carburizing mixture for definite time and at a definite temperature. Temperature and time, depend upon the depth of case hardening required and also upon the composition of steel. The temperature range is generally 900°C to 930°C and period of case hardening varies usually from 6 hours to 8 hours. Once the metal has been carburized, it is treated in one of the following ways to complete the process of case hardening.

(i) It may be quenched directly at carburizing temperature.

(ii) It may be cooled slowly in the carburizing box and then reheated and quenched.

(iii) It may be cooled slowly in the carburizing box and then reheated twice and also quenched twice.

The above mentioned process is the general process of case hardening. There are other processes of case hardening such as cyaniding, nitriding, flame hardening, induction hardening, but these processes adopt specially prepared carburizing mixture and specially designed furnaces. Depth of case hardening depends upon the nature of carburizing mixture, period of heating and temperature of the furnace during heating. Higher the temperature and more period of heating cause case hardening for larger depths.

Carburizing mixtures may be many. Commonly used mixtures may be following ones.

(i) 95% wood charcoal and 5% soda ash.

(ii) Animal charcoal.

(iii) Cyanides.

(iv) Finely cut leather pieces.

Precautions in case hardening.

(i) Alloy steels should be quenched in oil.

(ii) Quenching in water is preferred. But if articles are of unequal or uneven shapes they should be quenched in oil.

(iii) The article should be kept in such condition, that it can expand freely in all the directions.

(iv) The carburizing box should be totally free from air.

(v) Thickness of carburizing layer should be 25 mm at least.

4. Tempering. This process of treatment is applied on articles which have already been treated with the hardening process. In this the article which has been quenched in hardening process is reheated to temperature normally below critical temperature. The temperature is maintained for pre-determined duration which depends on the quality of steel required and composition of steel being tempered. After this the article is allowed to cool down in still air.

Tempering is adopted to achieve the following objects:

(i) To develop a desirable combination of ductility and hardness.

(ii) To relieve the article from high internal stresses developed during hardening process.

5. **Normalizing**. In this process, the steel is heated to temperature ranging from 840°C to 950°C and allowed to cool in air. As cooling is more rapid, less time is available to achieve equilibrium and as a result of this, the material becomes harder than fully annealed steel. The aim of normalizing is to promote uniformity of structure, secure grain refinement and to bring about other desirable changes in the properties of the metal.

13.10. Properties of Mild Steel

1. Its S.P. Gravity is 7.8 and melting point is about 1400°C.
2. It is malleable and ductile.
3. It has fibrous structure and not easily attacked by salt water.
4. It can be easily welded and forged.
5. It can be given heat treatment easily.
6. It can be magnetized.
7. It rusts easily.
8. It is harder and tougher than wrought iron.
9. It is used for all types of structural works.
10. Its ultimate compressive and tensile strengths vary respectively between ranges of 8 to 12 t/cm^2 and 6 to 8 t/cm^2.

13.11. Properties of Hard steel

1. It can be made permanent magnets.
2. It can be tempered and hardened easily.
3. It can be welded and forged easily.
4. It has granular structure and not easily attacked by salt water.
5. It is more elastic and tough than mild steel.
6. It also readily rusts.
7. Its S.G. is 7.9 and melting temperature about 1300°C.
8. Its ultimate compressive strength varies from 14 to 20 t/cm^2 and tensile strength from 8 to 11 t/cm^2.
9. Its tensile strength and shear strengths are almost equal.
10. It is used for edge tools, cutlery tools, and other situations, where frequent shocks and vibrations develop.

13.12. Corrosion of Ferrous metals

Conversion of metals into their oxides and other compounds by natural agencies is called *corrosion*. Corrosion is also referred by term rusting. Steels suffer from rusting difficulty to the maximum extent. There are a number of theories that explain the causes of rusting. These theories do not come under the perview of this topic and as such not explained. Preventive measures for rusting which are of importance for every body have been explained. Coaltar painting, painting with other paints, electroplating, enamelling, tin plating. etc., are the usual methods of preventing corrosion. A brief description of each method has been given here.

1. Tarring. The surface is covered by coalter which is applied hot with the help of brushes. This method is used on the surfaces, which remain embedded. Exposed surfaces get spoiled by it and hence not used.

2. Electroplating. In this method, ferrous metal surfaces are covered by copper, nickel etc. with the help of electric current. The surfaces covered by this method are smooth and shining.

3. Enamelling. In this method, iron surface is covered by melting a suitable flux on it.

4. Painting. Surface of iron is covered by paint. The paint may be applied on the surface by brushes or by means of spray guns.

5. Galvanizing. Thoroughly cleaned ferrous metal is dipped in a tub of molten zinc resulting in deposition of thin zinc layer, which protects the surface against rusting.

6. Metal spraying. In this method, iron surface is covered with a spray of vaporized, zinc, tin or aluminium. The layer gives very good protection against rusting.

7. Tin plating. Surface of iron or steel is thoroughly cleaned by dilute acid and then dipped in a bath of molten tin. House hold utencils and dairy equipments should be tin plated. Tin plating may be done by the process of electroplating also.

8. Parkerising. The article to be treated is kept immersed in hot solution known as Pareo for a period of about one hour. Due to chemical reaction of Pareco, insoluble phosphates are deposited on the surface of the article and protect the surface against rusting.

9. Sheradising. The article to be treated is cleaned and then embedded in pure zinc dust which is enclosed in an air tight box and heated to a temperature varying from 250°C to 450°C. Zinc melts in the box and forms a protective layer on metal surface.

10. Embedding in cement concrete. If steel is kept embedded in cement concrete, it is not affected by rusting or corrosion.

13.13. Market forms of steel

The steels are available in following forms in the Market. These forms are angles, channals, T-sections, I-sections, corrugated sheets, flat bars, square bars, round bars, etc. All these sections are also known as *structural steel sections* corrugated sheets, welded wire, fabrics, expanded metal and slotted angles are some other commercial forms of steel.

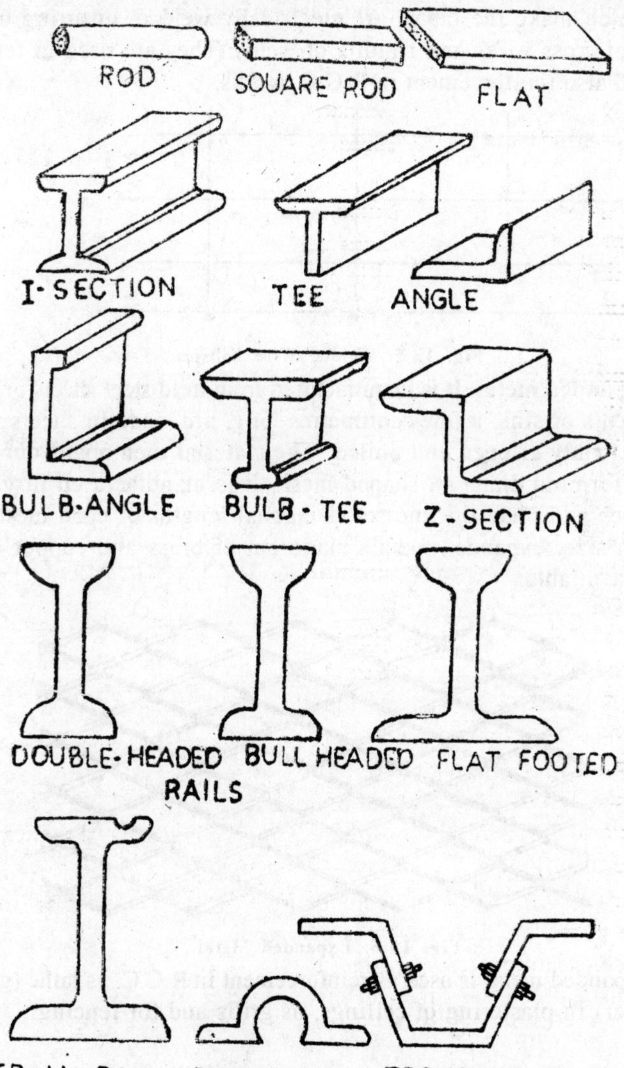

Fig. 13.4. Structural steel sections.

Corrugated sheets. Iron sheets are strengthened by providing corrugations that have the cross-section of sine curve. These sheets are protected against corosion by galvanising and are called galvanised corrugated iron sheets abbreviated as G.C.I. sheets. Without corrugations, they are abbreviated as G.I. sheets. These sheets are 66 cm wide and upto 3 m long. Their thickness varies from 24 gauge to 16 gauge. They are used as roof covering for trussed roofs.

Welded wire fabrics. These are manufactured in sheets, or rolls and available in rectangular or square mesh of steel wires. The cross wires which make the fabric are electrically welded, ensuring correct spacing of cross wires and rigidity of welds. They are used in fencing, grills and also reinforcement in R.C.C. works.

Fig. 13.5. Welded Wire Fabrics.

Expanded metal. It is manufactured from mild steel sheets or plates parallel cuts or slits, a few centimetres long, are made in sheets which are than firmly gripped and pulled. The material then opens out along the slits forming diamond shaped mesh. It is manufactured in various mesh sizes and plate thicknesses. Diagonal lengths of each mesh give the mesh size, expanded metals made out of brass and copper sheets also are available.

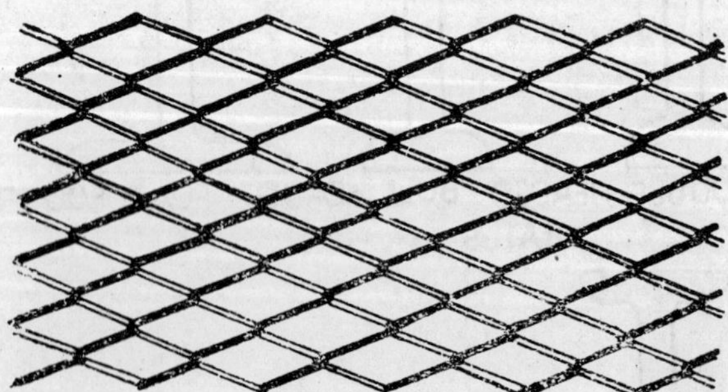

Fig. 13.6. Expanded Metal.

Expanded metal is used as reinforcement in R.C.C. as lathe (ground for plaster) in plastering of ceilings, as grills and for fencing.

Slotted angles. Angles with slots at regular intervals are marketed by different firms in different sizes. Lengths of each slotted angle is 3 m and the three commonly available sizes are 75 × 40 × 2.5 mm, 60 × 40 × 3.0 mm and 35 × 35 × 1.8 mm. Punched steel straps 38 × 2 mm are available in 3 m lengths. Two pieces of it are jointed by tightening nuts and bolts. These are good for assembly of structural components, scaffolds, benches and library or other storage racks. These may be used in combination with ply wood, hard board, Asbestos or wire mesh etc. It helps in easy and frequent fabrications and cutting down costs.

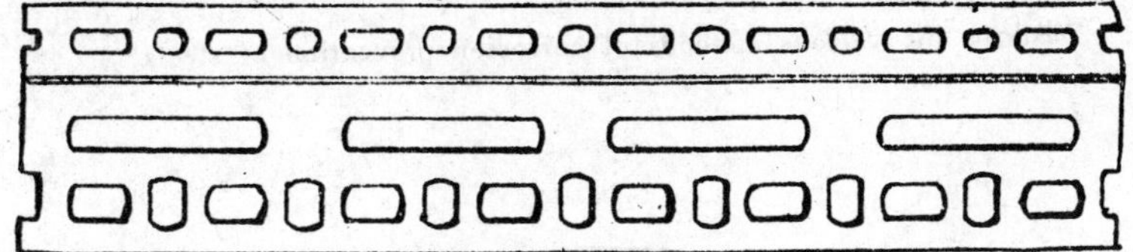

Fig. 13.7. Slotted Angles.

Stainless steel. It is an alloy of iron which is characterized by its pronounced resistance to corrosion. It is a steel having low carbon content and chromium content of over 12%. Now a days steels are manufactured in wide range of brands, each having distinct chemical composition as well as different physical properties. Stainless steel may be grouped in three categories.

First group of stainless steels. It contains chromium less than 14%, carbon less than 0.4% with small additions of nickel, copper, tungsten etc. Stainless steel of this category can be welded, machined, hardened by suitable heat treatment. This stainless steel is used for making steam valves, turbine blades, surgical instruments, scissors, knives, gears, ball bearings, springs etc.

Second group of stainless steels. This group of stainless steels contains chromium varying between 16 to 20% and carbon content not more than 0.45%. They are also known by *ferric stainless steels*. They can be forged, welded, rolled, machined, but do not respond easily to heat treatment. These steels can be used in the manufacture of valves, pipes, used in the chemical and food plants.

Third group of stainless steel. This groups of stainless steels, contains at least 24% chromium. There is nickel combined, but amount of chromium or nickel should not be less than 8%. Steels of this group cannot be hardened by heat treatment. They are non-magnetic in soft conditions. 18/8 stainless steel means, it contains 18% chromium and 8% nickel. This steel is used in daries, cooking and dining utencils, cutlery, chemical plants. etc.

QUESTIONS

1. Define 'mild steel. How does it differ from cast-iron, and wrought iron?
2. Describe the various processes adopted in the manufacture of steel ingots.
3. What do you understand by the term acidic or basic furnace? Describe in details the manufacture of steel by basic Bessemer process.
4. What are factors which effect the physical properties of steel?
5. (*a*) State the defects in steel.

   (*b*) State various uses of mild steel.
6. What are the operations involved in the mechanical treatment of steel?
7. What are purposes of heat treatment of steel? Discuss various processes of heat treatment.
8. Describe the various methods of corrosion prevention of steels.

14

NON-FERROUS METALS

14.1. Introduction

Like iron, non-ferrous metals also carry an equal importance in the field of their application. The use of non-ferrous metals is limited as far as engineering structures are concerned. In this chapter details of manufacture of all the metals will not be given. Only fundamentals of extraction, properties, and uses of principal non-ferrous metals has been given.

14.2. Aluminium

Aluminium is extracted from bauxite (Al_2O_3 $2H_2O$). Extraction consists of two operations namely.

(i) Purification of the bauxite ore and

(ii) Electrolysis of the purified bauxite, to get aluminium at about 1000°C.

The aluminium obtained is 99 to 99.5% pure metal.

Properties. Pure aluminium is a very soft metal and hence has to be alloyed with other metals, so as to make it useful for structural purposes. It is highly ductile, and malleable metal. Its melting point is 658°C and S.G. 2.7. It is very light metal and resists corrosion very effectively. It possesses large toughness, and tensile strength. Its colour is silvery white, having a high lustre. It can be rolled into sheets. It is a good conductor of heat and electricity.

Uses. I. This metal when alloyed with other metals is used for making pistons, cylinders, in aeroplane engines.

(ii) It is coming in use increasingly in form of electric cables.

(iii) It is used for making automobile bodies, utencils, etc.

(iv) Aluminium paints are made from it.

(v) It is used as a protective coating to structural steel work.

(vi) It is coming increasing is use for making show cases high class doors and windows, furnitures, etc.

14.3. Copper

This metal is obtained from copper pyrite ($CuFeS_2$) ores. It contains about 30% copper. This ore is found in Bihar, Rajasthan, Orissa states.

Extraction of copper from its ores involves a very complex process which may be divided into four stages *viz* ; *(i)* Roasting, *(ii)* Smelting, *(iii)* Converting and *(iv)* Electrolytic refining.

The ores are crushed to small pieces and roasted in a reverberatory furnace to dull redness in the presence of air. Most of the sulphur, present in the ore gets removed during this operation. Roasted ores are than mixed with lime stone and a small quantity of coke and mixture is charged into a blast furnace or reverboratory furnace, again. The mixture is smelted here and most of the impurities are removed from the metal in form of slag. The melted metal is oxidized in Bessemer converter and copper known as *blister copper* in obtained. Impurities from blister copper are removed by melting is a reverberatory furnace in the presence of air. The slag is removed from the top and copper with 99.70% purity is obtained. 100% pure copper is obtained by electrolysis process.

Properties of copper

1. It is soft and ductile metal.

2. It can be rolled and worked in cold and hot states. But it cannot be welded.

3. Its colour is reddish brown.

4. Its melting temperature is 1083°C.

5. Its. S.G. is 8.90.

6. It is not attacked by water at any temperature.

7. It is good conductor of heat and electricity.

8. It can be alloyed with other metals.

9. It can be made strong, hard, tough and malleable by suitable treatment.

10. It is highly resistant to atmospheric corrosion.

11. Its tensile strength varies between 3 and 4 Hcm^2 5t/cm^2.

Uses. It is very much used in electrical goods and cables, household, utensils, Alloys, electroplating etc. It is also used as material for damp-proof course, flashing etc. On exposure, to atmosphere, it forms a self-protecting film of oxide which resists further corrosion of the metal even, if it is used in polluted atmosphere. It is also used in the manufacture of thin sheets, water pipes, gutters, taps, tanks, hardware fittings, etc.

14.4. Lead

This metal is obtained from ore known as Galena (Pbs). This metal does not occur free in nature. Galena contains about 86% lead. The ore is first roasted to reduce the sulphur content. There after roasted ores are smelted in a blast furnace which produce a mass known as *Lead bullion*. It is an impure lead which consists of other impurities like copper, silver, antimony, etc. The impure metal is remelted in a reverberatory furnace and pure lead is obtained.

Properties. 1. It is a soft metal which can be cut by knife.

1. Its melting temperature is 326°C.

3. Its S.G. is 11.36.

4. It forms black impressions on paper.

5. It is lustrous metal having bluish-grey colour.

6. When heated strongly in the presence of air, it is converted into litharge.

7. Lead is not acted upon by atmospheric corrosion.

8. It is slightly soluble in certain soft and acid type of drinking water and may lead to lead poisoning.

9. It is resistant to the action of alkalies, sulphuric acid and Hydrochloric acid.

10. It is mostly used in form of oxides like white lead, red lead and litharge.

11. It is a malleable metal and can be rolled into thin sheets.

Uses. 1. Compounds of lead are commonly used as pigments for paints.

2. It is also very much used in chemical processing industry.

3. It is the only metal for making bullets, shots.

4. It is also used for storage cells, sanitary fitting, cisterns water proof and acid proof chambers.

5. It is also used for gas pipes, roof gutters, printing types, D.P.C. cable coverings etc.

14.5. Zinc

This metal does not occur in free state in nature. Zinc is obtained from ores named calamine ($ZnaCO_3$) and zinc blende (ZnS).

The process of manufacture of Zn consists of reduction of ores to the oxide form. Zinc oxide is then heated to 2000°F in an electric furnace and pure zinc is liberated in the form of vapour which is then condensed. The condensed zinc is taken out of the chamber in form of liquid, skimmed, and poured into moulds to form slabs or cast into ingots. The solidified zinc thus obtained is called *spelter*. Zinc may also be extracted by electrolytic refining.

Properties. 1. Its. S.G. is 6.86.

2. It is not affected by dry air.

3. Its colour is bluish white.

4. Its melting temperature is 419°C.

5. It can be rolled into sheets and drawn into wires between temperature range of 100°C to 150°C.

6. When strongly heated in air, it burns with a greenish white flame.

7. At ordinary temperature it is brittle.

8. It is not attacked by pure water.

Uses. 1. It is used in electric cells and batteries.

2. It is used for galvanizing the other metals.

3. It is very much used in paints and alloys.

4. It is also used in die casting, brass-making, engraving etc.

14.6. Tin

Tin occurs in nature in the form of oxides. The process of extraction consists crushing, roasting and then smelting of the ore to a temperature of about 1000°C in blast or reverberatory furnace. The tin ore is in oxide form (SnO_2). It is called tin stone or cassterite. The crude tin as obtained from reverberatory or blast furnace is further refined either by or heating or by electrolysis. Refined metal is cast in mould for further shaping.

Properties. 1. When a tin bar is bent, a peculiar sound occurs which is also known as *cry of tin*.

2. Tin is a silvery-white lustrous and malleable metal.

3. Its melting temperature is 232°C.

4. It becomes brittle when heated to a temperature of about 200°C.

5. It is not affected by dry air and pure water.

6. Its S.G. is 7.30.

Uses: 1. It is used in alloys with lead and other metals.

2. It is used in the form of protective and decorative coatings for metals like iron, copper, brass, lead etc.

3. It is used in form of foil for wrapping cheese and other products.

4. It is also used in the manufacture of collapsible tubes and pipes for toilet purposes.

14.7. Nobel Metals

Gold, silver, and platinum are the metals which come under this category of metals. They are very costly. A brief description of each has been given here.

1. Gold (Au). Gold occurs widely distributed through out the world, but its concentration is very low. Gold is generally found in veins among rocks and ores of other metals. It is also found in form of dust in the river beds.

Properties. It is a bright yellow metal having density 19.3. Its melting point is 1063°C and boiling point that at 2700°C. It is very malleable and ductile metal and it can be beaten to sheets as thin as 0.00001 mm. It readily dissolves in mercury to form amalgams. It is considered chemically least active metal. It does not oxidise, when exposed to air and maintains its brightness for years.

Uses. It is used for making coins and jewellery. It is also used in printing and decoration of porcelain. It is also used in electrical field.

2. Silver (Ag). It occurs as a free element in nature or in alloyed form with other metals like lead, copper, etc. It is mostly found in ores containing silver compounds. In malleability and ductility, it is next only to gold. Its density is 10.5. It is good conductor of heat and electricity. It cannot be oxidized by heat, but can be oxidized chemically and electrically.

Uses. *(i)* It is used very much in the production of photographic films and papers.

(ii) It is also used as a solder, where strong joints are required.

(iii) It is used for coinage, jewellery, and household wares.

(iv) Silver alloys are used for providing heavy duty bearings.

(v) It is used for electoplating.

(vi) A special alloy of silver called amalgam is most widely used by dentists as tooth filling material.

3. Platinum (Pt.). It is a greyish-white metal, very ductile and malleable. It is hard and does not corrode easily. Its density is 21.45 and melting temperature 1773°C. It can easily resist the attack of water, air sulphuric acid. Hydrochloric acid and other acids. It is readily attacked by *Aqua Regia*.

Uses. It is generally alloyed with gold, iridium and iron to produce more useful metals. It is used for making jewellery, pen-points, scientific instruments, surgical instruments, standard weights and temperature measuring devices.

14.8. Properties and uses of some other metals

1. Cobalt. It is obtained from ores named arsenide and sulphoarsenide. Purifide crushed ores are fused in blast furnace in which lime stone or sand has been used. The cobalt obtained in this way is impure oxide of cobalt which is purified by various processes.

Properties. It is a lustrous white metal which can decompose even steam in red hot state. It can absorb hydrogen about 150 times, its own volume when it is in finely divided state. It can be magnetized and it can retain magnetic properties even at a temperature of 1100°C. It is malleable and ductile metal which is not affected by alkalis. Its S.G. is 8.80.

Uses. It is widely used in the preparation of special alloy steels, ceramic products, T.V. Articles etc.

2. Chromium. It is never found in free state in nature. It is obtained on commercial basis from an important source called *spinal mineral chronite*.

The S.G. of pure chromium is 6.9 and melting point 1510°C. It is an intensively hard and brittle metal, having a silver white colour. It retains its colour and brightness indefinitely. It is not oxidized by moist air.

It is mostly used in electroplating and as an alloying element. It is considered to be one of the most important alloying elements and its alloys with tungsten, nickel, molybdenum and iron are particularly outstanding. It is also used in the manufacture of stainless steel and electrical resistance wires.

3. Cadmium. It is found generally associated with zinc minerals and as such, it follows very closely zinc in its properties. Pure metal carries very little application in industry.

It is a soft ductile, silvery white metal, having a specific gravity of 8.64 and melting point of 321°C. It is used mostly in alloyed form only.

4. Nickel (Ni). It is a plentiful element and occurs in three main classes of ores, namely arsenide ores, sulphide ores and silicate ores. It is mainly found in Norway, Sweden, Germany and Canada. Mostly it is extracted from sulphide ores. The ores are cleaned, roasted and smelted in blast furnace along with limestone, quartze and coke. The molten mixture of nickel and copper sulphide collects at the bottom which is lead to basic lined Bessemer converter. Nickel is obtained by repeated smelting and electrolysis.

It is greyish white lustrous metal, capable of taking high polish. It is hard, malleable and magnetic. S.G. is 8.9 and it is highly corrosion resistant. In powdered form it can absorb hydrogen to the extent of about 17 times its volume. It can decompose steam in red hot state.

Nickel is used widely as a protective coating on other metals. It is also very much used as an alloying metal. It is also used in coins of small denominations. Almost all the nickel produced is used in a variety of extremely important ferrous as well as non-ferrous alloys.

5. Magnesium (Mg). This metal does not occur in free state in nature. Its chief ores are magnesite ($MgCO_3$), Dolomite ($CaCO_3$, $MgCO_3$), Kieserite ($MgSO_4$ H_2O) and carnallite ($MgCl_2$ KCl, 6 CHO).

For producing magnesium on small scale anhydrous magnesium chlorite is heated with sodium in presence of coal gas. But for large scale production, magnesium is obtained by the electrolysis of carnallite Magnesium is sold in the market in the form of ingots, bars, rods,wires, tubes, sheets, etc.

It is a silver-white metal, ductile and malleable in nature. Its melting point is 651°C. If strongly heated, it can decompose steam, like nikel and chromium. It burns with dazzing white light when heated in air. Its S.G. is 1.75. It is harder than aluminium and its tensile strength is 17.5 t/cm^2, which is almost equal to the tensile strength of grey cast iron. It corrodes in moist air. It can be easily machined and polished. It is also used for flash light photography. It is used in fire works and signalling purpose in the army. In pure form it can not be used in any of engineering purposes but its alloys with other metals are quite important.

6. Manganese (Mn). It is a grey-white metal almost resembling iron. It is more brittle and harder than iron. It is obtained from ores of manganese oxides. It is one of the important metals. It is extensively used in the manufacture of steel to act as reducing agent and recorburizor. It is added as an alloying element in steel to improve its strength, toughness and head-treatment characteristics. Practically all the commercial grades of steel contain manganese. It is used in electric batteries, paints and varnishes, staining agent, etc.

7. Molybdneum (Mo). It is obtained from Molybdenite (MOS_2). It is a silvery white metal which resembles tungsten in some of its physical properties. Its density is 10.2 and melting point 2625°C. It alloys readily with several metals, particularly with iron and steel. Steel containing molybdenum is known as ferro-molybdenum and it is very much used in ordinance factories. High tensile steel tools and machine parts are also made from this ferro-molybdenum.

Stainless steel also contains about 2 to 4% of this metal. Molybdenum is very much used in the manufacture of anti-cathodes for x-ray tubes. Wires of this metal are commonly used for heating elements in industrial laboratory furnaces, where high temperatures are required to be generated. It is also very much used in the manufacture of chemical reagents, dyes, glazes and dis-infactants.

8. Tungsten (W). It is silvery-grey metal, having a density of 18.8. The melting point of this metal is as high as 3400°C. It is generally obtained in powder form, but it can be had inform of bars also. It is insoluble in acids and does not oxidize. Tungsten imparts a remarkable property of wear-resistance to steels. Hence, it is mainly used as alloying element for high speed steels and other cutting alloys. It is added to the extent of 5 to 6% to produce magnet steels. Steels containing about 2% carbon and 5 to 10% of tungsten are used for dies. It is also very widely used in radio tubes, electric lamps inform of filaments.

9. Vanadium (V). Its S.G. is 6.1 and melting point 1750°C. It is non-magnetic. It is brilliant white metal. It is soft and ductile, but because of its great affinity for oxygen, carbon and nitrogen, it is very difficult to obtain in pure form. It is an important alloying element in the steel industry. It imparts unique properties of extreme hardness and wear resistance to alloyed steel. It is used in the manufacture of tool steel. When added in small quantity, it improves the strength impact resistance, and weldability of the steel. Higher proportions are added in chrome-vanadium spring steels and in high speed cutting steels.

In this chapter uptil now we have discussed properties and uses of some important non-ferrous metals. Now important alloys of both ferrous and non-ferrous metals will be discussed in chapter 15.

QUESTIONS

1. Give the properties and uses for the following metals :
   (i) Nickel, *(ii)* Tungsten, *(iii)* Molybdenum, *(iv)* Zinc.
2. Describe the characteristic and uses of aluminium, copper and Tin.
3. What are the noble metals? Give their properties and uses.

15

ALLOYS OF FERROUS AND NON-FERROUS METALS

15.1. Alloys of Steel

The properties of steel can be modified by adding small percentage of other metals such as manganese, nickel, copper etc. Some of the common steel alloys have been given as follows :

1. Cobalt-steel. This alloy is formed by adding cobalt to high carbon steel. This alloy remains hard and tough even at red-hot condition. Cobalt helps maintain magnetic effect permanently in the steel. Alloy containing 5-12% cobalt is very much used for high speed cutting tools, 35% of cobalt in high carbon steel is used for making permanent magnets.

2. Copper steel. This alloy consists of copper to the extent of about 0.15 to 0.25%. This alloy can resist effects of atmospheric agencies in a better way that ordinary carbon steel.

3. Chrome Nickel Steel. This alloy is made by adding 0.55 to 1.75% chromium, and 1.10 to 3.75% of nickel to steel having carbon content varying from 0.17 to 0.43%. This alloy is durable tough, and highly resistant to dynamic stresses. It possesses high tensile strength. This alloy is used for bearings. gears, aeroplanes and various engine parts etc.

4. Chromium steel. It is also known a *chrome steel*. It is prepared by adding 0.7 to 1.20% of chromium to steel containing carbon content varying from 0.17 to 0.55%. This alloy can withstand impact, shock, and abrasion very effectively. Elastic limit of this alloy is very high. It is used for coil springs, ball bearings, files cutting tools, etc.

5. Chrome-molybdenum steel. It this alloy 0.4 to 1.1% chromium, and 0.2 to 0.4% of molybdenum is added to the steel having carbon content of 0.2 to 0.5%. This alloy is very hard tough and strong. It is very much used in air craft industry, oil industry etc.

6. Chrome-nickle stainless steel. It consists of 18 to 20% chromium and 8 to 12% of nickel. It is highly resistant to corrosion and can be cast, pressed, and machined. It is not affected by acids. It is very much used for vessels to store acids, diary plant equipment and house hold utensils etc.

7. Chromium-vanadium steel. This alloy is formed by adding 0.7 to 0.9% of chromium and 0.1 to 0.15% of vanadium to steel containing 0.17 to 0.55% of carbon. It is finely grained, weldable alloy, possessing very high strength. It is highly ductile and can be easily worked. This alloy is very much used for bolts, pistons, springs, marine. Engine constructions.

8. Manganese-steel. This alloy contains manganese 1.6 to 1.9% and steel containing carbon content varying from 0.30 to 0.50%. It is hard, strong, fairly ductile alloy. It possesses excellent resistance against abrasion. Its coefficient of expansion is low. This allow is used for gears, railway points, and crossing etc.

9. Molybdenum-steel. This alloy consists of molybdenum 0.2 to 0.30%, manganese 0.7 to 1.0% and rest as the steel containing carbon content of 0.3 to 0.7%. It is resistant against shock and impact and maintains its properties at high temperatures also. It can be easily welded. It is strong and hard alloy. It is used for springs, bolts, scraper blades, axles, etc.

10. Nickel steel. This alloy is made by adding 3 to 3.5% of nickel to steel containing 0.15% to 0.50% of carbon. This alloy is hard, ductile and resistant to corrosion. It is used as structural steel, and for propeller shafts, boiler plates, etc.

When nickel is increased in the range of 18% to 40%, it is called high-nickel steel. Invar is one of the high nickel steel alloys. It contain 36% of nickel. It possesses coefficient of thermal expansion very small. It is very much used in precision instruments and clock pendulum etc. If nickel content is increased to 80% the resulting alloy is known as perm alloy. It is used for transformer cores.

11. Nickel-molybdenum steel. This alloy contains 1.65 to 3.75% nickel, 0.20 to 0.30% of molybdenum, in a steel containing carbon content varying from 0.17 to 0.23%. This alloy may also contain small percentages of sulphur, phosphorus, manganese and silicon. This alloy can be given that treatment. It is very tough. This alloy is very much used in air craft industry, petroleum industry etc.

12. Nickel-chromium-molybdenum steel. It contains 0.4 to 20% nickel, 0.4 to 0.90% chromium 0.15 to 0.30% of molybdenum, in a steel having carbon content of 0.28 to 0.40%. It may also contain small percentages of phosphorus, silicon, sulphur and manganese. This alloy does not become soft at high temperature and it cannot be easily welded. It can withstand impact and shock effects. It is used for die-casting, dies, bucket teeth of dredgers, etc.

13. Tungsten steel. Steel having carbon content of 0.5 to 1.0% is alloyed with 5 to 7% of tungsten. It is a hard alloy which can maintain cutting edges sharp even at very high temperatures. This alloy is used for cutting tools, and drills etc.

14. Vanadium Steel. This alloy is formed by alloying about 0.20% of vanadium with steel. This alloy is ductile and has quite high strength. It is used for springs, automobile parts, etc.

15. Silicon steel. This alloy is made by alloying silicon with steel. This alloy is very tough. Steel alloy containing 3.5% silicon can hardly be bent up to 90°. More than 4% silicon develops brittleness in the alloy. It can be easily made magnetic and with equal ease, it can be demagenetized. This alloy is very much used for transformer cores.

16. Stainless steel. It has already been explained in chapter 13. It is an alloy of steel having very low carbon content and chromium content of over 12%.

15.2. Aluminium alloys

Important alloys of aluminium are the following.

1. Aldural. It is duralumin which remain coated with thin coating of pure aluminium. This layer prevents corosion of the core due to salt water. It is also known as Alclad.

2. Aluminium bronze. It contains about 10% aluminium and 90% copper. It is used for die-casting, pump rods, etc. It is hard, light yellow, brown coloured alloy. It does not rust.

3. Duralumin. It is an important aluminium alloy. Its composition is 94% aluminium, 4% copper, 0.5% each of magnesium, manganese, iron, and silicon. This alloy is quite strong, and is very good conductor of heat and electricity. It has got the property of age hardening. Its specific gravity is about 2.85. Its density is although one third, of that of mild steel, but its strength is equal to that of mild steel. This alloy is used for electric cables and air craft industry.

4. Y-alloy. It is also a very important alloy of aluminium, which is very good conductor of heat and maintains high strength at high temperature. It is used for gear boxes propeller blades, cylinder heads. Engine pistons etc. Composition of the alloy is 92.50% aluminium, 4% copper, 2% nickel and 1.5% magnesium.

5. Magnalium. It consists of 90-98% aluminium and 2-10%

magnalium. Its strength is equal to that of pure aluminium, where as it is lighter than it.

15.3. Copper Alloys

Copper alloys may be divided into two groups namely Brasses and Bronzes.

1. Brasses. Brasses are alloys of copper, zinc and minor percentages of other elements.

(i) Muntz metal. It consists of 60% copper and 40% zinc. It is used for castings and condenser tubes, etc.

(ii) Cartridge brass. It consists of 70% copper and 30% zinc. It is used for cartridges, tubes, springs etc. It is ductile and possesses a high tensile strength.

(iii) Delta metal. It consists of 60% copper, 37% zinc and 3 % iron. It is resistant to corrosion. This alloy may be used in place of mild steel.

(iv) Low brass. It contains 80% copper and 20% zinc. It is also known as Dutch metal.

(v) White brass. It contains 10% copper and 90% zinc. It resembles more or less zinc. Addition of copper makes it strong and hard. It is used for ornamental works.

(vi). Yellow brass. It contains 65% copper and 35% zinc. Its S.G. is 8.47. It is very strong. It is used for plumbing accessories, grill work etc.

(vii) Red brass. It consists of 85% copper and 15% zinc.

(viii) Naval brass. It is muntz metal in which 1% tin also has been added.

2. Bronzes. Bronzes are alloys of copper and tin. Following are some of bronzes.

(i) Bell metal. It contains 82% of copper, and 18% tin. It possesses resonance and is hard and brittle. It is used for making school bells.

(ii) Gun metal. It consists of 88% copper, 10 to 8% tin and 2 to 4% of zinc. It is tough, hard and strong. It is used for making guns, bearings etc.

(iii) Phosphorus bronze. It consists of 89% copper, 10% tin and 1% phosphorus. It is hard, strong, and corrosion resisting alloy.

(iv) Manganese bronze. It consists of 56 to 60% copper and remaining as zinc. It also contains manganese maximum 1%, aluminium 0.05 to 1% lead 0.4% maximum and iron 0.4% to 1%

This alloy is not affected by sea water and is not attacked by dilute acids. It is used for various ship fittings, shafts, axles etc.

(v) Speculum metal. It consists of 67% copper and 33% tin. It is a white silvery in colour. This alloy is used for making telescopes. It has a high reflective surface.

15.4. Nickel Alloys

1. Monel metal. It consists copper and Nickel. It consists of Nickel 70%, copper 27% and 2-3% iron. Its tensile strength is very high and it does not rust. Even acidic and basic reactions do not have any effect on it. It is very much used in plants manufacturing caustic soda.

2. German Silver or Nickel silver. It is a brass to which nickel is added. Its composition consists 50 to 80% copper, 10 to 35% zinc and 5 to 30% Nickel. It is highly resistant to corrosion. It is used for making ornaments emitating silver ornaments. It is used for making scientific instruments, utensils, fittings etc.

15.5. Some other alloys

1. Dow metal. It is a magnesium alloy. Its composition consists of 4 to 12% aluminium, 0.1 to 0.4% manganese and the rest is magnesium.

2. Bearing metal. It contains 82% tin, 14% antimony and 4% copper. This alloy is very much used in locomotives.

3. Britania metal. This alloy consists of 93% tin 5% antimoney and 2% copper.

4. Die-casting alloys. These are whitish coloured alloys containing zinc, copper, tin, aluminium, magnesium and Nickel. The moulds of very high class are generally made from them. Alloy containing 4% aluminium, 3.5% coper and 0.05% manganese and remaining amount as zinc, is generally used for die-castings.

5. Solder. It is an alloy of tin and lead. Melting point for solder is 182° to 250°C. Alloy goes on softening as lead is increased. Generally it consists of two parts of tin and one part of lead. It is used to join the different parts.

6. Babbit metal. In general the term 'babbit' is used to denote all white metal bearing alloys, which have lead, tin antimony, zinc and copper as the base metal. It is name given to numerous varities of white metal alloys which have great anti-frictional qualities.

15.6. Welding, Soldering and Brazing

Welding. It is the process, of joining metal surfaces by the application of heat. The heat for welding may be obtained by an electric arc, a gas flame or by some chemical reaction.

Soldering. In this process parts of metal to be jointed are heated and an alloy (solder) having its melting point lower than that of the parts to be soldered is applied over the junction in the molten state.

Brazing. In the process of brazing, the alloy which is usually in the form of fine grains, is placed between the two surfaces to be jointed and the alloy is then melted by heated in a furnace or by the use of a heating torch.

15.7. Corrosion

The corrosion is a process due to which gradual wearing away of the metal takes place. The process takes place due to chemical or electro-chemical reactions by which the metal is converted into an oxide, salt or some other compounds. The substance resulting out of corrosion is known as **rust.** The corrosion indicates the deterioration and loss of metal due to chemical attack. The corrosion may be dry corrosion or wet corrosion, Corrosion taking place in the absence of electrolyte is known as dry **corrosion.** Electrolyte is a substance which dissociates into ions in solution or when fused and thus becomes electrically conducting. If the electrolyte causing corrosion is an aqueous solution of acid salt or alkali, it is known as the **wet corrosion.**

The corrosion has always been a serious problem and hence to minimize its effects it is necessary for the engineer to understand, the mechanism of corrosion.

15.8. Causes of corrosion

The following are the factors which are responsible for causing corrosion.

1. Exposure of the metallic surfaces to atmospheric agencies.
2. Exposure to moist atmosphere.
3. Presence of active gases in the surrounding atmosphere.
4. Presence of harmful salts in the surrounding environment
5. Eddy electric currents.
6. Chemical composition of the metal itself together with its internal structure.

15.9. Theories of corrosion

So many theories have been put forward for corrosion. But the four accepted theories which carry importance are the following.

1. Direct corrosion or chemical action theory.
2. Electrolytic theory.
3. Galvanic action theory.
4. High - temperature oxidation.

1. Direct Corrosion Theory. According to this theory the corrosion takes place due to oxidation of all or apart of the surface of material.

$$Fe + O + 2CO_2 + H_2O \longrightarrow Fe\,(HCO_3)_2$$

$$2\,Fe\,(HCO_3)_2 + O \longrightarrow 2\,Fe\,(OH)\,CO_3 + 2\,CO_2 + H_2O$$

$$Fe\,(OH)\,CO_3 + H_2O \longrightarrow Fe\,(OH)_3 + CO_2$$

This theory involves action of oxygen, CO_2 and moisture on metal surfaces. As shown in the above reactions iron first turns in to ferrous bicarbonates, then to ferric carbonate and lastly to hydrated ferric oxide and CO_2 is liberated.

The chemical reaction may take place at the interface between a liquid and the metal in following three forms.

(i) The atom of liquid may diffuse into the surface of the metal and cause changes in the mechanical properties of the metal.

(ii) The liquid atmosphere may dissolve the surface of the parent metal by a simple solution action.

(iii) The liquid may react with the parent metal surface to form a compound similar to the oxide films.

The surface due to direct corrosion has etched or worn out appearance.

2. Electrolytic Theory of Corrosion. This theory is the most accepted theory of corrosion. In this theory corrosion is supposed to have taken place due to chemical reaction is combination with electrolysis. It takes place when the metal comes is contract with moisture, or salts, acids or bases. For electro-chemical corrosion to take place following conditions should be satisfied.

(i) There has to be a electrolyte.

(ii) Current must flow through the circuit.

(iii) Circuit must close.

(iv) There has to be difference of potential between a metal and its surrounding or between different parts of the same metal. The electrolytic corrosion involves the cathodic region and anodic region of the metal. The metal surface from which current leaves are termed as anodic regions and the metal surface on which current returns is called

cathode region. It is the anodic area which corrodes. The cathodic areas do not corrode.

The anodes and cathodes may be two separate independent units or different areas of the same piece of metal. The rate of corrosion depends on the intensity of current between anodic and cathodic sides and also on the nature of electrolyte. The instensity of the current depends upon standard electrode potential difference. The alloys and multi-phase metals corrode at higher rates than pure metals.

3. Galvanic action theory. The galvanic corrosion takes place when two dissimilar metals are in electrical contact with each other and are exposed to an electrolyte. For example a more noble metal such as copper will act as cathode and a less noble metal such as zinc will form anode. It is the anode metal which dissolves and thus subjected to corrosion. Hence is order to prevent corrosion of anodic metal, it is necessary to see that direct contact between two dissimilar metals is avoided.

4. High - temperature oxidation. The corrosion of ferous alloys at high temperatures forms scales and oxides. It is an example of high temperature dry corrosion. The other form of high - temperature corrosion occurs when liquid metals flow through other metals. The liquid metal attack may take place by any of the following forms.

(i) Formation of chemical compounds.

(ii) Simple solution of the solid metal.

(iii) Selective extraction of one of the component metals in a solid alloy.

15.10. Forms of corrosion

In order to denote a particular type of corrosion specific terms are used. These terms have been given here.

1. Atmosphoric corrosion : This type of corrosion mostly occurs on ferous materials. The moist conditions such as rain water and humid air act as electrolytes and are thus responsible for this type of corrosion.

2. Erosion corrosion : The combined effect of mechanical abrasion and the basic corrosion mechanism on a metal surface produce erosion corrosion. In this corrosion cavities are formed on the metal surface.

3. Corrosion fatigue : The combined effect of corrosion and repeated stresses give rise to corrosion fatigue.

4. Fretting corrosion : A fret indicates worn spot, a hole or path made by abrasion. This type of corrosion occurs when common surface of any two materials in contact are subjected to vibrations.

5. Intergranular corrosion : This corrosion develops when substantial difference in reactivity exists between grain boundaries and the remainder of the alloy. This corrosion is mostly observed in defective welding and heat treatment of stainless steel, copper and aluminium alloys.

6. Selective corrosion : When electro-chemical corrosion encourages preferential corrosion of one of the component metals, it is called selective corrosion. This type of corrosion is observed in brass pipes and for brass articles containing more than 15% of zinc.

7. Stress corrosion : The combination of corrosive environmental and mechanical stress produce this type of corrosion on the metal. This corrosion is usually confined to a local area which ultimately gives rise to small cracks.

8. Pitting corrosion : It is a localized type of corrosion. It is recognized by the presence of holes. This type of pitting is observed in copper, steel, aluminium and nickel alloys.

9. Uniform corrosion : In this corrosion the whole surface is corroded uniformly. This corrosion is commonly found on aluminium, lead and zinc surfaces.

15.11. Standard electrode potential

It is a scale which gives standard electromotive force of metals and alloy in relation to each other. Relative positions of the metals in the electro-potential series with respect to hydrogen are given here. Hydrogen gas is considered as a neutral element. The metal magnesium is the most reactive in the whole series and the reactivity decreases in the descending order until it is the minimum for brasses. The metals below hydrogen become inert in the increasing order and platinum is the most inert being last in the series.

Brasses are highly resistant towards corrosion where as Magnesium is the metal which is easily affected by corrosion. Any metal is capable to displace the metal below it in the series.

For example the iron can displace copper.

When two metals are in contact with each other the metal which is higher in the series will function as the anode and undergoes accelerated corrosion whereas the metal more nearer to the bottom of series acts as cathode and thus receives corrosion protection. Metal and alloys according to standard electrode potential *i.e.*, galvanic series are as follows.

(Anode or least noble)	Corrosion end
	Magnesium
	Zinc
	Aluminium (2S)
	Cadmium
	Aluminium (17st)
	Steel or Iron
	Cast steel
Decrease in nobility	Chromium iron
	Ni-resist call iron
	Molybdenium - Iron
	Lead-Tin Solder
	Lead
	Tin
	Nickel
	Basses
	Hydrogen
	Copper
	Bronze
	Copper-Nickel alloy
	Silver-solder
	Nickel (passive)
	Chromium - Iron (passive)
Increase in nobility	Titanium
	Silver
	Graphite
	Gold
	Platinum
(Cathodic or most noble)	(Protected end)

15.12. Preventive measures for corrosion

Following measures if taken in time prevent the corrosion of ferrous metals. Brief description of each measure has been gives here.

1. Coal tarring : The iron surface is applied a coating of hot coal tar which protects the surface from atmospheric actions leading to corrosion. Since the blackened surface with coal tar does not look good, this method is usually adopted on iron used in substructures.

2. Electroplating : In this method a thin protective layer of copper, nickel, cadimiums or chromium is laid on ferrous metal with the help of electrolysis process. The surface to be protected is made the cathode and the metal to be deposited is made the anode.

3. Galvanizing : The surface of iron is first thoroughly cleaned and then washed with dilute solution of HCl. After this the metal surface is dipped in a bath of molten zinc. The thin layer deposited on the surface protects the surface from corrosion.

4. Metal spraying : In this method the ferrous metal surface is covered with a spray of vaporized aluminium, lead tin or zinc.

5. Tin plating : It is similar to galvanizing method except that cleaned surface is dipped in bath of **molten tin.** If instead of tin bath, lead - tin alloy bath is used for coating the surface the process is known as **terne plating.**

6. Sherardising : The article to be treated is cleaned dried and then covered with dust of pure zinc. There after it is heated to a temperature from 250°C to 450°C in an air - tight steel box. The zinc melts and it combines with metal and forms a protective layer on the metal surface. The surface so formed is very durable and can be easily polished.

7. Parkersing : In this method the surface to be treated in kept immersed for a period of about an hour in a water bath of chemical known as parco. The insoluble phosphates are formed on the surface and protect the surface against corrosion.

8. Painting : In this method the surface is covered with a layer of suitable paint.

9. Enamelling : In this method the surface to be protected is covered by melting suitable flux on it in a muffle furnace.

QUESTIONS

1. What are the alloys of steel? Write down the composition of all the steel alloys.
2. Enumerate copper alloys, and aluminium alloys.

16

GLASS

16.1. General

Glass has been an important engineering material, since old times. Glass industry has progressed very rapidly and new techniques have been developed with the help of which glass of any type and quality can be produced. The art of glass making is very old and today the industry uses basically the same raw materials as did the ancient glass-makers. However, the methods of manufacture have changed and improved, resulting in higher production rates, superior glass, and large sheet sizes.

16.2. Classification of Glass

Glass is a hard brittle, transparent, translucent material. Its structure is amorphous. It is made by fusion of silica with varying proportions of oxides of sodium, potassium, calcium, magnesia, iron and other mineral. All these materials when melted, form a number of metallic silicates. Hence glass may be said as a material consisting of a number of metallic silicates. For the purpose of classification, glass may be grouped into following four categories.

1. Soda-lime glass (Na_2O, CaO, $6SiO_2$)
2. Potash-lime glass (K_2O CaO 6 SiO_2)
3. Potash-lead glass (K_2O, PbO, 6 SiO_2)
4. Common glass.

Composition of glass

The glass consists of so many compounds and thus it is very difficult to give any particular formula for its composition. Its composition may be expressed by following formula

ax_2O, bYO, $6SiO_2$

where a and b = numbers of molecules

x = an atom of an alkali metal such as Na, K, etc.

Y = an atom of a bivalent metal such as Ca, Pb, etc.

with this expression the chemical formulas for soda-lime glass, potash-lime glass and potash-lead glass become as follows :

(Soda-lime glass Na_2O CaO $6SiO_2$)

(Potash-lead glass K_2O PbO $6SiO_2$)

(Potash-lime glass K_2O CaO $6SiO_2$)

1. Soda-lime Glass. It is also called *soda-glass* or soft glass. It is a mixture of sodium silicate and calcium silicate. This glass is used in the manufacture of glass tubes and other laboratory apparatus, Plate glass, window glass etc. may also be of this type of glass. It is cheap, and easily fusible at comparatively low temperature. This glass can be welded with the help of simple heat.

2. Potash-lime glass (K_2O CaOCSiO$_2$). It is chiefly a mixture of potassium silicate and calcium silicate. It is also known as *hard glass* or *Bahemian-glass*. It is used in the manufacture of such glass articles which have to withstand very high temperatures, such as combustion tubes etc. This glass does not melt easily and thus fuses at high temperatures only. Water and other solvents do not affect this glass.

3. Potash-lead-glass. It is mainly a mixture of lead silicate and potassium silicate. It is also termed as *flint glass*. It is a very high class glass and is used in the manufacture of lenses, prisms, electric bulbs, artificial gems etc. This glass possesses bright lustre and very high refractive power. It fuses easily and turns black and opaque, when reducing gases of furnace during heating come in its contact.

4. Common glass. It is mainly a mixture of sodium silicate, calcium silicate and iron silicate. It is used in the manufacture of medicine bottles. It is always a coloured glass. Its colour may be yellow, green or brown. It fuses with difficulty and also easily attacked by acids. It is also sometimes called bottle glass.

5. Coloured glass. The colouring pigment is added to produce coloured glass. The colouring pigment is added to the raw materials at the time of preparing the batch for its manufacture. The whole mass is heated till it becomes homogeneous.

The colouring pigment is obtained from metallic oxides, finely divided metals, carbon, salts of metal, sulphur etc. It should also be noted that different quantities of the same substance may produce different coloured glass.

The coloured glass is used for window panels, fancy articles, decorative tiles etc. Different colouring substances for glass are as given in table here.

	Colour	Substances
1.	Red	Cu prous oxide (Cu_2O), Metallic gold.
2.	Violet	Manganese dioxide (MnO_2)
3.	Blue	Cobalt oxide, cupric oxide (CuO)
4.	Dark blue or dark brown or violet	Cobalt, manganese and iron oxide.
5.	Green	Ferroso-ferric oxide (Fe_2O_4) chromium sesqui oxide (C_2O_3)
6.	White opaque	Tin oxide, calcium phosphorite
7.	Yellow or brown	Antimony tri sulphide, charcoal silver borate etc.

16.3. Manufacture of glass

Glass is manufactured in following stages:

1. Collection of raw materials.
2. Mixing of material and forming a batch.
3. Melting in the furnace.
4. Fabrication.
5. Annealing.

Each stage has been explained in brief.

1. Collection of raw materials. Raw materials are collected depending upon the type of glass being manufactured. For soda-lime glass, chalk, soda-ash and clean sand are taken as raw materials. Similarly for *Potash-lime glass*, chalk, Potassium carbonate and clean sand, are used. For potash-lead glass, litharge, pure sand and potassium carbonate are used. For common glass. chalk, salt cake, coke and ordinary sand are used as raw materials.

In addition to above compositions for different type of glasses, cullet and decolorizer are also added as raw materials.

Cullet is nothing, but pieces of old broken waste glass. This when added to the mixture increases the fusibility of the resulting glass and also reduces its cost.

Decolourizers are added to avoid the colouring effect of traces of iron present in raw materials. Such substances are antimony oxide, arsenic oxide, cobalt oxide, mangnese dioxide, and Nickel oxide.

2. Preparation of batch. All the raw materials including cullet and decolourisers are separately ground to fine powders and then mixed together in pre-determined proportion. The mixture is mixed dry till a uniform dry mixture is prepared. This dry mix is known as *batch or frit*.

3. Melting in the furnace. Furnace used for melting is shown in Fig. 16.1. The batch prepared is charged in this pot furnace and heating is continued until evolution of carbon dioxide, oxygen, sulphur dioxide and other gases stops. Heating of the furnace is done by producer gas. After this, melted mass is removed from the furnace for further treatment. This pot furnace does not run continuously.

Fig. 16.1. Pot furnace.

Tank furnace. This furnace is used when glass is to be produced on mass scale and process of melting of the batch has to be continuous. This furnace is just like reverberatory furnace used in the manufacture of wrought-iron. The furnace is made from reinforced masonry. Its roof is given a peculiar shape, so as to deflect the flames of heated gas down wards and bring about heating of the batch. Tank of the furnace, in which batch is heated and molten mass collected. is divided into two unequal parts. The batch is heated in larger part. The batch contains some what impure glass. Molten glass flows into smaller part through the opening provided for the purpose from where it is taken out for further treatment. Floating impurities collected at the top of molten mass in larger part are removed from time to time. The floating impurities are also known as *Gall*. Tank of the furnace is provided with refractory lining. Doors and openings are provided for charging the furnace and taking out the molten mass.

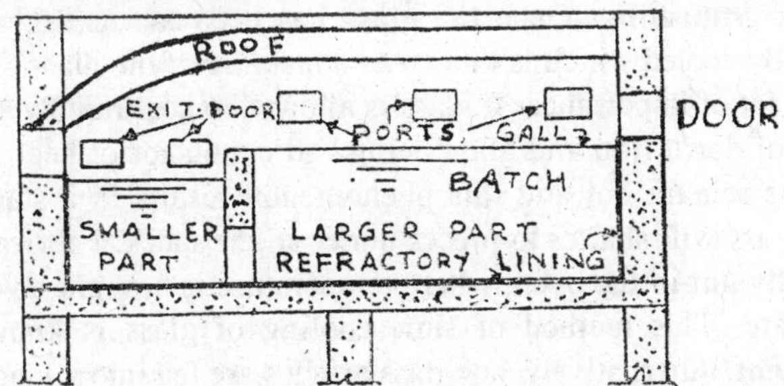

Fig. 16.2. Tank furnace.

4. Fabrication. The process of giving desired shape to the molten glass is known as fabrication. This process can be performed either by hand or by machines. Blowing, casting, drawing, pressing, rolling and spinning are the different ways of fabrication.

Blowing. Blowing process is performed with the help of a blow pipe 180 cm long and about 1.2 cm diameter. One end of the pipe is dipped in the molten mass and a lump of about 5 kg is taken out. This lump of glass will get lengthened to some extent due to weight of the lump itself.

Compressed air is now blown from the other end of the pipe. The blowing causes molten mass to take the shape at a cylinder. It is again heated for few seconds and blown again. The process of heating and blowing is continued till the cylinder of required size is formed. It is then put on an iron plate and is disconnected from blow pipe. The glass prepared this by method is known as crown glass.

Casting. Molten glass is casted in moulds like C.I.

Pressing. Molten glass is put in moulds and then pressed by hand or by mechanical means. This method is adopted to prepare ornamental articles, hollow glass, etc.

Drawing. An iron bar is dipped in molten glass and drawn side ways. In doing so it catches a sheet of molten glass. This sheet is then passed over several large sized rotating rollers and thin sheets of glass are obtained.

Rolling. Rolling methods may be two type. One of the methods consists passing glass through heavy iron roller and flat glass plates are obtained. In second method molten mass is poured on a flat iron casting table and it is then turned flat.

Spinning. In this case, molten mass of glass is spun at a very high speed. The glass obtained by this method is of very high class. It is not attacked by acids and it does not fade, decay or shrink. It is very soft and flexible.

5. Annealing. Once the glass has been fabricated, it has to be gradually cooled which is known as *annealing* of the glass. This process carries lot of importance. If glass is allowed to coal rapidly. Outer layers will cool down first and glass being bad conductor of heat, the interior portions remain hot and this phenomenon results in a state of strain. Such glass will shatter to pieces under slight shock. Fabricated glass is generally put in the oven, where temperature is brought down at a very slow rate. This method of slow cooling of glass is known as **oven treatment.** Alternatively, hot glass articles are fed into a long flue which has the maximum temperature at one end and cool at the other end. The temperature slowly goes on decreasing from hotter end to the colder end. As the glass comes out of this long flue, it is quite cold. The method of slow cooling in known as **flue treatment.**

16.4. Treatment of glass

Glass as manufactured above may be given following treatments:

1. Bending. Glass cannot be bent cold. It is heated first and then bent. Glass rods, sheets, tubes etc. can be bent by this method. The temperature in oven is regulated.

2. Cutting. Glass is cut by diamond pencil. Rough glass or small wheels of hardened steel can also be used for this purpose.

3. Opaque making. Glass can be made opaque by grinding the surface of the glass with emery. It can also be done by applying a wash of hydrofluoric acid.

4. Silvering. In this process a thin coat of tin is first applied and then silver is deposited. Lastly the surface is covered by a suitable paint to protect it against atmospheric effects.

16.5. Coloured glass

It is used in fancy articles, decorative tiles, window panels etc. To obtained coloured glass, suitable pigment is added and ground in the raw materials of the batch. Colouring pigments may be metallic oxides, carbon, salts of metal, sulphur etc.

16.6. Varieties of glass

1. Crown glass. This type of glass is practically absolete. It is manufactured by the process of blow pipe. This glass is slightly convex. This glass is free from colour and has a finer surface. It is used for special articles. This glass is superseeded by sheet glass due to demand for large sizes.

2. Sheet glass. It is made by blowing molten glass into a large hollow cylinder. The cylinder is then split longitudinally and then flattened over a plane disc. This glass is used of ordinary purposes.

3. Plate glass. This glass is made by pouring hot glass on casting table and then levelling the material to a uniform thickness by means of rollers running over the whole surface of the casting table. This process is followed by process of grinding, smoothing and polishing. This glass is stronger than sheet glass. It is used for looking glass, and large paned glass for high class houses. Glazing of shop fronts, wind screens of vehicles, are made from it.

4. Perforated glass. In this glass, perforations are made either during or after manufacture, with the help of projections attached to rollers. This glass is used for panels in ventilators.

5. Fluted or ribbed glass. It is a glass which has corrugations on both sides. It is used, to secure privacy without obstructing the light of the sun. This is a variety of obscure glass.

6. Wired glass. Wired mesh is put in the glass while rolling during manufacture of glass. It is used for fire resisting doors and windows, as it does not shatter into pieces. Embedded wires keep the pieces of glass held together.

7. Safety glass. A celluloid sheet is put between two sheets of plate glass and formed into one unit with the help of glue. Celluloid sheet prevents shattering of splinters when glass breaks.

8. Shielding glass. This glass is used for windows through which high radiations are to be observed. This glass contains lead oxide as one of the elements. It is a variety of potash lead glass.

9. Bullet-proof glass. This glass is prepared by sand wiching vinyl-resin plastic between several layers of plate glass. It consists of minimum four layers of glass and three layers of vinyl-resin in between them. The outer layers of glass are made thinner than inner layers. Total thickness of this glass may vary from 15 mm to 75 mm or even more. It does not allow bullet to pierce through it. It is extensively used for glazing bank tellers booths and cash booths, jewellery stores, display cases, etc.

10. Calorex. It is also caled *heat excluding glass*, as its most peculiar property is heat exclusion. It is opaque to ultra-violet light and thus cuts off the heat of the sun. It is used in factories, hospitals, kitchens, etc.

11. Insulating glass. This glass provides a very high resistance to heat flow. It is composed of two or more plates of glass separated by 6 to 13 mm of dehydrated captive air. The edges of the glass are kept sealed. The sealed air reduces transmission of heat and provides insulating effect.

12. Fibre glass. The fibre is composed of minute glass rods and each glass rod resembles the parent material in all respects. It is soft to the touch and is flexible in nature. It can be developed either in the form of continuous strands or in staple form.

13. Foam glass. Glass and carbon are finely ground and mixture of both is melted in a furnace. By melting, the mixture expands and takes the form of a black foam. This glass floats in water and it can be cut like wood. It is fire-proof, rigid, and an excellent heat insulator. It is prepared in form of rectangular blocks.

14. Ground glass or obscured glass. It is made either by grinding one side of the glass or melting powdered glass upon it. This glass is used, where light is required with out transparency. Thus this type of glass will be useful for public toilets office door, partitions etc.

15. Glass wool. Thin fibres of glass are spun out of molten glass. These fibres are fairly flexible and have high tensile strength and hence can be woven into mats. Glass wool is available in loose fibres, quilts, mats, rigid or semi-rigid slabs. Glass wool is used as filter in air conditioners for electric insulation, for heat insulation and for filteration of corrosive liquids.

16. Tempered plate glass. Glass plate is heated and then suddenly cooled to temper it. Tempered glass is much stronger than ordinary glass and is used for glazed entrance doors or in making table tops, shelves counters etc.

17. Laminated glass. Two or more sheets of glass can be attached with plastic resin between them. It is shock absorbent and provides a good acoustical medium. This glass does not fly off in splinters, when it breaks. It thus ensures safety at places where glass is liable to shatter.

18. Glass blocks. Glass blocks are hollow transparent units, produced by fusing together two pressed semi-blocks. They are used in the construction of non-load bearing external panel walls and partition walls. They are made 10 cm thick and 15 cm, 20 cm, and 30 cm square in sizes. Their edges are sealed with grit bearing plastic material so that a good bond is provided with mortar.

19. Soluble glass. This glass is prepared by melting quartz sand, grinding and thoroughly mixing it with soda ash, sodium sulphate or potassium carbonate. The melting is done in glass tanks at 1300°C to 1400°C. The resulting glass mass flows out from the surface and it cools rapidly and breaks up into pieces known as **silica lumps**. This glass is soluble in water. This glass is used for making acid-resistant cement.

20. Ultra-Violet ray glass. This glass is made from raw mixture with minimum admixtures of iron titanium, and chrome. This glass transmits 75% of ultra-violet radiation which is far more than common glass. It is widely used is window panes.

16.7. Properties of glass

1. It is extremely brittle and is available in beautiful colours.
2. It is affected by alkalies, but not by air or water.
3. It has âmourphous structure.
4. It has no definite melting point.
5. It can be polished.
6. It absorbs, and refracts light.
7. It is not easily affected by chemicals.
8. It can be cast into any desired shape.
9. Glass can be welded by fusion.

10. It may be transparent and translucent.

11. It is possible to modify some of its properties like hardness, fusibility, refractive power.

QUESTIONS

1. Describe the process of manufacturing glass.
2. Draw neat sketches of pot furnace and tank furnance and explain their working.
3. Give the classification and composition of glass.
4. Mention the properties and uses of various types of glasses.
5. Explain the properties of different varieties of glass.

17
PLASTICS

17.1. Introduction

Plastic was invented by Schonbein in 1856. He named the product as cellulose. John Wesley Hyatt developed a new material in 1890 and named it celluloid. In this century Dr. Bakeland, a Belgian scientists, produced a product known as Bakelite. Plastic is an organic material prepared from resins, natural or synthetic with or without fillers, plasticisers, solvents or pigments. Wax shellac, pitch, bitumen etc. are natural resins. The most significant development in plastics occured mainly in the period lying between two world wars. In 1924 an Austrian Scientist Mr. Pollak prepared a substance from urea and formaldehyde. This substance was as transparent as glass. Now the plastic has been improved to such an extent that it has assumed important place as engineering material.

17.2. Composition of Plastic

It is an organic substance prepared from natural or synthetic resins in which other materials like fillers, solvents, plasticisers, might have been added or not. In general terms, plastics may be stated as compounds of cabon with other elements such as oxygen, hydrogen nitrogen. Carbon combines with itself and other elements and forms more complicated compounds.

17.3. Polymerization

The simplest substances consisting of only one primary chemical are known as monoliths or monomers. They may be combined or synthesized to form polymers by the process known as *polymerization*. Plastics are high molecular weight compounds formed by polymerization and condensation of smaller molecules. The manner in which the polymer is formed affects certain fundamental properties of the final product.

The following three methods of polymerization have been given here.

1. Addition polymerization. In this method, similar or different molecules join together due to opening of double bonds and the molecular weight of the resulting polymer is equal to the sum of the molecular weights of the reacting molecules. The polymers developed by this method are polyacrylates, polypropylene, polystyrene, poly-vinyl chloride, polythylene, etc.

2. Condensation polymerization. In this process the low molecular substances are replaced from the high molecular substances formed from a large number of identical or different molecules. The polymers developed by this method are phenol formaldehyde, carbamide melamine-form aldehyde etc.

The condensation polymerization yields industrially more important byproducts such or H_2O, HCl etc. The reaction proceeds with an evolution of ammonia, hydrogen chloride and similar other low-molecular substances.

3. CO - polymerization. This method is nothing but addition polymerization of two or more different monomers. There are so many monomers which do not polymerize themselves but co-polymerize with other compounds.

The co-polymer may possess properties entirely different from those of either component member. Thus a wide variety of plastics can be developed by this process. Vinyl chloride acetate and butadiene - styrene co-polymers are the examples of co-polymerization.

17.4. Classification of Plastics

Based on behaviour with respect to heating, plastics can be primarily divided into two categories:

1. Thermo-setting plastics and 2. Thermo-plastic.

1. Thermo-setting plastics. Thermo-setting plastics set into permanent shape, when heat and pressure are applied to them. Reheating will not soften them again. They set at a temperature varying from, 127°C to 177°C. This plastic is soluble in alcohol and certain organic solvents when they are in thermo-plastic stage. This property is utilized for making paints and varnishes from these plastics. This plastic is strong, hard, and durable and is available in a variety of colours.

2. Thermo-plastics. Thermo-plastics, becomes soft when heated and harden, when cooled, regardless of the number of times the process is repeated. The process of softening and hardening may be repeated for an indefinite number of times provided the temperature during heating is not, so high as to cause chemical decomposition. It is thus possible to shape and reshape, these plastics by means of heat and pressure. Scrap obtained from old warn out articles can be effectively used again.

3. Classification according the structure of plastic. According to this classification, the plastics are of two types.

(i) Homogeneous plastic and

(ii) Heterogeneons plastic.

The variety of plastic containing only carbon chain is known as homogeneous plastic. They exhibit homogeneous structure.

The variety of plastic containing chain of carbon and oxygen, nitrogen and other elements is known as heterogeneous structure.

4. Classification based on physical and Mechanical properties. According to this classification plastics may be divided into following four groups :

(i) Rigid plastic

(ii) Semi-rigid plastic

(iii) Soft plastics and

(iv) Elastomers.

The Rigid plastics have high modulus of elasticity. They maintain their shape under external stresses at normal as well as increased temperatures.

Semi-rigid plastics have medium modulus of elasticity. Its elongation under pressure completely disappears when presure is removed.

Soft plastics have low modulus of elasticity. Its elongation under pressure disappears slowly on removal of pressure.

Elastomers are soft and elastic materials having very how modulus of elasticity. They deform considerably under load and return to their original shape on removal of the load. The elongation can range upto 10 times their original dimensions.

17.5. Types of Thermo-setting Plastics or resins

1. Phenol formaldehyde resin. Phenol is carbolic acid obtained as a by product during distillation of coal. It is also obtained from benzene. When phenol and formaldehyde react with each other, they form the resin known as *phenol formaldehyde*. Plastics prepared from this resin are used for paints, varnishes, electrical fittings WC seats, adhesives for ply wood etc. It is highly resistant to heat and possesses very good mechanical and electrical properties. It is not attacked by organic acids, dilutes mineral acids, oil, water, mild alkalies, etc.

2. Phenol furfuraldehyde resin. It can be produced from materials like rice husks, oat shells, ground nut and sugarcane waste products. When these materials react with some acid, furfuraldehyde is obtained. When furfuraldehyde reacts with phenol this resin is obtained. It is dark in colour and resists very high temperatures.

3. Urea formaldehyde. Urea is obtained by heating under pressure, a mixture of liquid carbon dioxide and liquid ammonia. It can also be prepared from calcium cyanamide. When urea reacts with formaldehyde this resin is formed. Plastic of urea are sometimes, designated as 'amino plastics'. This possesses excellent electrical properties. It is not easily attacked by dilute acids, alkalies, oils, chemicals, water etc. This plastic is widely used for making adhesives for wood and wood products. lighting fixtures such as lamps, reflectors etc.

4. Melamine-formaldehyde. Melamine is obtained from calcium carbide. When melamine reacts with formaldehyde this resin is obtained. It possesses very good electrical and mechanical properties. It is highly resistant to water. Plastics made from this resin are used for ceiling linings, decorative laminates, glass reinforced plastics, preparing papers having high strength in wet condition. It is also used for electrical insulators.

5. Casein plastics. This plastic is prepared from skimmed milk. It is not very strong. It can be given a number of colours. Buttons and ornamental articles can be prepared from it.

6. Alkyd resins. These are resins prepared by the combination of polyhydric alcohols and polybasic acids. The alkyds are resistant to heat, moisture and weathering conditions and hence are used in protective coatings. The alkydes are electrically insulated transparent and tough materials and can be easily coloured. They are flexible and can be joined to metals.

7. Polyesters. These are prepared by the condensation of a dialcohol and diacid. Many of them have long chain molecules which are characteristics of thermoplastics. A common polyester is made from ethylene glycol and phthalic acid. Tne molten material is extruded through an orifice and stretched to give a strong fibre known as terylene or Dacron. The same material in the form of film is known as Mylar. It has excellent electrical and mechanical properties.

8. Silicones. These have silicon-oxygen chain to which various organic groups are linked. They are available in a wide range of consistency. The thermo-setting silicon compositions are resistant to heat and water and have high electrical resistance. Therefore besides other applications, they are used to make insulations for high frequency equipment.

17.6. Types of Thermo-plastics resins

As already explained the thermoplastics soften or melt when heated. On cooling they become rigid. On reheating they again soften or melt and can be given the desired shape by moulding. Thermo-plastic resins are acrylics, celluloid, cellulose, acetate, polyamides, polyethylenes, polystyrenes and polyvinyls.

1. Acrylic plastics. The resin used in this plastic is acrylic which is derived from coal, petroleum and water by a very complicated process. It is light in weight and transmits, ultra-violet waves of light. It can be cut, sawn or turned. It possesses excellent optical properties and acts as a good electric insulator. Plastics prepared from this resin are used for safety glass, coloured and artificial jewels, roof lights, light fittings, bath and sink units etc. This resin is also known as Methyl-metacry late.

2. Styrene plastics. Ethyl benzene is converted with styrene by separating hydrogen from the rest of molecules. Styrene is obtained in liquid form. It boils at 145°C and can be soldified on polymerization. This plastic is particularly useful for storing materials like hydrofluoric acid, which damages the glass. Because of its very good optical qualities, it is used for the manufacture of lenses. It is extensively used in T.V. and radio industry.

3. Vinyl resins. Acetic acid and vinyl resins are prepared from acetylene gas. By altering the degree of polymerization of vinyl resin a variety of plastics can be made. Some of the plastics thus formed are polyvinyl acetate, polyvinyl chloride, polyvinyl aldehyde, vinyl chloride etc.

Polyvinyl chloride (P.V.C.)— It is made by polymerization of vinyl chloride. Kerosene oil, acid and other chemicals have no effect on P.V.C. It is used for, flooring, sullage water, and rain water pipes, and insulation of electric wires.

Polyvinyl acetate (P.V.A.) is obtained by polymerization of vinyle acetate. It is similar to PVC in use and properties.

4. Polyethylenes. They are prepared by polymerizating ethylene under high pressure and moderately high temperatures. The polymer is then subjected to substitution and other reactions to develop the plastics, which are resistant to chemicals, have good electrical resistance, low specific gravity, low water absorption and flexibility. They are much cheaper then the other plastics.

5. Ethyl cellulose. These plastics are very strong, tough, resistant to moisture, and are good insulators. It is used largely in coatings on adhesives.

6. Cellulose nitrate. It is quite hard and brittle material. It can be used as plastic material only after incorporating a plasticizer like camphor. Rods, sheets and tubes of cellulose nitrate are available in various colours. These plastics are highly inflammable, unstable at high temperatures, sensitive to sunlight and are affected by acids, alkalies and organic solvents like alcohols, ethers and ketones.

7. Cellulose acetate. It is developed by first preparing cellulose triacetate by acetylating cellulose. When the acetate content is about 62.5% it is hydrolysed, precipitated, washed and dried. The product is kneaded in a mixer with a plasticizer. These plastic are stable, transparent, show burning, tough, easily moulded, wear resistant, strong but not very resistant to moisture. It is used in automobile industry.

17.7. Compounding of Plastic

The materials described above are the resins or binders and are the chief ingredients of plastics objects. They have plasticity or binding property, but need other ingredients to be mixed with for fabrication of useful shapes.

Almost invariably plasticizers have to be added to the thermoplastics, because the thermoplastics are inflammeable and lack flexibility and toughness. Plasticizers reduce these defects and also improve the flow-property of the plastics. The plasticizers should dissolve the resins at the working temperature and should not evaporate. Plasticizers are not used with thermosetting resins, because the two are incompatible.

Thermo-setting resins gradually lack elasticity and crack under stress. To remove this defect, filler or extenders like wood floor' cotton or cloth fibres, asbestos, mica clay etc., are added. To give decorative effect, dyes and pigments are added. To prevent the plastics from sticking to the moulds lubricants like oils, waxes, and soaps are added.

In addition to pigments, lubricants, fillers, plasticizers given above catalysts, solvents and hardners are also used. Catalysts are used to accelerate the hardening of resin. Easter is used as catalyst for urea formalydehyde. Hardners are added to increase the hardness of the resin. Hexamethylene tetramins act as hardner for phenol formaldehyde. Alcohol is used as solvent in cellulose nitrate plastics to dissolve camphor.

Moulding Compounds. In order to develop certain favourable properties to the plastic and also to facilitate moulding of the articles. Some compounds have to be added. Such compounds are known as moulding compounds. These compounds are (1) Catalysts, (2) Fillers, (3) Hardners (4) Pigments (5) Plasticizers (6) Solvents (7) Lubricants. Brief discription of all these compounds has been given here.

1. Catalysts - Ester is used to act as catalyst for urea formaldehyde. Catalysts assist and accelerate the hardening of resin. They also help in quick and complete polymerization.

2. Fillers. The fillers are the inert materials. They impart strength, hardness and other properties to the plastics. The fillers may be in form of fibrous material, laminated material and powder materials. Asbestos, wood and glass fibres are the fibrous fillers. Paper, wood veneers, cotton, card boards are laminated fillers. Where as quartz powder, chalk, wood flour are the powder fillers.

3. Hardners. Hardners are used to increase hardness of the resin. Hexa-methylene tetramine acts as hardener for phenol formaldehyde.

4. Pigments. Pigments impart desired colour to the plastic beside acting as filler. Zinc oxide, barytes etc., are the usual pigments.

5. Plasticizers The plasticizers are the organic compounds, oily in nature and having low molecular weight. They give flexibility to the material and act as lubricants. They should be non-toxic, inert and poorly volatile. The usually used plasticizers are comphor, triacetin tributyl phosphate etc. The proportion of plasticizers in plastic should not exceed 10%. Plasticizers separate the polymer chain by a greater distance to make crystallization difficult.

6. Solvent. These compounds help in disolving the plasticizers. Alcohol acts as a solvent to dissolve camphor in cellulose nitrate plastics.

7. Lubricants. Lubricants are used on the surface of moulds, to avoid stricking to the moulds. Graphite, parafine, wax etc. are the common used lubricants.

17.8. Fabrication of Plastics

To give suitable shapes to plastics, several methods of fabrication are in use. The method chosen depends upon the type of the plastics *i.e*, thermo plastics or thermo setting plastics, and the shape of the finished product.

1. Blowing. This methods is similar to that used in the glass industry. The thermo plastic material is softened and then blown by air or steam into a closed mould. Jars, bottles, toys, are casted by this method.

2. Casting. Molten resin is poured in moulds which are usually made of lead and cured at about 70°C for several days. During curing low pressure may be applied, if necessary. This process is most suitable for cellulose plastics.

3. Calendering. In this method, the plastic material is made to pass through cylinders. The process consists of four sets of revolving cylinders. First three sets are kept heated and the last one is kept cold. While passing through first three heated cylinders set, the plastic is turned into thin sheets. It is cooled while passing through the fourth cylinder. Rollers may be provided with artistic designs so as to reflect them on the finished product. If cloth is to be given plastic coating, it is inserted along with plastic material between second and third heated rollers.

4. Laminating. This process is adopted in case of thermosettiing plastics. Paper sheets; asbestos etc. are applied with this plastic to from plastic laminates. Thickness of sheets varies from 0.12 mm to 15 mm. They possess excellent mechanical and electrical properties. Due to pleasing finished surface, they are used for ornamental and decorative purposes.

5. Moulding. Moulding is the most common method for the fabrication of platic articles. Following are some of the commonly adopted moulding processes.

(i) Compression moulding. This is the most widely used method of moulding. This is used both for thermo plastic resins and thermo setting resins. The moulds are preheated. The plastic moulds are put in preheated moulds and moulds are then closed. They are then heated at a temperature of 100°C to 200C° under a pressure varying from 100 to 500 kg/cm^2. On account of heat and pressure the plastic material gets the shape of the mould.

In case of thermo plastics, the moulds have to be cooled, before articles are taken out of them. Hence in this case moulds will have to be heated and cooled alternately. In case of thermo-setting plastic cooling of moulds is not required as setting takes places by chemical action only.

(ii) Cold moulding. It is adopted for phenol formaldehyde resins for moulding electrical fixtures. The moulding is done by pressure only. In case of thermo setting resins the article has to be cured in heated ovens.

(iii) Injection moulding. This method is used most for moulding thermo plastic resins, The plastic material is loaded, heated and then injected into the mould and allowed to cool, before taking out of the mould.

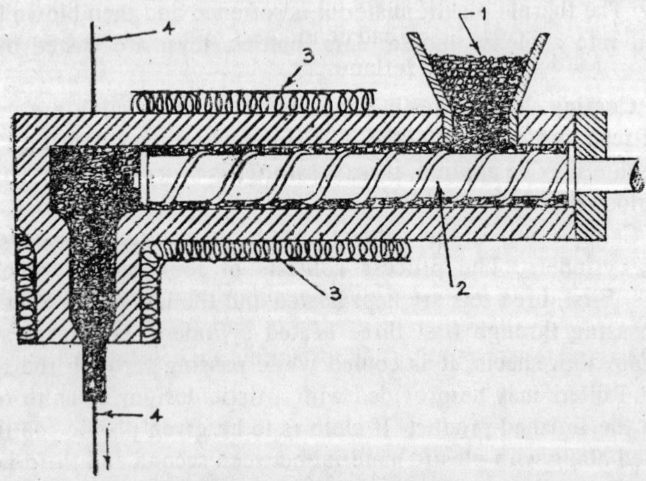

Fig. 17.1. Extrusion Method.

(iv) Extrusion moulding. It is again similar to injection moulding and is used for thermo-plastics only. The material is forced by a screw drive into a heated chamber, where it softens and is forced out through a die. The finished product coming out from the die is cooled by blowing air or spraying water. It is used for making continuous shapes like rods, tubes, sheets etc. See. Fig. 17.1.

(v) Jet moulding. In this, the plastic is slightly heated and then allowed to pass through nozzle, which is preheated to a high temperature. This mehtod is useful for both the types of plastics.

(vi) Transfer moulding. This method is almost exclusively used for thermo-setting plastics and has been developed to make compression moulding applicable to more complicated shapes. The material is heated in a chamber to melt it and then forced into a hot mould. The mould is opened after the plastic has set.

Engineering properties of plastics

The use of this material has been increasing, because of their several advantages over other materials, notably high strength-weight ratio, corrosion resistance, low thermal and electrical conductivity and transparency. Its S.G. varies from 1 to 1.6. Tensile strength of plastics is about 700 kg/cm^2. The stress-strain relationship of plastics is similar to that of the metals. Humidity also effects the strength of the plastics.

Most plastics are electrical insulators and find large scale use in the electrical industry.

Most plastics are clear and transparent. They can be given beautiful and brilliant colours.

Most plastics cannot be used at higher temperatures. Thermoplastics generally cannot be used above 100°C and thermo setting above 150°C. Plastics being bad conductors of heat are useful for making handles. Most plastic are inflammable, but some are, fire proof.

Optical clarity combined with strength, makes them suitable for making wind screens for automobiles, air crafts etc.

Short comings of Plastics

1. Most of the plastics possess low resistance.
2. They are not very hard.
3. They exhibit high creep.
4. They have high coefficient of thermal expansion.
5. Plastics disintegrate gradually and because of the effects of light, air and temperature. They lose strength, become soft and get dull as time passes.

Properties of Plastics

Following are the properties of plastics.

1. Chemical resistance. Plastics offer great resistance to chemicals, solvents and moisture. Most of the plastics have excellent corrosion resistance and as such are used to convey chemicals. Degree of chemical resistance depends on composition of plastics.

2. Appearance. The plastic can be developed to any attractive shade and design by adding suitable pigment.

3. Durability. The plastics are quite durable if they are sufficiently hard. However Thermo-plastic varieties one likely to be attacked by termites and rodents. Since plastics have no nutritional value there is no likely hood of any such attack.

4. Ductility. The plastic are not ductile and hence its members may fail with out any warning.

5. Electric insulation. The plastics have excellent electric insulating property.

6. Fire resistance. All the plastics are combustible but the degree of resistance varies from plastic to plastic. The cellulose acetate plastics burn slowly. The PVC plastics are non inflammable. The phenol formaldehyde and urea formaldehyde resist fire and are used as fire-proofing materials.

7. Weight. The plastics have S.G. of about 1.30 to 1.40. Being light material its transportation is very cheap.

8. Weather resistance. Phenolic resin plastics are good weather resistants. Some plastics are badly affected by ultraviolet light in the presence of sunlight. The resistance to sunlight can be improved by incorporating fillers and pigments which absorb or reflect the ultra-violet light at the surface.

9. Thermal property. The thermal conductivity of plastic is comparable to that of wood which is low.

10. Optical property. Plastics may be transparent and translucent.

11. Sound absorption. The acoustical boards are made by impregnating fibre glass with phenolic resins. Its absorption coefficient is about 0.67.

12. Melting point. Most of the plastic have very low melting point. Some of the varieties has as low as 50°C as its melting point. Thus the plastic cannot be used for carrying boiling water. The thermo-setting varieties of plastics are less susceptible to heat than thermo-plastic varieties. The glass fibre reinforcement improves the heat resistance of plastics.

13. Strength. No plastic structural section has yet been designed. The plastics are reasonably strong. The strength of plastic can be increased by reinforcing with fibrous materials. The plastics are costly, poor in stiffness, sensitive to temperature changes and are subjected to creep under constant heavy load. The plastics can be used as tensile members as their strength to weight ratio is very nearly equal to that of metals.

14. Maintenance. Practically there is no maintenance as plastic surface do not require any protective coat of any paint.

15. Fixing. The plastics can be easily fixed in position. They can be drilled, glued, clamped, bolted, screw - T hreaded.

16. Finishing. Any surface treatment can be given to plastics. It is also easy to exercise control during manufacture of plastics.

Fibre glass reinforced plastic (FRP)

The fibre glass reinforces plastic (FRP) in obtained by using two materials in conjunction with each other. It is a composite material of altogether different properties. In FRP, the glass fibres provide stiffness and strength while resin provides a matrix to transfer load to the fibres. Aesthetic appearance, corrosion resistance, durability, dimensional stability, light transmission, light weight are the favourable properties which have made FRP, the most commercially successful composite material of construction.

Uses of plastics in building construction

Plastic is a versatile material whose properties can be changed to suit varying requirements when used at different places and in different situations in a building. The important uses are as follows :

1. Flooring. Thermo plastics or polyvinyl (P.V.C. or P.V.A.) are used for floors inform of sheets or tiles. Polyvinyl chloride (P.V.C.) is resistant to abrasion and is unaffected by many chemicals.

(*a*) **Thermo plastic vinyl tiles**. These tiles are cut out of rolls of masticated hot mixture óf plasticised P.V.C., lime stone, asbestos and required pigments passed through hot rollers. These tiles are laid on dry floor free from dust, grease or loose scales. The tiles are laid on cut back bitumen adhesive spread on the sub-base hot and rolled with light rollers. These tiles are unaffected by water, oil or grease and with stand wear well.

(*b*) **P.V.C. sheets or Tiles**. Masticated P.V.C., its compounding in gredients and the required pigments are passed through hot rollers. The rolls are annealed and coold before cutting them into tiles. These sheets are 1 mm thick and are provided with cheaper backing material. To ensure better adhesion to sub floor, the underside of these sheets is roughened. Sheets with Hessian or felt as backing are also produced. These flooring tiles have excellent wearing properties and are unaffected by greasy or oily stuff.

(*c*) **Poly-Vinyl acetate floors**. Floors laid with poly-vinyl acetate are jointless inritre finishes and are also termed as plastics.

(*d*) **Emulsion floor finishes**. Cold mix of poly-vinyl acetate emulsion, fillers, and pigments are spread evenly on a smooth sub-base to provide a tough floor finish on drying. To have a thick finishing layers, successive thin layers are spread.

These plastic floor finishes are wear resistant, dampen noise, are non-slippery and comfortable to walk. Though these floors can be washed without any damage yet these should not be allowed to get saturated as then they soften and have poorer resistance to wear.

2. Roofing. Corrugated sheets of phenolic-resin-bonded paper laminates manufactured in rather darker shades provides light, strong and corrosion resistant opaque roofing material.

Corrugated plain or curved sheets in glass reinforced polyester resin, or of a crylic resin are translucent and when used for roofing they provide ample day light.

3. Pipes. Plastic pipes are finding more and more usage in water supply, sanitation and in specialized industrial applications. Polythylene and P.V.C. pipes are the most extensively used ones. Plastic pipes are excellent in use at low temperatures, particularly when there is fear of metal pipe bursting due to freezing but they become soft at temperature higher than 65°C. PVC pipes are ductile, can be threaded and can be welded with hot gas stream and a PVC rod.

4. Decorative laminated plastic veneer. These are versatile sheets marketed under trade names of Formica, sunmica, sungloss, Decolum etc. Veneers of 1.6 mm thickness and panels of 3.2 mm thickness are available in sheets of sizes 244 cm × 122 cm and 274 cm × 122 cm in various shades and patterns.

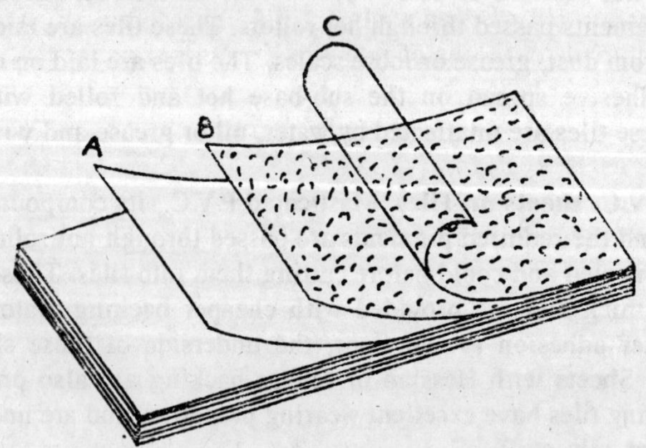

Fig. 17.2. (Laminated plastic veneer).

It is a surface material, a smooth ready finished decorative veener or board of exceptional toughness and durability. It is made from sheets of paper impregnated with selected resins. The impregnated papers are assembled into packs A is the tough core laminae and B, last but one layer carries the colour-printed pattern. These visible laminae are coloured and patterned in a wide range. This is protected lastly by a transparent top sheet (C) which is impregnated with a colourless resin of extreme toughness. The assembly is then subjected to very high pressure and accurately controlled high temperatures. In the closely compacted paper layers, a chemical reaction, polymerisation occurs. This fuses the combination into one homogeneous sheet of superb decorative finish unobtainable in any other material. It can be cut and sawn as ordinary plysheets. It can be bonded to any other material provided suitable adhesive is used. Synthetic resins are the most commonly used adhesives for bonding it with a wooden base like plywood, block board, chipboard etc.

It is extensively used for table tops, wall panels, counters in kitchens and bathrooms, interior of bodies of trains, buses, aircrafts and every where when decorative finish is required.

5. Concrete shittering The moulds and forms of FRP give the cast concrete shapes of very high quality. Very complicated concrete shapes can be moulded in FRP.

6. Doors and window frames. The light weight Flush doors and standard window frames can be made of FRP. They have long life easy to maintain and overall cheap in cost. The use of FRP doors for bathrooms and toilets eliminate the problems of rotting warping, swelling etc.

7. Internal partitions and wall parelling. FRP sheets can very well be used for internal partitions of industrial and commercial buildings. The various designs of FRP for wall parelling and ceilings can be made in shape, form and colour.

8. Stractural sections. The FRP sections have much better properties in flexure and tension. They are corrosion resistant and grant a choice of colours. They can be machined, riveted, bolted just like steel sections.

9. Temporary shelters. The FRP modular systems are ideally suitable for temporary shelters at project sites, watchman cabin, green houses, defence shelters, vehicle parking sheds etc. They can be easily dismantled and re-erected at other site with minimum cost.

10. Water storage tanks. The FRP water storage tanks are found to be superior to steel and concrete tanks. Sintex tanks and so many other plastic water storage tanks have come in the market. These tanks are almost exclusively used as over head water storage tanks in all the buildings.

11. Furniture items. FRP chairs, and benches have come in big way in the market and are being used for auditoriums, hotels, restaurants, gardens, parks, waiting rooms, theatres etc.

QUESTIONS

1. What are the processes involved in fabrication of plastic articles?
2. Enumerate general properties of plastic.
3. What are the compositions of plastics? How are they classified?
4. Discuss various types of thermosetting plastics.
5. Discuss various types of thermo-plastics.

18

ASPHALT, BITUMEN AND TAR

18.1. Introduction

The material in which asphalt, bitumen or tar are associated in some form are termed as bituminous materials. Bituminous materials have been known and used in road construction since ancient times. They were used as a mortar and water proofing agents as early as 3800 B.C. Early bitumen was of natural origin, found in pools and lakes. Many of these pools and lakes exist even to-day. The bitumen lake on the Trinidad island and the Bermudz deposit in venezuela are the largest known sources of natural bitumen. Now a days bitumen is mainly used in the construction of roads. It is also used in building industry inform of timber preservative, D.P.C. and leak proofing of the roofs. It is also used in so many other fields but its use in those field is not predominant.

18.2. Bitumen and Asphalt

There is some confusion in regard to terms 'Asphalt' and 'bitumen'. In U.S.A. the term asphalt is used to refer the both. But else where including India the last product or residue left in the petroleum distillation in termed as 'bitumen' and the mixture of bitumen with some inert mineral matter is known as 'asphalt'. Hence asphalt is nothing, but adultrated bitumen with some inert minerals like sand, crushed stone etc. Chemically bitumens are *hydro carbons* having extremely complex composition.

18.3. Asphalts

As already explained that asphalts are nothing, but bitumen mixed with inert minerals like sand, gravel and crushed stone. It is available in natural state or it can be prepared artificially. In natural from it is found in the name of lake asphalt, and rock asphalt. If asphalt is naturally found in forms of lakes it is known as *lake asphalt*. In some countries there are certain rocks which contain lot of bonding bitumen in natural form. These rocks can be used in road construction after slightly heating.

Such naturally occuring rocks and containing bitumen content, are known as *rock asphalt.*

Artificial or mastic asphalt. It is a preparation made by using natural asphalt, bitumen and sand. It is water proof, fire proof, and elastic to some extent. It is largely used as a D.P.C. water proofing layer over flat roofs, and for making floors. It is not used much for road consrtruction, as roads paved with this, become soft in summer and slippery in winter.

18.4. Bitumens

As per I.S. 334-1951 bitumen is defined as a non-crystalline solid or viscous material having adhesive properties, derived from petroleum either by natural or refinery process. It is substantially soluble in carbon disulphide.

The greatest proportion of bitumen is obtained from crude petroleum. It is obtained by fractional distillation process in whicch the simpler components of the crude petroleum such as white spirit, kerosene, fuel oil, light, medium and heavy lubricating oils which have lower boiling points are evaporated, leaving behind the bitumen. It is black or brown in colour. Bitumen may be extracted by distillation process or cracking process. Mostly distillation process is used.

1. Straight run bitumen. The bitumen which has been distilled to a definite viscosity or penetration without further treatment is known as straight run bitumen. During processing, by regulating rate of flow and temperature, bitumen from very soft to a very hard consistency grade can be produced. Before this bitumen can be used it has to be processed to reduce its viscosity either by heating, addition of cut, or emulsifying agent. This bitumen is mostly used for road construction.

2. Air blown bitumen. Special properties can be developed in semi-solid bitumen by blowing air through the residue, still in hot condition. This bitumen is sometimes called *oxidized bitumen* also. This bitumen is not used in paving mixes, but is a useful material for roofing, battery boxes, water proofing, etc. It is widely used, as crack and joint filler material, for concrete pavements.

3. Cut back bitumen. Cut back is defined as a bitumen, whose viscosity has been reduced by the addition of a volatile diluent. Volatile diluents are gasoline, kerosense and high boiling-point light oils. Cut back is used, when it is essential to have a fluid binder which can be readily poured or sprayed at relatively low temperature. The important features of a cut back are its viscosity at the temperature of its use and also the rate at which it sets. The rate of setting is the rate at which solvent evaporates from cut back.

Cut backs are commercially manufactured in three groups namely rapid curing (R.C.), medium curing (M.C.) and slow curing (S.C.). R.C. cut backs contain naphtha or gasoline, M.C. cut backs contain kerosene and S.C. cut backs contain light oils as the fluxing agents. Each group of cut backs is further divided into six categories varying from 0 to 5. The six different viscosities are named by numbers from 0 to 5, in the increasing order of viscosity. Zero grade has the lowest viscosity and grade 5 the highest. Hence, rapid curing (R.C.). Medium curing (M.C.) and slow curing (S.C.) cut back may be written as follows. RC-0, RC-1, RC-2, RC-3, RC-4, RC-5, MC-0, MC-1, MC-2, MC-3, MC-4, MC-5, SC-0, SC-1, SC-2, SC-3, SC-4, SC-5.

4. Emulsions. It is a combination of water, bitumen and an emulsifying agent. Bitumen does not dissolve in water. But when heated bitumen and water are mixed together and agitated. The bitumen disperses in water inform of spherical globules of about 2 micron diameter. To prevent bitumen spheres from coalescing, an emulsifying agent is added in the emulsion which remains dissolved in water. Soap is used mostly as an emulsifying agent. Depending upon the stability of the protective coating of emusifying agent the emulsion may be classifed as Rapid setting (R.S.), Medium setting (M.S.) and slow setting (S.S.). Emulsions are always stored in air tight drums. It is used mostly for the construction of roads. It is not required to be heated, before use and as such are very useful for the places' where heating of the bitumen has to be avoided. Emulsion is mixed with road metal and applied. When emulsion changes its colour from brown to black, it is said that emulsion has started breaking. As the emulsion starts breaking, it starts binding the aggregate. Emulsion can be used for soil stabilization, patch repair works of bitumenous roads, etc. Its main feature is that it can be used in wet conditions also.

18.5. Tests for Bitumen

In order to ascertain the properties of the bitumen, it may be subjected to tests as follows.

1. Penetration test. This test is used to determine the hardness of the bitumen. This test consists of a needle of standard dimension which is loaded by 100 gm and made to penetrate vertically in the bitumen at 25°C for a period of 5 seconds. The penetration of the needle is measured in units of 1/100 cm. Bitumen is graded according to the penetration. It is written as 30/40, 80/100, 60/70, etc. 30/40 grade bitumen means that under standard conditions of temperature, the needle penetration varies from 0.30 to 0.40 cm.

2. Softening point. This test is done to determine temperature susceptibility of the bitumen. This test is done by ring and ball equipment. The softerning temperature is that temperature at which a ball of bitumen will flow vertically for 2.54 cm through the ring on which it was placed. This temperature for usual bitumens lies between 35°C and 70°C. As per IS 702-1961 bitumen has been classified into grades such as 62/25, 75/15, 75/30, 85/25, 85/40. The first figure gives softening temperature in degres centigrade and second figure gives penetration in 1/100 cm units at 25°C.

3. Ductility Test. This test is carried out to ascertain the ductility of the bitumen. A standard briquette of bitumen is prepared from bitumen and stretched at predetermined rate at 75°C in a stratching machine. The distance of stretch of the briquette, before it breaks determines the ductility of the bitumen. Ductility for various grades of bitumen varies from 5 to 100. For satisfactory use in road pavement, value of ductility should not be less than 50.

4. Float test. This test is carried out to determine the consistency of the bitumen. For this test an aluminium float having standard sized hole at the bottom is used. The specimen of bitumen to be tested is filled in the coller fitted in the hole and temperature of the water bath in which this float is left, is raised to 50°C. The temperature of the bath is maintained at 50°C. The time required in seconds for water to force its way through bitumen plug is noted. The higher the float test value, the stiffer is the bitumen.

5. Flash point and fire point test. Flash point is the lowest temperature at which the vapour of a bituminous material momentarily catches fire in the form of a flash under specified conditions of test.

Fire point is the lowest temperature at which bituminous material gets ignited and burns under specified conditions of test.

The knowlege of these points is of interest mainly to the users, since bitumen must not be heated beyond these points. The flash point tells the critical temperature at and above which suitable precautions are required to be taken to eliminate the danger of fire during heating.

6. Spot test. This test is made to ascertain wheather bitumen being used has cracked or not. Cracked bitumen should not be used in road pavement construction.

7. Loss on heating test. Loss in weight after heating at 163°C for 5 hours should not be more than 2%.

There are other tests also, but they are not of much significance.

18.6. Tar

Tar is a bye product obtained from the destructive distillation of coal. It can be obtained from many organic substances also.

Tar as received directly from, process, is known as Crude Tar. Crude Tar is then sent to tar refining plants, where it is first dehydrated and then fractionally distilled to produce various types of road tars and tar pitches.

Road tars are manufactured in five grades viz RT-1, RT-2, RT-3, RT-4, and RT-5. All the grades vary in viscosity and other properties. To what use every grade of tar can be put, is given in table below.

Grade of Tar	*Uses*
RT-1	Surface painting under exceptionally cool weather.
RT-2	Surface painting under normal climatic conditions.
RT-3	Surface dressing, renewal coat, premix carpet.
RT-4	Premix Tax Macadam in base courses.
RT-5	Grouting purposes.

Like Bitumen, Tars are also tested for S.G. softening point water content, etc. Suitable properties of Tars are given below.

Property	*RT-1*	*RT-2*	*RT-3*	*RT-4*	*RT-5*
Softening point in 0°C	-	-	-	-	45-50
Specific gravity at 27°C	1.16-1.26	1.16-1.26	1.18-1.28	1.18-1.28	1.18-1.28
Viscosity by 10 mm size Tar Viscometer. Tar 0°C	36	44	45	55	-
II. in seconds	33-35	30-55	35-60	40-60	-
Equi-Viscious tempe- rature range 0°C(EVT)	32-36	37-41	43-60	53-57	63-67

QUESTIONS

1. Explain the terms bitumen, asphalt and Tar. What is difference between these products?
2. Explain the terms-lake asphalt, rock asphalt, cracked bitumen, straight run bitumen, air-blown bitumen.
3. Discuss various tests performed on bitumen.
4. Explain the term cut-back bitumen. Under what circumstances, they are used in road construction? Briefly discuss the tests carried out on cut-backs.
5. (*a*) What is difference between R.C., M.C. and S.C. cut backs?
   (*b*) Explain Tar and its properties and grades.

19

MISCELLANEOUS MATERIALS

19.1. Fuels

Fuels are the substances which are capable of creating heat energy This energy is utilized to run machines and other useful works. The fuels may be classified into following three groups.

(1) Solid fuels (2) Liquid fuels (3) Gaseous fuels

1. Solid fuels. Charcoal, coal coke, wood etc. are the examples of solid fuels. Charcoal is obtaiined by burning wood in kilns in the presence of limited air. Coal is excavated from coal mines. Its colour may be black or brown. It is a natural solid fuel. It is formed by the decomposition of vegetable matter under great pressure and in the absence of air. Coke is prepared by heating the powdered coal and then quenching the heated mass. It is a high class solid fuel and is used for metallurgical purposes. Wood is obtained from natural trees.

2. Liquid fuels. Alcohol, crude oil, Petroleum, etc. are the exmples of liquid fuels. Petroleum is the main source of liquid fuels, which on distillation gives several fractions. The lower boiling fractions find use into internal combustion engines and the higher boiling fractions in diesel engines and in oil fired furnaces. Alcohols, tar, and colloidal fuels are used to a lesser extent.

The chief disadvantages of many of the liquid fuels are that they are highly inflammable and are volatile.

3. Gaseous fuels. Coal gas, natural gas, producer gas, are the examples of gaseous fuels.

Coal gas is a mixture of several gases and is obtained by the distructive distillation of coal in fire clay retorts. The average composition of the coal gas is 45-50% Hydrogen, 25-35%, marsh gas, 5-10% carbon monoxide, 2-5% Ethylene, benzine, 2-10% Nitrogen, 0-3% carbon dioxide and 0-2% Oxygen.

Producer gas is produced by passing a regulated supply of air through a stack of red hot coke. it is mixture of carbon monoxide and nitrogen. It is used as a cheap industrial fuel.

Natural gas is obtained from natural under ground sources. it is always associated with petroleum under pressure. Gaseous fuels do not leave any residue. They ignite readily and require less air for combustion. They require large space for storage.

19.2. Rubber

Rubber is an important engineering material. The whole of tyre industry is based on rubber and practically the whole of transportation system is dependent on tyres.

1. Natural rubber. It is obtained from latex or milk tapped from rubber trees. These trees grow in hot climate regions. This tree is found in abundence in countries like Cylon, Malasia, Mexico, Singapure, North Africa. This tree is very fast growing and starts giving latex within 5 years of its plantation

The latex collected from trees is cleared from impurities like leaves, sand, debris etc. and coagulated. Acetic acid is usually used as a coalgulant. Coagulated latelx is just like curd. The curd like mass is passed through rollers and water is separated from it. The resulting mass is natural rubber which may be in form of sheets or globules.

2. Synthetic rubber. Natural rubber cannot fulfill the large world wide demand. Hence artificial rubber was developed. Artificial rubber is used to indicate rubber like materials which are produced by chemical processes. These are generally obtained from acetylene gas. This rubber possesses certain unusual properties which are not found in natural rubber. Synthetic rubber is more elastic than natural rubber and also resists light rays more effectively. With the growth of petro-chemical industries production of synthetic rubber has increased. Buna-S, Buna-N, Butyl rubber, Neoprene, Thiokol, are the usual forms of synthetic rubber.

Vulcanization. Crude rubber becomes hard and brittle in winter and soft and sticky in summer. In order to make rubber useful for all seasons, it has to be vulcanized. Vulcanization of rubber is brough about by adding small quantity of sulphur in the crude rubber. When a mixture of crude rubber and sulphur is heated, a complicated chemical reaction takes place which renders rubber hard and resistant to changes in temperature. 1 to 5% of sulphur produces soft rubber. If the percentage of sulphur is increased to about 30% hard rubber is obtained. The heating temperatures for soft and hard rubbers are respectively 130°C and 170°C. The soft vulcanized rubber is used for shoe soles and other ordinary things. Hard variety is used for tyres and belts etc.

Vulcanization brings about the followiong changes in rubber.

(i) Rubber becomes more durable and permanent set of it becomes very small.

(ii) Such a rubber offers great resistant to friction and solvents and its tensile strength is considerably increased.

(iii) Such a rubber is less susceptible to temperature changes.

Compounding of rubber. In order to make rubber more useful, certain compounds have to be added to it. These compounds are accelerators, accelerator activators, anti oxidants fillers, hardners, plasticizers, pigments and vulcanizing agents. All these compounds bring about improvement in the desirable properties of rubber. Pigments are added to impart desired colour to rubber. Plasticizers are added to impart softness to rubber. Wax, resin, vegetable oil etc. are the commonly used plasticizers. Barium sulphate, calcium carbonate, sealing wax etc. are the usually used hardners. They increase tensile strength and hardness of rubber. Hardened rubber can withstand high temperatures. Fillers are added in the form of carbon, cotton etc. to increase the strength and rigidity. Accelerators and activators reduce the preparation period of rubber and also improve its properties.

Anti-oxidants prolong the oxidation process of rubber. Wax, phenols, phosphates etc. are the usual anti-oxidants.

Forms of Rubber

(i) Sponge rubber. This rubber is prepared by adding sodium bicarbonate during vulcanization. Small pores are left on evaporation of moisture and spong rubber is formed. It is very good material for insulation of sound and heat.

(ii) Gutta percha rubber. This is natural rubber prepared from the leaves of trees known *dischopsis Gutta* and *Palaquim Gutta*. It is considered as the best material for making ropes for submarine use. It absorbs comparatively less amount of water and becomes sticky and soft at a temperature of about 100°C.

(iii) Foamed rubber. This rubber is widely used for pillows, packing pads etc. It is prepared by adding some foaming agent. Foamed rubber is then converted into slabs of suitable thickness and put to varying uses. In the liquid latex the chemicals producing gases are added and the mixture is well stirred till foam is formed.

(iv) Crepe rubber. This rubber has irregular surface. It is prepared by passing coagulated latex throughy rollers. It is available in form of rolls. This variety is one form of crude rubber.

(v) Guayule rubber. It is prepared from branches of guayule tree.

Its composition is 70% hydro-carbon, 20% resin 10% insoluble materials like cellulose, lignin etc. It is also a natural rubber.

(vi) Smoked rubber. It is also a variety of crude rubber. After coagulation, the rubber pieces are dried in room filled with smoke at a temperature of about 40°C to 50°C. Since drying is done in a smoke - room, it is known as smoked rubber.

(vii) Polybutadiene rubber. It is a variety of synthetic rubber. It is produced by the Indian petrochemical corporation Ltd. (IPCL) near Baroda IPCL has given commercial name as CISRUB to this rubber. This rubber has wide variety of applications. It is found excellent where high abrasion resistance and strength are the main requirements. Engineering moulded goods, floor Tiles, foot wear, gaskets, hoses, seals, tyres belts are the man areas of application of this rubber.

The rubber has very high scrap value. Old rubber can be reclaimed and used again. The old worn out rubber articles are cut and ground into fine powder. The metallic material is removed, with the help of a magnet. The required ingredients are then added and crude rubber is formed. Reclaimed rubber although proves cheaper than new rubber, but its properties are markedly inferior to the new rubber. Hence reclaimed rubber is used for unimportant situations. It can be used for vehicle tyres, hose-pipe, etc.

Properties of Rubber

1. It is bad conductor of heat and it can contain liquids and gases.
2. It absorbs shocks or impacts.
3. It can be extended by applying force.
4. It is flexible and abrasion resistant.
5. It can be moulded to any desired shape.
6. It is possible to modify its properties by vulcanizing and compounding.
7. Natural rubber should be protected from sun light and from coming in contact of oils, organic liquids etc.
8. It can under go large deformation without breaking.
9. Synthetic rubber is resistant against petroleum, acids etc.

Uses of rubber. It is used for tyres of vehicles, gaskets, lining for parts subjected to heavy friction, rubber ropes, shock absorbants, hose-pipes, rubber soles, lining for reservoir, thermal insulation, etc.

19.3. Adhesives

Adhesive is a substances naturally or artificially prepared, which is used to join two or more parts, so as to form a single unit. Adhesives develop quite strong bond, between the joined surfaces. They can join the surface of glass, timber, plastic and metals. But there is no adhesive developed, so far which could be used universally for all the materials. A particular adhesive can be used for joining particular surface only. Secondly adhesive generally lose their grip at higher temperatures. The use of adhesives in the manufacture of laminates such as ply wood, laminated glass, laminated plastics is unquestionable. Adhesives are generally referred by term glue. Following are some of the commonly used glues.

1. *Blood albumin glue*. It is a special animal glue made for use particularly with leather and paper. It has only moderate bonding power with wood. It has good resistance against heat and cold, but very poor against water. It is sold as dry powder which has to be mixed with water before use.

2. *Animal protein glues*. It is obtained by boilding waste pieces of skins, bones etc. of animal with hot water. It is affected easily by damp and moist conditions. It is used in the manufacture of ply wood and other laminated timbers.

3. *Synthetic glues*. These glues are based on synthetic resins. They are the resins used in the manufacture of plastics. Plastic glues are Malamine resin, Phenolic resins, Urea resins, Resoricinal resins, Nitro cellulose glues, Polyvinyle resins, etc. All these plastic glues are resistant to moisture, heat, fungi etc. and develop a very strong bond, between joined surfaces. They are used for permanent and high class works.

4. *Gun arabic*. It is a glue obtained from acacia tree. It is the most useful natural adhesive which is soluble in water.

5. *Starch and dextrin glues*. They are available in both dry and liquid states. They have good bond with paper or leather and fairly good bond with timber, but strength does not compare with those of animal or casein glues. They have fair resistance to heat and cold, but poor resistance to water. They dry at room temperaturte. Starch glues are made by mixing wheat or rice flour with hot water. Acid or alkalies are also used as modifiers. They are quite, cheep. Dextrine is a glue prepared by treating starch with acid. They are expenbsive as compared to starch glues. It is used in paper and textile industry.

6. *Casein glues*. It is obtained from skimmed milk. The mass is washed, pressed and dried to a white powder, which is casein glue. It is sold in market either in form of glue powder or as wet-mix glues. These glues form strong water proof wood joint.

7. *Natural resin adhesives*. Asphalt, shellac, Rosin, are the common natural adhesives.

8. *Sodium silicate glues.* It is used in the manufacture of paper boxes and card board. Fused mass of sodium silicate as obtained from fusion furnace is cooled and dissolved in water to form this glue.

9. *Nitro cellulose glue.* It is prepared from pyroxilin a product of nitrated cellulose. It is obtained by treating cellulose with nitric acid.

10. *Araldite.* It is special glue, used to join light metals and glass surfaces.

11. *Rubber glues.* These glues are prepared by dissolving rubber in benzene. It is used for joining plastics, glass, rubber, etc.

19.4. Abrasives

An abrasive is a hard material used to remove excess of material by grinding or rubbing action. Abrasives are used inform of abrasive stones, abrasive papers or cloths, grinding wheels, grinding pastes with oil etc. Abrasives may be classified as hard, soft, silicious, and artificial.

Diamond, emergy, corundum and garnet are the varieties of hard abrasives. Lime stone, metallic oxides etc. are the examples of soft abrasives. Silicious abrasives are flint, quartz, sand stoné, quartzite and pumice. Artificial abrasives are also artiflicially formed. Silicon carbide, steel shots, crushed steel, basic acid, fused aluninium oxide are the examples of artificial abrasives.

Grinding wheels are made by bonding abrasive powder on the cast iron wheels with the help of suitable adhesives. Artificial abrasives have following advantages.

1. Amount of abrasive material is more.
2. Exactly similar grinding products can be manufactured.
3. They can be made exactly as per desired properties, size and shape.

19.5. Asbestos

It is a naturally occuring fibrous substance. It is composed of hydrous silicates of calcium and magnesium. It may also contain traces of iron and alumina. It is mostly found in India, Russia, Cyprus, and Canada. Its varieties may be white, amosite etc. It is white asbestos ($3MgSiO_3$) which is used practically in all the products of asbestos.

Properties. It is an excellant insulator of heat and electricity. It is fire proof, acid proof, soft, flexible material which can be drilled screwed and cut into pieces. Its colour may be grey, white or brown and its surface is smooth like glass. Its S.G. is 3.1 and melting point 1200°C to 1550°C. It has high durability and mechanical strength. It acts as a reinforcing agent, when mixed with cement.

Uses. It is used to form paint, fire-proof cloths, ropes etc. It is used for insulating furances and boilers. By mixing with cement, sheets and pipes can be manufactured. Sheets are very much used for roof covering and pipes are used for sanitary purposes and rain water drainage purposes. Plain A.C. sheets can be used for panelling purpose. It may be used for damp-proof layers also. It is used for covering magnetic coils. It is also used as lining material for fuse box and switch box.

19.6. Cork

It is obtained from the bark of oak tree. The bark is ground, cleaned and baked during, its manufacture. During baking process the natural resin present in the cork comes out and binds the material into a homogeneous mass known as *cork*. Its structure is cellular and its specific gravity is 0.20. Cork may be mixed with cement and bitumen to form its light slabs. The weight of the cork slabs is about 210 kg/m^3. It is a porous and light weight material which is not attacked by heat and moisture. It is resilient and reasonably elastic. It is a good insulator of sound and electricity. It is mainly used for preparing cork sheets and boards, bottle stoppers, packing gaskets etc. It can be cast into tiles also.

19.7. Lath

It is used for plastering the roofs, to support covering of tiles or slates.

Plasters lath is a thin strip of wood 2.5 cm wide and about one metre long, but its thickness varies to suit the work for which, it is meant. Tiling or slate lath or batton is generally sawn boards about 3 m long, but its section varies from 2.5 × 2.5cm to 7.5 × 2.5 cm.

19.8. Gaskets

It is a material used as packing material in joints. Cotton A.C. flat sheets, hemp, jute, yarns, are the material mostly used as packing materials. They fill the empty space and make the joints leak proof. Gaskets are also some times used for absorbing shocks.

19.9. Lubricants

It is a material which prevents direct contact of a moving part of a machine with another part stationary or moving. It presents a thin film between the surfaces. Lubricants reduce wear and tear of moving parts and also make easy motion of moving parts, as friction reduces to very small amount. Life of the moving parts is also prolonged.

Lubricants may be classified in two categories.

1. Solid lubricants 2. Liquid lubricants.

1. Solid lubricants. Mica, soapstone, graphite are the examples of solid lubricants. They are suitable under conditions of very high temperature and pressure. The solid lubricants are slowly converted into powder and they prove harmful to the moving parts. Hence use of the solid lubricants is recommended for limited circumstances only.

2. Liquid lubricants. Animal oils, mineral oils, vegetable oils, greases are the usual varieties of liquid lubricants. Lard oil, Neat's foot oil, Tallow oil, whale oil, are the animals oils. They are used for lubrication of delicate machines. Grease is a product consisting of liquid oil to the extent varying from 50 to 98% and soap varying from 50 to 2%.. It is a semi-solid lubricant and is used in conditions, where dust is more in air and also it is not possible to maintain oil film either due to presssure or due to intermittent operations. It is also used, when lubrication is to be carried out under moist conditions. Oils drived from crude petroleum are known as mineral oils. Castor oil, Rape seed oil, olive oil, palm oil, are the examples of vegetable oils. They are also used for delicate machines.

Lubricant is applied to the moving part by force feed method, gravity feed method, or mechanical feed method. In force feed method lubricant is forced under pressure at the desire point. In gravity feed method lubricant is made to drop from a vessel under gravity. In mechanical feed method moving chain is used to carry and convey the lubricant to the desired point of application.

19.10. Turpentine

It is obtained from the juice or gum of certain varities of pine trees. The collected juice is heated and distilled to obtain turpentine. It is mainly used as solvent for paints and varnishes. It also acts as a solvent for rubber. It is used for making printing ink, synthetic camphor etc. It is a transprarent, volatile liquid, of the consistency of water.

19.11. Gypsum

It is a hydrated sulphate of calcium. It is mainly used in the manufacture of cement to increase its setting time. It is also used to prepare plaster of Paris and gypsum boards. Gypsum boards are made by mixing gypsum with asphalt. They are quite hard and strong boards having insulating properties. It is mostly found in Rajasthan in India.

It contain 79.1% calcium sulphate and 20.9% water of crystallizaton. It is a good binding material and sets within 4 to 6 minutes after addition of water.

Gypsum plaster. When finely ground gypsum is heated to a temperature of 170°C. about two third its water of crystallization is lost and the resulting product is known as hemihydrate of calcium sulphate. It is also known as plaster of Paris or first settle plaster. When water is added to this product, it sets almost immediately and hence requires addition of retarders to gain time to carry out miixing, placing and finishing etc. Clay, gum, starch, sugar, glue are the usual retarders. Hemihydrate gypsum plaster means Paris plaster with retarders added to it.

When gypsum is further heated to say 200°C, the entire water of crystallization is drivern out and the resulting product is known as gypsum *an hydrite*. The setting time of gypsum an hydrite is quite large and in order to reduce it, alum, raw gypsum or pottassium sulphate are added as accelarators. Following are some important properties of gypsum plaster.

1. It is fire resistant and hence used as an insulating material to protect wood or metal columns and beams from high temperatures.

2. It is very light metal. Its weight can be further decreased by adding materials like saw dust, granulated cork etc in it. By addition of these materials gypsum plasters become more insulated against heat and sound, both

3. It has good adhesion on fibrous materials and it suffers very little shrinkge on drying.

4. Its setting takes places by the process of crystallization.

5. Sand is added, when used for base coat and lime putty is added in the final finishing coat.

6. It is used for ornamental castings. Boards and blocks of gypsum are used for ceilings, internal lining of partition walls.

7. It is slightly soluble in water and as such cannot be used for exposed damp conditions.

19.12. Heat Insulating Material

Rock wool, slag wool, fibre boards, flexible, blankets, saw dust, wood savings, cork board slabs, mineral wool, light aggregate, cement concrete products, gypsum boards, A.C. boards, chip boards, foam glass, gasket, cork sheet, etc are the materials which are mostly used for the purpose of heat insulation. The choice of an insulating material depends on its cost, area to be covered and standard of insulation required. Thermally insulated materials should be non-absorbent of moisture, able to resist attack of insects, and reasonably fire proof.

19.13. Sound Absorbent materials

The materials which absorb sound are known as *sound absorbent materials*. These materials are extensively used in cinema halls, auditorias, lecture halls, T.V. and radio station. Hair felt, acoustic plaster, acoustic tiles, straw boards pulp boards, compressed fibre boards, perforated ply wood, wood wool board, quilts and mats are the materials used for giving acoustic treatment to the buildings. All these materials have porosity. More the porosity, higher is the sound absorbing capacity of the material. Sound absorbing materials being excessively porous, are light materials. Sound absorbing capacity of any particular material depends upon its coefficient of absorption which in turn is dependent upon so many factors. But porosity is definetly a predominent factor affecting absorption coefficient.

19.14. Glazier's Putty

It is prepared by mixing finely powdered chalk with raw lineseed oil to form a stiff paste. The paste is well kneaded left for 12 hours and then worked up in small quantities at a time until quite smooth mass is obtained. Mixture of white lead and putty in the proportion of 1:2 will be very much stronger than ordinary putty.

Glazier's putty is used for fixing glass panes. The putty may be softened to remove the glass panes by the following mixture. 1 kg of perl ash is mixed with 3 kg of quick lime slaked in water. Plasterer's putty is lime punning

19.15. Mica and its Products

It is found as an impurity in the natural stones. Its variety muscovite is considered as the best variety of mica. It is used for insulating purposes. It can be developed into thin sheets by gluing together by means of varnishes. It has a high dielectric strength. It is a vary good insulator. Its thickness may vary from 2.5 to 0.50 mm.

19.16. Ropes

Rope may be of following types. Steel wire rope, manilla rope, hemp rope, coir rope, jute rope. Steel wire rope is used, where very large strength is required. It is made from strands of thin wires. Coir rope is very much used for securing and tying scaffoldings. Ropes are used for hauling and fastening the things. Jute rope is used where practically no strength is required.

19.17. Belts

The belts are used to run engines and for driving machines or for transmitting power from engine to machine or from one machine to the other. Brief description for various types of belts are as follows :

1. Cotton belts. These belts, are used for driving fans in automobiles, conveyor belts etc. They may or may not be impregnated with rubber compounds.

2. Canvas. They are made by impregnating canvas with different resins. They may be 2 to 10 ply in thickness.

3. Balata. These belts are formed by impregnating canvass with balata which is a milky fluid present in rubber trees and similar other plants. These belts are water proof. The grease or oil does not affect them.

4. Leather. The leather belts are available in suitable widths. Special water proof leather belts are also available which can be used in moist places. These belts should not be allowed to get dry and brittle. The good leather should not stretch by about 15% of its length. Its tensile strength is about 175 Kg/ cm^2.

5. Rubber belts. These belts are quite cheap and are available in any length and width. They have better grip on pulleys. These belts are reinforced with cotton, jute, canvass etc. These belts should not be allowed to come in contact of oils and grease. They also resist deterioration by moisture. Their tensile strength is about 400 kg/cm^2

19.18. Electrical materials

These materials can be classified into:

(i) Conductor materials

(ii) Magnetic materials and

(iii) Insulating or dielectric materials.

1. Electrical conductors. Cables, wires, and filaments are the electrical conductors. They are made from metals, metallic alloys or metalloid, copper, copper cadimium alloys, steel cored aluminium etc. are commonly used conductors.

Fuse wires may be made of tin, lead, or tin-lead alloy for currents up to 30 amperes. For higher currents copper alloy is used as fuse wire. For very high voltages high rupturing capacity fuses (HRC) are used.

Lamp filaments may be of carbon (Vapourishing point 3500°C) Tantalum (melting point 2800°C) and tungsten (melting point 3400°C). Tungsten is mostly used.

2. Magnetic materials. They may be classed as magnetic soft material and magnetically hard materials. Pure iron, cast iron, carbon steel, silicon steel and manganese and nickel steels are the magnetically soft materials. These materials have high permeability and are used in electrical machines in form of poles, cores of transformers and electro-magnetes.

Magnetically hard materials are used for making permanent magnets. Tungsten steel, chromium steel and cobalt steel, are generally used as magnetically hard materials.

3. Electric insulators or dielectrics. These are non-metallic materials of high specific resistance against the passage of electricity. These are called non-conductors. The dielectric strength to a material is a measure of the material to withstand high voltage.

Mica, Asbestos, Porcelain, Marble, slate, ebonite, Bakelite, Shellac, Rubber, Wax are the solid insulators. Paraffin oil, chlorinated diphenyl are the usual liquid insulators used in switches, transfoermers, and rheostates. Insulators are used to separate the conductors carrying electric currents.

19.19. Lenoleum

Lenoleum is made by fixing a paste prepared by mixing ground wooden cork and colouring pigment with linseed oil on convas or jute. It is prepared in form of rolls in beautiful colours. It is used for covering the floors. It is particularly used in English dancing rooms such as twist. It is not affected by oils, but acids affect it slightly. It is available in thicknesses of 1.6, 2.0, 3.2, 4.5 and 6.7 mm.

19.20. Thermocole

It is a light and cellular plastic material which is a very good insulator against electric flow. It is quite strong, durable and damp-resisting material. It does not disintegrate due to heat and its strength is not affected due to shrinkage and expansion. It is manufactured by "Thermocole Indoplastic Limited" a firm at Bombay. It can be manufactured in any colour, but mostly it is white. It is so soft that is can be easily broken by finger nails.

It is used in refrigeration, air-conditioning, cold storages, roofs etc. It is also used for packing purpose, as well as acoustic treatment of buildings.

19.21. Sun Glass

Some varieties of plastics are transparent just like glass. Such plastics are known as *sun-glasses*. Such plastics can sustain impact effect and do not shatter like glass when broken. Acrylic plastic is mostly used, 92% light passes through sun glass, where as actual glass allows only 88% passage of light. This is very much used in air craft and car industries for safety purposes. Styrene, Perspex etc. are some of the varieties of sun glasses. It is also used in the manufacture of lenses.

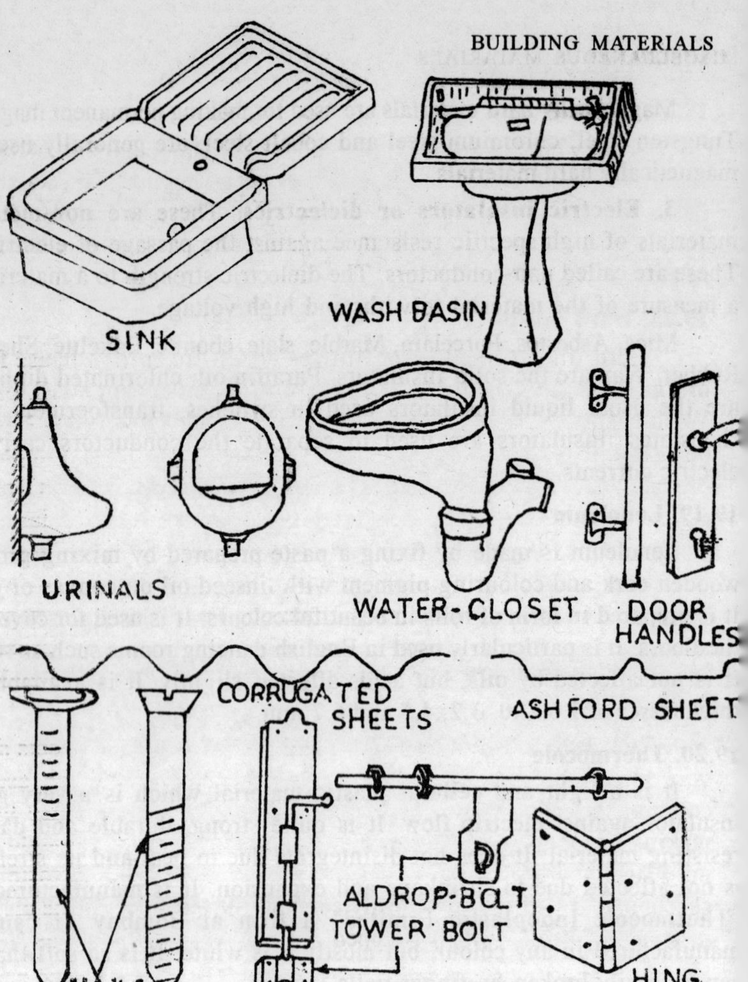

Fig. 19.1. Hard wares.

19.22. Bakelite

When equal amounts of formaldehyde and phenol are heated in the presence of a base an amber coloured substance called Bakelite resin 'A' in formed. This substance is used with fillers for forming different materials. By subjecting this resin A to further heat treatment an amber coloured insoluble infusible transparent and hard substances known as Bakelite resin C commonly known as only Bakelite is obtained. It is widely used for electrical insulations, decorative fittings and for bearings in roller mills, propellar shafts, pumps etc.

19.23. Leatheroid

It is synthetic leather and is used in making coverings for furniture and for interior decoration work.

19.24. Ebonite

It is obtained by vulcanising rubber with large amount of sulphure. Ebonite becomes soft on heating and can be moulded to any shape. It takes good polish, remain unaffected by moisture or light acids and is durable. Its colour varies from grey to dark black. It is extensively used in electric insulations.

19.25. Hard Wares

Hard-wares include such articles which are used in house fittings, drainage etc. Various types of pipes, pipe appurtinences. W.C. bath tub, Wash basins, Sinks, Sheets, are included under hard wares. Pipes may be made of C.I., mild steel, copper, wrought iron, A.C. simple, A.C. pressure, A.C. Hume, Lead, Cement, R.C.C., P.V.C. etc. C.I., A.C. pressure, R.C.C. pipes are mostly used for large drainage lines or large water supply mains. G.I. pipes, are mostly used in house fittings. Copper, steel, lead pipes are used for specific purposes. P.V.C. pipes are also increasingly coming into use and in future may replace all other pipes. Every pipe line requires some attachments to make a fulfledged pipe line. Various types of valves like sluice valve, foot valve, hydrant etc. also come under hard wares.

Galvanised iron sheets (G.I.) and Asbestos cement sheets are also very important engineering materials. They are very much used as a covering material in the case of sloped roofs. They are also used for making temporary partitions etc. G.I. sheets are made of wrought iron or mild steel and are coated by zinc to protect them from corrosion. A.C. sheets and G.I. sheets are mostly corrugated, but A.C. sheets also come in trough shape.. Trough shapped A.C. sheets are known as 'Big six' sheets. Door attachments, nails, bolts etc. also come under name hard wares.

Fly-ash. Fly-ash is obtained where-ever the coal in used for heating purpose. It is in form of fine powder and is a waste material which remains lying near its source. The Modern Thermal poweer stations in the country are its major contributors. In property in resembles pozzolana. It does not have its own cementing properties but has constituents which combine with the lime to form a material having cementing properties. Fly-ash contains some amount of unburnt carbon. It is acidic in nature and its main constituents are silica, aluminium oxide and ferrous oxide.

The fly-ash driven away from the boilers by flue gases is extracted by mechanical collectors or electro-static precipitators or combination of both. Following problems are being created by fly-ash.

1. Surrounding environment is polluted.

2. Ecology of the region is disturbed.

3. Disposal involves heavy expenditure.

4. Lot of land in the vicinity of the thermal power stations is wasted due to dumping of fly-ash.

Investigation regarding producing by products from fly-ash reveal that the fly-ash can be used profitably in many ways.

The following are three main practical applications.

1. Fly-ash building bricks.

2. Cellular concrete blocks.

3. Addition to the mass concrete.

1. Fly-ash building bricks. Fly-ash building bricks are made using fly-ash, lime, sand and a small quantity of magnesium chloride.

The fly-ash, sand and lime are taken in ratio of 12:2:1. To this mixture a small quantity of magnesium chloride is added to act as accelerator. The bricks are moulded in hydraulic press. The semi-dried bricks are cured in the steam chamber.

Fly-ash bricks are superior to conventional bricks in all respects. They are about 20% lighter and 10 to 15% cheaper.

2. Cellular concrete blocks. This block is light in weight. These blocks are produced by autoclaving a set mixture of fly-ash and lime. These blocks possess many advantages such as better strength to weight ratio better sound insulation,. resistance to fire, low thermal conductivity etc.

Blocks being machine made, they possess uniform size and thus they require less mortar both for masonry and plaster work.

Addition to the mass concrete

Adding fly-ash to mass concrete acts as an admixture and imparts the following good properties to the concrete.

1. Presence of fly-ash reduces the cement aggregate reaction.

2. Evolution of heat is reduced.

3. Concrete becomes more dense and thus water tightness of the concrete in greatly improved.

4. Workability of the concrete gets improved.

5. Strength of the concrete is improved.

6. Fly-ash replaces 20 to 25% of cement by weight or by volume without affecting the strength of the concrete.

In addition to the above said applications, the fly-ash can also be used as aggregate for concrete as well as mortar, as filler material and as stabilizer of the soil for roads etc.

Sealants for joints. Sealants material are used to seal the joints of the structures. Sealants have to undergo changes in shape due to stresses and strains. It is always in tension. A good sealant should posses good bond property and should be soft and remain flexible. It should not deteriorate either due to weather effects or due to stress and stress relief cycles. The sealants possessing, these properties are classed as elastometric sealants. The sealants are silicone based, a crylic based, urethane based and poly sulphide based. But of all these polysulphide based sealants are most popular.

Poly sulphide based sealants. These sealants are available in form of thick paste and are applied cold. They are cured chemically to form a firm synthetic rubber. These sealants are available in one part system and two part systems.

1. One part system. In this case the sealants are supplied in premixed ready to use condition. They cure chemically by absorbing moisture from atmosphere. Time of curing varies from 3 to 4 weeks.

2. Two part system. These sealants are supplied in two parts; namely base and accelerator. This system achieves curing after the base and accelerators are thoroughly mixed. They become touch dry with 48 hours, but they require about one week for full cure. Two part poly sulphide based sealants are available in two forms such as gun grade and pour grade. Gun grade in used for inclined, over head and vertical applications which latter is used for the horizontal applications.

QUESTIONS

1. **Explain the uses of gypsum. What are its various products and uses?**
2. **(*a*) Explain different types of lubricants.**

   (*b*) Enumerate the types and properties of fuels.
3. **Explain the properties and uses of rubber. What are its various varieties? What is importance of vulcanization?**
4. **Explain various type of electrical materials.**
5. **Enlist the materials included under heading hard-wares? Give their brief description.**

20

PROPERTIES OF BUILDING MATERIALS

20.1. Introduction

Different types of materials are required for different types of engineering structures and other industrial purposes. The use of a particular building material is governed by the characteristics and properties of that material. The properties of building materials may be classified into various heads such as :

1. Physical properties. These are the properties which can be appreciated by physical examination of the material. Appearance, bulk density durability, porosity etc are the usual physical properties. These properties help in superfical evaluation of the material.

2. Chemical properties. The chemical properties of the material reflect their tendency to combine with other substances, its solubility reactivity and effects like corrosion, chemical composition, acidity, alkalinity etc.

3. Electrical properties. Electrical properties include conductivity, resistivity and dielectric strength of the material. In other words these properties are related to the flow of electric current.

4. Magnetic properties. The magnetic properties of the material like permeability, hysteresis and coercive force are required to be studies for materials to be used for generators, transformers etc.

5. Mechanical properties. Elasticity, hardness, toughness, pasticity are some of the examples of mechanical properties of the materials. These properties govern the behaviour of material when external forces are applied.

6. Thermal properties. These properties of the material show their response to the thermal changes. Specific heat, thermal expansion, and conductivity are the important thermal properties.

7. Optical properties. The optical properties such as colour, light transmission, refractive index, are the important optical properties.

Out of all the above said types of properties it is the physical and mechanical properties which are useful for engineer and as such only these two type of properties have been explained here.

20.2. Physical properties of materials

Various physical properties of materials are as follows. Brief description of each material has been given here :

1. Density. The density of a material is mass of unit volume of homogeneous material. It is obtained by working out the ratio of mass of material to the volume of material. The physical properties of a material are greatly influenced by its density.

2. Bulk Density. The term bulk density is the mass of a unit volume of material in its natural state. It includes pores and voids. The properties of material such as strength, heat, conductivity etc. are greatly influenced by its bulk density. For most of the materials the bulk density is less than its density. Bulk densities of some of the commonly used materials are as follows.

Name of material	*Bulk density in kg/m³*
Limestone	1800 to 2400
Granite	2500 to 2700
Gravel	1400 to 1700
Cement concrete	1800 to 2500
Light concrete	500 to 1800
Sand	1450 to 1650
Steel	7850

The ratio of bulk density of a material to its density in known as its density index. It reflects the degree to which its volume is filled up with solid matter. The density index of most of the building materials is less than unity.

3. Chemical resistance. The resistance of the material against actions of acids, alkalies, gases and salt solutions in known as its chemical resistance. This property is particularly important for the material used in sewer pipes, hydraulic installations, sanitary fittings and other situations where chemical reactivity is predominant.

4. Durability. The property of a material to resist the combined action of atmopheric and other factors is known as its durability. The maintenance cost and the life of a building naturally depends upon the durability of the materials used in its construction.

5. Fire resistance. This is the ability of the material to withstand the action of high temperature without lossing its load bearing capacity without substantially undergoing deformation. This property of material carries great importance because in case of a fire, temperature rises very high and for extinguishing fire water is used and thus temperature comes done suddenly. So here this property is tested by the combined action of high temperature and water. Hence materials used in fire prone situations should be sufficiently fire-proof to afford safety and stability.

6. Coefficient of softening. The ratio of compressive strength of material saturated with water to that in dry state is known as the coefficient of softening. Glass, and metals are not affected by presence of water and hence their coeffficient of softening is unity. On the other hand the materials like clay easily loose strength when soaked in water and hence their coefficient of softening in zero. The material having softening coefficient of 0.8 or more are called as water-resisting materials. It is advised to avoid the use of materials with coefficient of softening less than 0.8 for situations which are likely to be exposed to the action of water permanently.

7. Specific heat. The quantity of heat required to heat 1 kg of material by 1°C is known as specific heat. It is expressed in kilo-calories. This property of material carries importance when heat accumulation is to be taken into account. The specific heat of steel, stone and wood are as follows.

Wood	-	0.57 to 0.65 kcal/kg°C
Steel	-	0.11 kcal/kg°C
Stone	-	0.18 to 0.22 kcal/kg°C.

8. Thermal capacity. The thermal capacity of the material is its property to absorb heat. It is determined by the following equation.

$$T = \frac{H}{M(t_2 - t_1)}$$

where M = Mass of material in kg.

T = Thermal capacity in kcal/kg°C

t_1 = Temp. of material in °C before heating

t_2 = Temp. of material after heating in °C

9. Thermal conductivity. It is the amount of heat in kilo calories which will flow through unit area of the material with unit thickness in unit time where difference of temperature in its faces is unity. The thermal conductivity of the material depends on its density, porosity, moisture content and temperature.

The thermal resistivity of a material is used to mean the reciprocal of its thermal conductivity.

10. Frost resistance. The frost resistance of a material is its ability to resist repeated freezing and thawing without considerably decreasing the mechanical strength in saturated condition. The frost resistance of a material depends upon the density of material and its degree of saturation with water. The dense materials are generally frost resistant.

11. Hygroscopicity. This is the property of the material by which it absorbs moisture from atmosphere. It is controlled by the nature of substance involved number of pores, air temperature, relative humidity, etc.

12. Porosity. This term indicates the degree by which the volume of the material has been occupied by the pores. It is expressed as a ratio of volume of pores to that of the specimen. The porocity of the material is indicative of its various properties such as strength, bulk density, water absorption, thermal conductivity, durability etc.

13. Refractory property. The ability of the material to withstand prolonged action of high temperature without loosing shape is known as its refractory properties.

14. Water absorptions. It is the ability of a material to absorb and retain water. It depends on the volume, size, and shape of pores present in the material.

15. Water permeability. It is the capacity of a material to allow passage of water under pressure.

16. Weathering resistance. It is the ability of the material to resist the effect of wetting and drying alternately, without seriously affecting the shape and mechanical strength of the material. It is a measure of the behaviour of the material when exposed to changing conditions of humidity.

17. Spalling resistance. It is the ability of a material to withstand a certain number of cycles of sharpe temperature variations without falling. This property mainly depends on the coefficient of linear expansions of its constituents.

20.3. Mechanical properties of materials

The mechanical properties are the basic or fundamental properties which decide the importance of the material and possible practical applications. Regidity, ductility and strength elasticity are the main mechanical properties. Brief description of these properties is as follows.

1. Elasticity. When a load is applied to a material there is change in its dimensions and shape. The term elasticity is used to indicate the ability of the material to restore its initial form and dimensions as soon as the load is removed. The deformation of the material is said to be elastic if the deformation produced by the external load vanishes as soon as the load is removed from the material. This deformation obeys Hook's law and the elastic strain of the material is directly proportional to the applied force. This condition of deformation persists up to the elastic limit of the material.

If the material is loaded beyond elastic limit, the deformation produced by external load does not vanish completely and some change in shape remain persisting even after the load is removed. The deformation which does not vanish after removal of the load is known as the plastic deformation. The plastic deformation is thus observed when the stress exceeds the elastic limit and its rate is controlled by the strain rate, applied stress and temperature. This can occur under tensile, compressive and tortional stresses.

2. Hardness. It is a measure of resistance to penetration. This property is the major factor in deciding the workability and use of a material for various applications. The hardness is not a fundamental property but it is combination of compressive, elastic and plastic properties. The hardness bears an almost constant relationship to the tensile strength. Out of the two materials the material which can cause scrach on the other is said to be harder.

3. Creep. The creep is a time-dependent deformation of a material. This deformation with time may grow large and may even result in final fracture of the material without any increase in load. The deformation which continues even when the load is constant with time is known as *creep*. Most of the materials when subjected to constant load, undergo creep to a certain extent at all temperatures. Metals such as steel, aluminium and copper creep very little at room temperature. At higher temperatures process of creep increase which often leads to micro-structural changes.

4. Impact strength. Impact strength of a material indicates the toughness of the material. Impact testing machine is used to determine the impact strength of any material. Impact strength is a complex characteristic which takes into account both the toughness and strength of a material.

5. Plasticity. This is a property of a material which defines its ability to change shape under load without cracking and to retain its shape even after the removal of load. Steel, copper, hot bitumen etc. are the examples of plastic materials.

6. Brittleness. The brittle materials fail suddenly under pressure without appreciable deformation preceding the failure. Concrete, cast-iron, stone, glass etc. are the brittle materials. These materials offer poor resistance to bending, impact and tension.

7. Strength. The ability of a material to resist failure under the action of stresses caused by a load is known as its strength. The loads to which a material is generally subjected to are tension, compression, and bending. The corresponding strength is obtained by dividing the ultimate load with the cross-sectional area of the specimen. The stresses in the building material are not allowed to exceed a certain limit. A margin of safety is provided and the terms factory of safety is used which denotes the ratio of ultimate stress to safe stress. The values of factors of safety are specified by design standards and they are fixed by taking into account various factors.

8. Wear. The failure of a material due to its constant use is known as its wear. It involves abrasion as well as impact actions. It is expressed as a percentage loss in weight.

9. Abrasion. When one material slips over the other it, is known as abrasion. The resistance to abrasion of a material in found out by dividing the difference in weights of specimens prior to and after abrasions with the area of abrasion.

21

AN INTRODUCTION TO MATERIAL SCIENCE OF METALS

21.1. General

The material science is a specific branch of science. It deals with many characteristics reflected by various materials during their behaviour in use. We have given various properties of materials in chapter 20 of this book. The material science gives the fundamentals and clues as to why these properties exist in a particular material. Thus material science sets relationships between the engineering properties of materials and structures of materials. The material science being a fulfledged subject in itself and hence can not be discussed in one chapter. Here it has been tried to give some introduction in this respect.

The metals in particular are important engineering materials. They possess properties like resistance to corrosion, electrical and thermal conductivity, property of being magnetised and pleasing metallic lustre. All these properties in metals are the result of following two factors.

1. Atomic structure of the metals and

2. The manner in which atoms are distributed within the body of the metal mass.

In this chapter important topics related to the material science of metals have been described is brief.

21.2. Atomic structure

All the materials may be in form of gases, liquids or solids, are composed of small atoms. An atom is an electrical structure whose diameter is nearly 10^{-10} metres. An atom is further made of following three things.

1. Electron. Electrons are very small components of an atom of the material. They always carry very small negative electrical charge. Its mass in comparison to hydrogen atom, is about $\frac{1}{1850}$ th. The comparison is made with hydrogen atom because it is the lightest of all the known atoms.

2. Proton. It is small element of atom and always carries positive electrical charge. This electrical charge in just equal to the negative charge of the electron of that material. The mass of proton is very nearly equal to that of one atom of hydrogen.

3. Neutron. This is the third element of an atom. It carries no electrical charge. It is 1.0008 times heavier than the proton. The mass of each neutron is very nearly the same as that of the proto 1.

Each atom has a central part known as nucleus. Both protons and neutrons remain housed in neucleus and the electrons continuously remain moving is an orbit around the nucleus in circular or elliptical paths. The entire mass of an atom is practically concentrated in its nucleus. Since the electrons remain revolving around the nucleus just in the same manner as the planets of the solar system do round the sun, they are known as *planetary* or *orbital electrons*. Also since the atom is electrically neutral, the number of protons in the nucleus must be equal to the number of electrons in the surrounding orbits. The volume of an atom is only due to the number of orbits of the orbital eletrons.

21.3. Atomic number and Atomic weight

Atomic number denotes the number of protons present in the nucleus. It is always in whole numbers for various elements. It is designated by letter Z.

It has already been said that almost whole mass of an atom is concentrated in the nucleus of the atom. Thus the mass of the nucleus is proportional to the total number of protons and neutrons. This is known as *atomic weight* of the element. Let it be represented by letter A. The difference between atomic weight and atomic number of the element represents the number of neutrons inside the nucleus.

The nucleus of hyrogen contains practically no neutrons because atomic weight (A) of hydrogen is 1.0008 and atomic number (Z) is 1 and A-2 is 1.008-1.0 = 0.008 which is nearly zero.

Similarly for oxygen the atomic weight (A) is 16.00 and atomic number (Z) is 8. Hence 16.00 - 8.0 = 8.00. Hence number of neutrons in case of oxygen nucleus is 8. In other words the nucleus of oxygen contains equal number of protons and neutrons. Hence atomic nucleus of oxygen will be stable.

Now take an example of uranium. It is atomic weight (A) is 238.07

and atomic number (Z) in 92. Hence number of neutrons in necleus of uranium is 238.07 - 92 = 146.07. We see that the nucleus of uranium contains 146.07. neutrons and 92 protons *i.e.* number of neutrons is far more than protons. Thus the uranium nucleus is hightly unstable in its behaviour and thus it continues to emit radiation constantly. This act of emitting nuclear radiation makes uranium nucleus *radio active* and this property is known as *radio-activity*

21.4. Periodic Table

A Russian Scientist Mr. Mandeleev arranged various discovered elements and their compounds according to the periodic law. This table in known as *Periodic table*. This table is based on the principle that the properties of the elements and their compounds are a periodic function of their atomic numbers. This table comprises both horizontal as well as vertical rows. The horizontal rows are known as series and the vertical columns are known as groups. In the table there are seven series and eight groups each group being further sub-divided into two sub-groups namely A and B. The elements of these sub-groups form families. The data and other details contained in the periodic table are very useful because the elements from same group have similar chemical properties.

21.5. Building of solids

The atoms of a solid element are held together by inter-atomic forces and this process of holding atoms together is known as the *bonding*. The physical, chemical, and electrical properties of the solid elements are dependent on the nature of the binding force.

The orbital electrons remain distributed on different circles depending upon the nature of the element. The circles containing orbital electrons are also called shells. The shells are nothing but a set of hypothetical spherical surfaces centred on the nucleus of an atom. The maximum number of orbiting electrons in each shell is controlled by following two rules.

Rule 1 - If C indicates the number of shell counted from the nucleus, the maximum number of orbital electrons that can be present in shell C in equal to $2C^2$.

Rule 2. The outermost shell cannot contains more than eight electrons and the penultimate shell cannot contain more than 18 electrons. Based on first rule, the first shell from nucleus, which is also called innermost shell, can contain $2 \times (1)^2 = 2$ oribital electrons, the second shell $2 \times 2^2 = 8$, the third shell $2 \times 3^2 = 18$ and forth shell $2 \times 4^2 = 32$ electrons. The last shell is known as outermost or ultimate shell and the one immediately preceding the outermost shell is known as the penultimate shell.

Both these rules control the arrangement of orbital electrons of the element having the atomic numbers upto 38.

The elements which have 8 electrons in their outermost shell are termed as *saturated element*. Such elements do not take part in any chemical reaction.

The elements having electrons less than eight in their outermost shell are called the *unsaturated elements*. Such element take part in chemical reactions and form the new chemical compounds.

21.6. Metals and non-metals

The orbital electrons present in the outermost shell are called the *valency electrons*. The valency elctrons have the capacity to participate in forming chemical bonds with other atoms.

It is the natural tendency of an atom to acquire eight electrons in its last shell. It is also seen that the atom of an element tends to complete its outermost shell by the smallest possible charge. Thus an element having less than four valency electrons in the outermost shell will lend and an element having more than four valancy electrons will borrow electrons to complete its eight electrons. The elements which have tendency to lend electrons are called *metals* and those which have tendency to borrow electrons are called non-metals. The metals are elctropositive elements because they retain positively charged valency electrons after lending. The non-metals are electro-negative elements becasue the extra borrowed valency electrons will impart the negative charge Fig. 21.1 and 21.2 show the arrangements of the electrons for magnesium (metals) and chlorine (non-metal). The magnesium metal atom nucleus contains 12 neutrons and 12 protons. The first shell around the nucleus has 2 electrons, second shell contains eight electrons. Since number of electrons has to 12 in this case hence the third shell contains only 12-8-2 =2 electrons.

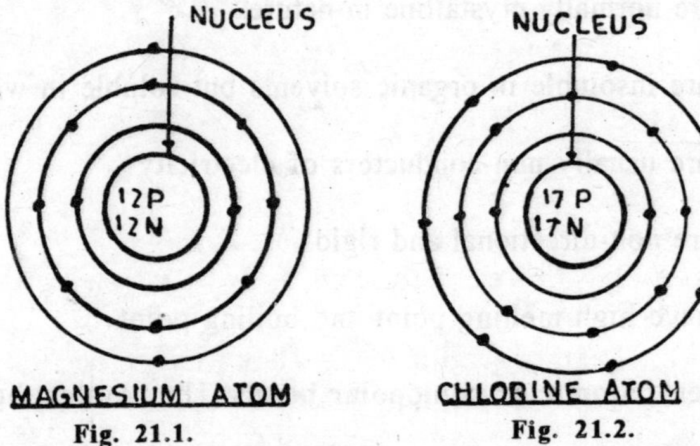

Fig. 21.1. Fig. 21.2.

Similarly Fig 21.2 shows the arrangement of electrons in the shells of chlorine atom. The nucleus of chlorine atom contains 17 Neutrons, 17 Protons. It contains three shells. There are 2 and 8 electrons respectively in first and second shells. The third shell will contain 17 - 2 - 8 = 7 electrons.

21.7. Bonds in solids

The bonds in solids can be of following three categories.

1. Primary bonds.
2. Secondary bonds and
3. Mixed bonds.

1. Primary bonds. Primary bonds are formed due to inter-atomic force. They are also termed as the attractive bonds and are considered as the strongest bonds. The primary bonds can be further classified into following three kinds.

(i) Electro-static or ionic bonds

(ii) Covalent, atomic or homopolar bonds and

(iii) Metallic bonds.

I. Electro-static or ionic bonds. The ionic bonds are formed due to mutual attraction between positive and negative ions. The main features of ionic bonds are as follows :

1. They are normally crystalline in nature.
2. They are insoluble in organic solvents but soluble in water.
3. They are usually non-conductors of electricity.
4. They are non-directional and rigid.
5. They have high melting point and boiling point.

II. Covalent, atomic or homopolar bonds. The covalent bond is formed when electrons are shared between atoms and not transferred from one atom to the other atom. This type of binding takes place due to sharing of valence electrons between identical atoms. The covalent bonding alone is not sufficient to build three dimensional solids. Only a few solids are held together by these bonds. Fig. 21.3 shows a chlorine molecule in which the outer shells of each atom have seven electrons. Each chlorine atom requires one electron to form a stable octet. The way they form octet by sharing electrons is clear from Fig. 21.3.

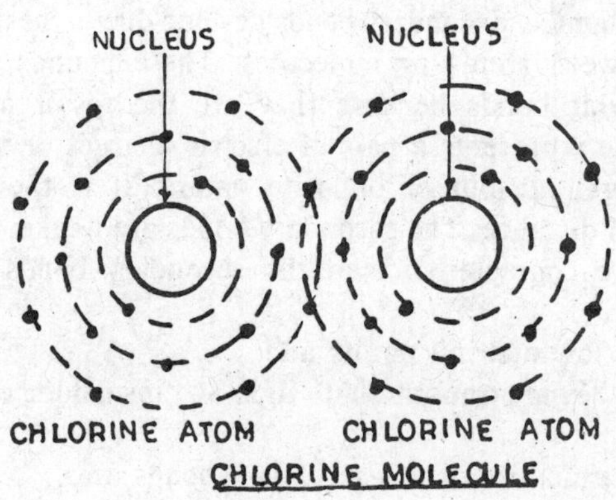

Fig. 21.3.

The properties of covalent-compounds are as follows :

1. They are directional in nature.

2. They are usually electric insulators.

3. They are insoluble in water but soluble in non-polar solvents like alcohol, benzene, paraffins and chloroform.

4. They are homo polar in the sense that the valence electrons cannot move freely through the material as in the case of metallic bonds.

5. They have low melting and boilding point

6. They are usually soft except diamond and graphite.

7. They can be observed in all states of matter like gases, liquids and solids.

8. They form a variety of structural materials commonly known as plastics.

III. Metallic bonds. All the commercial metals contains one, two or three valence electrons in their respective valency shells of the atoms. These electrons can be easily released to the common pool. An electron cloud is formed which surrounds the solid metal. The valence electrons are not bonded directly to the undividual atoms, but keep moving freely in the sphere of influence of other atoms. They are bonded to different atoms at different times for a short period of each time. These bonds are weaker than ionic bonds. The characteristics of metallic compounds are as follows :

1. They are crystalline in nature.
2. They are good conductors of heat and electricity.
3. They are non-directional.
4. They are not very strong.
5. They have high melting point.
6. They possess high reflectivity and good lustre.

2. Secondary bonds. Secondary bonds develop due to the attractive forces existing between atoms or molecules. These bounds are also called inter-molecular bonds because they are the result of dipole attractions. A dipole represents a pair of electric charges or magnetic poles of equal magnitude but of opposite nature. It is the polarity separated by a small distance. The secondary bonds are weaker than the primary bonds. The characteristics of the secondary bonds are the following :

(i) They have low melting points and

(ii) Generally they are transparent to light and insulators, exception being water.

The common examples of the secondary bonds are :

(i) Hydrogen bond and *(ii)* Van der waals bond.

(i) Hydrogen bonds. In these bonds there is no sharing of electrons betwen atomic groups. These bonds mostly occur in organic materials where hydrogen often plays an important role. These bonds are responsible for the unusual physical properties of ice and water. This bond is also referred as a hydrogen bridge.

(ii) Van der waals bonds. Van der waal bonds develop due to van der waals forces of attraction arising from electrical dipoles. These bonds also develop between molecules that have no permanent dipoles. Such type of binding is common in polar compounds such as HCl and PVC. These bonds are non-directional.

3. Mixed bonds. A few materials are found to have pure bonds of one type or the other. In many substances the bonding between atoms is a mixture of pure bonds. Such bonds are known as mixed bonds. These types of bonds are observed in the common materials.

21.8. Cristal structure

The structure of a solid can either be non-crystalline or crystalline. When constituent molecules or atoms are arranged in a systematic manner a crystal is formed. The crystalline solids are made of a number of crystals which may be similar or of widely varying sizes and may be metallic or non-metallic.

The non-crystalline solids do not have any difinit form and lack in specific shape. Non-crystalline solids are also referred as amorphous solid. The internal structure of an amorphous solid is without any regular repetition pattern.

In the liquids the atoms are very active and their mobility increases with the rise in temperature. The metal assumes the shape of a crystal when it freezes from the state of fusion. While solidification takes place, the atoms of the liquid metal arrange among themselves in a systematic pattern. A crystalline solid may consist of only are crystal or it may contain an aggregate of many crystals separated by well-defined boundaries.

The pattern or arrangement of atoms difffers in different metals and alloys. If the metal exists in two or more stable but different crystal structures it is known as *allotropy*. It means that the same metal will have more than one grouping of atoms under different conditions of temperature and pressure. Lot of change in the properties of the metal is noticed when re-grouping of the atoms takes place. For example the pure iron is magnetic at room temperature but when it is heated to red heat, the re-grouping of the atoms occurs and it becomes non-magnetic.

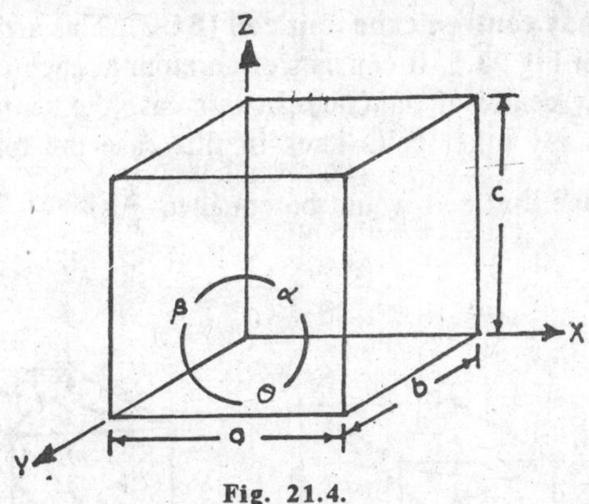

Fig. 21.4.

21.9. Space lattice and unit cell

The space lattice is three dimensional geometric construction. It shows the arrangement of ions or molecules in a crystalline solid.

The smallest component of the lattice structure is known as unit cell. Fig. 21.4 shows a cubical unit cell. The distance from one atom to another atom measured along one of the axes is called the lattice constant and it has the same value in all three dimensions for a cubical cell.

The unit cell is in the shape of a paralleos-piped solid with six faces, each being a parallogram. The lengths of the unit cell (*a*, *b* and *c*) may be equal or unequal depending upon the fact whether angles between the edges are right angles or not. The lengths *a*, *b* and *c* and angles α, β, and θ are known as the lattice parameters.

'The space lattice provides a very useful information regarding the arrangement of atoms within a crystal. It also helps in comparing arrangements of atoms among the crystals of different types.

21.10. Crystal structures of metals

In the case of metallic elements, the arrangement commonly found in the unit cells in the space lattice are as following.

1. Plain cubic unit cell (PCS)
2. Body - centred cubic unit (BCC)
3. Face - centred cubic unit cell (FCC)
4. Hexagonal close - packed unit cell (HCP).

1. Plain cubic unit cell (PCS). This is the simplest possible unit cell. This cell contains eight atoms, one at each corners of the cube. These eight atoms can be shared by the adjoining eight cubes. Thus the share of each cube = $\frac{1}{8} \times 8 = 1$ atom only. In this case it seems that unit cell consists of eight atoms but the share of each cube is only one atom. See Fig. 21.4

2. Body centred cube unit cell (BCC). This arrangement of atoms is shows in Fig 21.5. It consists of an atom at each corner and another at the body centre of the cube. In this case the centre atom cannot be shared by any other cell. Thus in this case the total atoms in body centred cube unit cell would be equal to $\frac{1}{8} \times 8 + 1 = 2$ = 2 atoms.

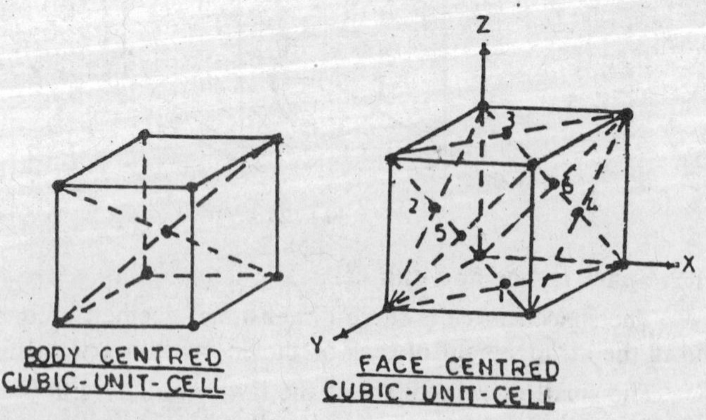

Fig. 21.5. Fig. 21.6.

3. Face-centred cubic unit cell (FCC). This arrangement of atoms is shows in Fig. 21.6. In this case six atoms are located at the centres of the six faces and each will be equally shared by the two neighbouring cells. Thus the total atoms in FCC unit cell would be $\frac{1}{8}\times 8+\frac{1}{2}\times 6=4$ atoms.

4. Hexagonal close - packed unit cell (HCP). The arrangment of atoms is shown in Fig. 21.7. In this arrangement there are six atoms at the six corners of the hexagon. Besides there are two atoms at the centre of the hexagonal faces and also there are three atoms located in the body of the hexagonal structure. Thus the total atoms in HCP unit cell will be $3+\frac{1}{6}\times 12+\frac{1}{2}\times 2=6$ = 6 atoms.

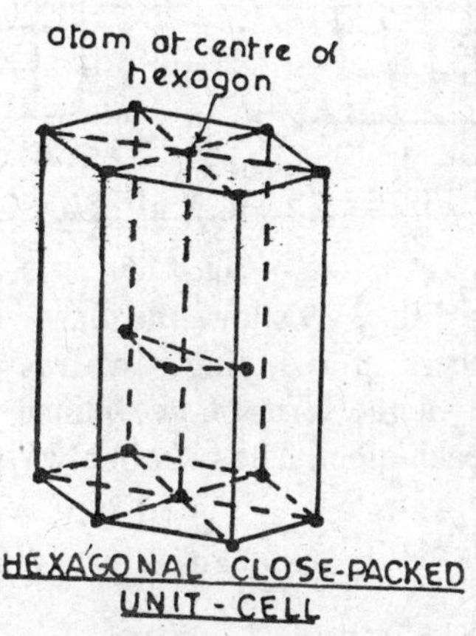

Fig. 21.7.

21.11. Plastic deformation of a single crystal

The plastic deformation of a crystal takes place by following two mechanisms.

(1) Slip and (2) Twinning.

1. Slip. The slip is also sometimes referred as the shear deformation because slip occurs due to shear load only. The slip may occur on certain planes known as slip planes and in certain directions known as slip directions. The slip plane is normally the most dense atomic plane. The slip may occur in any direction and at any angle between the horizontal and vertical planes. The slip planes are clearly evident and the slip bonds are all parallel in individual crystals. But they differ in direction and magnitude in the neighbouring crystals. The stress to cause slip is the same in all crystals even though the load required to break an individual crystal may be different.

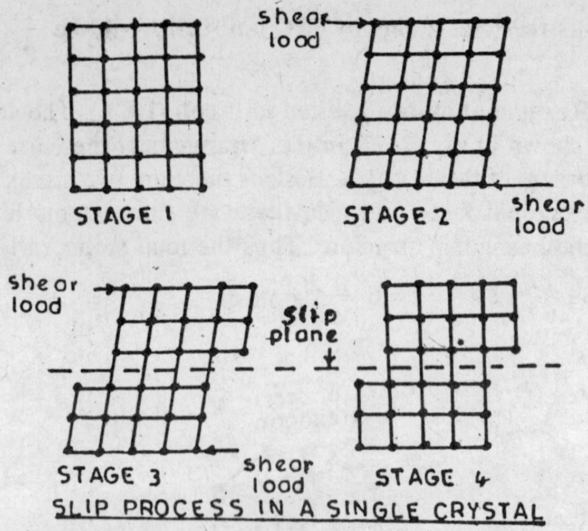

Fig. 21.8.

2. Twinning. Fig. 21.9 shows the plastic deformation by twinning process. The process of twinning involves converting the twinned portion of crystal in the form of two joined similar parts which are dependent upon each other. The twin in always three-dimensional. The

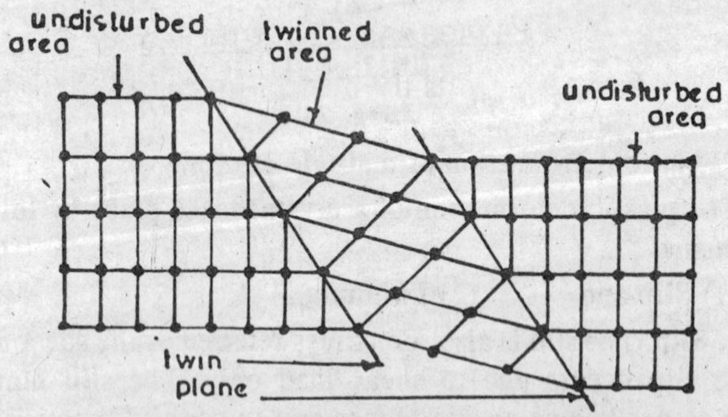

Fig. 21.9.

twined area within a crystal differs in orientation from the untwinned area of the crystal. The twin extends right into the body of the crystal. Under the effect of applied force on Twinning planes, one of the twinning plane will move parallel to the other. The area between the twin planes will shear homogeneously and the untwinned region of the crystal remains undisturbed.

The actual deformation produced by twinning in small but it produces sound because it occurs suddenly. The causes of Twinning are impact, plastic deformation and thermal treatment. The twinning also changes the shape of the surface.

21.12 Types of imperfections

An ideal crystal structure consists of an arrangement of atoms which remain arranged in a very regular way. But still defects or imperfections are found in the lattice of the most of the alloys. These imperfections considerably affect various properties of the crystal like electrical properties, chemical reactions, mechanical strength etc. The defects in crystal can be divided into following three categories.

1. Line defects or dislocations
2. Point defects
3. Surface and grain boundary defects.

1. Line defects or dislocations. The disturbance of the atomic arrangment which occurs easily on the slip plane through the crystal is known as the linear defect or dislocation. This defect may occur as edge dislocation or screw dislocation. In edge dislocation all the points which were coincident across the slip plane before dislocation, are displaced relative to each other by the same amount. A pure edge dislocation can slip in a direction perpendicular to its length.

In the case of screw dislocation, the displacement is parallel to the linear defect but it also distorts the plane. Thus in this case the atoms are displaced is two separate planes perpendicular to each other and the atoms are arranged around dislocation as if it is a screw or spiral staircase. The formation of screw may be right-handed screw or left-handed screw. The following are the effects of dislocations.

1. A new stress is developed by the dislocation in a crystal and hence it is strengthening mechanism.

2. Large number of dislocations occuring simultaneously in several directions change the shape of the crystal which is accompanied by progressive plastic deformation.

3. The dislocations are continuously generated during the process of mechanical working, heat treatment etc. and their formation can be accelerated.

4. The dislocations influence the important properties of metals and alloys.

5. The process of dislocation occurs like a chain reaction. Dislocations create more dislocations. They often interact with each other and increase the density of dislocations.

6. The total number of dislocations present in a given metal account for only a small permanent deformation of the metal.

2. Point defects. These deflects occur due to missing atoms, displaced atoms or extra atoms. They are always present in crystals and their effect is localized. The simplest defect of this kind in shown in Fig. 21.10 and it involves a missing atom within a metal. The atoms around the missing atom tend to be closer and may result into the distortion of the lattice planes.

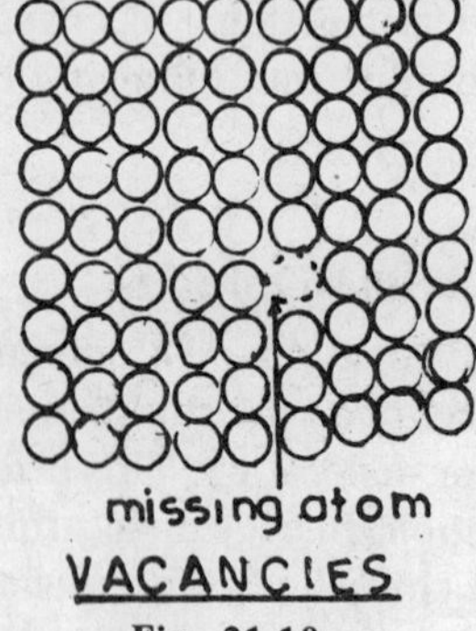

Fig. 21.10.

3. Surface and grain boundary imperfections. These imperfections occur due to a change in the stacking of atomic planes on or across a boundary. They are two-dimensional in nature. The surface imperfections and grain boundary imperfections are shown in Fig. 21.11. The surface atoms, in the case of surface imperfections, have neighbours on only one side where as the atoms inside the crystals have neighbours on both sides. From Fig. 21.11 (*a*) it is clear that surface atoms are not entirely sorrounded by other atoms and as such they possess higher energy than internal atoms. Fig 2.11 (*b*) shows the area of disorder at grain boundaries. The atomic packing is imperfect in grain boundaries and there is a transition zone between two adjacent grains.

21.13. Electrical conductivity

The elctrcial conductivity is based on the conception that a rapid flow of electrons occurs through an electron cloud under the direct influence of an electrical potential. Metals are the most efficient electrical conductors. It is assumed that current flow represents the migration of an electron cloud through a metallic crystal structure. In other words it also means that there is freedom of movement for valence electrons in the direction of the current in the crystal lattice of the conductor. In a solid, large number of electrons are very close to each other which result in the formation of energy bonds. The solids are classified as metals, semi-conductors and insulators on the basis of their band structure. A band in a restricted range of very closely spaced electron energy levels in solids. The distribution and nature of these ·bands determine the electrical properties of a material. The bands may be partly filled, completely filled or empty or may be entirely filled except one or two bands . If one or more bands are partly filled, the crystal behaves like a metal. If the bands are entirely filled except one or two bands, the crystal will act as a semi-conductor. For bands which are completely filled or the electrons cannot move in an electric field and the crystal will behave as an insulator. As per band theory the following three results can be easily arrived at.

1. In a completely filled band the electrons cannot move freely in any direction and hence no conduction of electric current can take place.

2. An empty band also does not contribute to conduction of electric current since empty band contains no charge.

3. In partly free bands there is always free movement of electrons and as such these bands contribute to conduction of electric current as in case of metals.

The conditions which obstruct the rapid flow of electrons cause electrical resistance. Impurities, temperature and number of valence electrons are the three causes which cause resistance to the flow electric current.

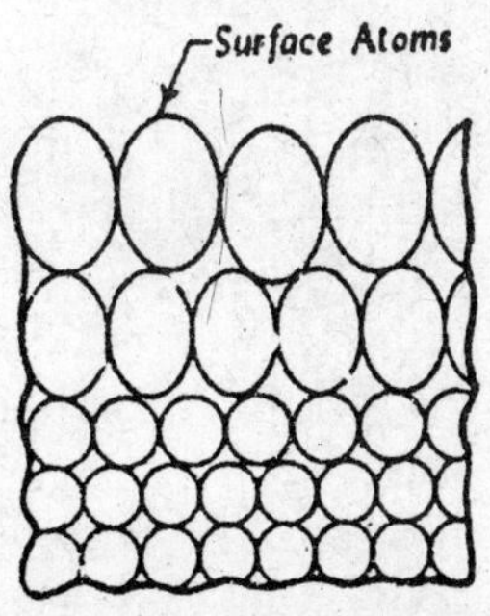

(a)

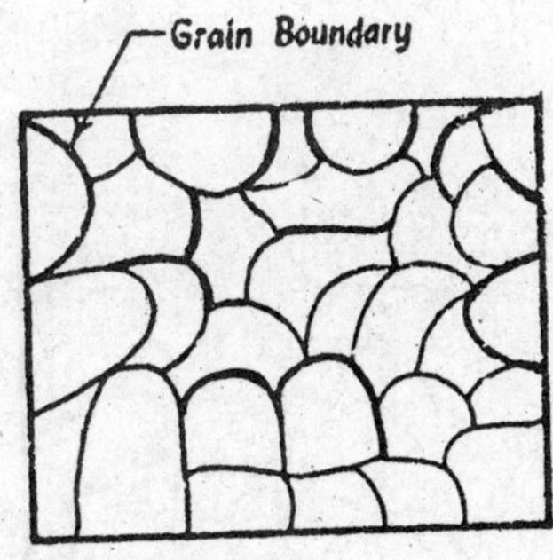

(b)

Fig. 21.11.

1. Impurities. Presence of alloying elements and other impurities cause obstruction in the flow of electric current and thus increase electrical resistance.

2. Temperature. The atomic nucleus of all the metals vibrate at all the temperatures. Higher the temperature the higher will be the amplitude of the vibration. This cause resistance to the electrical flow. This is because the collisions of the rushing valence electrons increase due to higher amplitude of the vibrations.

3. Number of valence electrons. All the metals contain 1, 2 or 3 valence electrons in the valency shell. The binding force of these valence electrons with their atomic nucleus is the highest where there are three valence electrons. It is the least when there is only one valence electron. Thus the force required by one valence electrons to detach itself from the nucleus is the least and its flow is made easy through the electron cloud. Hence the univalent elements have the highest conductivity.

QUESTIONS

1. What is a space lattice?
2. Explain the arrangments which are commonly found in the unit cell in the space lattice
3. Why is it necessary to study the structure of an atom.
4. Explain the process of slip in a single crystal
5. When does a matter become conductor of electricity.
6. What is meant by dislocation ?
7. Explain the concept of the crystal structure ?

LIST OF OUR OUTSTANDING PUBLICATIONS

CIVIL ENGINEERING

Effective July. 1, 1996	Y. of Pub.	Pages	Rs. P.
Arora K. R. : Fluid Mechanics, Hydraulics & Hydraulic Machines	7/E 1993	1312	140.00
Arora K. R. : Soil Mechanics and Foundation Engineering in S.I. Units	**4/E1996**	**1060**	**175.00**
Arora K. R. : Introductory Soil Engineering	1/R 1996	630	60.00
Arora K. R. : Irrigation, Water Power & Water Resources Engineering	**1/E1996**	**1120**	**200.00**
Arora K. R. : Civil Engineering Objective Type with Answers	2/E 1994	220	50.00
Bangar K. M. : Principles of Engineering Geology	**1/E 1995**	**480**	**75.00**
Bangar K. M. : Text Book of Engineering & General Geology	3/E 1995	264	40.00
Charan H. D. : Soil Testing (Laboratory Manual)	1/E 1991	84	30.00
Gupta B. L. : Roads, Railways, Bridges and Tunnel Engineering	**5/E 1995**	**1088**	**100.00**
Gupta B. L. : Engineering Hydrology	2/E 1992	380	50.00
Gupta B. L. : Text Book of Railway Engineering	/E 1995	520	50.00
Gupta B. L. : Taxt Book of Concrete Technology	/E 1995	478	50.00
Gupta B. L. : Construction Management & Accounts	/E 1995	496	50.00
Gurcharan Singh : Standard Hand Book of Civil Engineering	**7/E 1996**	**1512**	**200.00**
Gurcharan Singh : Environmental Engineering Vol. 1 (*Water Supply*)	**4/E 1995**	**518**	**50.00**
Gurcharan Singh : Environmental Engineering Vol 2 (*Sanitary Engineering*)	**4/E 1996**	**590**	**75.00**
Gurcharan Singh : Highway Engineering	**4/E 1995**	**710**	**75.00**
Gurcharan Singh : Design of R.C.C. Structures in S.I. units (*Limit State Design*)	3/E 1994	1312	120.00
Gurcharan Singh : Civil Engineering Drawing	**7/E 1995**	**408**	**75.00**
Gurcharan Singh : Materials of Construction (Building Materials)	**3/E 1996**	**388**	**60.00**
Gurcharan Singh : Design of Steel Structures	1/E 1982	856	50.00
Gurcharan Singh : Text Book of Engineering Drawing (*Plain and Solid Geometry*)	2/E 1996	528	50.00
Gurcharan Singh : Building Planning, Designing and Scheduling	**2/R 1995**	**428**	**75.00**
Gurcharan Singh : Estimating Costing and Valuation	**1/E 1993**	**720**	**100.00**
Jain V. K. : Text Book of Computer Science	2/E 1995	382	75.00
Jain V. K. : Basic Programming	1/E 1994	154	40.00
Jain V. K. : Computer Fundamentals	1/E 1994	230	40.00
Kukreja C. B. : Structural Mechanics Vol. I (*Determinate Structures*)	1/E 1991	498	55.00
Kukreja C. B. : Experimental Mthods in Structural Mechanics	2/E 1991	142	30.00
Kukreja C. B. : Material Testing Laboratory Manual (*For Quality Control*)	**2/E 1996**	**240**	**75.00**
Kaushal Kishore : Method of Concrete Mix Design with Chemical Admixtures	1/E 1992	40	30.00
Roy L. B. : Application of Graphics in Engg. (*Statics, Stresses and Structures*)	**1/E 1992**	**232**	**45.00**
Sushil Kumar : Building Construction	**16/E 1996**	**840**	**90.00**
Saxena, S. Narayan : Construction Planning Equipment	3/E 1990	200	30.00
Suresh R. : Soil and Water Conservation Engineering	1/E 1993	350	65.00
Suresh R. : Watershed Hydrology	**1/E 1996**	**430**	**100.00**
Pandey P.H. : Post Harvest Technology (Hindi Ed.)	**1/E 1995**	**320**	**65.00**
Punmia B.C. : Irrigation and Water Power Engineering	11/E 1990	892	75.00
Punmia B.C. : Introductory Irrigation Engineering	3/E 1985	616	40.00
Punmia B.C. : Strength of Materials & Mechanics of Structures Vol. I. S.I. units	9/E 1991	890	65.00
Punmia B.C. : Strength of Materials & Mechanics of Structures Vol. 2 S.I. units	8/E 1989	852	65.00
Punmia B.C. : Reinforced Concrete Structures Vol. I, as per ISI 456/78	6/E 1990	1096	85.00
Punmia B.C. : Reinforced Concrete Structures Vol. 2, ISI 456/78, 1343/1980	4/E 1991	1030	100.00
Ram Chandra : Applied Mechanics	3/E 1993	912	75.00
Arora K.C. & N.C. Goyal : Hotel Maintenance & Building Services	**1/E1996**	**410**	**100.00**